MODERN UGC NET: HISTORY

MODERN UGC NET/SLET
HOME SCIENCE

By

A Team of Experts

ANMOL PUBLICATIONS PVT. LTD.
NEW DELHI - 110 002 (INDIA)

ANMOL PUBLICATIONS PVT. LTD.
H.O.: 4374/4B, Ansari Road, Daryaganj,
New Delhi-110 002 (India)
Ph.: 23278000, 23261597
B.O.: No. 1015, Ist Main Road, BSK IIIrd Stage
IIIrd Phase, IIIrd Block,
Bangalore - 560 085 (India)
Visit us at: www.anmolpublications.com

Modern UGC NET/SLET: Home Science

[Responsibility for the facts stated, opinions expressed, conclusions reached and plagiarism, if any, in this volume is entirely that of the Chief of the Team of Experts. The Publisher bears no responsibility for them, whatsoever.]

PRINTED IN INDIA

Printed at Mehra Offset Press, Delhi.

CONTENTS

Preface (ix)

SECTION I
COMPREHENSIVE READINGS

1. **The Early Age** 3
Geographical Situation • Original Sources of History • The Early Period

2. **Civilization of Indus** 9
The Remnants • Horticulture and Agriculture • Business and Trade • Social Fabric • Economy • Religion • Harappan Script • End of Harappan Culture

3. **Before Vedas** 13
North-West • North-East • Belan Valley • Bihar/Mid Ganga Valley • South India • Important Features • Banas Culture or Ahar Culture • Kayatha Culture • Malwa Culture • Jorwe Culture • Settlements in South India

4. **Vedic Age** 19
Early Vedic-Age • Later Vedic Age • Literature • Religion

5. **Empire of Mauryas** 29
Administration • Ashoka's Dharma • Decline of Mauryas • Socio-economic Conditions • Art and Culture

6. **Post-Mauryan Era** 33
Small Kingdoms • Chetas of Kalinga • Satvahanas • Indo-Greeks • Shakas • Kushanas • Sangam Age

7. **Age of Guptas** 39
Samudragupta • Chandragupta Vikramaditya • Administration • Business and Trade • Society • Religion

8. **Regional Powers** 43
Northern India • Rashtrakutas • Pratiharas • Palas • Senas • Rajput Dynasties • Gahadavalas • Paramaras • Chahamanas • Chalukyas • Kalachuris • Chandellas • Southern India • The Cholas • Administration • Economy • Society • Art and Architecture • Religion

9. **Religion and Culture** 53
Religious Conditions •Temples and Monastic Institutions •Adi Sankaracharya •Literature in South India •Islam and Sufism •Literature •Science •Art and Architecture

10. **Sultanate of Delhi** 61
Mahmud of Ghazni •Muhammed Ghori •Slave Dynasty •Khaljis •Tughlaqs •Lodhis

11. **Small Kingdoms** 75
Bengal •Assam •Orissa •Gujarat •Malwa •Mewar •Marwar •Jaunpur •Kashmir •Khandesh •Bahmani Kingdom •Vijayanagar Kingdom

12. **Advent of Mughals** 83
Babur •Humayun •Sur Dynasty •Bhakti Movement •Growth of Regional Literature •Art and Culture

13. **Mughal Empire** 89
Akbar •Jahangir •Shahjahan •Aurangzeb •Shivaji •Mughal Painting •Architecture •Culture and Literature •Economy

14. **Fall of Mughals** 107
Later Mughals •Causes of Decline •Rise of New States

15. **Arrival of the British** 115
Anglo-French Rivalry •Carnatic Wars •Mysore •Anglo-Maratha Struggle •Economic Impact

16. **Social Reform Movements** 125
Brahmo Samaj •Derozio and Young Bengal •Ishwar Chandra Vidyasagar •Prarthana Samaj •Arya Samaj •Ramakrishna Mission •The Theosophical Society •Social Reform among Muslims •Social Reform among Sikhs •Movement of the Parsis •Depressed Classes Movement •Trade Union Movement •Peasant Movements

17. **The Revolts** 131
Early Uprisings •Revolt of 1857

18. **Movement for Freedom** 137
Moderate Phase •Growth of Militant Nationalism •Partition of Bengal •Growth of Revolutionary Terrorism •Ghadar Movement •Surat Split •Home Rule League •Lucknow Session •Gandhi and his Thought •Swaraj Party •Other Political Developments •Civil Disobedience •First Round Table Conference •Second Round Table Conference •Third Round Table Conference •Phase II of Civil Disobedience Movement •The Communal Award •The August Offer •Individual Satyagraha •Cripps Mission •Quit India Movement •Other National Movements •The Left Movement •Subhash Chandra Bose and the Indian National Army •Separatist Trends in Indian Nationalist Politics •Muslim League •Two-Nation Theory and Pakistan Movement •Hindu Mahasabha •Post-Quit India Movement •Wavell Plan •Elections of 1945-46 •Cabinet Mission Plan •The Interim Government •Attlee's

Announcement •The Mountbatten Plan •Partition of India •The Indian Independence Act, 1947

19. **India after Independence** 157
The Constitution •Five Year Plans and Industrialization •Agrarian Reforms •Foreign Policy

SECTION II
OBJECTIVE QUESTIONS WITH ANSWERS

Set I 171
Set II 181
Set III 191
Set IV 201
Set V 211
Set VI 225
Set VII 237
Set VIII 249
Set IX 259
Set X 269
Set XI 279
Set XII 291

SECTION III
SOLVED TEST PAPERS

Model Test Paper I 305
Model Test Paper II 311
Model Test Paper III 317
Model Test Paper IV 325
Model Test Paper V 331

SECTION IV
GUIDELINES FOR PAPER-III

Comprehensive History 339
A.Ancient Period •B.Medieval Period •C.Modern Period
Sources 341
•Ancient Period •Medieval Period •Modern Period

Preface

There is a dearth of good books for reference purpose, for the aspirants of UGC Examinations. Hence, this book, a work of worth, to say the least. It is an humble attempt to fulfil the requirements of students, appearing for UGC-NET, SLET Examinations. Model test papers for UGC Paper I and II have been provided. Guidelines for Paper III have also been given duly. For Paper I and II, adequate study material is provided to help solve all sort of Questions. A number of questions of all varieties viz., Multiple Choice, Matching Type, Reason and Assertion, Multiple Statement type etc., are included in this book. Further, memory based questions asked in previous examinations have also been added. This book should serve as a complete revision tool and reference material, for the examination preparations.

The undersigned is confident enough that this 'ready to refer' book would prove to be beneficial for all its readers.

Editor

Section I

COMPREHENSIVE READINGS

One

THE EARLY AGE

Our country, India is bounded on north by Himalayas and on the south by Indian ocean. A part of Jambudvipa, the scriptures called it Bharatvarsha or where the descendants of Bharatas live. The name Hindu or India is given by the Persians. They call it Hafta-Hindu or Sapta-Sindhu, a land watered by the river Sindhu. The ancient name Bharatvarsha has its authenticity in ancient literature that refers to Bharat clan that dominated the large area of the country.

Geographical Situation

On the north the huge range of Himalayas render a very strong frontier to this country. The other mountains like Hindukush and Vindhyachal have equally played decisive roles in moulding the history of the land. These features are important factors in the study of civilisation. These mountains have several passes that served as routes of movement and invasion in various periods of history. The five passes of Himalayas-Khyber, Bolan, Tochi, Gomal and Kurram served as important ways for invasion and migrations that influenced the formation of the history of the land. Khyber and Bolan passes are the major ones. Rig-Veda refers to Tochi-Kurram pass used by Aryan invaders. The Khyber route also finds its mention in the treatise. The invaders could have come down through the pass to the valley of Kabul river to Peshawar. These five natural routes, known as five fingers, connect Iran and central Asia with India. The passes eased the movement and the invaders used these to conquer the land ultimately changing the entire course of history and moulding the civilisation.

Hindukush range has two passes-Qora-Kottal and Dandan-Shikan that connect Western Afghanistan and Hari Rud Valley with Balkh (Bactria). This route facilitates the eastward movement towards Kabul.

Between Kabul and Kandhar, a series of valleys and mountain passes offer several ways to Punjab frontiers. These areas have remained historic shelters of warlike races. Once these people settled themselves in those strategic and difficult mountain belts it became easier for them to command the Indian plains. Thus, the peaceful tenor of life of Punjab and Western India was recurrently endangered by those strategic factors. The Huns, Persians, Greeks,

Sakas, Turks and Afghans entered the country through these passes. They not only politically dominated the land but also influenced the culture and the society.

The long structured sea coasts in Southern Plateau have also remained a powerful source of contact with the world. The vast coastline had activated the maritime activities and led to the establishment of a number of harbours. The trade relations with Rome, China, Malaysia, South-east Asia were developed.

The plains of north India were fertile land that rendered prosperity to the country. This was the cause of numerous invasions from outside. The climatic changes in north-western India changed the history-of the region. The monsoon currents did not remain as strong as earlier as a result of dry land and extension of desert. It extended from east Iran to Rajputana serving as a natural barrier repulsing the invasions through Khyber pass.

The various races that entered the region as invaders settled down here. In course of time they lost their identity. The Indian society is a mixture of various races like Aryans, Dravidians, Persians, Greeks, Turks, Mughals, Huns, Sakas, Kushans, etc. This led to the formation of a composite culture in India.

The literature of ancient India offers six geographical divisions of the country.: 1. Middle region (Madhya Desa), 2. Himalayan region (Himavanta), 3. North-West region (Uttarpatha), 4. Deccan (Dakshinapatha), 5. Eastern India (Purvanta), 6. Western India (Aparanta).

The Anthropologists consider India a land of multi-races. The geographical feature of the country attracted people from outside during various periods. The Indus Valley and the Gangetic plains had such climate that brought out bumper harvests and eventually prosperity. The races from outside coveted the prosperity of the land. They invaded the country and were impressed with the environment which made them settle here. After a few centuries the invaders mingled with the local population and it was not possible to identify them.

There are references when the groups from outside were called Sudras, but later on they assimilated to the national stream and were called Kshatriyas. India is not a land of geographical integration but it is a land of pious ceremonies. The sacred cities and lakes, rivers and mountains are scattered throughout the country. The seven holy cities, seven holy rivers and seven holy mountains give it a spiritual unity. The sacred points like temples are placed either on the sacred mountains, seacoasts or on the river banks. People from all ethnic groups, religious groups and social groups have quest for unity, peace and immortality. Indian myth, religion and art introduce into man's life an overtone binding into a greater universe. The principles set since Dravidian culture have been re-moulded through the various stages in history. The peace prayer of the country includes not only men and animals, but all the living creatures in this universe. Through ages the country has experienced vast movements and has gone through many renaissances. All this has contributed to the emergence of a composite culture. Despite diversities in the land due to geographical and other features there is an underlying unity in the country.

Original Sources of History

History is not a myth. The whole saga is based upon the testified sources. The historians use various sources to establish the authenticity of events which depends upon the authenticity of the sources. The essence of literary sources in Indian history keeps the scholars guessing about the incident which is evident from other sources. The historian has to use indirect sources. Some Europeans opine that the ancient Indian did not have proper knowledge of language. But the vast literature of the period proves it baseless. Though the literature is religious and deals with the spirituality, the chronologies offered in Vedic literature, Buddhist and Jain literatures bring forth the quest of ancient India's keeping records. The works are master pieces demonstrating the talent of the author. But in most cases the historian has to depend upon the indirect sources.

Literary Sources: The Vedas and the literatures pertaining to them are religious in spirit. The four Vedas try to divulge the secret of this universe. They discuss how the supreme power of God can be pleased. The later Vedic literature contains the philosophy part of the religion. The Puranas and Epics deal with the events in detail and give vast chronology of various dynasties who ruled the country. The Vedic literature though religious in nature, accidently gives the condition-political and social. The Jain literature and the Buddhist treatise deal extensively with the religion but they narrate the social incidence to assert, their sayings. The treatises on astronomy and grammars are also helpful in reconstructing the history of the period.

From Mauryan age onwards, there are number of political treatises. The *Arthashastra* of Kautilya gives details of the political systems, and of the society of the period. Banabhatta's *Harshacharita* is also informative about the social conditions and about the people. *Gaudavaho, Vikramankadeva Charita, Ramacharita, Rajatarangini* and *Navasahasankacharita* are all very valuable informative works. During the medieval period there are works on life and achievements of the kings. The Mughal king were fond of getting their biographies written in the court. Some of them had also written autobiographies. The literary pieces of medieval age are very helpful in reconstructing the history. These works give very accurate chronology of the past. During the British period, the government records and numerous books produced during the period are the main sources.

Archaeological Sources: The building in archaeology are palaces, tombs, temples and the other building. The remains of these personal or public buildings serve as powerful source of history. The remains of Mohenjodaro, Harappa and other places of Indus Valley are the main sources for reconstructing the history of prehistoric period in India. The planning of the towns, the bricks used, the objects found there, the graves, the seals, all speak of a developed and civilised society. The inscriptions on the walls of the temples or the tombs inform about the period they belong to. The decorations on the walls tell about the aesthetic values. The information engraved on the pillars is usually of two types:

(i) instructions of the king to his subjects; and

(ii) eulogies of kings:

These engravings on the stone also inform about the language in the period. There are rock-cut edicts belonging to Ashoka's period. The inscriptions inscribed on the copper plates, silver and gold plates are also eulogies. These inscriptions are also found in medieval period.

Foreigner's Accounts: India has attracted the people of other lands from time to time. The foreigners visited the country, stayed here, observed and wrote their experiences.

Some of them stayed here and learnt the languages recorded. They came here to study the religion. Many of them were on a special mission. On returning to their countries these travellers wrote their experiences. In Maurya period Megasthanese, the Greek ambassador lived in India for quite a long period, and wrote one book in Patliputra, the capital of Mauryan Empire during the reign of Chandra Gupta. The book is lost now. But the references to this book by other scholars, helps in reconstructing the history of the period. The book is named as *Indica*.

Alexander's admiral Nearchos has written an account of his journey and referred to the coastal areas.

The Chinese Traveller Fa-Hien and Hieun-Tsang had also written their accounts about the social, political and economic condition of the people. Fa-Hien visited India in fourth century A.D., during the reign of Chandragupta Vikramaditya, Hiuen Tsang came in 6th century A.D. during Harshavardhana's period. These records are authentic. On their stay in the country, the travellers collected large material. Hiuen-Tsang's record is supported by his biography written by Huai-li. He included in his record information collected by Hieun-Tsang. I-Tsing, who visited India in 7th Century A.D. had also recorded genuine accounts.

Alberuni, an astronomer from Arabia, wrote *Tahkik-e-Hind,* throwing light on society, customs, manners, literature and philosophy of Hindu society. Thus, the record is very useful for reconstructing the history.

Numismatic Sources: The numismatics or the coins are very vital source for reconstructing the history of the country. The coinage gives idea about the prevailing economic conditions of the society and their metallurgical art. Coins also carry the date or period of a particular reign. The imprints on the coins tell about the individual. Like Samudragupta is shown playing Veena. This tells that the King was an expert artist. The seals showing a woman ready to kill an animal speaks about their belief in animal sacrifice.

The Early Period

Before the dawn of civilisation, the early man also called the cave man, lived in few parts of the earth. From the tools he developed for his use, experts can derive the antiquity of the man. He first lived in Indus Valley, China and Malaysia. The scientists study the tools excavated these areas and derive conclusions. The primate had to counter the natural forces. For his protection and for food he used tools made either of stone or of bones of animals. The quality of the man is that he not only uses various tools for various purposes but also improves upon them. It is because of this nature of the man we are in the present modern age. The archaeologists have traced the early species of humans like the Poking Mar, and others.

On the basis of collected facts, the archaeologists have classified the early history of man in three stages-Stone age (new and old), Bronze age and Iron age. These three ages did not occur at the same time in all parts of the world.

Old Stone Age (Palaeolithic Period): This period in the progress of humanity occurred 5,00,000 years ago. In India this culture developed in Ice Age, a geographical period. In the earliest phase of this stage, the man lived on hunting and food gathering. He was using the hand axes and other tools. The notable point is that during this stage, there is improvement in the tools of stone. The sites of this age in India are mainly situated in the valley of river Soan in Punjab. The flakes of the stones are used. The tools are mainly bones, blade and axes. This stage is a stage of savagery.

Mesolithic Age: In 9000 B.C., after the end of the upper Palaeolithic Age, began an intermediate stage in stone age culture, which is called the Mesolithic Age. It intervened as a transitional phase between the Palaeolithic Age and the Neolithic Age. The characteristic tools of this age are microliths. The mesolithic sites are found in good numbers in Rajasthan, South Uttar Pradesh, Central and Eastern India. Adamgarh in Madhya Pradesh and Bagor in Rajasthan provide the earliest evidence for the domestication of animals. The mesolithic people were hunters and herders.

New Stone Age (Neolithic): This state developed about 10,000 years ago. The stone of the tools is refined in this age. The weapons and tools are sharper and refined. These are scattered in north, south, east and western India. By this time the man had control over the supply of food. He cultivated and bred animals. The age was still called barbaric age. The spinning wheel, use of pottery, cotton woven into thread came into being. A large number of flint arrow heads, bone harpoons, blades and sickles are found in large number. The later settlers of this age are agriculturists. The granaries or store houses for keeping wheat are also found.

Bronze Age: About 5,000 years ago the man started using bronze along with the stone. Now the man had developed to a great extent. The population is mainly urban including the priests, writers and clerks during this stage. Though the tools available suggest that there was over-lapping in use of stone and the metal, the similarity in the shape and types of stone and bronze tools shows simultaneous use of bronze and stone. Tin mixed with the copper was the major material used. That is why, the period is called Bronze age. The specialists were needed to manufacture goods with the metal, like smiths, miners and smelters. During this period, the discovery of wheel revolutionised the whole system. The transportation was improved which eventually brought about the complexities in life of the man. Commerce was developed. The production in all fields was surplus i.e. he could sell it away for luxuries. This gave rise to capitalism. The person with more resources was able to control the power. The status of rich and poor developed and along with this came exploitation. This age is witnessed in Indus Valley Civilisation that spread to a long belt along the western India.

Iron Age: In India the iron age commenced around 1000 B.C. The use of weapons with iron heads is found in western Uttar Pradesh. Iron is a common element easily available as compared to copper. But in the beginning it has remained a rare element. It was not possible to clear iron from its ore. It needs more heat for the process. It is believed that its production must have been guarded by the tribals who first discovered. The metal became common only later on. It was cheaper after it became easily available. Later on iron revolutionised the techniques like agriculture, industry and also weapons. Its easy availability brought about great changes in the society.

Two

CIVILIZATION OF INDUS

It was in 1922-23 that during the construction in Baluchistan a destroyed city was discovered. The archaeologists started working on it and they surmised that it was a pre-Aryan settlement in India. The city culture was spread in one thousand kilometres of area. From the Arabian Sea coast in Sind and Gujarat it extended upto Meerut. A recent excavation carried out in Kalibangan in Rajasthan revealed a third city as large as Harappa. As called Indus Valley Civilisation, it was not confined to the valley only. It was the Bronze Age when this civilisation flourished.

The Indus civilisation occurred at the time when the civilisations of Mesopotamia and Egypt were flourishing. The discovery of this civilisation has dated back the pre-history, period of India. Before this it was believed that the Aryans were the first inhabitants of this land and Aryan civilisation was the first civilisation in India.

The Remnants

The important source of information for restructuring the history of the Indus valley is the remnants of the city at various sites. The planning of the town and the level of urbanisation surprises the people. The cities of Mohenjodaro, Harappa, Lothal are built on the similar plans. The public buildings in these cities were built on a platform. The platform was defended by a wall. The town was below this building. In the town the planning is marvellous. The houses are constructed in a line. Each lane has crossing. The streets meet at the main streets. The houses are built on both the sides of the streets and are built of burnt bricks. The houses of varying sizes, generally two or more storeys, consist of rooms constructed around a court-yard. Most of the houses built on the land measured around nine metres. There were big houses also, perhaps for the rich people. The row of the houses perhaps were for poor people.

The Great Bath at Mohenjodaro is the most striking feature. It is a large tank which has a few stairs to reach the bottom. It was perhaps; for some important ritual. The drainage system of the cities is another striking feature. All the houses have drains that reached the main drain in the street. The drains were covered. There were also public baths and wells. There were manholes for cleaning the drains.

At Harappa the granary is the most important. It is built on raised platform to protect it from the flood waters. The granary is divided into many blocks to store grains of various types.

Horticulture and Agriculture

In the early stage there was less cultivation and pastoralism was practised. Sheep and goat were domesticated. But later on there is evidence of permanent village life. Mud bricks, boulders, and cut stones were fully used. Wheat and barley were the main food crops. There were two varieties of wheat and barley. Mustard and sesamum were used for oil. From the main sites cultivation of rice was not indicated. The fields were irrigated by irregular floods in the Indus region.

Business and Trade

No currency is found. It is assumed that barter system was practised. The Harappans knew the use of wheel. They used wheeled carts for transportation. Many seals have been found belonging to Harappan from Mesopotamia and Egypt, which clearly indicates the trade links. This is supported by reference in Mesopotamian texts.

The remains from these sites include objects made of bronze. It seems that the people of these civilisations were great admirers of art and knew the art of copper. The potter's wheel was used.

In absence of any written evidence it is very difficult to know about the social and political organisation. The Harappans knew the art of writing. It is evident from the seals found from there.

Social Fabric

The Indus Valley people pursued a colourful social life. They were very fond of ornaments and dressing up. This information is derived from the spindles which indicate that both cotton and woollen threads must have been spun. An idea of the dresses worn by them can be had from the statues and carvings of different seals found in those cities. The women wore skirts and men wrapped themselves in knee-length cotton clothes tied to the waist.

Ornaments were used by both the sexes of all classes. Necklaces, fillets, armlets, finger rings, and bangles were worn by both men and women, whereas nose-studs, earrings and anklets were used by women only. The Indus Valley people knew the art of toileteries and cosmetics.

Hunting was indulged in by the Harappans. The potter's wheel was in full use. The people also used many tools and implements of stone. Bronze was made by mixing tin with copper.

The uniformity of patterns in civil life and the planned structure of the cities suggest some sort of political organisation. The fire cult at Lothal and the Great Bath at Mohenjodaro, suggests that the priests ruled in Harappa. But there are no temples on any sites of Harappa. So, historians believe that the Harappan rulers were more concerned with commerce than with conquests, and Harappa was possibly ruled by a class of merchants.

Economy

A wide variety of crafts were developed, which formed an important basis of liveliood, and were also traded. Specialized crafts included flint tool-work, shell-work, bangle-making, pottery-making, copper-and bronze-working, gold-smithy, stone-working, brick-making and seal-cutting. The raw materials for these works came from different sources: gold from north Karnataka, silver from Afghanistan or Iran, copper from Khetri and Baluchistan, turquoise from Central Asia and Iran, and *lapis lazuli* from Baluchistan.

There was a well-knit system of external and internal trade. The internal trade was carried on through river, sea and land routes. This is clearly evident from the clay boats represented on the seals and the discovery of a dockyard at Lothal. Cultural influence of the Harappan civilization found its way to the neighbouring regions. Harappan seals and other Harappan materials were found in Mesopotamia. Weights and measures of accuracy existed in the Harappan culture.

Religion

Mother Goddess was one of the main objects of worship of the Harappan people. Many figurines of this Mother Goddess on pottery, seals and amulets have come to light. In one figurine, a plant is shown growing out of the embryo of a woman. The image probably represents the goddess of earth looked upon as a fertility goddess. The male deity was also worshipped. On a seal, a figure with horned head-dress, surrounded by wild animals, and sitting in an erect meditative or yogic posture was noticed. This is described as 'proto-Shiva' by Marshall. The Phallus worship was also prevalent. Numerous symbols of the phallus and female sex organs, made of stone, have been found in Harappa.

The Harappan people also followed 'animism' implying worship of stones, trees and animals under the belief that these were abodes of spirits, good or evil. Perhaps, peepal tree was regarded as sacred. Some forms of Naga worship was also practised. The representation of swastik and the wheel on some seals, perhaps, indicate that the sun was represented symbolically. They also worshipped demi-gods who had human body with the hoofs and tails of a bull, and closely resembled the demigods of Sumeria. Many forms of our modern Hindu worship have their precedence in the Indus Valley civilization.

Harappan Script

Historically, of all the objects discovered from the Harappan sites, the seals which have scripts are most interesting. Although the complete script was discovered in 1923, it has remained undeciphered so far. The Indus script is supposed to be proto-type of the Brahmi script. This view cannot be accepted as the similarity between the two scripts is only external. Some historians claim to have deciphered it with the help of proto-Dravidian languages or with the Sanskrit language.

The script is not alphabetical but pictographic. There are about 600 undeciphered pictographs.

End of Harappan Culture

The mature phase of the Harappan culture continued from 2200 B.C. to 2000 B.C. By 1800 B.C., this culture completely declined. There are several theories regarding the decline of Harappan culture. The natural causes such as frequent floods, environmental and ecological changes, the social break-up of the Harappans, demographic changes, etc., are the mainly listed possible causes leading to the end of the Harappan civilization. Foreign invasion and the decline of foreign trade are also projected as the causes of the decline. In the later phases of the Harappan culture, some exotic tools and pottery indicate the slow percolation of new people in the Indus basin. It is true that the new groups of people came and settled there, but there is enough evidence to indicate that there was bitter confrontation between these new settlers and the Harappan people.

Three

BEFORE VEDAS

Human communities entered a new stage of culture when, instead of depending entirely on the resources of nature for survival as in the Palaeolithic and the Mesolithic Age, they started producing their own food by cultivating cereals like barely, wheat and rice and started domesticating some species of animals both for supplies of milk and meat as well as for harnessing their labour for various purposes. These main characteristics are the important features of the Neolithic stage of culture. The people of this age used tools and implements of polished stone, particularly stone axes.

The only Neolithic Settlement in the Indian sub-continent attributed to 7000 B.C lies in Mehrgarh, situated in Baluchistan. Some of neolithic sites found on the northern spurs of the Vindhyas are considered as old as 5000 B.C. The Neolithic Settlements found in South India are not older than 2500 B.C., in some parts of Southern and Eastern India they are as late as 1000 B.C.

Domestication of plants and animals led to:

* the emergence of village communities based on sedentary life.
* the beginning of agriculture technology, and
* greater control over nature by exploitation of natural resources.

North-West

The earliest evidence for the beginning of agricultural communities in this area comes from Mehrgarh in Baluchistan attributed to 7000 B.C.

The Kashmiri neolithic culture was distinguished by its dwelling pits, the range of ceramics, the variety of stone and bone tools, and the complete absence of the microliths. Village settlements appeared in the Kashmir Valley by about 2500 B.C. Excavations at Burzahom and Gufkral throw significant light on the Neolithic cultures of this region. In Burzahom, which means 'the place of birth' situated 16 km Northwest of Srinagar, the neolithic people lived on a lake-side in pits and probably had a hunting and fishing economy. They seem to have been acquainted with agriculture. The people of Burzahom used coarse grey pottery. The Burzahom domestic dogs were buried with their masters in their graves. Pit dwelling and the placing of domestic dogs in the graves of the masters do not seem to be the practice with neolithic people in any other part of India. The people of Gufkral (literally the cave of the potter) a neolithic site 45 km south-west of Srinagar, practised both agriculture and domestication of animals. Other than polished tools of stone, the neolithic people in Kashmir used numerous tools and weapons made of bone. The only other place which has yielded considerable bone implements in India is Chirand, situated 40 km west of Patna.

North-East

Neolithic tools have been recovered in the hills of Assam (2500 B.C.), Garo hills in Meghalaya.

Belan Valley

The relevant excavated sites of the Belan Valley which indicate transition from the food-gathering stage to the food producing stage are Chopni-Mando, Koldihawa and Mahgara. It has been suggested that Neolithic farmers of the Belan Valley emerged as the earliest rice farming community in India (6th millennium B.C.) Pottery makes its appearance in the late mesolithic/proto-neolithic phase at Chopni-Mando (9th-8th Millennium B.C.) Chopni-Mando, thus provides the earliest evidence of the use of pottery in the world. The Neolithic culture of the Belan Valley shows a developed and advanced sedentary life.

Bihar/Mid Ganga Valley

The lower central Gangetic Valley was occupied by sedentary village settlements much later (2000-1600 B.C.). Excavations at Chirand, Chechar, Senuwar and Taradib, etc., throw significant light on the life pattern of the Neolithic people of this region. Both Chirand and Senuwar are known for their remarkable bone tools. At Senuwar, the neolithic farmers cultivated rice, barley, pea, lentil and some millets. The grains cultivated at Chirand were, wheat, barley, rice and lentil.

South India

The neolithic settlements in South India are mainly found South of the Godavari river, and they usually settled on the tops of granite hills or on plateaus near the river banks. They used stone axes and also some kind of stone blades. Fire-baked earthen figurines suggest that they kept a large number of cattle. They used rubbing stone querns, which shows that they were acquainted with the art of producing grains. Excavated sites, which throw light on the various aspects of Neolithic culture, of the South India are Maski, Brahmagiri, Hallur, Kodekal, Sanganakallu, T. Narsipur and Takkalakota in Karnataka and Paiyampalli in Tamil Nadu. Piklihal and Utnur are important Neolithic sites in Andhra Pradesh. The neolithic phase in South India seems to have covered the period from about 2000 B.C to 1000 B.C.

By the second millennium B.C. several regional cultures sprang up in different parts of the Indian sub-continent. These were non-urban, non-Harappan and were characterised by the use of stone and copper tools. Hence, these cultures are termed as Chalcolithic cultures which means the stonecopper phase. The Chalcolithic people occasionally used low-grade bronze. They were primarily rural communities spread over a wide area in those parts of the country where hilly land and rivers were available. The Chalcolithic cultures are identified on the basis of their geographical location. they are:

- Banas culture (located in the Banas basin) in Rajasthan or Ahar culture (2100-1500 B.C.)
- Kayatha culture (type site Kayatha) and represented by other sites in Central India. (2000-1880 B.C.)
- Malwa culture (1700-1200 B.C.)
- Jorwe culture (1400-700 B.C.)

Important Features

1. The people belonging to this culture used tiny tools and weapons made of stone in which the stone-blades and bladelets occupied an important position. In certain settlements, copper objects are found in good numbers.
2. The people of the Chalcolithic phase used different types of pottery, one of which is called black-and-red and seems to have been widely prevalent from nearly 2000 B.C. onwards. It was thrown on wheel and occasionally painted with white linear designs.
3. The people domesticated animals and practised agriculture. In addition to the staple crops such as wheat and rice, they also cultivated bajra. They produced several pulses such as the lentil, black gram, green gram and grass pea. Almost all these food grains have been found at Navdatoli situated on the bank of the Narmada in Maharashtra. In Eastern India, fish hooks have been found in Bihar and West Bengal which suggests that the Chalcolithic people in the eastern regions lived on fish and rice.
4. The Chalcolithic people were generally not acquainted with burnt bricks, which were seldom used, as in bricks around Gilund 1500 B.C. Occasionally their houses were made of mud bricks, but mostly these were constructed with wattle and daub, and seem to have thatched houses. However, the people in Ahar lived in stone-built houses.
5. The Chalcolithic people were expert coppersmiths and also good workers of stone. Tools, weapons and bangles of copper have been found. They manufactured beads of semi-precious stones such as carnelian, steatite and quartz crystal. People knew the art of spinning and weaving because spindle whorls have been discovered in Malwa. This shows that these people were well acquainted with manufacture of cloth. In addition to these artisans who practised these crafts at various sites we find potters, smiths, ivory carvers, lime makers and terracotta artisans at Inamgaon.
6. In Maharashtra people buried their dead in urns under the floor of their house in the north-to-south position; unlike the Harappans who used separate cemeteries for this purpose. Pots and some copper objects were deposited in the graves for the use of the

dead in the next world. In South-India, the dead bodies were placed in the east-west position.

7. Terracotta figures of women suggest that the Chalcolithic people venerated the mother goddess, which has been found in Inamgaon. In Malwa and Rajasthan, stylised bull terra-cottas show that the bull was the symbol of a religious cult.

8. Both the settlement pattern and burial practises suggest beginning of social inequalities.

Banas Culture or Ahar Culture (type site Ahar)

Located in the Banas basin in Rajasthan, this is represented by the type site Ahar. Unlike the other contemporary Chalcolithic farming cultures, Ahar practically did not use microlithic tools; stone axes or blades are almost absent here. Its objects include several flat axes, bangles, several sheets; all made of copper, although a bronze sheet also occurs. The people of Ahar practised smelting and metallurgy from the very beginning. The old name of Ahar is Tambavati or a place possessing copper. The Ahar culture is placed between 2100 and 1500 B.C. and Gilund is considered a regional centre of Ahar culture. In Gilund only fragments of copper appear. Here, we find a stone-blade industry.

Kayatha Culture

The Kayatha Culture (2000 -1880 B.C.) is named after the site of Kayatha (25 km east of Ujjain) located on the bank of the Kalisindh. It has some pre-Harappan elements in pottery, but it also shows Harappan influence.

Malwa Culture. (1700-1200 B.C.)

It is found in Maheshwar, Navdatoli, Eran and Nagda and considered to be non-Harappan. The Malwa ware, typical of the Malwa chalcolithic culture of central and western India is considered the richest among the chalcolithic ceramics. It is to some extent coarse in fabric and has a thick buff slip over which patterns are executed in black or dark brown colour.

Jorwe Culture. (1400-700 B.C.)

Named after the type-site Jorwe, situated on the left bank of the Pravara river, several chalcolithic sites, belonging to this culture have been excavated such as Jorwe, Newasa, Daimabad, Chandoli, Songaon, Inamgaon, Prakash and Nasik. Although the Jorwe culture was rural, some of its settlements such as Daimabad and Inamgaon had almost reached the urban stage. The settlements at Daimabad and Inamgaon was fortified. At Inamgaon, large mud houses with ovens and circular pit houses have been discovered in its early phase (1400-1000 B.C.). In the later phase, the houses of the artisans were located on the western periphery of the principal habitation area, whereas those of well-to-do farmers were in the central part. The position and size of houses (artisans houses were smaller than those of the well-to do) demonstrate social differentiation. Daimabad is famous for the recovery of a large number of copper hoard, such as elephant, rhinoceros, two wheeled chariot with a rider, buffalo, etc.

Several chalcolithic sites have also been found in the Vindhyan region of Allahabad district. In eastern India, besides Chirand on the Ganga, mention may be made of Pandua Rajar Dhibi in Burdwan district and Mahishdal in Birbhum district in West Bengal. The Prabhas and Rangpur cultures respectively, are known after the type sites Prabhas Patan and Rangpur in Gujarat.

In addition to cultural material of this phase, found at excavated sites, copper hoards have been found. The largest hoard comes from Gungeria in M.P; it contains 424 copper tools and weapons and 102 thin sheets of silver objects. Nearly half of the copper hoards are concentrated in the GangaYamuna doab. At Saipai (Western U.P.) a copper harpoon has been found in association with a pottery known as Ochre-coloured Pottery (OCP). As more than a hundred sites have yielded this characteristic pottery in the Ganga-Yamuna doab, these sites are described as belonging to the OCP culture. This pottery is made of medium grained clay, under fired and has a wash of ochre ranging from orange to red. The period covered by the Ochre-coloured Pottery Culture may roughly be placed between 2000 B.C.-1500 B.C. At some of the OCP sites (e.g., Lal Qila, Atranjikhera, Saipai) excavations have revealed no signs of regular inhabitation. At Hastinapura and Ahichchatra there is break in occupation between the OCP culture and the succeeding Painted Grey Ware culture (PGW), while at Atranjikhera the OCP settlements are succeeded by Black and Red Ware Pottery (BRW).

Cultures associated with Black and Red Ware (BRW) and Painted Grey Ware (PGW) mark the coming of Iron Technology in India. Carbon - 14 dates for PGW culture given them a period between 1025 - 500 B.C. Important PGW sites include Ahichchatra, Hastinapura; Ropar, Panipat, Indraprastha (Purana Qila), Mathura, Bairat, Sonepat, Atranjikhera, Alamgirpur and Sravasti in Doab, Noh in Rajasthan. Further east the characteristic pottery was BRW and the important sites are Kausambhi, Rajghat, Buxar and Chirand. The PGW iron period was primarily an age of iron weapons and did not contribute much to develop handicrafts and agriculture.

Settlements in South India

The Neolithic Chalcolithic Settlements excavated in South India are Piklihal, Brahmagiri, Sanganakallu, Tekkalakota, Hallur and T. Narsipur. The available radio carbon dates for this phase suggest a time span covering 1800-1500 B.C. In this phase new pottery types like the perforated and spouted vessels appeared replacing the red and black slipped wares of the neolithic phase. In the later chalcolithic phase (1400-1050 B.C.) there was increase in the number of copper and bronze tools and new ceramic types occur. The grey and buff ware with a harder surface and a wheel thrown unburnished ware with purple tint were the prominent ceramics used. There is continuity of occupation from the neolithic phase to the later chalcolithic phase with no significant change in the economy.

The use of iron in South India began sometime around 1100 B.C. The earliest phase of iron age in South India is recovered by the excavations at Piklihal and Hallur and possibly by the burial pits at Brahmagiri. Most of the information about the iron age in South India comes from the excavations of the Megalithic graves. These graves are called Megaliths because they were encircled by big pieces of stone. They contained not only skeletons of people who were buried but also pottery and iron objects. The megalith builder used various types of pottery including red ware, but black-and-red ware seems to have been popular with them. Arrowheads, spearheads, hoes and sickles, tridents which later came to be associated with Shiva, all made of iron have been found in the megaliths. Compared to the number of agricultural tools that were buried, those meant for fighting and hunting are larger in number, which shows that megalithic people did not practise an advanced type of agriculture. The megaliths emerged around the end of the second and beginning of the first millennium B.C. but in many cases the megalithic phase lasted from about the 5th to the 1st century B.C. Megalithic burials have been reported in large numbers from Maharashtra (around Nagpur), Karnataka (Maski), Andhra Pradesh (Nagarjuna Konda), Tamil Nadu (Adichanallur) and Kerala. This phase merged into the early historic South India when the literate tradition began.

Four

VEDIC AGE

The term Veda stands for knowledge. The treatise-the four Vedas are the chief source of information about the Vedic life. The Rig-Veda, the first Veda refer to a conquest of Aryan in Punjab. It is surmised that these wars were with the original inhabitants of the land. Later on the Aryans settled down there and later on extended their sphere of influence upto north India and central India. About the original home of the Aryans there are a number of theories. The most accepted one is that they arrived from Asia steppes as is evident from their language, references to their original home in Rig-Veda.

Early Vedic-Age

The four Vedas are Rig Veda, Yajur Veda, Sama Veda and Atharva Veda. Rig Veda is a collection of 1028 hymns in praise of God. Yajur Veda contains sacrificial formulae in prose and poetry to be used by the priests. The Sama Veda is a collection of verses from Rig-Veda. Atharva explains the magical spells and charms. To each Veda is attached Brahmanas which offers explanatory prose. The last portion of Brahmanas is called Aranyakas or the literature to be taught in forest only.

The Vedic literature has been secretly held sacred, for it is believed that it derived from divine mouth. The author received those directly from the mouth of the God. Vedas were transmitted orally from generation to generation. These were compiled later on.

The Vedas can be divided into two parts: early Vedic period (1500 to 1000 B.C.) when Rig-Veda was composed and the later Vedic period where the remaining Vedas were composed.

Rig-Veda mentions the rivers like Gomal as Gomti, Kurram as Krumu, and Kabul as Kubha. The Rig-Vedic culture seems to be concentrated in Punjab and Indus areas. Delhi was the extent of Rig Vedic Aryans. They mention Yamuna river and nothing beyond this.

Rig-Veda refers to the land of seven rivers and tribal wars that took place. But the Aryans chief opponents were the indigenous people who were of non-Aryan origin. They hated the Dasas or Dasyus who were survivors of Harappan site. They are described as black skinned people, who do not perform sacrifices. They spoke a different language.

Agriculture: The Aryans were pastoral people. They knew about the ploughs, about the seasons, and they used several animals in their daily life. The Rig-Vedic Aryans knew sowing, harvesting and fishing. In spite of all such knowledge they give importance to cow.

Polity: Early Aryans established a number of tribal states. The first kingdom was founded by four tribal chiefs known to be sons of Manu. The tribal chief was called Rajah. The king was assisted by Purohita or the priest, Senani, the head of the army. Sabha and Samiti were the two political bodies in the state. Vidatha, *gana* and *parishad* are also mentioned in the treatise. These bodies also had women as their members. The women was attributed very respectable position. She was given education and in certain cases she was given higher education. She participated in Vedic Seminars. There were illegal practises and spies were employed to control these.

Society: The Society was divided on the basis of occupations but there was no system of the sub-castes as at the present times. Vama was the term used for colours. They repulsed the people of dark vama. The defeated dark people were treated as slaves. The Rig-Vedic Aryans worshiped nature. Indra was their most powerful God. He was the rain God who broke the forts of the enemy. The other Gods are Agni, Varuna, Aditi and Usha. The Aryans offered prayers by reciting and sacrifice.

Later Vedic Age

Later Vedic Age is considered from 1000 B.C. to 600 B.C. During this period the Vedas were composed. The Aryans during this period had moved further. Then they occupied the land between Ganga and Yamuna. That was called Aryavrata. It covered the land up to Western UP.

Polity: The King became more powerful. The theory of kingship became stronger. The new tribes had now emerged. The kingship had been accepted by the people. The hereditary succession to the throne was accepted. The other organisations became weaker before the kingship. In later vedic period the assemblies declined. The society now was divided into four Vamas called Brahmans, Rajanyas or Kshatriyas, Vaishyas and Sudras. Brahamans are the intellectual elites who devoted themselves to the performance of social rites, study and teaching. Second are Kshatriya who protected the people. They are the rulers and warriors. The third is Vaishyas who kept themselves engaged in trade to produce wealth. Rest of the people were Sudras who were supposed to serve the above three groups. The peculiarity of the caste system is that these groups were linked with birth. This is the basis of Indian caste system. A person had to follow certain profession not because he had aptitude but because he was born in that particular group. Slowly all the occupations became caste groups. All the three Varnas were entitled to Upanayana ceremony or the sacred thread ceremony. The fourth group, the Sudras were deprived of it. Only the Chariot maker were given this right. The institution of Gotra came up in this period. Gotra means having common ancestors. The position of women was not as graceful as it was in the early period. She was not allowed to participate in the assembly meetings. The learned women of the period can be regarded as exceptions. The kings performed Rajasuya Yagya. The Asvamedha Yagyas were performed by the king to ascertain his authority over larger area. The king collected taxes from the people and the treasurer was known as Sangrihitri. In administration and other duties of the state the king was assisted by the priest, the commander and the chief-queen. The local administration was carried on by the lower bodies and by the village level bodies. The king did not keep the standing army but depended upon his chieftains.

Religion: In the later Vedic period the Rudra, god of animals and the Vishnu, the preserver of the universe were prominent. The Indra and Agni of the Early Vedic Age were now in oblivion. In mode of worship the prayers were included but the sacrifices gained importance. The rituals in religion gained prominence and for this large number of priests were required. The people were now depending more on magic, spells and charms for their problems like diseases or destroying of the enemies. People were advised by the authors of literature to meditate upon. The doctrine of Karma, Maya, Mukti were popular. The Upanishads deal with the underlying reality. But along with this, there is reference to Gods in human form like Vishnu and Rudra. Pushan was the god of Sudras. The offerings to God also changed. In place of milk and vegetable food, animal sacrifices were made. The ceremonies were not simple now. Those were elaborate and lasted for months together. The Soma sacrifices were largely elaborated. The horse sacrifice known as Asvamedha became a prestigious sacrifice. There were sixteen classes of priests. Brahmans were one of them. The sacrifices and rituals dominated the religious scenario. The people were depending on charms and spells to cure the disease or to defeat the enemy. The Vedic literature emphasises doctrine of self, Karma, Maya, Mukti and transmigration of soul. Man is advised to meditate upon the self which is made up of intelligence and endowed with a body of spirit; and a form of light. He is told that there is one reality variously called 'the brahman', 'the holy power' or 'the atma'. The Upanishads highlight the philosophy behind life and death. They discuss the attainment of next birth on the performance. The doctrines were perfectly in harmony with the people of India. The philosophy has remained the basis to intellectual class in modern times.

Society: By the later vedic period the four groups emerged in the Aryan society. These were Brahmans, Rajanyas or Kshatriyas, Vaishyas and Sudras. The Brahmans are the intellectual elites, who remain involved in teaching and performance of religious rites. The Rajanyas or Kshatriyas protect the people. They are rulers and warriors. They defend the frontiers and maintain the social order. The Vaishyas are the common people who were involved in production and controlled the trade. In the beginning they were engaged in agriculture, cattle breeding and other jobs of artisans. It is only in later period that they started controlling trade. Rest of the people are Sudras who were supposed to stay separate from the society. The three higher groups had right to Upanayana ritual or investiture. It is wearing one sacred thread by the man. This ritual was denied to the sudras. Certain workers like the Rathakaras (chariot makers), were entitled to this ceremony. One more class was there in the society, called Nishadas, who were non-Aryans and lived in their own villages. The Vratyas was the Aryan group who led nomadic life. This caste structure developed in a peculiar way. The caste or the social group was linked with the birth. This is the unique feature of Indian society. A man is brahman not because he is intellectual but because he is born to brahman priests. The marriages took place within the same caste group. This in course of time became rigid. The society was patriarchal. The power of father in the family increased. Though women was respected her power had decreased in late Vedic period. She did not attend the assembly meetings. Though there are a few examples when the women theologian like Maitrey stands agains her own husband in the discussion of the highest metaphysical truth. These can be regarded as exceptional cases. Women were not inherited to the property. The birth of a girl was a source of misery. Sati and Paradah were not heard of. The elites married for more than once. The education during the period aimed at developing the character of the person. The list of subject for study includes a wide range like Itihasa, Puranas, grammer, astronomy, military science, dialects and knowledge of portents. The doctrine of Ahimsa or non-violence was not fully developed. In later Vedic period the concept of Gotra developed. This stood for the same ancestors. No marriage could take place between the persons of same gotra. This developed from cow-pen or where the cows of whole clan were kept. Asramas or the four stages of life, popularly attached with the Vedic time are the later developments. These are referred to in post-vedic literature: Brahamachari or the student, Grihastha -the house holder, Vanaprastha or the semi retirement and the Sanyasa- the complete retirement. These stages were not well defined in the vedic texts explaining that the concept of Asramas was not develogd in its full. The last Asrama i.e. Vanaprastha is not mentioned at all. Towards the end of later vedic period, many well known cities like Kasi, Ayodhya, Videha, Indraprastha, Kausambi and Hastinapur had sprung up. The Aryans used grey ware and iron. The use of iron formed the technological basis of overall economic development. The transition from the pastoral to the food producing economy is a landmark in Indian history.

Literature

Veda is the term derived from the term Vid of knowledge. The wisdom and knowledge of the Aryans is included in their sacred literature. These are not only Vedas but include the later works like Brahmans, Aranyakas and *the Upanishads*. Rigveda consists of 1028 hymns and has mythological contents. During this period the natural phenomena was personified. Sama Veda includes the verses from the Rig-veda arranged for sacrifices. The informations attached to this is very important for Indian music. It is also called the book of chants. The Yajur Veda is a collection of hymns to be recited at the time of sacrifices. This is the only Veda in prose in sharp contrast to Rig Veda. Atharva Veda is a book of spells and deals with witchcraft current among the lower classes of the people. The first three Vedas are collectively called as Trayi. The Brahmans are prose commentary on the Vedic Mantras. They explain the mutual relationship of sacred texts with their symbolic and ceremonial meaning. These texts, at some places, offer some information about the political scenario. The Aranyakas or "The Forest Books" are the concluding parts of Brahmans. These are composed for the hermits residing in forest. They deal with mysticism and symbolism of sacrifice and priestly philosophy. Upanishads are the main source of Indian philosophy. These mark the culmination of Indian thought. The doctrine of Karma, Liberation of Soul, Maya and Transmigration of soul are elaborated in the Upanishads. With the new social, economic and political order the literature also took a new turn. Now the Sutras were composed. These are Srauta Sutras, Griha Sutras and Dharma Sutras. Vedangas are part of Vedic texts and six in number: Kalpa, Siksha, Vijakarana, Nirukta, Chhandas and Jyotisha. There are Upa-vedas dealing with the secular subjects. The Puranas are very detailed eulogies of various gods. The Epics, *Ramayana* and *Mahabharata* also influenced the thought of India. Ramayana is in 24,000 verses, and Mahabharata includes eighteen books.

In sixth century B.C. many republics and kingdoms emerged in northern India that gave certainty to the history of the country. There is a vast literary material available, which is religious in character. The Palicanon is associated with the two Buddhist councils-one at Rajagriha, immediately after the death of Buddha, another hundred years later held at Vaishali.

Of these Canon, Vinaya and Suttapitaka deal with society. Moreover, another source of the period is the archaeological remains like cities and Ashoka's inscriptions.

During the period the rural economy was based on village communities. The concept of wealth changed from the cattle to the land. This was the reason for the increase in the categories of labour.

Sresthin the head of the trading guild or bank was the most important person in society. The use of metal coins were first made in this age. The Buddhist literature refers to the coins of different values: Nishka and Suvarna-the gold coins, *masha,* the *pada, kakini* and *kamsa* are bronze and copper coins, *shippikani* are shells.

By this period the tribal community was categorically divided into four varnas. Village was the autonomous unit of corporate life. Dharmashastras laid down the duties of each of the four vedas. But the Sudras were deprived of the religious and legal rights. The sub-castes had emerged in the society. Women were not denied of learning. This was the period of social transformation when the agricultural economy, based on the private property was emerging. The Vaishya of Vedic period period had now emerged as agriculturist, traders had become wealthy. The gahapati the head of the family was the rich man. He was no longer bound by any tribal regulations. The surplus created by the traders, manufacturers and the agriculturist crossed the tribal boundaries.

During this period, urbanisation started in Indo-Gangetic plains. This was the condition when Buddhism emerged. It has its germs in Vedic techniques. This can be seen in devotion to abstract speculation in Vedas. At a number of places in Upanishads it is made clear that there is no personal god as there is no personal man. Man is one of the all 'atoms' capable of apprehending the essence of the process, and of achieving inner liberation. The treatises proceed from the doctrine of Karma to moral law. It declares the man the judge of his actions. This part of the vedic philosophy influenced the philosophies of later period. "Buddhism was originally but a modification of Brahmanism, and grew slowly up to the position of a rival and opposing system," says Max Muller.

Religion

At this time numerous religious movements arose in northern India. The most common were Buddhism and Jainism.

Buddhism: The Indian society was divided on the basis of Varna and the divisions were followed rigidly during the period of study. The lower caste was badly mistreated, the higher class always oppressed the lower ones. The society was tension ridden. At this time Siddhartha Gautam of Sakya clan was born. He was born in 563 B.C. and died in 483 B.C. Sakyas were Kshatriyas and ruled Kapilvastu on the foot hills of Nepal. From his childhood Siddhartha showed a meditative bent of mind. Though he was married but could not be involved in the affairs of the world. At the age of 29 he left home when he was moved with the scene of the sick, old dead and an ascetic. He wandered from place to place for six years. Buddha got nirvana at the age of 35 years under a peepal tree in Gaya. His first sermon was delivered at Sarnath in Benaras. Buddhism forwards a direct personal experience that involved intuition and a higher form of reason. It did not give any importance to the institution, cultures or opinion in the beginning. It emphasised the feeling of equal individuals. There is no authority in Buddhism as in Catholicism, Judaism or Islam. Buddha encouraged each individual to do his or her seeking. Buddhism does not include ritual except meditative techniques. It does not have theology or philosophical speculation involved. Buddha was concerned with the release of individuals from suffering and spiritual realisation. Buddha rejected most of the traditions of Hinduism and produced a religion of intense self-effort. Any sort of spiritualism, super-naturalism, concept of spirits or souls was rejected. Buddhism was scientific in approach as it emphasised the personal experience as the final test of truth rather than reasoning, inference or argument. It was concerned with problem solving rather than with theological or philosophical speculation. Like, it brings forward the way to eliminate the evils rather than the problem of existence of evil in the universe. It is psychological in approach, in that it begins with human beings rather than with the universe and works at dealing with their problems, their nature, and the dynamics of their development. Buddhism rejects governments, caste systems, and any other ranking of human beings, each individual is important in it. Buddha made the religion and its purpose very clear, "Here is the problem and here is the solution". For this he recognised four truths called the Four Noble Truths. These are sorrow, desire, annhilation or desire and Eight Fold Path.

The Eight Fold Path was the guidance by Buddha to people to remove the sorrows. Buddha denied Atman or soul but believed in Karma or action. He believed that man gets according to his actions. Buddhism was accepted by a large number of people. The reason behind this was that Buddhism attacked the weakness of the existing religion, Hinduism or Brahmanism. Brahmans occupied the highest position in the society. The lower caste was looked down upon by them. Buddha declared that the laymen could rise higher in spirituality by leading moral life. The religion particularly won the support of lower classes because it attacked the Varna System of Hindu Society. Buddha established the Sangha. Woman were brought on a par with the men and were admitted to the Sangha or the Church. The lower classes immediately joined Buddhism. The liberal and democratic attitude of Buddhism made it extremely popular with the people. The Magadha kingdom, excluded from Aryavrata since it was being ruled by a sudra embraced the religion readily. Buddha used Pali language for his sermons. It was the language of the people. This helped the people of the lower strata to follow and understand. The doors of Sangha or the religious order were open to all irrespective of caste and sex. Each Sangha became a centre of learning. It also worked as place of assembly for the followers where the teachings of the religion were imparted. The Sanghas became living examples of Buddhism where the monks were groomed. There were three aspects of Buddhism — Buddha, Sangha, Dharma. Buddhism had two sects: Hinayana and Mahayana. It was Mahayana Buddhism that help spread the religion. Its philosophy that the highest ideal of an individual is not to attain nirvana for himself but for others also, provoked the monks and nuns for propogation of the faith. Nagarjuna, Aganga, Vasumitra, Dharmkriti, and Vasubandhu were Buddhist scholars of the period. Buddhism was supported by various rulers like Bimbisara and Ajatsatru, Udayin and Prasenjit. King Ashoka brought a new epoch in Buddhism. The faith crossed the national boundaries and reached Asia (West and Central). Kanishka patronised the faith and fourth Buddhist council took place in his period.

Brahmanism: It was in fourth century A.D. that Brahmanism started reviving and it was also the declining period of Buddhism. By sixth century A.D. the decadence of Buddhism and invigoration of Brahmanism were well advanced. The new theistic religions, however centred round the idea of a supreme God conceived as Vishnu, Shiva or Shakti. Salvation was possible only through his grace, through devotion. Of this new system two sects remained prominent-Saivism and Vaishnavism. Vaishnavism owed its origin to the Upanishads. It laid stress upon the idea of a supreme God called Hari, and suggested the necessity of worshipping him with devotion. It gave preference to devotion than the previous methods of sacrifices and austerities. The rituals were not altogether done away with. Thus there was a reformed form of previous Brahmanism. It recommended devotion to Lord Hari and the principles of Aranyakas.

At a later stage, the faith which originated from Mathura spread to other regions. Krishna gave a definite shape to the faith. His philosophical teachings led to regular growth of an independent sect and Vasudeva was looked upon as a supreme deity. There are inscriptions referring to worship of Vasudeva in Maharashtra, Rajputana and Central India. One of the inscriptions explains that the Greek ambassador Heliodorus of Taxila styled himself as a Bhagvata and erected a pillar in honour of Vasudeva. Like Buddhism, Vaishnavism also made conversion of the foreigners. A Syrian legend refers to the cult of Krishna worship. The legendary exploits of Krishna formed the subject of dramatic representations. Krishna became incarnation of Vishnu and there is clear identification between Vishnu and Krishna. This demonstrates the reconciliation between the Brahmanism and the Vaishnavism. Saivism represented in Rig Veda in concept of Rudra is represented as malignant and destructive phenomena in nature. In further texts the Rudra is described as benevolent when his wrath on nature is thoroughly appeased. Shiva, as he is called, is the object of worship not of one particular sect but of the whole Aryan society.

Jainism: The other religious movement that had reformative attitude in sixth century B.C. was Jainism. The propounder of the faith was Vardhaman Mahavira who was born in 540 B.C. in Vaishali, Bihar. His father was a tirbal head and mother belonged to famous Lichchhavi clan. The tradition of Jaina religion can be traced back to the Vedic era when Rishabhadeva and Arishtanemi were Tirthankaras. The twenty third tirthankar was Parshvanath in the 8th century B.C. Mahavira was the last tirthankara. Jainism emphasised liberation through practice of three jewels: right faith, right knowledge and right conduct. It is explained in it that the right faith can be attained either by learning or initiation by some one. It is an attitude of respect towards truth. It is always expected of the aspirant to gain right knowledge and not to depend upon what is taught by the spiritual teachers. He must study the religion himself and grow more faith. It is surmised that perfect knowledge would cause perfect faith. For this, the removal of action is the requisite. Good conduct helps in removal of Karmas. This is the way of getting rid of actions that lead to bondage and suffering. Jainism refers to five doctrines: (i) Non-violence, (ii) Truth, (iii) Do not step!, (iv) Not to acquire property and (v) Celibacy.

Mahavira himself wandered in search of truth for 12 years. On gaining Kaivalaya he discarded clothes and lived naked. He suggested his followers to discard the clothes so that they did not have to depend upon any body. The previous Trithankar allowed covering of body. Later Jainism was divided into two sects over this point- Swetambars i.e. those who wear white dress, and Digambaras or those who remain naked.

Jainism placed Jina above god though it did not discard the presence of God. It did not discard the caste system of Hindu society like Buddhism. It believed that the person is born according to his previous karmas and he gets the caste group according to his actions or virtues he acquires. But the people of lower caste can also gain liberation through pure and meritorious life. The three gems or ratnas of Jainism are: full knowledge, action and liberation. Jainism spread to West and South India. But it failed to attract the masses on large scale as Buddhism did. During Mahavira's lifetime the number of followers rose to 14,000. Jainism adopted, like Buddhism, the language of people. Apbhransha, a form of Prakrit was used for Jaina literature. It discarded Sanskrit patronised by the brahmans. The earliest Jain literature was composed in Apbhransha, thus giving the language the first grammer. The literature includes many treatises in the form of epics, puranas, novels and dramas. A large literature was composed in Kannada since the place became the centre of the faith. It is mentioned in Jain literature that Chandragupta Maurya became Jaina during his later days. He lived in Karnataka as an ascetic. Jainism discarded the rituals of Vedic religion. But it failed to attract the people like Buddhism because it remained the part of its original faith i.e. Brahmanism. It did not categorically distinguishe itself from Hinduism. Jainism favours meditation and strict discipline. It emphasises on concept of nonviolence and lays down strict discipline. It had dogmatic approach towards the principal faith.

Jainism penetrated into Gujarat, Malwa and Rajasthan at a later stage. The Jainas adopted Prakrit and Apbransha as their language of literature. This language developed under their patronage. Kannada also developed since a large literature was written in the languae. The original text of Jains was called Purvas. Later on these were re-arranged and were called Angas. The Angas were not recognised by the Digambars. Jainism gave some of the best specimens of Indian architectrue and sculpture. The temples of Abu, the elephant caves of Orissa, the idols of Gomateshwara in Mysore and Jain tower of Chittorgarh are a few of them. Jainism was divided seven times during the course of history. The final division which is noticeable into two sects -Digambaras and Shwetambara. Both the sects have almost the same religious and philosophical beliefs. The only difference between the two is the belief over the sex of one of the Tirthankar-Malli. The Shvetambers believe that she was a woman, while the Digambaras consider her to be a man. They consider women incapable of attaining salvation or Nirvana. Digambaras believe that all Jaina ascetics should follow the example of Mahavira and discard clothes. While Shvetambaras believe that the leading teachers of Jaina church gave up the practice of living nude after a few generations of Mahavira. The other point of difference between the two is over intake of food by the ascetics. It is called Kevali. Digambaras believe that no Kevali is required by these ascetics while the Shvetambaras believe other way though it is an academic point. Both the groups believe in techniques of Mahavira but they behave at social and religious plains in a different manner. The early literature of both the sects is silent over the point. But in later literature there are various versions. It is clear that the final separation came in 80 A.D. The Digambaras have a long history since the eighth century. For first five or six centuries, after Mahavira, there is no particular reference to Digambaras. The reason apparently could be that they had not emerged as a separate sect. In the first century A.D. the tradition of Acharyas emerged. In south Karnataka, Kunda Kunda a great prolific author of books on Jainism lived during this period. He wrote in Prakrit which was close to Mathura region language. He has written on Jain philosophy with immense authority as if he was one of the immediate disciples of Mahavira. The new Acharya was Umaswami who lived during A.D. 135 to 219. He wrote *Tattavartha dhigamasutra* i.e. the manual of the understanding of the true nature of the things. This was written at Pataliputra in Sanskrit. It is an authority on Jaina dogmatics. This is a popular work on the sect. In private houses this work is read by all Jains. Umaswami is said to have written 500 books. The next Acharya was Samanta bhadra who was referred to as swami with reverence by the late acharyas. His period is around 120 A.D. to 185 A.D. Among other works, his important work is a commentary of Umaswami's *Tattavartha dhigamasutra*. Its only one part is left now. It is also known as Devagama-Sutra or Aptamimansa. It explains in detail the Jain philosophy. It was also discussed by non-Jain philosophers of the later period like Kumarila and Vachaspati Mishra.Upto 8th and 9th century Jain scholars of Karnataka produced distinguished works.

From ninth to seventeenth century Digambara church saw immense progress; During this period there were bhattarakas or the persons who looked after the Jain temples. In ninth centry a treatise on medicine was written by Ugraditya called Kalyankaraka. It contains 8,000 slokas in Sanskrit. This prescribes the medicines which do not contain animal product or intoxicants. in other words it prescribes only medicines which a Jaina can safely take. During this period a mathematician flourished known as Mahaviracharya who wrote *Ganitasara Sangraha* in 850 A. D. Another discovery related to mathematics was use of logarithms. Shvetambaras developed a separate church only after the Valabhi council that was held 980 years after the death of Mahavira. This council completed *Kalpasutra* of Bhadrabahu. It has three sections-1) Jainacharita-containing biographies of Jinas, 2) Theravali-the list of games sakhas, 3) Samachari-rules for the ascetics. Kalpasutra is a sacred work for every Shvetambara. The Valabhi council put to writing the saying of Mahavira which it thought had been authentically handed down. These are 45 books called Angas and Upangas. But Digambaras did not accept these canons as authentic. Many scholars have written commentaries on these Angas and Upangas which are called Niryuktis. All this forms a part of Shvetambar literature. The mythologies worked upon them are called Charitras. The Shvetambar monks composed a large number of commentaries between 6th and 9th centuries. These commentaries are known as Chumis. One of these works known as Nandichumi mentions that a council had been held in Mathura also in 676 A.D., which was presided by Skandila or Sandilya. However, the results of this are not clear. Another imporant Chumi of the period is *Avashyaka-sutra* by Jinadasagani. This work offers a detailed account of Mahavira's various journeys when he travelled for 12.5 years before he attained Kaivalyaj. The author must have obtained this information from a reliable source of his period. This work seems to be authentic.

During the fifth and sixth centuries there was a significant development in Jaina iconography. The sculptue of the period was standardized. The basics of the iconography were similar to both sects of Jaina-Digambara and Shvetambara. The only difference was that Digambaras do not, give clothes and ornaments to that images. The Tirathankaras were accompanied by Yakshas. These Yakshas were very popular during Mahaviras period. Later on these were diminished as attendants of Tiranthankaras. A few set of goddesses developed called Vidyadevis which were known by the sixteen different names. From sixth century A. D. an intellectual movement started which lasted upto 12th century A. D. in Shvetambara sect. It was initiated by a prolific writer Haribhadra. Suri in eight centruy A.D. He has written 1,444 works of which only 88 are available. Suri is the honorific title of learned Jain monks. Haribhadra became a monk and wandered from one place to another. He was originally a brahman and was very well versed in Buddhist studies also. He used both the languages: Sanskrit and Prakrit. There were many Jaina scholars like Udyotanaswimi who wrote *Kivalayamala,* Jayasinha wrote *Dharmapadesh mala* in 9th century. Because of their learning aptitudes the Jains were able to enter the court of flourishing Chalukya dynasty. Jainism also attracted the mercantile community.

The learning programme started by Haribhadra culminated in Hemachandra Suri in eleventh century. He wrote epics, grammer, poetry and fiction. Hemachandra has written on the life of 63 great persons of Jain mythology-Trishashtishalaka-Purusha Charita. Its appendix is known as Parisistaparvan which gives 14 generations history of Jaina Church *Siddha hema- -habada nushasana,* a famous grammar is by the same author. The main part of the work deals with the grammer of Sanskrit, language and the rest with the Prakrit language. In the Sanskrit part the author shows his acquaintance with nearly all grammatical systems of the language. He tried to elucidate many aspects of grammer to make it understandable. He deals with all Prakrits of the time. Kumarpalacarita is a long political work of Hemchandra. He has also compiled four lexicons. 1. Abhidhanachintamani, 2. Anekarthasangraha, 3. Nighanta (medical plants), 4. Deshinamala. There are a few works on poetics by this prolific writer. From 11th to 16th century a school of miniature paintings flourished in and around Gujarat. The Kalpa-sutra was the subject of Jain paintings. From 11th to 13th century A.D. the Shvetambaras were divided into various groups and these were called gachchhas. The canonical books of the Shvetambaras are not the works by Mahavira himself, but these are his discourses to the devotees. The Jains think that originally since the time of first Tirthankara, there were two kinds of sacred books. These were the purvas which numbered 14, and angas which were numbered 11. The 14 Purvas were lost by the time the canon was written. The eleven Angas are the oldest part of the canon. There are twelve Upangas, the ten Prakirnas, six Chhedasutras, individual texts and four Mulasutras. Tirthankara is a central figure in Jaina temple. His image is shown either standing or sitting in Yogasana posture. Since the images of the tirthankaras look alike they have to be distiguished by their animal depicted below the seat of the tirthankara. The tirthankaras were always accompanied by attendants called Yakshas. Digambaras have different emblems.

There is a big difference between Hindus and Jainas as regards treating of the ascetics. For Hindus an ascetic is practically outside the society. There is no relationship between him and the society, unless he becomes the god man. But in Jain community an ascetic is very much part of the society. He has a life long relationsip with society and is treated as a religious teacher. The society takes responsibility of providing the food and if necessary shelter. But society also maintains a watch upon his behaviour as he has to maintain the religious vow. Jaina Sadhu needn't worry about food and basic amenities but he has to remain under constant watch of the society. An ascetic spends his time in writing and reading. In writing on the religious aspect there is no scope for speculation. The works composed on Jain mythology do not have any poetic value since the monks keep their works away from sexual love. During the middle age the whole literature in India was devotional. The Jains remained away from the devotional favour. The writings of Jain Sadhus may not have literary value, but the ascetics have to lead studious life for this they have to be provided with the books. Wherever a group of Jain families live there is book collection known as 'Granth bhandar'. There are 100 such collections in Rajasthan only. These include books on various subjects apart from Jainism.

Five

EMPIRE OF MAURYAS

The history of Maurya's, unlike that of the early ruling houses, is rendered reliable by a variety of evidence drawn from the sources like, the *Arthashastra* of Kautilya or Chanakya, various Greek accounts like 'Indica' by Megasthenese, the inscriptions of Ashoka, coins of various metals, etc.

Chandragupta, the founder of Maurya dynasty succeeded to the Nanda throne in 321 B.C. at the age of 25. Indian tradition has it that a Brahaman, Kautilya, also known as Chanakya or Vishnugupta, who wanted to avenge upon the Nandas, was his mentor and his guide. Indian and classical sources state that he overthrew the last Nanda ruler and occupied his capital Pataliputra (Patna). The Greek accounts also render further information that he moved further towards north-west India and occupied Greek garrisons left behind by Alexander.

The sources indicate that Alexander's general, Seleucus Nikator gained control of most Asiatic provinces of the Macedonian empire, and he met Chandragupta in battle. The Greek general had to surrender and sign a treaty. He entered into a marriage alliance with the Mauryan king giving away his daughter to Chandragupta he obtained the territory across Indus. Seleucus sent his ambassador Megasthanese to the Pataliputra court where he lived for many years. He travelled the country extensively and he wrote an informative book '*Indica*' which is lost now. But it is referred to in many other works.

A Greek writer Justin writes that Chandragupta Maurya overrun the whole of India. With corroboration to other sources, it is clear that he built up a vast empire that included Bihar, portion of Orissa and Bengal, north portions of Deccan and part of north-west frontier. Jaina sources say that the Mauryan king embraced Jainism towards the end of his life and turned ascetic.

In 297 B.C. Chandragupta was succeeded by his son Bindusara, or according to Greek sources Amitrochates (orAmithaghata in Sanskrit). He had relations with Antiochus I, the king of Syria. Bindusara is said to have won "the land between two seas" which means he included peninsular India to Magadhan empire.

In 273 B.C. Ashoka ascended the throne who, according to Buddhist sources usurped the throne after killing many rivals and began his reign as a tyrant king. Though this view is not supported by any other source. Ashoka waged a war against the Kalinga state in south east India. The horror of war changed the monarch and he embraced Buddhism. This was the most important event of Ashoka's life and his religious period. Ashoka became an ardent Buddhist, and reigned like a noble king. The Buddhist church was reorgnised and the third Buddhist council met at Pataliputra in 250 B.C. under the chairmanship of Mogalliputta Tissa.

For the first time Maurya King contributed to the unification of a large part of the country. Ashoka's inscriptions refer to this certification. Ashoka annexed Kalinga after a great war and built the city of Srinagar thereafter including Kashmir in Mauryan empire. There are references to the rulers of Hellenic world-Syria, Egypt, Macedonia, Cyrene and Epirus. The Ceylonese traditions indicate very cordial relations with Mauryan King Ashoka who ruled upto 232 B.C.

Administration

Mauryan kings definitely had an efficient administration. Chandragupta Maurya was the father of the administration system. As indicated in *Indica* of Megasthanese and refered to in *Arthashastra* of Kautilya, the king was the supreme head of the state. The administrative network was guided by Chanakya who was also minister and advisor to the king. According to Kautilya, the royal order supercedes all other sources of authority including dharma, which could be interpreted by the King in changing context of time. The state controlled all spheres of life through its four fold bureaucracy—Judicial, military, executive and legislative. Though a despot, Chandragupta devoted himself whole heartedly to serve the people. As the highest military commander, he would consider plans of operation with his commander-in-chief (Senapati). The military was divided into six boards: admirality, infantry, cavalry, chariots, war elephants, transport and army service. The king was the head of the judiciary. As head of the executive government, Chandragupta appointed all high officials of the states like Sachivs, Amatyas, Mantris, and the Purohitas. Adhyakshas maintained correspondence with *mantri parishad*. The legislative functions included issuing of royal orders, maintenance of ancient tradition. The administration of Pataliputra was carrried on by six committees dealing with sanitation, foreigners, registration of birth and death, regulation of weights and measures and others.

The empire was divided into provinces and province into the districts. The village was the unit of the administrative system.

The Maurya state exercised a rigid control through a number of superintendents over all trade and including that which yielded profit. The superintendents were employed in the fields of commerce, markets, weights and measures, ships and tolls.

The land tax formed the chief source of revenue. There was water cess, share cropping was another source of income to the state. Custom and Ferry charges were other important sources of income to the state exchequer. The *Arthashastra* refers to the superintendent of mines and superintendent of salt. The state enjoyed monopoly over all mines in the empire. This derived its total control over the manufacture of metal weaponry for army and the supply of tools and implements needed for agriculture and industry.

The social order did not function as smoothly as envisaged by the Brahman law givers. The upper two castes were not ready to give equal status to third caste i.e. Vaisyas. The Vaisyas being a commerce class controlled the trade and urban institutions. Their support for Buddhism and Jainism is an expression of resentment against the higher caste groups. The Sudras were no less hostile to the higher groups.

Ashoka's Dharma

Buddhism, that was confined to Magadha and Kosala, had emerged as a powerful force to be developed into a distinct religion. Ashoka became Buddhist after the Kalinga war. His conversion brought about a great change in his policies. His administration, though on the same pattern, became noble. The king himself became a noble and a kind king.

In his inscriptions, specially in Bhabru inscription, he admitted that he believes in the principles of Buddhism, but what he taught to his subjects was an ethical code aimed at building the attitude of social responsibility among the people. His policy of Dhamma sought to make a strong case for the recognition of the dignity of man. The concept of Dhamma was very likely conditional by the vastness of the empire, whose unity would be preserved by overcoming tensions generated by existence of divergent social, religious and cultural elements. Ashoka laid emphasis on tolerance as a basic principle of Dhamma. By pleading for consideration towards slaves and servants, obedience to mother and father, generosity towards friends, relatives and towards priests and monks, Ashoka recommends a harmonious life both in family and community. Religious tolerance occupies an important place in the inscription of Ashoka.

In spite of his religious fervour, Ashoka denounced all useless ceremonies and sacrifices which resulted from superstitions.

Ashoka's Dharma emphasised non-violence. Overhwelmed by the horror of the Kalinga War he is said to have renounced all future blood shed, and in one of his edicts he prohibits animal slaughter. It is likely that Ashoka sought to prevent only the ritual sacrifice of animals and did not recommend a general prohibition.

The policy of Ashoka's Dharma also included several social welfare measures. He inaugurated, in the tenth year of his reign, a system of royal tours as described in an edict. Perhaps those tours brought him into direct contact with the people, and he was able to explain to them his Dhamma.

Ashoka created a new rank of officers and called then Dhammamahamatras who were to take care of *bhikshus*, brahmans, *ajivkas* and *nirgranthas*. These officers were directly responsible for working of Dharma. They were given special rights to enter any house or any section of the society. Ashoka also propagated his religion through monolithic pillars. 37 of his edicts under this category have come to light.

Buddhism under Ashoka had inspired art to a great extent. The best specimens of contemporary art are highly polished columns standing free in space, often crowned with animal figures. At least 14 such pillars are known, a few of them may date before the time of Ashoka. The excavated halls of Barabar and Nagarjuni caves belong to the time of Ashoka and his successors.

Decline of Mauryas

The Maurya empire began to decline with the death of Ashoka in 232 B.C. The western part of the empire was threatened by the Greeks and to whom it was finally lost by 180 B.C. In south the Satvahanas or the Andhras became powerful. The eastern part of the empire continued to be governed by Ashoka's successors. In 180 B.C. a Brahman general of the empire killed the last ruler Brihddratha, and Sunga dynasty was founded.

For the causes of the fall of Maurya Empire Ashoka's policies are blamed. His pro-Buddhist policies antagonised the Brahmans. His policy of non-violence is said to have weakened the army. But the economic policies of Ashoka are largely ascribed to the fall of the empire. His large army which fought no war became a burden on the state. The appointment of new officers, charitable public works though indicative of his paternal affection for his people, largely strained the exchequer. To these causes is added, undoubtedly the incapacity of later Mauryan successors.

Socio-economic Conditions

Kautilya's *Arthashastra* and other contemporary literature offer a vivid picture of the socio-economic condition of the people. The peace and security ensured by the monarchs offered great opportunity to the people for development in various fields. The internal trade flourished, the state controlled and organised the agriculture, industry, trade and commerce of the country. Agriculture was the main occupation. The crown lands were directly controlled.

Ship building was the state's monopoly. The trade and commerce with other states was directly regulated. Textile industry was one of the major industries. The *Arthashastra* refers to the manufacture of iron, copper, lead, bronze and tin. The Maurya period witnessed the development of many industries like drugs, gums, dyes, perfumes, potteries, etc.

Kautilya and Megasthanese both testify to the society being grouped on the basis of caste. Women were not held in high esteem. The staple food was rice.

Art and Culture

Mauryans contributed to arts singnificantly. This includes architecture, sculpture, engineering, polishing, etc. The wooden carving was magnificent as is evident from the excavations from Kumrahar. The wooden palace of Chandragupta was wonderful. Ashoka further improved the wooden walls and build the capital by adding many attractive edifices.

The Buddhist tradition tells that Ashoka built as many as 84,000 stupas. They were made of rock or bricks. The art of rock cutting reached its zenith during the period. The caves are a beautiful example of Mauryan period. These were used for assembly halls or for religious ceremoneis. The monuments, pillars and caves have a polishing, which is a unique feature. The engineering was of high level.

Six

POST-MAURYAN ERA

Small Kingdoms

The dwindling Mauryan empire came to an end in 180 B.C., when the last ruler Brihadratha was killed by his own commander Pushyamitra Sunga. This founded the Sunga dynasy. Sungas were Brahmins, and very likely they hailed from Ujjain. The centre of Pushyamitra Sanga was Vidisha in Madhya Pradesh. He is said to have performed Ashavamedha sacrifices. While the Buddhist scripture describe him as persecutor of Buddhists, destroyer of monasteries, the Buddhist remains at Barhut, assigned to the Sunga period contradicts this. Pushyamitra reigned for 36 years i.e. upto 148 B.C. He was succeeded by his son Agnimitra. He ruled for eight years. Agnimitra was succeeded by his son Jyeshtha. Vasumitrà was the next important king of the dynasty. Bhagbhabra and Bhagvata are other kings of the Sunga dynasty. Puranas mention Devabhuti the last Sunga king who was incapable and ease loving. He was put to death by his minister called Vasudeva Kanva.

Sungas fought back the invasion of Hunas and are known for cultural development of the country.

Kanvas ruled the throne of Magadha for 45 years. During this duration 4 kings of the dynasty ruled the Kingdom. These kings are also known for their brahmanical faith.

Chetas of Kalinga

Kalinga became independent of Maurya kingdom after Ashoka. The Hathigumpha inscription near Bhubaneswar records the exploits of King Kharavela belonging to Cheta dynasty. According to the inscription, Kharavela ascended the throne of Kalinga at the age of 24, after having served apprenticeship as prince for eight years. When he became the king he assumed the titles of Kalingadhipati or Kalinga Chakravartin as a mark of his paramountcy. The inscription mentions that the king Kharavela sent his armies as far as south and victorious. He was able to defeat Rashtrakutas and Bhojakas. Kharavela was an ardent Jaina and he constructed a cave for Jain monks.

Satvahanas

Satavahanas, the successors of Mauryas in Deccan and Central India are also known as Andhras. Satavahanas took advantage of Maurya disintegration and extended rule upto western coast. The first king Simuka is believed to have destroyed the Sunga power. The Satavahanas had to suffer a defeat at the hands of Shakas. This is suppoprted by the coins and inscriptions available at Nasik referring to Shaka chief Nahapana indicating Shaka dominance in the area towards the close of the first century A.D. or the beginning of the second. But under the most illustrious ruler Gautamiputra Satkarani. The Satavahanas recovered the western possessions. Gautamiputra and his son Vasishtiputra, who ruled in first half of the second century A.D., extended their territory and gave Satavahanas a position of eminence. A matrimonial alliance was concluded between Gautamiputra and Rudradaman of Shaka clan who gave his daughter in marriage to Gautamiputra. Upto the end of the second century Satvahanas ruled over Kathiawar, and upto northern Tamil Nadu. In the third century, however, there was gradual weakening of the Satavahanas as power and many local governors claimed independence.

Satavahanas have a prominent place in their history. They ruled according to Dharmashastras. The King was the upholder of Dharma and was represented as possessing the qualities of ancient gods. Satavahanas administration had similarities with the Mauryas. The Kings claimed to be Brahmins, and performed vedic rites, worshipped large number of Vaishnava gods. There are examples that the Kings gave grants to Buddhist monks. Mahayana Buddhist sect had considerable following. Nagarjunakonda and Amaravati in Andhra Pradesh became important seats of Buddhist culture under them. Art and commerce also flourished during their period. Many monasteries and temples were cut out of solid rock in the North-Western Deccan. Chaitya or the Buddhist temple and monastery or the Viharas were constructed in this period.

Indo-Greeks

The most significant development after the fall of Mauryan empire was the onslaught of foreigners from the north-west. The unguarded north-western frontier attracted Greeks. In second century B.C. Demetrius, son of Euthedemus, passed further into India. Menander the famous Bactrian king in India, reached Patliputra. He ruled from 155 B.C. to 130 B.C. and gave some stability to Greek power in India. This Indo-Greek King is best known as Milinda as a Buddhist text refers to him in *Milinda Panho* (Milinda Prashna) which records his discussions with Buddhist philosopher Nagasena, resulting in his conversion to Buddhism.

Shakas

The Indo-Greek kindgom in India did not last long. Due io disturbances in Central Asia the Scythians or the Shakas, a nomadic tribe attacked Bactria and later invaded Greek kingdom in India. By the middle of first century B.C. only a few Greek chiefs ruled in India, and the Shaka power extended as far as Mathura. Towards the close of the first century B.C. the Palavas or Indo-Parthians controled north-west India. The most popular of these is Gondopharnes to whose court St. Thomas came to propagate Christianity. Indo-Parthians power broke down soon.

Kushanas

The Parthians were followed by Kushanas who are also known with the name Yuechis or Tocharians. In Kabul and Kashmir the first ruler of the dynasty known as Kujula was succeeded by Vima Kadphises. He was eventually succeeded by Kanishka. Kushanas issued gold coins.

The Kushan dynasty flourished under Kanishka. The most accepted date of his accession to the throne is 78 A.D. This year is also marked for beginning of an era known as Shaka era. In India the suzerainity of Kushanas reached the height of its power and extended to far south till Sanchi and East Benaras. Purushpura or Peshawar was his capital. Mathura was a flourishing city of the Kushanas.

Kanishka is known for his association with Buddhism. He convened the fourth Buddhist council to bring forth the theology and doctrine of the faith in Kashimir. He is said to have constituted at Peshawar a multi-storeyed relic tower enshrining the relics of the Buddha. The Chinese traveller Hieun Tsang who came to India in Harshavardhan's period has written about his stupa.

Kanishka's interest in Buddhism is futher verified with the reference of several Buddhist theologians like Ashvaghosa, Vasumitra, Parshva, Sangharaksha and Kasyapa Matanga.

The most striking feature of the post Mauryan period is the thriving trade between India and the western world. With the improvement of the internal communication by the Mauryas, the construction of highways gave impetus to the internal trade. The conquest of north-west India by the West Asian powers promoted closer contacts with western and central Asia. The Indian merchants participated as intermediaries in the Chinese silk trade. Central Asia acted as a link between India and China. With the emergence of Roman empire as a permanent power the western world started trade with India and became the chief customer of its luxury goods. This led to the growth of money economy and coins were used for trade. Apart from gold and silver coins, the coins of low value of lead and potin are also found from Deccan. In north west India the Kushans circulated the copper coins.

Increased commercial activity and the consequent growth of money economy led to a proliferation of arts and crafts leading to greater specialisations and to the achievements of greater technical skills in certain spheres of production. The period also witnessed progress in the techniques of textile manufacture. It is testified by the later status of special celebrity states attained by Mathura in the manufacture of textiles, especially shataka, a kind of cloth. The influx of Chinese silks into India stimulated the silk industry here.

Increase in trade demanded an efficient organisation of production and distribution. The individual artists got together and formed guilds and the merchants also organised themselves into corporations. Around two dozen guilds of artisans existed in this period. The guild system became a general pattern of production, facilitating high output. Inscriptions attest the existence of many of them in the Mathura region and western Deccan. These guilds sometimes acted like the banks. The membership of the guild provided social status and security to the artisans. Artisans and craftsmen in the post Mauryan period were drawn from the Shudras who gained wealth and status. The distinction between Vaishyas and Shudras became blurred.

The traditional social order based on Varna was threatened by the influx of foreign people's during this period. The absorption of foreigners into Indian society was made easier through their adoption of Buddhism, which did not raise difficulties as to caste. This explains why a number of foreign rulers patronised the religion of Buddha.

In this period the art mainly centered around Buddhism. The foreigners who settled here lost their identity and craftsman among them developed a different school of art. The devotees of Jainism patronised a school of sculpture at Mathura, here at an early period the artists working for centuries in the white spotted red sand stone of the locality, produced pieces of art depicting the cross legged naked figure of the Tirthankara in meditation. The Mathura school, as it came to be known, is said to have begun at the end of the first century B.C. Later it received the patronage of the Kushan rulers, some of whose portrait statues have also been discovered near Mathura, the most well known being that of Kanishka without its head. The Mathura school is said to have produced the first image of Buddha, his presence in the earlier stupa sculptures being indicated by the symbols. In technique and artistic execution the Mathura craftsman owed a great deal to the earlier Indian traditon. But they also borrowed more than one, Graeco-Roman motif from Gandhar. In the north-west, a distinct and prolific school of art flourished from about the middle of the first century B.C. to the fifth century A.D. known as the Gandhara art. The Mathura tradition inspired another school of art, that of Sarnath, in the succeeding period.

The Gandhara school, often called Graeco-Buddhist was influenced less by Greek than by Roman art. It enjoyed the greatest prosperity under the Kushana emperor. The subject matter of the Gandhara art was predominantly Buddhist, but many of the sculptural motifs are of Hellenistic or Roman derivation. The mother of the Buddha resembled the Athenian matros.

During the period discussed, terracotta was the medium used for artistic expression. The female figures found are well balanced depicting a great variety of ethnic tribal and normal fashions, especially prominent in male figures from Mathura. The literary activity in the post-Maurya period took various forms. The *Gathasaptashati,* an anthropology of 700 self contained graceful stanzas on love, is a fine creation in Prakrit. It is said that it was written by a Satavahana king though later additions were made to it. But Sanskrit emerged as a chief medium of literary expression in this period. In second century B.C. Patanjali wrote *Mahabhashya* which was a commentry on Sanskrit grammer written by Panini. Ishtis or new grammar rules were formulated to supplement the earlier ones. This was transformation in the Sanskrit language. *Charaka Samhita,* the well known medical treatise was written in this period. *Sushruta* is also another medical treatise of this period. The most important legal text of India the *Manusmriti* was compiled between 200 B.C. and 200 A.D. The *Natyashastra,* the first important work on deamaturgy, is also believed to have been written by Bharat Muni in this period. In poetry, *Buddha Charita* is valuable as it deals with the life of Buddha by Ashavaghosha. He has composed another poetical composition known as *Saundarananda* that depicts the conversion of Buddha's brother to Buddhism. *Svapanavasvadattam* is the complete play written by Bhasha.

Sangam Age

Sangam Age is the period from the first century A.D. to fourth century A. D. in south when the literary work of various literatures were approved by the societies or the academies. Tamil is the language of the literatures. These scholars flourished in Pandya kingdom, where three Sangams (college of Tamil poets were held). Of those the literature of two are lost. The third Sangam contains only anthologies and epics. These are from the Tamil classics. From the first Sangam nothing has been preserved. From the second Sangam only a single work, Tolkappiyam has come down to us. It is a grammatical treatise written in form of Sutras, though it also throws enormous light on the manners, customs, thoughts and beliefs of the people.

The other Tamil classics of the age known to us belong to the Third Sangam. These are anthologies and epics and grouped in schematic anthologies: 1. Narrinai, 2. Kuruntogai, 3. Aingurunuru, 4. Padirru Pattu, 5. Paripadal, 6. Kalittogai, 7. Aganandru, 8. Purananura, 9. Pattuppattu. The entire collection includes 2,279 poems of various lengths-from three to eight hundred lines by 473 poets. There are notes giving the name of its author, the occassion of the composition and other details at the end of each poem. Only a part of the vast literature has survived. Many inscriptions referring to Pandyas, Cheras and Cholas mention about the Sangam literature. The translation of *Mahabharata* in Tamil, Bharatam by Perundevanar are also mentioned. The three kingdoms offered patronage to the poets and other authors from time to time. The Sangam literature reflects the maturity of the Tamil language and started serving as a powerful elegant medium of literary expression. After the age of Sangam the language assimilated many words and ideas from the Sanskrit sources.

The poems offer geneologies of various dynasties of the three kingdoms and refer to many events, personalities, etc. There is also reference to battles and valour of the brave soldiers is sung of. With corroboration of the events a political scenario of the Sangam age is established.

About the socio-economic and cultural ideas, Sangam literature provides a true picture. The literary pieces bring forward the composite character and a result of blend of the two cultures-Dravidian and Aryan. It can be understood this way that the stories of *Ramayana* and *Mahabharata* were very well known to the people of South, mention of God Shiva, struggle between Krishna and Asuras, presence of great fine under the ocean and Uttara-kuru-the northen country.

The Sangam literature throws light on the political conditions of the country. Hereditary monarchy was the prevailing form of government and there were disputed successions and civil wars. The Sabha of the king, also known as Manram, was the highest court of justice. Land and trade were the main sources of the royal revenue. Foreign trade was important and *Pattinappalai* gives a detailed account of the custom's department. Moderation of taxation was the advice to the kings by the wise.

Kings patronised poets and supported the development of various arts like music and dance. Various kinds of musical instruments were described, like the drums and the flutes. The courts of the kings were enlivened by the bands of the musicians followed by the women who danced to the accompaniment of the music, mixed dances in which men and women danced together are also mentioned. Here a systematic attempt was made to synthesize the indigenous pre-Aryan modes with those known as Aryans.

The poems refer to the popular beliefs and customs. The people believed in omens and astrology. There were fortune tellers, the rites were practised which were supported to avert the mischief of demons. The banyan tree was considered the abode of gods, the eclipses were the result of snakes eating up the sun and moon. Crows were believed to announce the arrival of the guests. The Tamil poems speak of trade and commerce as well. This information is supported by the archaeological finds. Ships from other countries poured out on the beach precious merchandise they brought from the other countries. The markets had huge buildings used as trading centres at the lower floors and families at the upper one. Saliyur in Pandyan, Muziris in Chera are the famous ports mentioned in the poems. Horses were imported, the ships and light houses were also repaired. The life in ports was cosmopolitan since people from various parts stayed there. The author of *Periplus* gives enormous information about trade between India and Rome. The large quantities of gold and silver coins struck by the Roman emperors upto first century A. D. are found in the interior of Tamil land. These testify to the extent of the trade, the presence of Roman settlers in Tamil country. Internal trade was also brisk, caravans of merchants with carts and pack-animals carried their merchandise from place to place and from fair to fair. Salt was an important commodity of trade. Barter played an important part in all transactions.

Agriculture was the mainstay of the national income, most of its operations were carried on by the women of the lowest class whose status appears to be little different from a slave. The bulk of land was owned by an agriculturist of high rank known as Vellalar. He did not plough the land himself but employed labourers to do it. The Sangam literature often mentions the weaving of complex pattern on cloth and silk. Uraiyur was a great centre for cotton.

The influence of northern ideas over philosophy and religions are marked. The Vedic religion had made its place in South India is clear from the references to costly sacrifices made by the monarchs. The religious duties were held high in the society. The followers of Vedas had to face a disputation with other sects. But Hinduism was the dominant creed of the age and the worship of Subramanya (Murugan) was very prominent. The other member of the pantheon are Shiva, Balarama, Vishnu, Krishna, Ardhanarishvara and Anantashayi. Music and dance were intertwined with the religion since early times.

Seven

AGE OF GUPTAS

After centuries of political disintegration an empire came to be established in A.D. 319 under the Guptas. Their origin and original home cannot be determined with certainty. But very likely they were initially a family of landowners who acquired political control. The first Gupta ruler known to be is Chandragupta I. By marrying a Lichchhavi princess he sought to gain in prestige, though Vaishali does not appear to have been a part of his kingdom. His rule remained confined to Magadha and parts of eastern Uttar Pradesh. He got the title of Maharajadhiraja and his accession in about 319-20 A.D. marked the beginning of Gupta era.

Samudragupta

Chandragupta I was succeeded by his son Samudragupta in 325 .A.D The details of his reign and his exploits are known from a lengthy eulogy composed by Harishena and inscribed in Ashoka pillar at Allahabad. This Prashasti informs us that Samudragupta uprooted Achuta of Ahichchhatra, Nagasena of Padmavati, Ganapatinaga of Mathura, and captured the prince of Kota family. He defeated the kings of eastern Himalayan states and some frontier states like Nepal, Assam, Bengal. He further conquered the forest kingdoms in Vindhya region known as 'atvikarajyas'. He further conqured the twelve states of Deccan. Some Shaka and Kushana chieftains were also conquered. He followed the policy of conquest. Digvijaya was his motto. He is compared with Napoleon of Europe.

Samudragupta was also adept in fine arts. He was a great poet, musician and a patron of learning. Though his poetical compositions have not survived, but his love of music is attested by the coins which have the king playing Vina. It has also been suggested that he was a great patron of the Buddhist scholar Vasubandhu.

Chandragupta Vikramaditya

Samudragupta was succeeded by his son Chandragupta II (375-415). The main source of his period, the drama Devichandraguptam, tells that Samudragupta was succeeded by his brother Ramagupta. He was defeated by Shaka ruler whom he decided to give his wife. Later Chandragupta killed Ramagupta and himself became the king.

Chandragupta, who assumed the title of Vikramaditya, led a campaign agaist the Shakas and totally uprooted them. This led to the annexation of western parts of India to the reign of Guptas. This also gave control over sea ports in the area. He also extended matrimonial alliance with a number of dynasties. He married Kuberanaga of the Naga family and had a daughter named Prabhavati Gupta. She was given in marriage to Rudrasena II of Vakataka dynasty which ruled the territory roughly corresponding to the area ruled by Satavahana dynasty. Prabhavati ruled over the kingdom as regent after the death of her husband. This way Chandragupta virtually ruled the Vakataka kingdom.

Chandragupta II took the title of Vikramaditya. His reign is often remembered not for wars but for his patronage of art and literature. Kalidas the great Sanskrit poet and play writer, is said to have lived in his court.

Kumaragupta (415-454) succeeded his father Chandragupta II. A branch of the Huns from Central Asia had occupied Bactria and were threatening to cross the Hindukush mountains, but they remain a distant threat during his rule. Otherwise his reign period is peaceful.

The Hun threat naturalised in the reign of Kumaragupta's successors, on whom fell the real task of defending the empire. Skandagupta, the successor of Kumaragupta, fought bravely against the Huns. It seems that at this time his feudatories asserted themselves at home, further complicating the situation. His debased coins indicate a deep economic crisis in the region.

After the death of Skandagupta in about 467. D. there was succession of Kings who were weak and could not keep the empire intact. Towards the end of fifth century the Huns poured into north west India and the disintegration of empire took place. The Gupta empire disintegrated not because of Hun invasions only but there are many other reason attributed to it like number of feudatories within the empire. Only Bengal, Bihar and Uttar Pradesh were the regions directly under the rule of imperial rulers. As soon as the opportunity emerged the chieftains asserted their independence. There is no evidence that Gupta's had a big army. The Chinese traveller Fa-hien, who visited Chandragupta II's reign does not mention any military set up. Perhaps the army was supplied by the feudatories at the time of war.

Administration

The Guptas had a different set up of administration. It was from princes and the royal blood that the important officers were choosen. Though the King appointed the high officials but one person had control of several offices. Administrative posts also became hereditary. This led to the weakening of royal power. Decentralisation of administrative authority was also caused by grants of lands and villages with fiscal and administrative immunities to priests and temples. This practice also included the transfer of royal right over salt and mines, which were the royal monopolies in Maurya period and evidently signs of sovereignty. But now the villages were granted in perpetuity to the beneficiaries, often with administrative rights. Such land grants paved the way for feudal development in India. Several inscriptions refer to emergence of serfdom, which meant the peasants were attached to the land even when it was given away. During the Gupta period, position of peasant was also undermined on account of the imposition of forced labour (vishti) and many other levies and taxes.

The Guptas issued large number of gold coins which are regular in size and weight. Those vividly portrayed Gupta Kings, indicating their love for war and arts. There was large assimilation of foreigners in Indian society. There was increase of many sub-castes due to absorption of many tribals into brahmanical society through the process of land grants. Every tribe become a kind of caste in its new incarnation. The Shudras in the period were improved and were allowed to listen to the epic and puranas. The women were dependent on men in higher calss. The women of high varna did not have any access of livelihood but the gifts given to her were in her custody and she could sell it. It was called Stridhana.

Business and Trade

There seems to be a decline of trade in the Gupta period. There were guilds of artisans and merchants but they did not have importance during the later or the Post-Gupta period. Silk and spices were the chief Indian export articles of Indo-Roman trade. But there seems to be decline of the trade in silk. The Guptas issue gold coins but these did not flow into day-to-day private economy, as Fa-hien tells cowries or the corals became common. The weakening of the commercial links with the western world due to certain reasons arrested the movement of the artisans and traders from one part of the country to other part. They remained limited to their own village.

Society

Owing to the proliferation of castes, the varna system had been considerably modified. The guilds of craftsmen were transformed into castes. The ruling class often used religion for maintaining the social order. Bhagvatism centered round the worship of Vishnu or Bhagvat, and originated in post Maurya period. He was now merged with the god Narayana. He was supposed to bestow good fortunes on his devotees and in return the devotee offered his devotion or love. The great epic Mahabharata refered to Krishna as Vishnu. By this period the worshippers of Vishnu were known as Bhagavatas. Bhagvatism became a popular belief. *Vishnu Sahasranama* was composed for the benefit of the devotees. Vishnu became a member of the trinity of gods along with Shiva and Brahma. He comes in all the previous incarnations as a saviour of dharma. During this period female deities, of non-Aryan origin also became important. Now they were associated with the gods as their consorts. Sri or Lakshmi, the goddess of wealth became very popular among the masses. The earlier epigraph referring to this union is found of Skandagupta's time. This cult of mother goddess assimilated into the brahmanical pantheon and led to the growth of the shakti cult with superiority of female. Under Gupta rule, the brahmanical sect of Vaishnavism became very popular. It spread in various parts of the country and also travelled across the sea to south east Asia. Vaishnavism adopted various deities, beliefs and superstititions leading to assimilations of different cults and substitute faith for logic. It acted as an effective instrument for reconciling the masses to their lot and maintaining the social division based on varna.

Religion

During this period Shaivism, like Vaishnavism received the royal support. But there are evidences that Shaivism promoted extreme practices like human sacrifice or immolation, hence was less popular.

On the other hand Buddhism had split into two major sects, each into a number of subsects. Mahayanism, through its cult of devotion, worship and its enlarged pantheon with male and female deities, had come closer of brahmanical religion. Fifth century onwards the sect came under the influence of Tantra that was transformed into Vajrayana in the later countries. On the other hand Jainism had also developed icons. Two Jaina councils were summoned simultaneiouly at Mathura and Valabhi in 313 A.D. The canonical text of the sect was standardised and were later committed to writing at another council at Valabhi in 453 A.D. In certain areas in Deccan, Jainism received support from the local ruling houses, though in the later period this patronage stopped. Christianity, that first appeared on Indian soil in pre-Gupta period, remained restricted to Malabar where a Syrian church existed.

The Gupta period is said to be a landmark in the development of philosophical ideas. The six schools of thought developed known as (1) Nyaya or school of logic and epistemology. Vatsyayan was its main expositor, (2) Vaisheshika was atomic philosophy interested mainly in physics, Uluka Kannada was its principle commentator, (3) Sankhya, i.e. popularity of Purusha and Prakriti, (4) Yoga dealt with control of body physically, with its basic text *Yoga sutra* of Patanjali, (5) Mimansia that sought to explain revive the vedas. The earliestwork of the school is Sutras of Jaimini, (6) Vedanta or Uttarmimansa, that forcefully rejected the theories of non-brahmanical schools.

Religion was intimately connected with the developments in architecture and plastic arts. The growing importance of image worship led to the construction of free standing temple with a sanctum in which the central cult image was placed. This was known as *garbh-griha*. Several shrines that have survived from Gupta period have central shrine. These are at Sanchi, Ladh Khan, Deogarh, Tigawa and Bhumara. A fragmentary temple at Deogarh is the most beautiful temple and well ornated as a Vishnu temple.

Gupta age is the culmination of arts. The plastic arts reached climax in this age. Under the influence of Mathura tradition, a distinct school of art flourished in this age. At Sarnath a distinct school of art developed whose best specimen is image of the Buddha seated in *dharmachakra pravarttana* attitude. This is Buddha giving his first sermon, a fine expression in stone of meditative and compassionate attitude. The impact of this school could also be felt in eastern and Western India during Gupta age.

During Gupta age painting was a very well developed art. Apart from professional artist, men and women of the upper class also knew it. The murals at various caves depict a consummate skill in delineating animal and human figures. Some of those are master pieces.

In literature also the Gupta period witnessed excellence. Sanskrit language and literature, after centuries of evolution, through lavish royal patronage reached the level of classical excellence. The Puranas were compiled, the Mahabahrata was rewritten, Panchatantra was elaborated. Aryabhatta, the author of *Aryabhattiya* flourished in fifth century A.D. He was first to use place-value system. Varahmihira wrote several treaties on astronomy and horoscopy,. Laghu and Brihatjataka are his works on horoscopy. Kalidasa is the greatest name in Sanskrit poets. *Meghaduta, Raghuvamsha* and *Shakuntalam* are his famous works. *Abhijyana Shakuntalam* is his most famous play.

Eight

REGIONAL POWERS

Northern India

After the disappearance of the centralized polities in northern India, the period between 800 -1200 A.D. saw the emergence of regional kingdoms. Centralized states gave way to decentralized political systems based on local interests. This change took place due to the emergence of a politico-economic structure termed as feudalism. Since the Gupta period the political structure in northern India was increasingly becoming feudal. The relationship of the king to his subordinates was more like vassal and lord. Feudatories were granted land along with certain rights on the land. Later they were given the right to sub-infeudation i.e. making a further grant of the land, thus building a hierarchy of officials. The feudatory had certain military obligations towards the king and was required to supply the king with armed men whenever needed. Theoretically the feudatory was a claimant of the land revenue and the land was re-assigned after his death, but in reality the feudatory held the land in perpetuity and this tended to become hereditary with time. Gradually these feudatories assumed criminal and judicial functions and administered territories with minimum possible allegiance to the central authority. They also began to assume high sounding titles as Mahasamanta, Mahamandaleshwara, and so on.

The outcome of the growth of feudalism was the carving out of independent principalities by the various vassals in different parts of the country. It is under these conditions that decentralized regional power flourished in the eighth-ninth century A.D. in northern India. This period is also known for the tripartite struggle between the Rashtrakutas, the Palas and the Pratiharas who established themselves in different regions.

Rashtrakutas

Dantidurga of the Rashtrakuta family, who was a feudatory of the Chalukyan king Vikramaditya II, founded this dynasty in A.D. 756 with Manyakhet or Malkhed near modern Solapur as his capital. He was succeeded by his uncle Krishna I, who finally defeated the

Pallavas. Dhruva, the next important ruler (780 A.D.) led campaigns in north India against Palas and Pratiharas. His successor Govinda III (792 A. D.) made an incursion into north India and fought the Pala ruler Dharmapala and his protege Chakrayudh. He also repelled an attack of a confederacy of the Pallava, Kerala, Pandya and Ganga rulers. His successor Amoghvarsha I is the most well known ruler of this dynasty and came to power in 814. A.D. He fought long drawn battles with the eastern Chalukyas and the Gangas. His son Krishna II emerged successful against the Pratihara Bhoja. Krishna III defeated the Chola king Parantaka I and reached Rameshwaram where he set-up a pillar of victory and a temple. His successors were weak and could not hold the empire together.

Pratiharas

The Pratiharas were also called Gurjara-Pratiharas. The earliest well-known king of this dynasty was Nagabhatta I, who was known for repulsing an attack of the Mlechhas, possibly the Arabs of Sind. His grand nephew Vatsaraj was known to have ruled in 813 A.D. He included Jodhpur in his kingdom. He defeated Dharmapala, the Pala ruler of Bengal but himself suffered a defeat at the hands of the Rashtrakuta king Dhruva. His successor Nagabhatta II exterminated Yasovarman's dynasty and shifted his capital from Bhinmal to Kannauj. Govinda III of the Rashtrakutas defeated him and occupied Malwa. Later his hold over Kannuaj was reinstated. The greatest king of this dynasty was Mihir Bhoja, under whom the Pratiharas became powerful. He defeated the Gauda king, Devepala and pushed the boundary of his kingdom to the east and Sindhu in the west. Bhoja is credited with the establishment of the city of Bhojpura. His son Mahendrapala I lost Punjab on the west but annexed Magadh and Gauda to his kingdom. After 915 A. D. the fortunes of the Pratiharas were affected under Mahipala who surrendered Kannauj to the Rashtrakuta king Indra III. The disintegration of the Pratihara dynasty occurred under Mahendrapala II.

Palas

The Pala dynasty was founded by Gopala in A.D. 750 at a time when Bengal was under anarchy without a king. Gopala was elected by different chiefs and nobles as their king. Dharmapala (780-810 A.D.) the son and successor of Gopala was the most powerful king of the dynasty. He is credited with the establishment of the Vikramshila University. He was a devout Buddhist and assumed the title of Paramasangata. During the reign of Dharmapala the Pala kingdom extended from Pataliputra to Rajshahi. He was defeated by the Pratihara king Nagabhatta II near Monghyr. His successor Devapala (815-854 A.D.) won victory over the Gurjara King and reached the Kamboja country. He conquered Assam and Orissa. Under Gopala II and Vigrahapala II, the Palas regained their power. During the reign of Mahipala I (992-1040 A.D.), the Palas were attacked by Rajendra Chola I in 1023 A. D but they went back without annexing any territory. The Palas maintained relations with distant rulers. The empire began to disintegrate under Kumarapala who reigned till about 1120 A.D.

Senas

The Senas of Bengal called themselves Kshatriya and Bramha-Kshtriya and were originally the inhabitants of Dakshinpatha. Vijayasena ascended the throne in A.D. 1095 and conquered Vanga defeating Bhojavarman. He occupied a large part of Bengal from the Palas. Vijaysena was succeeded by his son Ballasena in 1158 A.D. He conquered Mithila and a portion of east Bihar. He was succeeded by Lakshmansena who defeated Jayachandra of the Ghadavala dynasty. He was a learned man and patronized art and literature. His successors continued to rule in east Bengal till about the thirteenth century.

Rajput Dynasties

With the breakup of the Pratiharas, a number of Rajput states came into existence in north India. The most important of these were the Ghadavalas of Kannauj, the Paramaras of Malwa and the Chauhans of Ajmer. The other Rajput dynasties were Kalachuris of Jabalpur, Chandellas of of Bundelkhand, Chalukyas of Gujarat and Tomars of Delhi.

The origin of the Rajputs is obscure. Many Rajputs claim their descent from the solar and lunar families of Kshatriyas. Various legends connect them to these families of the epic age. The traditional view speaks of them as indigenous people whereas the other view talks of them as foreigners who were assimilated into the Hindu society of their times. Many propagate the view that the Rajputs were of mixed origin. According to the Agnikula myth, the founder of the Paramara dynasty originated from the fire pit of Sage Vashistha on Mount Abu. This fire origin is also ascribed to the Chalukyas of Gujarat and the Chahamanas of Ajmer. However, these myths have no semblance with reality and are mostly creations of the bards. One aspect of the early medieval Indian polity is that these creations of myths demonstrate the Kshatriya symbol as a way of legitimization of the newly acquired power of these families. It was done in order to gain recognition, politically and also to rise high in social status.

Gahadavalas

The Ghadavalas ruled from Kannauj from the later half of the eleventh century A.D. Chandradeva was the first ruler of the dynasty. He seized Kannauj and made it his capital. He also included Ayodhya and Varanasi in his empire. Govindachandra, his grandson proved to be a capable ruler and extended the boundaries of his kingdom both by war and diplomacy. He advanced as far as Patna and Monghyr. Govindachandra's kingdom in the east was up to Danapur in Bihar. His son Vijaychandra was also a capable ruler and kept the boundaries of the empire intact. He is known for the defeat inflicted on the Ghaznavids of Lahore. Jayachandra was the last ruler of the Gahadavalas. His empire included the entire Uttar Pradesh and a part of Bihar. His advance into east India was checked by the Sena ruler Lakshman Sena. He was famous for his bitter relations with Prithviraj Chauhan of Ajmer on account of his daughter's elopement with Prithviraj.

Paramaras

The Paramaras began their political domination as the feudatory chiefs of the Rashtrakutas. They established themselves in the Malwa region with their capital at Dhar. The founder of the dynasty was Upendra Munja. He was a capable commander and defeated big powers as Kalachuris, the Huns and the Guhilas. Both the Chalukyas and the Paramaras were annexing the territories of the disintegrated Rashtrakutas and were close rivals of each other. Munja successfully repulsed the attack of the Chalukyas several times. Munja was succeeded by his brother Sindhuraja. He was also a capable commander. He is credited with wars with the Huns and the Latas. Bhoja was the greatest ruler of the Paramaras who raised the power of his dynasty to an imperial rank. He is known as a great scholar as well as an able commander. With the death of Bhoja, the glory of the Paramaras declined. His successors continued as local rulers till about the thirteenth century A. D.

Chahamanas

There were several branches of the Chahamanas better known as the Chauhan Rajputs. The most important of them ruled in Sakambhari (Sambhar) in Rajasthan. The Chahamana rulers were feudatories of the Pratiharas till Vigraharaja II who declared the independence of the dynasty in the last quarter of the tenth century. One of his successors, Ajayraja founded the city of Ajaymeru or Ajmer, Vigraharaja IV extended his kingdom up to the Punjab, where he confronted Mahmud of Ghazni. The next important king Prithviraja III began his reign in 1177 A. D. He is said to have carried away the daughter of Jayachandra Ghadavala, Sanyukta and married her against Jayachandra's wishes. His achievements are narrated in the Hindi epic *Prithviraja-Raso* authored by Chand Bardai. His greatest victory won was at Tarrain over Muhammed Ghori in 1197 A.D. But the next year he was defeated by Ghori and executed.The Chahamana dynasty ended with his defeat.

Chalukyas

The Solankis or Chalukyas were divided into three branches. The branch at Gujarat was founded by Mularaja I in Anhilvad. During the reign of Bhimadeva I, the great grandson of Mularaja in 1025 A.D. Mahmud of Ghazni overran Gujarat and plundered Somnath. After the withdrawal of Mahmud he regained his capital. Karna, the successor of Bhimaraja fought against the Paramaras of Malwa and Chauhanas of Marwar. The Solankis were finally overthrown by Alauddin Khalji in 1207 A.D.

Kalachuris

The Kalachuris of Chedi started as feudatories and called themselves the descendants of Haihayas. The Kalachuri power was restricted to Dahala near Jabalpur. Their capital was Tripuri. The dynasty was founded Kokkalla (875-925 A.D.). He strengthened the dynasty through matrimonial alliances with the Rashtrakutas and the Chandellas and by friendly relations with the Pratiharas. The Kalachuris played an important role in the history of north India under Gangeyadeva Vikramaditya (1030-1041 A.D.). Gangeya occupied Allahabad, raided Punjab, Bengal and Orissa and defeated the Chalukyas of Kalyani. He was finally defeated by Bhoja I Paramara. Laxmi- Karna was Gangeya's son. He made extensive conquests. He overthrew Bhoja with the aid of Chalukyas of Kalyani and Anhilvad. He conquered the Chandellas and the Palas. His rule extended from Gujarat to Bengal and from Ganges to Mahanadi. The Kalachuris were conquered by the Delhi sultans.

Chandellas

The Chandellas were regarded as a clan of aboriginal chiefs who were promoted to the rank of Kshatriyas. They ruled over the region of Bundelkhand. The area was called Jejakabhukti. The founder of the dynasty was Nannuka. Dhanga, (954-1002 A. D.) the son and successor of Yasovarman proved to be the greatest king of the Chandellas. He built some grand temples at Khajuraho. His kingdom extended from Yamuna to Chedi and from Gwalior to Kalinjar. The next important ruler of the dynasty was Vidyadhara. The last king Paramardideva was defeated by Prithviraj III in 1182 A.D.

The basis of the Rajput society was the clan. Every clan traced its descent from a common ancestor, real or imaginary. The clans generally dominated particular territories. Attachment to land, family and honour was a characteristic of the Rajputs. They were chivalrous and valued their honour as utmost. Each Rajput state was supposed to be ruled over by the ruler in conjunction with his chiefs who were mostly his blood brothers. The social organization of the Rajputs was bound by a strong sense of brotherhood which was mostly egalitarian in nature and often created problems within them. But their basic weakness was their tendency to form exclusive groups, each claiming supremacy over the others. They could not tolerate the inclusion of non-Rajputs within their clan. This often created a hostile relation between the minority Rajputs and the majority of the population. The Rajputs treated warfare as a sport. Their struggle for land and cattle often engaged them in various wars with the other Rajput states. They were followers of Hinduism and gave large grants of land to Brahmanas and temples. In return for these concessions the Brahmanas were ready to recognize the Rajputs as descendants of solar and lunar dynasties of Kshatriyas.

Southern India

During the period of 800-1200 A.D. south India became the center of political activity. In the beginning of the ninth century, the Pallavas who were a great force were on the decline. The Chalukyas of Badami were by now overthrown by the Rashtrakutas. The latter were engaged in several wars and alliances with northern and southern kingdoms. The Cholas who were the feudatories of the Pallavas began to assert their power and were able to replace the Pallavas. The emergence of the imperial Cholas marked the beginning of a new stage in south Indian history. Under their domination art and culture reached new heights whose influence was felt even in the countries of South-East Asia.

The Cholas

The founder of the Chola Empire was Vijayalaya, who was the first feudatory of the Pallavas of Kanchi. He captured Tanjore in 850 A. D. He established a temple of goddess Nishumbhasudini (Durga) there. Aditya I succeeded Vijayalaya. Aditya helped his overlord the Pallava king Aparajita against the Pandyas but soon defeated him and annexed the whole of the Pallava kingdom. By the end of the ninth century, the Cholas had defeated the Pallavas completely and weakened the Pandyas capturing the Tamil country (Tondamandala) and including it under their domination. He then became a sovereign ruler. The Rashtrakuta king, Krishna II gave his daughter in marriage to Aditya. He erected many Shiva temples. He was succeeded in 907 A.D. by Parantaka I, the first important ruler of the Cholas.

Parantaka I was an ambitious ruler and engaged himself in wars of conquest from the beginning of his reign. He conquered Madurai from the Pandya ruler Rajasinha II. He assumed the title of Maduraikonda (captor of Madurai). He, however, lost to the Rashtrakuta ruler Krishna III at the battle of Tokkolam in 949 A.D. The Cholas had to cede Tondamandalam to the adversary. At that point of time the Chola kingdom almost ceased to exist. It was a serious setback to the rising Chola power. The revival of Chola power began from the accession of Parantaka II who recovered Tondamandalam to re-establish dominance of the dynasty.

The climax in Chola power was achieved under the successor of Parantaka II, Arumolivarman, who crowned himself as Rajaraja I in 985 A.D. The next thirty years of his rule formed the formative period of Chola imperialism. The Chola kingdom grew under him into an extensive and well-knit empire, efficiently organized and administered and possessing a powerful standing army and navy. Rajaraja began his conquests by attacking the confederation between the rulers of the Pandya and Kerala kingdoms and of Ceylon. Polonnaruva became the capital of a Chola province. Elsewhere several parts of modern Mysore were conquered and annexed which intensified their rivalry with the Chalukyas. Rajaraja built the magnificent Shiva temple of Brihadeshwara or Rajaraja temple at Thanjavur which was completed in 1010. It is considered a remarkable piece of architecture in South Indian style.

Rajaraja was succeeded by his son Rajendra I in 1014 A. D. He ruled jointly with his father for a few years. He also followed a policy of conquest and annexation adopted by his father and further raised the power and prestige of the Cholas. He followed the expansionist policy and made extensive conquests in Ceylon. The Pandya and Kerala countries after being conquered were constituted as a viceroyalty under the Chola king with the title of Chola-Pandeya. Madurai was its headquarters. Proceeding through Kalinga, Rajendra I attacked Bengal and defeated the Pala ruler Mahipala in 1022 A.D. But he annexed no territory in north India. To commemorate the occasion, Rajendra I assumed the title of Gangaikondachola (the Chola conqueror of Ganga). He built the new capital near the mouth of the Kaveri and called it Gangaikondacholapuram (the city of the Chola conqueror of the Ganga). With his naval forces, he invaded Malaya Peninsula and Srivijaya Empire that extended over Sumatra, Java and the neighbouring islands and controlled the overseas trade route to China.

Rajendra was succeeded by his son Rajadhiraja I in 1044 A.D. He was also an able ruler. He put down the hostile forces in Ceylon and suppressed the rebellious Pandeyas and subjugated their territory. He celebrated his victory by performing the Ashwamedh Yajna but lost his life in about 1053 A.D. in a battle with the Chalukyan king Someshwara I at Kappam. His brother Rajendra II succeeded him. He continued his struggle against Someshwara. He defeated Someshwara in the battle of Kudal Sangamam. Next came Virarajendra I, he too defeated the Chalukyas and erected a pillar of victory on the banks of Tungabhadra. Virarajendra died in 1070 A. D.

He was succeeded by Kullotunga I, the great-grandson of Rajaraja I. He defeated the rulers of the Pandya kingdom and that of Kerala. The Chola empire continued for more than a century after him. Weak rulers succeeded him. The Cholas and the later Chalukyas clashed for the overlordship of Vengi, the Tungabhadra doab and the Ganga country. The Chola empire continued in .a flourishing condition during the twelfth century but declined by the end of the thirteenth century. The Pandyan king Sundara rendered the final blow by seizing Kanchi in 1297 A. D. The place of the Cholas was taken over by the Pandyas and the Hoysalas. This marked the end of the Chola power.

Administration

The king was the head of the administration of the Cholas and all powers were concentrated in his hands. The form of the Chola government was hereditary monarchy. The rule of primogeniture generally prevailed. The Chola rulers took high-sounding titles as Gangaikondacholapuram. The royal household also run on an elaborate scale. The royal priest Rajguru became the close confidant of the royal family. The king had council of ministers to aid and assist him. They often advised him on important matters. An elaborate and complicated bureaucracy ran the government. The general tendency was to make the officers hereditary. The officials were paid by assignments of land called jivitas according to their status.

The whole empire was divided into *mandalams* or provinces. Sometimes princes of the royal family were appointed governors of the provinces. Further they were divided into *valanadu* (districts) and *nadu* (villages). Village was the basic unit of administration. There was remarkable autonomy at the village level. Chola officials participated in village administration more as observers than as administrators. The Cholas are best known for their local self government at the village level. We hear of two assemblies called the *ur* and *sabha* or *mahasabha.* The *ur* was a general assembly of the village. The mahasabha was a gathering of adult men in the Brahmana villages called *agraharas.* These were villages settled by the Brahmanas and most of the lands here were rent-free. The ur consisted of all the tax paying residents of an ordinary village. Most of the information regarding the Chola administration is gathered from their inscriptions. The other kind of division was called the *nagaram.* These were found more commonly in the trading centers since it catered mostly to the mercantile interests. The working of these assemblies differed according to local conditions. A description of the functioning of the local sabha is found from the Uttaramerur inscription from a temple wall of the tenth century. The Mahasabha possessed proprietary rights over community lands and controlled the private lands within its jurisdiction.

Village Assembly: It assisted the state in assessing the land revenue. It collected revenue and in cases of default, had the power to sell the land in question by public auction. It looked after the reclamation of wasteland and forests that were within its jurisdiction. The judicial committee of the mahasabha called the Nyattar settled both civil and criminal cases of dispute. It looked after the roads, cleanliness, lighting, tanks, rest houses and security of the villages.

Economy

Land tax constituted the single largest source of income of the Chola state. It was generally assessed at one-third of the produce. The village assembly took land tax and local levies. Cattle rearing was a subsidiary occupation. Trade with foreign countries was an important feature of the Cholas mercantile activities. The rulers built a network of royal roads that were useful for trade as well as for the movement of the army. There were gigantic trade guilds that traded with Java and Sumatra. South India exported textiles, spices, drugs, jewels, ivory, horn, ebony and camphor to China. Trade brought considerable prestige and affluence to the Cholas.

Society

The caste system was the basis of the social organization under the Cholas. Society was divided into a number of social groups or castes. Each caste was hereditary and constituted an occupational group. Brahmanas occupied a privilege position in the society. They combined both religious authority and economic power. They were exempted from taxes, owned and enjoyed land with full royal support. Their main duties included learning and teaching of the Vedas and performing rituals and ceremonies. Some of them served as chief priests of the temple. Some of them were more adventurous and engaged themselves in trade. They were given lighter punishments in case of offences committed.

Women were well treated in the Chola Empire. They enjoyed the right to property. Some of them participated in governmental activity as well. Monogamy was the rule under ordinary people. Girls were generally married at the age of twelve. Devadasis were common in the temples. Courtesans and upper caste women had a certain freedom of movement in that they could defy social conventions. Slavery existed in the Tamil society under the Cholas. Sometimes they were sold to the temples. Slavery was adopted in a few cases in order to escape starvation.

Art and Architecture

Temple architecture in the South attained its climax under the Cholas. The style of architecture came to be known as Dravida. The main feature of this style was the building of storey upon storey above the chief deity room (*garbagriha*). They had a typical style that came to be called *vimana* and a pillared hall called *mandapa* with elaborately carved pillars and a flat roof, was generally placed in front of the sanctum. The lofty gates that decorated the temples were called *gopurams*. The Rajarajeshwara and the Brihadeshwara temple is the best example of this style.

Religion

The period is marked by the revival and expansion of Hinduism and a continued decline of Buddhism and Jainism. Buddhism remained confined to eastern India and was propagated by the Pala rulers. Decline of the Palas marked the end of Buddhism in the eastern region. The deterioration of Buddhism was primarily due to the rise of Mahayana school that regarded and worshipped Buddha as god. The worship became more elaborate and a lot of importance was attached to uttering of mantras. Buddhism during this period took different forms that made it indistinguishable from Hinduism.

Jainism continued to be popular amongst the trading communities. The Chalukyas of Gujarat patronized Jainism. The Jain temple of Dilwara at Mount Abu was built during this time. The Paramara rulers also built many images of Mahavira. The Ganga rulers of Karnataka too patronized Jainism.

On the other hand the revival and expansion of Hinduism took different forms. Shiva and Vishnu became the chief deities and magnificent temples were built to proclaim their supremacy. Buddha became absorbed as an incarnation of Vishnu. Image worship increased substantially. In the process many local gods of popular level as well as tribal gods were absorbed into Hinduism. It became more popular in nature. The importance of rituals resulted in the supremacy of the brahmanas. In south India, popular saints as Nayanars and Alvars were known as worshippers of Shiva and Vishnu.

At the intellectual level, the most serious challenge to Buddhism and Jainism was offered by Sankara, who reformulated Hindu philosophy. Sankara was born in Kerala probably in the ninth century. He propagated the philosophy of *advaitavad*. This is the doctrine of non-dualism. According to Sankara, god and the created world was one; the differences were apparent but not real and arose due to ignorance. The philosophy is called Vedanta and regarded the Vedas as source of true knowledge.

Among the Muslims, Sufism became popular. It is an old religious sect. It had penetrated into India prior to the establishment of the Delhi Sultanate. The philosophy of Sufism believes in one god and regards every individual and everything as part of him. The Sufi saints preached that all is in god and god is one. The Sufis were devout Muslims who moved within the Shariat (Muslim law). They emphasized inner purity and love for god as a means of attaining salvation. They did not believe in image worship of any kind. Music brought them closer to God and they engaged themselves in music and dance. They believed in the guru whom they called Pir. None could approach god without the assistance of Guru.

The Sufis were divided into different sects, most important being the Suhrawardi sect and the Chisti sect. The influence of the Suhrawardi sect remained limited only in Sind, Punjab and Multan region. The Chisti sect became popular in Uttar Pradesh, Bihar, Bengal, Orissa and south India. Many sufi saints became popular during the period and the most important among them were Shaikh Moinud-din Chisti, Baba Farid-ud-din, Nizam-ud-din Auliya, Chirag-i-Dehlavi, and so on.

Nine

RELIGION AND CULTURE

In the evolution of Indian culture in general, the early medieval period has its own significance, for it was marked by the growth of several regional cultures. In this process of growth of the regional cultures, the three main factors of developments are, the emergence of regional kingdoms, the transformation of Brahmanism into a new kind of popular Hinduism, and the evolution of regional languages and literature. The regionalisation of Indian culture had begun with the emergence of the great regional kingdoms. This change of political structure was then paralleled by a religious transformation. The more or less unified Brahmanism of an earlier age was disrupted by the rise of popular religious movements, which in turn, led to the formulation of new philosophical doctrines. Almost simultaneously, regional languages produced a rich literature which challenged the monopoly of Sanskrit literature. All the heritage of the early medieval period was in many ways enriched by the influence of Islam.

Religious Conditions

The early medieval period (750-1200 A.D.) is marked by a revival and expansion of Hinduism and a continued decline of Buddhism and Janism.

During this period, Buddhism was gradually confined to eastern India. The decline of the Pala powers who were patrons of Buddhism after the 10th century was a blow to Buddhism. The association of Buddhism with magical cults accelerated the process of decline. As a result of the influence of tantric ideas on Buddhism, much of its original ethical teachings were further submerged in rituals. Thus, Buddhism did not so much decline, as it assumed forms which made it indistinguishable from Hinduism.

Jainism continued to be popular particularly among the trading communities. The Chalukyan rulers of Gujarat patronised Jainism. It was during this time that some of the most magnificent Jain temples, such as the Dilwara temple at Mt. Abu were built. The Paramara rulers of Malwa also built many huge images of Jain saints and of Mahavira. In South India, Jainism attained its high water-mark during the 9th and 10th centuries. The Ganga rulers of Karnataka were great patrons of Jainism. During this period, many Jain basadrs (temples) and *mahastambhas* (pillars) were set up in different parts. The colossal image of Gomateswara at Sravana Belogola was set up during this time. The Rashtrakutas continued to support it but later the rise of Lingayatas undermined its strength. The growing rigidity of Jainism and the loss of royal patronage led to the decline of Jainism.

The revival and expansion of Hinduism took many forms. Shiva and Vishnu became the chief god and magnificent temples were built to proclaim their supremacy. In Eastern India, Tara, the consort of Buddha, Durga the consort of Shiva, Kali, etc, became themselves the chief object of worship. The rise of the worship of Shiva and Vishnu signified the growth of a process of cultural synthesis. But the religious revival also increased the power and arrogance of the Brahmanas. The growth of Tantrism in North India is attributed to the orthodox Brahmanical ritual and its ordering of society.

The most important religious movement was the Bhakti movement in South India. It was led by a series of popular saints called Nayanars (Shaiva Saints) and Alvars (Vaishnava Saints) There were 63 Nayanars, most important were Appar, Sambandhar and Sundarar. There were 12 Alvars, important ones being Poyagi, Padam, Pey, Andal (a woman), etc. These saints rejected austerites and looked upon religion as a living bond based on love between the god and the worshipper. The path of Bhakti advocated by these saints was open to all, irrespective of caste and this movement won many adherents of Buddhism, Jainism and tribals to its fold.

Another popular movement which arose in the twelth century was the Lingayat or Virshaiva movement founded by Basava and Channabasava who lived at the court of the Kalachuri kings. They worshipped Shiva and strongly opposed the caste system and rejected fasts, feasts, pilgrimages and sacrifices. In the social sphere, they opposed child marriage and allowed remarriage of widows.

At the intellectual level, the most serious challenge to Buddhism and Jainism was posed by Sankaracharya who reformulated the Hindu philosophy. His philosophy is called advaitavada or doctrine of non-dualism. Ramanuja another famous scholar founded Visistadvaita Siddhanta or qualified monism and Shivaishnava sect. He tried to build a bridge between the popular movement based on Bhakti and the upper caste movement based on the Vedas.

Temples and Monastic Institutions

Indian temples symbolised the very mundane human urges and were centres for varied activities of the community as a whole. Temple was not merely a place of worship but the hub of social and cultural life as well.

To begin with, general education within the temple was of great importance. Many endowments to temples were specifically made for establishment of colleges (Ghutikas) which were incorporated into temple complexes. Music and dance generally formed part of the daily ritual of the temples and during special celebrations and annual festivals these played a particularly dominant role. The institution of devadasis was attached to the temples. Regular festivals (such as annual rathayatra of the Jagannatha temple at Puri) and the undertaking of pilgrimage was the mechanisms through which the participation of the community in temple activities was facilitated. As temples provided work and the means of livelihood for a large number of persons, they were able to exert a great influence upon the economic life of people.

The rise of the great royal temples (Kandariya Mahadeva Temple-Khujuraho, Rajarajeshwara templeTanjore, Udayeswara temple-Udaipur, Lingaraja temple-Bhuvaneswar, etc.) symbolised the power and religious identity of the respective realm. The temples were evidently meant to be a counterweight to the division forces (increasing Samantisation) prevailing in the kingdoms. The settlement of Brahmins and foundation of royal temples served the purpose of creating a new network of relations-political, economic and ritual which worked as an antidote to the centrifugal tendencies of the Samantachakra.

The monastic institutions such as the Viharas and Mathas served as educational institutions and played a significant role in the cultural and educational life of the Indian people. It also served as a place of religious discussions. The notable monastic institutions were at Odantapuri, Vikramshila, Nalanda, Valabhi, Jagadalla, Somapura, Kanchipuram, etc. Kashi with its Shaiva monastries was also a flourishing seat of Brahmanical learning.

Adi Sankaracharya (788-820)

Born at Kaladi in Kerala, Sankaracharya is considered to be one of the greatest Indian philosophers and thinkers. Sankara's philosophy is called *advaitavada* or the doctrine of non-dualism or monism. According to him, God and the created world was one: the differences were apparent but not real and arose due to ignorance. The way Forward to Salvation was devotion to God, strengthened by the knowledge that God and the created beings were one and the same. This philosophy is called Vedanta. Thus, Sankara upheld the Vedas as the fountain head of true knowledge.

All his philosophical thoughts are explained by him in his works, mainly consisting of commentaries known as Bhashyas on Upanishads and also commentaries on Brahmasutras and Bhagawad Gita. Besides, one of his chief original works exposes his view on Stan-Bodha, i.e., understanding of the soul.

He is called the Aquinas of Hinduism since he reduced the self-contradictory passages of the Upanishads into the consistent system. Sankaracharya is also known and remembered today as the propounder of Jnana Marga or the way of wisdom as one of the three ways to salvation in contrast to the Bhakti Marga and the Karma Marga. He considered Atma (soul) to be identical with the absolute or the Nirguna Brahman. In this world, man's sufferings arise from the fact that he fails to realize this identity and this is due to ignorance (*avidya*) and illusion (*Maya*). Therefore, it is only vidya or knowledge which alone shall lift the veil of ignorance and which shall allow man to realize his identity with Brahman. According to him it is this realization of self that constitutes liberation or salvation and this he sums up in the Upanishadic Phrase-Tat-Vam-Asi. After his death four maths were established in Sringeri (Karnataka) Dwarka (Gujarat) Puri (Orissa) and Badrinath.

Sriharsha in the reign of Jayachandra wrote *Naisadhacharita, Khandana-Khanda-Khadya* (Vedanta Treatise) in Sanskrit.

Senas— The reign of Lakshmanasena was remarkable for patronising considerable literary activity. Jayadeva the author of *Gita Govinda,* Dhoyi the author of *Pavanduta* and

Govardhana the author of *Aryasaptasati* lived at his court. Ballalasena the Sena king wrote *Danasagara* and *Adbhutasagara* (on astronomy)

Literature in South India

1. Cholas— The period was marked by the growth of Tamil classics. Kamban's *Ramayana,* Jayangondar's *Kalingattupparani,* Pugulendi's *Nalavenbu* and Sekkilar's *Periya Puranam* are some of the important literary works.
2. Chalukyas of Kalyani— Among the Sanskrit works Bilhana's *Vikramankacharita,* Vijnanesvara's *Mitaksara,* a commentrary on Yajnavalkya Smriti and Somesvara II's Manasollasa are important.
3. Rashtrakutas— Amoghavarsha wrote *Kavirajamarga,* the earliest work on poetics in Kannada. Sanskrit literature was also patronised. Trivikrama wrote *Nalachampu,* Halayudha wrote *Kavirahasya* in the reign of Krishna III. Jaina literature made great progress and Akalanka and Vidyananda wrote *Ashtasati* and *Ashtasahasri,* two commentaries on the Aptamimansa. Manikyanandin wrote *Pakikshamukhasashta.* Jinasena wrote *Parsvabhudhya.* Amoghavarsha's reign saw the composition (on grammar) and Ganitasarasamgrahaka of Viracharya (Mathemetics), Pampa the greatest of the Kannada poets wrote *Adipurana* and Vikramarjunavijaya and Ponna wrote *Santipurana.*

Islam and Sufism

After the conquest of Sindh by the Arabs in 712 A.D., Islam was established in Sindh from the 8th and in Punjab from the tenth centuries. Arab travellers had also settled in Kerala between the 8th and 10th centuries. While it is difficult to determine the precise extent of the influence of Indian philosophic ideas, it made a definite contribution to the development of Islamic philosophy in its formative phase. A considerable number of people living in the provinces having contact with Arabs were compelled to embrace Islam. With the rise of orthodox schools based on the Quran and Hadis and of the Sufi mystic order in the 10th century, Islamic history witnessed an important change.

Mystics, who are called sufis, had risen in Islam at a very early stage. Most of them were persons of a deep devotion who were disgusted by the vulgar display of wealth and degeneration of morals following the establishment of the Islamic empire. The goal of the sufi was emotional communion with God and service of humanity. The monastic organisation of the sufis (*khanqah*), and some of their practices such as penance, fasting and holding the breath are sometimes traced to the Buddhist and Hindu yogic influence. After the Ghazanavid conquest of the Punjab, a large number of sufi saints appeared in India. Shaikh Ismail of Lahore was the first among them. He was followed by Shaikh Ali bin al Hujwairi, better known as Data Ganj Baksh. His tomb at Lahore is a popular shrine in Punjab. He might be described as the founder of the Sufi cult in India and was the author of the celebrated manual on sufism entitled Kashful Mahjub. Another Sufi Saint of this period was Sayyid Ahmed Sultan Sakhi Sarwar, popularly known as Lakhdata. He died at Shahkot near Multan in 1080. Abdul Karim al-Jili was profoundly influenced by Hindu Vedanta. The Chisti order was founded by Khwaja Moinuddin Chisti who came to India around 1192 A.D.

Literature

The rulers of the various dynasties patronised arts and letters during this period. While Sanskrit was regarded as the language of high culture and a number of kings as well as scholars wrote in it, a remarkable feature of the period was the growth of literature in the language of the areas.

1. Pratiharas— The great Sanskrit poet and dramatist Rajashekar who lived at the court of Mahipala has to his credit a number of literary works—*Karpuramanjari, Bala Ramayana, Bala* and *Bharata, Kavyamimansa.*

2. Palas— Devapala's court was adorned with the Buddhist poet Vajradatta, the author of *Lokesvarasataka.*

3. Paramaras— Bhoja wrote Samaranganasutradhara, an excellent work on art and architecture.

4. Chahamanas— Vgraharaja composed the drama *Harikeli Nataka.*

5. Gahadvalas— In Govindachandra's reign, Lakshmidhara wrote *Kritya kalpataru* (on law and procedure) or Kalpadruma.

Science

The growth of science in the country slowed down during the period so that in course of time, 'India' was no longer regarded as a leading country in the field of science. Astronomy was gradually pushed into the background by astrology. The Lllawati (on Mathematics) of Bhaskara II was written during this period. Mahesvara wrote *Sekhara* and *Laghutika* on astrology. Some advance was made in the fields of medicine by the use of minerals, especially mercury.

Reasons for stagnation of Indian science: •During the period society was becoming increasingly rigid and narrow in character. •Tendency of the Indians to isolate themselves from the main currents of scientific thoughts outside India which is also reflected in the writings of Alberuni.

Alberuni's "India": Muhammad Ibn Ahmad Alberuni or Abu Raihan was born in 973 A.D. in the territory of Khawariz, now called as Khiva in Central Asia. He came to India along with Mahmud of Ghazni and lived here for about 10 years during the early part of the 11th century. All this enabled Alberuni to write a classic account of the country—*Kitab-ul-Hind.* He was a great scientist and noted scholar and was also famous as *manujjim* (astrologer cum astronomer). He took keen interest in Hindu learning and conversed with Brahmin philosophers. In his book *Kitab-ul-Hind* (Reality of Hindustan) he gives a graphic description of India as he had seen it. He was profoundly impressed by the intellectual subtlety and metaphysical speculation of the Brahmin philosophers but was shocked by their close-mindedness.

Writing about the country in general he observes, 'They believe that there is no country like theirs, no kings like theirs, no science like theirs.' He further says "if they travelled and mixed with other nations they would soon change their mind for their ancestors were not so narrow minded as the present generation." Talking of the Brahmins in particular he says, "They are haughty, foolish, vain, self-conceited, stolid. They are by nature niggardly in communicating that which they know and they take the greatest possible care to withhold it from men of another caste among their own people, still much more, from any foreigner." Thus, though a great admirer of Indian science and learning, he noted also the insular attitude of the learned people of the country.

Discussing the Indian society, he mentions of various castes and distinctions among the people. He also bears testimony to the prevalence of child marriages and sati, as well as the prohibition on widow-remarriage. Regarding religion, Alberuni says that image worship was confined to the ignorant common people but the educated Hindus, believed god to be one, eternal without a beginning and end; obviously a reference to the proponents and followers of Bhakti movement. On the whole, he observes, there is very little dispute about theological topics among the Hindus; at the utmost they fight with words, but they will never stake their life or body or property on religious controversy. Uniting them all were the common customs to Aryavarta. Weights and measures may differ from province to province but wherever you went, you find the same brahmanic culture and the same outlook on life.

Speaking of the economic conditions, Alberuni says that 1/6th of the produce was taken by the king from the peasants, but is silent about the exploitation of the peasants by the hereditary feudal chiefs. The brahmins, according to him were exempt from the payment of taxes, while the rest paid taxes on their incomes.

Dealing with the adverse effects of Mahmud's invasion, he says, 'Mahmud utterly ruined the prosperity of the country and performed those wonderful exploits by which the Hindus became like atoms of dust scattered in all directions.'

Art and Architecture

The Nagara and the Dravida style of temples reached a mature style of evolution during this period, which may be further classified on the basis of the region of their occurrence.

Nagara Style: The salient features of the Nagara temples found all over North India are the cruciform ground plan and curvilinear Shikara (tower).

A. *Temple of Orissa:* The Orissa temples have rightly been described as exhibiting the Nagara style in its greatest purity. The Parasuramesvara temple (8th century) and the Muktesvara Temple at Bhubanesvar represents the Nagara style in Orissa. The temple of Lingaraja at Bhubanesvar (11th century) built by Anantavarman Choda Ganga represents the Orissa style in its maturity. The Jagannatha Temple of Puri (late 12th century), the Sun-temple at Konark (built by Narasimha I, (1236-64 A. D.) are the other well-known temples.

B. *Temples of Central India* are usually *saptaratha* in plan (Seven-faceted on each side) and two *amalaka-silas* crown the summit of the Shikara. The Khajuraho temples built by the Chandeias of Jejabhukti between A.D. 950-1050 comprises Kandariya Mahadeva, Devi Jagadamba, Parsvanatha, Visvanatha temples.

C. *Temples of Western India:* This western Indian variation of Nagar style is also called the Solanki style after the rulers. Nilakantha Mahadeva temple at Sunak, and the Rudramal temple are the famous temples. Of the famous Jaina temples at Dilwara, Mount Abu the most noteworthy are the ones built by Vimala in 1031 A.D. and by Tejapala in A.D. 1230.

D. *Temples of Malwa and Khandesh:* The Nagara style in this region is also designated as the Paramara type. The Nilakantesvara temple or Udayesvara temple at Udayapur in MP is the finest monument of this type.

Dravida Style: Intricately carved vimana on top of the sanctum and pillared halls. Temple architecture, particularly the Dravida or South Indian style reached the pinnacle of glory under the Cholas. The chief feature of a Chola temple is the *vimana* or the storey which was later eclipsed by the richly ornamental Gopuram or gateway. Among the early Chola temples are the Vijayalaya Cholesvara temple at Narthamalai and Koranganatha temple at Srinivasanallur. The famous Rajarajesvara (Brihadesvara) at Tanjore and the Gangaikondacholesvara temple are the finest specimen of the mature phase.

The Vesara style also called the Chalukyan type possessed the Dravidian Vimana and the Nagara type faceted walls. The Jain temple of Lakkundi, the Muktesvara temple of Chauddadampur and the Mahadeva temple at Ittaggi are some of the examples of the Vesara style.

Sculptures: The early medieval period also witnessed the evolution of the sculptural art. The broad wall of the temples offered ample facility for the sculptors to exhibit their talent. Free standing stone images and bronzes have also appeared on the scene.

The non-iconic figure sculptures of Puri and Konark represents the Orissa sculpture at its best. An image of Goddess Saraswati installed at Saraswati Mandir at Dhara is one of the best specimens of Paramara art. The sculptures on the ceilings of the Jain Neminatha temple of Mount Abu are characterised by the sharp and pointed angularity of the limbs. Ellora, Aurangabad and Badami in the Deccan are virtual store-houses of sculpture. The three main classes of Chola sculptures are the portraits, icons and decorative sculptures. The Siva temple at Tiruvalisavaram is a veritable museum of early Chola iconography. The Cholas are particularly known for their Nataraja bronzes, the best example is the Nataraja image in the Nagesvara temple at Kumbakonam.

Paintings: The principal painting-specimens of the period are on the walls of the temples such as the Kailasa temple at Ellora, the Brihadesvara temple at Tanjore and Vijayalaya Cholesvara temple at Narthamalai.

Ten

SULTANATE OF DELHI

The rise and growth of Islam is regarded as a significant event for world history. Its first converts, the Arabs were a powerful force in the politics of Asia. Islam inspired a war-like spirit and national consciousness among the Arabs who wanted to carry on military conquests all over the world.

Hajjaj, the Muslim Governor of Iraq sent a powerful army under the command of his nephew and son-in-law Muhammad Bin Qasim in 711 A.D. to attack Sind. The desire to extend the empire and the allurement of wealth of India were the primary reasons behind the attack. The local Hindu chief of Sindh, Dahir had failed to punish the enemies of Hajjaj and that became the pretext for the Arab attack on Sindh.

At that time India was divided into many states that constantly fought each other. Muhammad defeated Dahir and captured Sindh in 712 A.D. In 713 A.D. he captured Multan as well. But very soon the Arabs failed to make any further incursions. The main reasons for the success of the Arabs in Sindh can be attributed to the meagre economic resources of the region coupled with its military weakness and sharp social divisions. However, the presence of the powerful Rajput states in India also checked the further incursion of the Arabs in the region.

Mahmud of Ghazni

The period from 1000 -1200 A. D. saw rapid changes both in the west and central Asia and in North India. By the end of 9th century A.D. the decline of the Abbasid Caliphate saw the rise of several states ruled by the Islamised Turks. They had been mercenary palace guards in the Abbasid Empire. These rulers titled themselves as Amirs and Sultans. The strife between different Muslim sects and different regions made the period a restless one. The Turkish tribesmen brought with them the practice of ruthless plunder. The credit of establishing the Muslim rule in India went to the Islamic Turks. The Turks captured the leadership of Islam from the Arabs first and then by the Persians. In the beginning they were barbaric hoarders and their strength was their arms. But gradually they converted themselves into extremely cultured people.

Meanwhile the break up of the Gurjara-Pratihara empire in the north India had led to a period of political uncertainty. As a result little attention was being paid to the incursions of these Turks from northwest of the empire.

Towards the end of the ninth century A.D. Trans-Oxiana, Khorasan and parts of Iran were being ruled by the Samanids who were Iranian by descent. Among the Samanid Governors was a Turkish slave Alptgin who with time established an independent capital at Ghazni. Sabuktigin a successor of Alptgin was a capable and ambitious ruler. During his rule he started attacking the boundaries and occupied some forts and cities. Jayapala, the Hindushahi ruler could not ignore these attacks and attempted to crush the power. Since then began the long struggle of the kingdoms of Ghazni and the Hindushahis.

Twice Jayapala attacked Ghazni. He was supported by some other Rajput rulers also who sent their contingents to help Jayapala. But all his attempts failed and Sabuktigin succeeded in capturing all the territories that lay between Lamghan and Peshawar. Thus the Hindushahis failed to check the growing power of the Ghaznavids towards the east. One of the successors of Alptgin, Mahmud ascended the throne (998 1030 A.D.) at Ghazni. He belonged to the Ghaznavid dynasty and claimed its origin from the family of Persian rulers.

Mahmud was closely associated with the renaissance of the Iranian spirit that took place during this period. A climax in Iranian renaissance was reached with Firdausi's *Shah Namah.* He was the poet laureate of Mahmud. These Turks not only became Islamized but Persianized as well.

From 1000 to 1027 A. D. Mahmud invaded India 17 times. The first invasion took place in 1000 A.D. when he attacked some frontier fortresses. The initial raids were directed against Hindushahi rulers who at the time held Peshawar and the Punjab. The first confrontation between Mahmud and Jayapala took place at Peshawar where the forces of the Hindushahi ruler were routed. He captured a good booty after that. It is said that unable to bear the humiliation Jayapala burnt himself to death. His son Anandapala succeeded him in 1002 A.D.

In 1004 A.D. Mahmud attacked Multan and in 1006 A.D. captured it. Next he occupied Punjab. The Hindushahi rulers had opposed the Ghaznavids from the very beginning. It had pursued an aggressive policy against the Muslim ruler. Again in 1009 A. D. its ruler Anandapala sought support of other states and went ahead to fight a war with Mahmud. Both the armies met at Wahind where Mahmud and his forces defeated Anandapala. Mahmud marched as far as Nagarkot in Punjab and captured it. The defeat of Anandapala reduced the strength and territories of the Hindushahi Kingdom

The subsequent raids of Mahmud into India were aimed at plundering rich temples and cities in northern India in order to continue his struggle against his enemies in Central Asia. Mahmud's raids advanced as far as Thanesar near Delhi. In the Ganga-Jamuna doab he first attacked and looted Mathura. Next he captured Kannauj in 1018 A.D.

The most daring expedition of Mahmud was in Somnath in Gujarat in 1025 A.D. in the west of Kathiawar. The temple received offerings in different forms from lakhs of devotees daily and had a regular income from a large number of villages. The temple of Somnath had the pride of its devotees that no one could harm its deity Lord Shiva and it is said that this pride attracted the attention of Mahmud and prompted him to loot and destroy the temple. He returned with huge booty.

Mahmud came back to India for the last time in 1027 A.D. to punish the Jats who had troubled him on his return journey from Somnath. Mahmud looted their wealth and enslaved their women and children. He died at Ghazni in 1030 A.D. He was never defeated in India.

Within a short span of Mahmud's death his empire met the fate of other empires. The Ghaznavid's possessions in Khurasan and Trans-Oxiana were thus annexed first by the Seljuks and later by Khwarizm Shah. Towards the middle of the twelfth century A.D. two new powers emerged into prominence. The Khwarizmi empire based in Iran and Ghurid empire based in Ghur in Northwest Afghanisthan. The power of the Ghurids increased under Sultan Alauddin who earned the title of Jahan Soz or the world burner because he burnt Ghazni and razed it to the ground. The rising power of the Khwarizmi Empire severely limited the Central Asian ambition of the Ghurids. Khwarizm Shah soon conquered Khurasan that was the bone of contention between the two. This left no option for the Ghurids but to look for expansion towards India.

Muhammed Ghori

In 1173 A. D. Shihabuddin Muhammed also known as Muizuddin Muhammad bin Sam ascended the throne at Ghazni. Proceeding by way of the Gomal Pass, Muhammad bin Sam also known as Muhammad Ghori conquered Multan and Uchch in 1175 A. D. In 1178 A. D. he tried to penetrate into Gujarat but was defeated completely routed by the Chalukyan King Mularaj II near Mount Abu. After that Muhammad Ghori attacked Punjab using the Khyber Pass. By 1190 A.D. Muizuddin Muhammad conquered Peshawar, Lahore and Sialkot. By 1182 A. D. the whole of Sindh was captured.

His conquest of Punjab and further inroads into northern India led to inevitable contest between him and the Rajputs. While Muhammad was over-running Multan and Uchch, Prithviraj III known as Prithviraj Chauhan ascended the throne of Ajmer at the age of 14. He was very powerful and made several conquests. He invaded Bundelkhand and defeated the Chandellas in the battle at Mahoba.

The conflict between Prithviraj and Muhammed Ghori started for the fort of Tarabhinda (Bhatinda). The enemies met each other in the battlefield at Tarain known as the First Battle of Tarain in 1191 A. D. Muhammad was defeated in the battle and his forces were severely routed. Little attempt was made by Prithviraj to oust the Ghurids from the Punjab. This gave Muhammad Ghori time to re-group his forces and make another bid for India the following year. He met Prithviraj for the second time in the battle field of Tarain in 1192 A.D. Prithviraj was decisively defeated this time. Though the numerical strength of Prithviraj's army was more, the superior organization and skill of the Turkish cavalry decided the issue. Soon after Prithviraj was captured and put to death.

The second battle of Tarain paved the way for the ascendancy of the Turks. From this point Rajput power entered a phase of irreversible decay. Thus the area of Delhi and eastern Rajasthan passed under the Turkish rule. Muhammad came back to India in 1194 A.D. This time his target was the kingdom of Kannauj. Jayachandra the ruler of Kannauj and Muhammad fought a battle at Chandawar. Rajputs were defeated and Jaychandra was killed in the war. Muhammad proceeded as far as Benares and captured all the important places of the Kingdom of Kannauj. The battle of Chandawar laid the foundation of Turkish rule in northern India.

Slave Dynasty

After Tarain, Ghori returned to Ghazni leaving the affairs of India in the hands of his trusted slave Qutubuddin Aibak. During his governorship Aibak had to face a serious rebellion in Rajasthan that was suppressed. Thereafter Aibak attacked Anhilwara in Gujarat in 1197 A.D. and defeated Bhima II. He also conquered Badaun, Benares and Chandawar and consolidated the conquest at Kannauj. One of the most important conquests of Aibak was that of Bundelkhand. Aibak attacked in 1203 A.D. the fort of Kalinjar that was regarded impregnable. Aibak was successful in ousting the Chandellas and occupying the region. He also occupied Mahoba and Khajuraho.

The conquest of Bengal and Bihar was not attempted either by Muhammad Ghori or Aibak but by a petty noble named Bakhtiar Khalji. He began his career as an ordinary soldier and received some villages as jagirs from his master at Oudh. Here Khalji gathered a small force of followers and started raiding the nearby territories of Bihar. He began expanding his area and gradually conquered Nalanda and Vikramshila as well. Making careful preparations Bakhtiar Khalji marched with an army towards Nadia, the capital of Sena Kings of Bengal. Lakshman Sena felt that the Turks had made a surprise attack and fled out of fear. He plundered the city and later established his capital at Lakhnauti in North Bengal. Lakshman Sena and his successors continued to rule South Bengal from Sonargaon. Bakhtiar Khalji tried to conquer Tibet but his expedition failed miserably. Later his own army men murdered him.

The rulers who ruled Delhi between the period 1206-90 A.D. are popularly known as Slave dynasty. But neither of them belonged to one dynasty. Qutubuddin Aibak was the founder of the Qutubi dynasty, Iltutmish that of Shamsi dynasty and Balban of Balbani dynasty. They were also called the llbari Turks or the Mameluk Sultans of Delhi.

The death of Muhammad Ghori in 1206 A.D. created a tussle for supremacy among his three important generals, Tajuddin Yalduz, Nasiruddin Qabacha and Qutub-ud-din Aibak. Tajuddin held the area from Afghanistan to upper Sindh, Nasiruddin Qabacha who held Uchch, Multan and Qutub-ud-din Aibak became the governor of the Indian provinces of Muhammad. He functioned as an independent ruler. He has been regarded as the real founder of Turkish rule in India. Qutubuddin not only helped Muhammad in all his Indian campaigns but also consolidated and extended his conquests in his absence. Though technically still a slave, the title of Sultan was conferred upon him soon after the death of his master. Qutubuddin severed all connections with Ghazni.

In his brief reign of four years (1206-10 A.D.), he moved his capital to Lahore in order to frustrate Yalduz's ambition of annexing Punjab. He strengthened his position by matrimonial alliances with influential rival Turkish chiefs. He married the daughter of Yalduz. Next he married his sister to Nasiruddin Qabacha of Sindh and married his own daughter to Iltutmish. He earned the title of Lakh Baksh (giver of lakhs). He built the Quwwat-ul-Islam Mosque at Delhi and another at Ajmer called Adhai Din Ka Jhopra. He started building the Qutub Minar at Delhi but could not complete it. Aram Shah his immediate successor was mostly probably not his son. He was later killed by Iltutmish.

Qutubuddin was succeeded by his son-in-law Iltutmish. His accession was opposed by the Turkish nobles. Ali Mardan Khan had declared himself independent in Bengal and Bihar, while Qabacha, a fellow slave of Aibak had declared himself as an independent ruler of Multan and seized parts of Lahore and Punjab. The Rajput rulers of Jalore, Ranthambore,Gwalior and Ajmer became independent and Turkish power was thrown out of the doab. At the same time the Delhi Sultanate was threatened by the Mongols from the northwest. They appeared under Chenghiz Khan in pursuit of Jalal-ud-din a prince of Khwarizm. He was refused asylum by Iltutmish and thus saved the Turkish empire from the wrath of the Mongol warlord. He was also able to subdue the rebellion in Bengal and do away with other rivals one by one. He won back Gwalior, Bayana, Ajmer and Nagor. He also sent expeditions against Ranthambor and Jalore to reassert his sovereignty. He attacked and occupied Mandor in 1226 A.D. the capital of Paramaras. In 1234-35 A.D. Iltutmish attacked Malwa and plundered Bhilsa and Ujjain. Iltutmish requested the Caliph of Baghdad to grant him the title of Sultan. This gave Iltutmish legal claim over the Delhi Sultanate. It also helped him in making his rule hereditary. He made Delhi his capital. He issued coins and had Khutba read in his name. He gave a governing class or an official nobility to the Sultanate called Chahalgani or the "forty". He introduced the *Iqta* system. The *iqtadars* retained a part of the revenue from the *iqta* rendering military service to the Sultan. Large iqtadars were put in-charge of maintaining law and order in their iqta, in addition to sending troops to the Sultan in times of need. He died in 1236 A. D. He completed Qutab Minar of Delhi. Iltutmish had nominated his daughter Razia as the successor on his death-bed. However, nobles elected Rukn-ud-din Firoz as the ruler. But his reign proved short lived. He engaged himself in sensual pleasures while his mother Shah Turkan created dissatisfaction among the nobility. It resulted in revolts. At the capital Razia took advantage of Firoz's absence. She succeeded in getting the support of the people of Delhi and declared herself the Sultana of Delhi in the absence of Firoz. The accession and deposition of Firoz proved one point that the provincial governors proved the actual middlemen who could make and unmake the kings.

Once Razia ascended the throne she cast off the seclusion of the harem and wore male attire, administered justice in open court and personally led armies against rebellious chiefs. Jalal-ud-din Yakut, an Abyssinan slave became her favourite, which was not liked by the other nobles. Her bold and independent ways were not liked by the Chahalgani. Razia tried to concentrate power in her own hands and succeeded. Her primary aim was to make the Turkish slave nobles subservient to the throne. They planned to oust her from the throne. The first to revolt against her was Ikhtiyar-ud-din Altuniya, the governor of Sirhind. On her way to Delhi she was killed by one of the nobles.

After Razia's fall two weak rulers Bahram (1240-42 A.D.) and Alauddin Masud (1242-46) followed in quick succession. Their brief and inglorious reign was marked by the invasion of the Mongols. In 1246 A.D. Nasir-ud-din Mahmud, another son of Iltutmish ascended the throne. Nasiruddin placed all power into the hands of his Prime Minister Balban. On one occasion Balban was removed from office for a brief period at the instigation of Imaduddin Raihan, an Indian Muslim. Balban however was continuously regrouping his forces.

After Nasiruddin Mahmud, Balban ascended the throne. Balban's original name was Ulugh Khan. With his accession began the Balbani dynasty, an era of strong centralized government. He realized the need to strengthen the authority of the Sultan and wanted to curtail the power of Chahalgani. Balban in his attempt to curtail the power of the nobility increased the power and prestige of the Sultan. It was an age when power was exclusive to the persons born in noble houses. Hence Balban tried to strengthen his claim to the throne by declaring that he was the descendant of the legendary Iranian king Afrasiyab. Likewise Balban stood as the champion of the Turkish nobility.

Balban built up an aura around the throne and associated it with certain traits. He refused to entertain persons outside Turkish descent. It naturally meant the exclusion of Indian Muslims from all the positions of power and authority. He beleived in a semi-divine theory of kingship - a shadow of God on earth. He modelled his court in that of Persian manners and introduced Persian etiquette like *paibos* (prostration) and *sijda*. (Kissing of the monarch's feet). He maintained a dignified reserve and did not allow anyone to indulge in frivolity in his presence. He introduced the Persian Nauroz ceremony in the court.

While claiming to act as a champion of the Turkish nobility, Balban was not prepared to share power with anyone. He did not hesitate to poison his cousin Sher Khan to achieve his objective. The main instrument of Balban's despotism was his army. The credit of organizing a separate department of army (Diwan-i-Arz) goes to Balban. He reformed the financial side of the military administration and pensioned off those soldiers and troopers who were no longer fit for service. The strong centralized army that he built was to deal with both internal and external disturbances and mainly to tackle the Mongol menace. Balban also appointed spies in every department. The Barids or spies appointed were to watch the activities of his governors, military and civil officers and that of his own son. Balban administered justice with extreme, impartiality. Not even the highest in the land were to be spared if they transgressed his authority.

Balban did not undertake any fresh conquest largely because of the Mongol menace. He instead, concentrated on consolidating the territory already in possession. He suppressed the revolts in the doab and Oudh and tracked down recalcitrant elements in the region of Rohilakhand in Katehar.

In Bengal Tughril Khan revolted in 1279 A.D. and declared himself independent. This rebellion was easily suppressed. The region of Delhi had been rendered unsafe with the operation of robbers and dacoits to the extent that communication with the eastern areas became difficult. The Mewatis had become bold enough to plunder people on the outskirts of Delhi. Balban adopted a policy of 'blood and iron' and mercilessly subdued them. Balban had to face another invasion of the Mongols in 1285A.D. He sent his eldest son to repel the attack but lost him during the encounter. He could no longer recover from this tragedy and died in 1287 A.D. His greatest contribution was heightening of the dignity of the Sultan and of strengthening the army. He was also a patron of men of letters and showed special favour to the poet Amir Khusrau.

On the death of Balban, his grandson Kaiqubad succeeded him. The affairs of the state fell in disorder. Jalal-ud-din Khalji, placed himself at the head of a powerful faction and routed the Turkish amirs. Eventually Kaiqubad was murdered and Jalal-ud-din placed himself on the throne. Thus, the rule of the Ilbari Turks came to an end in 1290 A.D.

Khaljis

Jalaluddin Khalji: The Khaljis were another group of Turks who had settled in the

Khalji region of Afghanistan. With the accession of Jalaluddin Khalji on the throne of Delhi, the supremacy of the Turks finished in India. It established the strong position of the Indian Muslims. Kind by nature, Jalaluddin Firuz, the first Khalji ruler, he was lenient in his treatment of the rebels. When the rebels were brought before him he excused them and treated them with respect. Likewise he ordered that thugs who were a serious menace to the people and property around Delhi should be taken to far off places and set free. Only in the case of Sidi Maula he showed no clemency. Jalaluddin ascended the throne at the ripe age of seventy years and the weakness of old age affected his attitudes and activities. In 1290 A.D. he attacked Ranthambor. On the way he attacked Jhain. On reaching the fort the sultan realized the futility of attempting to capture the fort. He withrew the same day and told his nobles that he did not consider ten such forts worth a single hair of a Muslim. In 1292 A.D., Mandawar was captured from the Rajputs. The same year the Mongols under the command of a grandson of Halaqu, Abdullah attacked Punjab and reached near Sunam. Jalaluddin immediately marched against them and reached the banks of the river Indus. The sultan succeeded in defeating an advance guard of the Mongols and captured many of their officers. But afraid to face the main force of the Mongols, he tried for peace that was agreed upon by the Mongols. The invaders agreed to withdraw but Ulugh, a descendent of Chenghiz Khan accepted Islam and decided to stay in India.

Jalaluddin's ambitious nephew, Alauddin who had succeeded Malik Chajju at Kara, began to establish an independent kingdom for himself. In 1292 A.D. Alauddin had attacked Bhilsa and a part of the booty was sent to the Sultan. As a reward Alauddin got the governorship of Awadh in addition to that of Kara and Manikpur. This increased his desire for power. All those nobles who were dissatisfied with the weak policy of Jalaluddin had gathered round him. Alauddin needed wealth to strengthen his position.

He had heard about the fabulous wealth of Devagiri during the campaign of Bhilsa. Ramchandra Yadav, the ruler of Devagiri had not anticipated an attack from the north. Alauddin did not disclose his plans to anybody. Even from the Sultan, he sought permission simply to attack Chanderi. In 1296 A.D. he proceeded towards the South and passing through Chanderi and Bhilsa he reached Ellichpur, the northernmost outpost of Devagiri. Ramchandra was completely taken unawares. His son had gone with a large army to a neighbouring kingdom. On his return the two armies of Alauddin and Singhana, (Ramachandra's son) met each other. At the site of the approaching Muslim army, the troops of Singhana retreated in confusion. Alauddin got a huge indemnity. The enormous booty that Alauddin got from Devagiri helped him become the Sultan of Delhi. Jalaluddin was later murdered by a planned action by Alauddin in 1296 A.D.

Alauddin Khalji: The reign of Alauddin Khalji (Ali Gurshap as he was known), marks the zenith of the power of the Delhi Sultanate. His reign witnessed the expansion of the Muslim rule in terms of larger territorial conquests. He was unpopular among his subjects, as he had treacherously murdered his uncle. However, he soon won over the nobles by the lavish use of gold. For sometime he had to face some rebellions from nobles as well as his relations. Alauddin dealt with all of them with a severe hand. After consolidating his position and firmly establishing himself at Delhi, Alauddin undertook the first expedition to Gujarat in 1297 A.D. Possibly he was attracted by the wealth of Gujarat whose flourishing trade had always lured invaders. Alauddin sent an expedition under Ulugh Khan and Nusrat Khan to

Gujarat. On the way Ulugh Khan conquered Jaisalmer. The invaders plundered Gujarat and its capital Anhilwara and went as far as Cambay, destroyed the temple of Somnath and returned to Delhi with immense booty. He also sent an army to Multan soon after his accession. He faced resistance from the sons of the late Sultan and wanted to subdue them forever. Ulugh Khan and Zafar Khan were entrusted the task of eliminating Akrali Khan at Multan. After his capture, Multan once again came to the control of the Delhi Sultans.

The next to fall was Ranthambor, a stronghold of the Chauhana Rajputs. Its ruler Rana Hamir Deva, had extended his influence and provided shelter to the Mongol rebels. Alauddin desired to conquer it for its strategic importance too. He sent Ulugh Khan and Nusrat Khan to attack Ranthambor. The fort was besieged but Nusrat Khan was killed following which the invaders retreated. Alauddin himself captured the fort later in 1301 A.D. with the help of Ran Mal, the Prime Minister of Hamir Deva who had come over to his side.

An expedition against Mewar was organized in 1303 A.D. after the capture of Ranthambor. Another center of power of the Rajputs was Chittor. Alauddin was successful in capturing the fort. It was renamed Khizrabad after the sultan's son Khizr Khan. In traditional accounts Rani Padmavati the beautiful wife of Rana Ratan Singh is said to be the main cause of invasion of Mewar. However, territorial expansion seems to have been the most obvious reason. In 1305 A.D., Alauddin sent Ain-ul-Khan to attack Malwa. He defeated the Koka Pradhan, the minister of Rai Mahalak Dev in a battle and captured the fort of Mandu. Later Ujjain, Dhar and Chanderi were also captured.

Malwa was followed by Siwana. The fort was finally besieged in 1309 A.D. after a prolonged struggle. The ruler of Siwana, Rai Shital Dev was killed in action and the fort was put under the charge of Kamaluddin Gurg. In the same year, Jalor ruled by Raja Kanera Deva was attacked. The fort was annexed and its ruler was killed.The conquest of Jalor completed the conquest of Rajputana by Alauddin. The regions of Bundi, Mandor, Tonk and probably Jodhpur also surrendered to Alauddin. By the end of the first decade of Alauddin's rule the frontiers of the Delhi Sultanate had expanded to cover whole of north, west and central India. The Mongols, however, continued their inroads into Punjab in 1297 A.D. but were repulsed by Zafar Khan.

Between 1308 and 1312 A.D., Alauddin began the southward expansion of his empire. The prosperous state of Devagiri was ruled by the king, Ramachandra Deva. Alauddin invaded Devagiri in 1306-07 A.D. The immediate cause for this was unduly long delay in sending the annual tribute. He sent an army to attack Devagiri under Malik Kafur. His careful handling of the affairs of Devagiri enhanced Sultan's confidence in him and he was entrusted the responsibility of making further inroads into southern India. Acquisition of wealth rather than territorial expansion seems to have been the real motive of the Sultan. Kafur was able to defeat Ramachandra easily and in return captured a huge booty. Later Ramachandra became a feudatory of Alauddin.

In 1309 A.D. the Kakatiya kingdom was attacked. Its ruler Prataparudradeva accepted the suzerainty of Delhi and surrendered vast treasures. In 1310 A.D. the Muslims attacked the Hoysala kingdom. Its ruler Vira Ballala III surrendered all his treasures. Gradually Kafur subdued the Pandyas as well of Madurai. None of these territories were annexed by Alauddin directly but the flow of wealth was ensured from these regions.

Alauddin was an ambitious and capable ruler. He was so overwhelmed by his success at conquests that he dubbed himself as the 'Second Alexander'. He assumed the title of Sikandar-i- Sani. He dreamt to conquer the world and even thought of starting a new religion. After consolidating his position, he started the task of administering the empire with an iron hand. He established a strict system of administration. As a continuation of Balban's policy of kingship, Alauddin too strengthened the position of the Sultan through some tough measures. After deliberate thinking he came to the conclusion that there were four reasons of rebellion. Sultan's disregard to the state's affairs; drinking of wine; closeness among the nobles through get together and over affluence of the subjects. To start with, Alauddin struck at the power of the nobles and took four important measures. (a) He forbade the nobles to visit each other. Their private meetings were banned and there could be no marriage alliances between them without the permission of the Sultan. (b) Prohibition of drinking parties. (c) Strict vigilance through an efficient espionage system and (d) Confiscation of all lands given to the chiefs and in religious endowments.

As per the decision all grants of land and pensions were revoked and all lands that were held by people as gifts, pensions, endowments from the state were confiscated. He organized an efficient spy system to report all-important occurrences to the Sultan. The system worked so successfully that even the high officers of the Sultan feared talking aloud in public. The third ordinance prohibited the sale and use of wine and other intoxicating drugs at Delhi. The fourth measure prohibited all social gatherings and inter-marriages without the permission of the Sultan. The nobles remained terrorized till the last days of his reign and no further revolt occurred during Alauddin's lifetime.

Alauddin carried strong revenue reforms as well. He was the first monarch who insisted that in the doab, land revenue would be assessed on the basis of measurement of the land under cultivation. All lands given as assignments were reclaimed as Khalisa lands (crown lands). The size of these Khalisa lands whose income were directly collected for the Sultan's own treasury expanded quite considerably under Alauddin Khalji. Land tax was raised to fifty percent of the produce and other taxes were also collected with great harshness. Alauddin soon attacked the privileged position of hereditary revenue officers like *khuts, chaudhuris* and *muqaddams*. Alauddin abolished their privileges and snatched away their right to collect revenue. They were asked to pay equally as the other taxpayers.

The maintenance of a huge army by Alauddin was one of the special attributes of his rule. To avoid any kind of fake registration he devised the muster roll for identifying the soldiers personally called Chehra. Similarly to ensure the best kinds of horses by the soldiers the horses were branded (Dagh) and the troops were reviewed regularly. He personally recruited the army and paid it in cash. Alauddin's aim was to maintain a large standing army at a minimum cost. So, he devised the market control policy. Through this policy he sought to fix the cost of all commodities from food grains and other articles. The market control department was called Diwan-i-Riyasat and the chief officer Shahana-i-Mandi. Severe punishments were given to those who violated these measures. This market regulation was applicable to Delhi and its neighbouring regions. His measures were effective only during his lifetime. In the long run they affected trade and commerce adversely.

Alauddin was the first Muslim ruler who disregarded the position of the ulema (guardians of Islam). He refuted the suzerainty of the Caliph and did not allow any power independent of the state to guide his policies. He also gave patronage to many artists and learned men. Amir Khusrau flourished in his court. He built the Alai Darwaza beside the Jamat Khana Masjid at the Dargah of Nizam-ud-din Auliya, the Siri Fort and the Hazar Sutun (the palace of thousand pillars). He also built the magnificent tank, Hauz-i- Khas or Hauz-i- Alai.

On the death of Alauddin Khalji, his general Malik Kafur set aside the claims of the heir apparent Khizr Khan and crowned the infant son of the late Sultan. Soon after, another son of the Sultan murdered Kafur and ascended the throne as Qutubuddin Mubarak Shah Khalji. He was in turn murdered by Ghazi Malik who ascended the throne as Ghiyas-ud-din Tughlaq in 1320 A.D.

Tughlaqs

Ghiyas-ud din Tughlaq: Ghiyas-ud din Tughlaq laid the foundation of the Tughlq dynasty. It is stated by some writers that the Tughlaqs belonged to the race of Qarauna Turks and were a people of mixed breed. The Sultanate at this time was suffering from unsettled political conditions and demanded attention of the new ruler. The administrative set up established by Alauddin was destroyed by his successors and Ghiyas-ud-din had to address these problems urgently. He pursued a policy of reconciliation with the nobles and the people who were severely restricted under Alauddin. He succeeded in getting the support of the Turkish nobles on the basis of his race. He resumed the grants that were revoked and allowed them to enjoy their privileges. Ghiyas-ud-din succeeded in getting the support of the nobles and the people through these measures.

Ghiyas-ud-din attempted to improve the finances of the state and persued a policy to encourage agriculture. His twin object was to increase land under cultivation and improve economic condition of the cultivators. The state demand of revenue was fixed between one-fifth and one-third of the produce. He ordered the revenue to be increased only gradually and in no case could increase beyond one-eleventh to one-tenth. The privileges of the previous Hindu rulers were restored. The practice of measurement and survey of land was abandoned. The measures of Ghiyas-ud-din succeeded and the area under cultivation increased and the condition of the farmers improved.

Ghiyas-ud-din continued the system of *dagh* and *chehra* instituted by Alauddin. However, the market regulations were also abandoned under him. He insisted on paying the army better to increase its efficiency. He was successful in increasing the strength of the army.

He also pursued a policy of annexation. Prataprudra Deva, ruler of Warangal had reasserted independence and had not paid the annual tribute. In 1321 A.D. he sent his son Prince Jauna to Warangal to suppress Prataprudra Deva. He moved swiftly and besieged the fort. After a period of six months, Prataprudra Deva surrendered and agreed to pay the annual tribute. The name of Warangal was changed to Sultanpur. Telangana was annexed into the territories of Delhi Sultanate. Jauna Khan next attacked Orissa (Jajnagar). The expedition in the eastern part was a consequence of the wars in the south. Bhanudeva II the ruler of Jajnagar in Orissa had supported the ruler of Warangal at the offensive by the Sultans. Ulugh Khan in 1324 marched against Jajnagar. After plundering it, the region was annexed to the Delhi Sultanate.

In 1323-24 as a response to the request by nobles of Firoz Shah, the independent ruler of Lakhnauti, Ghiyasuddin marched into Bengal. In the ensuing battle, Bengal ruler was defeated. On his way back from Bengal, Ghiyas-ud-din also defeated the Raja of Tirhut in north Bihar. East and south Bengal were also annexed to the Sultanate. Ghiyas-ud-din patronized literary men as Amir Khusrau. He also built a strong fort called Tughlaqabad near Delhi.

Muhammad bin Tughlaq: Jauna Khan succeeded his father in 1325 A.D. with the title of Muhammad bin Tughlaq. He was a very learned man and proficient in many branches of learning. He began his career with the expedition of Khurasan. Ultimately the project was abandoned as an unrealistic scheme and the army was disbanded. It led to a tremendous financial loss to the state exchequer. He did not take into account the geographical and transportation difficulties.

His first administrative measure was to enhance land tax in the doab that led to widespread discontent as it was introduced at a time when the entire region was in the grip of a severe famine due to failure of rains. The Sultan raised the tax from five to ten percent. Therefore the peasants instead of paying the taxes, abandoned their lands and adopted highway robbery. The tax collectors continued to collect taxes by oppression. It resulted in extensive revolts. The Sultan suppressed the revolts severely.

The next venture of Muhammed Bin Tughlaq was the shifting of the capital to Devagiri that was renamed Daulatabad. In 1326-27 he involved almost a wholesale transfer of the population. Muhammed wanted to locate his capital in the central part of the empire and he also wanted to make it safe from the Mongol invasions. Every care was taken to provide a comfortable travel to the people to the new capital. But when some of the people resisted to the transfer, the Sultan ordered every one to shift as a punitive measure without realizing the sufferings carved due to this complete evacuation. Soon the Sultan discovered the unsuitability of the new capital. He ordered the people to shift back to Delhi once more. Daulatabad was abandoned largely because he soon found that he could not control north India from Daulatabad. The order of going back to the old capital caused much distress to the people.

Another of his novel and daring experiment was the introduction of the token currency of bronze coins in 1329-30 A.D. He was inspired by a similar system prevailing in Iran and China. The Sultan made these token coins legal tenders and kept their value on a par with the gold and silver coins. Now the Sultan issued *tanka* (rupee) of a silver and copper coins. People soon began to manufacture counterfeits of bronze in large numbers. As a result bad money drove out goon money. Trade came to a standstill and business was paralyzed. Finally Muhammed Tughlaq decided to withdraw the token currency. The Sultan readily gave gold and silver coins in exchange for bronze coins. The loss to the exchequer was immense. As a result the treasury that he wanted to fill was completely empty.

Muhammad Tughlaq carried out many measures for improvement of the administration of revenue. One of these was the preparation of a register in which income and expenditure of all provinces were recorded. All provincial governors were asked to submit the reports of income and expenditure to the center. Tughlaq established a separate department of agriculture called Diwan-i-Kohi. A special scheme was extended to improve cultivation in the doab. In 1333-34 A.D., loans were provided to peasants. However the scheme failed miserably because the men chosen for the purpose proved to be inexperienced and dishonest.

Firoz Shah Tughlaq: After the death of Muhammad Tughlaq his first cousin, Firoz Tughlaq became the Sultan in 1351 A.D. He overtook the administration in a chaotic condition. Firoz Tughlaq primarily paid attention to domestic affairs. He appointed as his wazir(chief minister), Malik Maqbul originally a Brahmin from Telangana. Firoz Shah started his reign with liberal ideas. He assured protection to all members of the royal family. He tried to please the nobles and set to ameliorate the distress caused to the people during long and troubled reign of Muhammad. Firoz Tughlaq abolished many irksome taxes keeping only those allowed by Quranic law. He looked after the interests of the cultivator, provided irrigation facilities by constructing five canals and advanced loans to the needy. He created a department of charity Diwan-i- Khairat. He worked towards winning over the confidence of the ulema. Firoz increased the salaries of his officers and gave them jagirs.

Firoz is known to have established several towns, Fatehbad, Hissar, Firozpur, Jaunpur and Firozabad, the favourite city of Firoz now popularly known as Kotla Firoz Shah. He revived the jagirs system abolished by Alauddin and reorganized army on feudal basis. He marched twice to capture Bengal in 1353 and in 1359 A.D. but failed on both the occasions. While returning from Bengal Firoz Tughlaq attacked Jajnagar in Orissa. In 1365 A.D. he started on a campaign to Thatta to avenge the wrongs done there to his predecessor but ended up granting pension to its ruler whose brother was reinstated in Sind.

When Firoz Tughlaq died in 1388 A.D. a civil war broke out among his successors. The Mongol conqueror Timur marched into India in 1398 A.D. and Nasiruddin Mahmud who came to the throne was defeated and fled to Gujarat. Timur plundered Delhi and returned to Samarqand leaving his Indian possessions under Khizr Khan of Sind.

Sayeds: The Sayed rule was established by Khizr Khan in 1414 A.D. He claimed to be the descendant of Prophet Muhammad. Even though there is considerable doubt on the claim it is known from sources that the family hailed from Arabia. Firoz Shah appointed him governor of Multan. He never assumed the title of Sultan and continued to send the yearly tribute to Shah Rukh, the son of Timur. His rule ended in 1421 A.D. His son Mubarak Shah (1421-34 A.D.) succeeded him. He assumed the title of Shah and got the khutba read in his name. It was during his reign that Yahiya Bin Ahmed Sarhindi wrote *Tarikh-i- Mubarak Shahi.* He carried on punitive actions against jagirdars who refused to pay the land revenue. He was succeeded by his son Muhammad Shah (1434-45 A.D.). He remained an incapable ruler. After his death the nobles declared his son Alauddin Alam Shah (1445-50 A.D.). He was the weakest ruler of the Sayed dynasty. By the time of his death the empire was limited to the city of Delhi. Alauddin was deposed by Bahlul Lodhi, the powerful governor of Lahore and Sirhind.

Lodhis

Bahlul Khan, the founder of the Lodhi dynasty, belonged to the Shahu Khel clan of the

Lodhis which was an important branch of the Afghans. He was helped by Muhammed Shah against the ruler of Malwa and was also granted possession over Punjab. Bahlul later attempted to capture Delhi twice but failed. When wazir Hamid Khan called him to Delhi, he got an opportunity. He proclaimed himself the Sultan in 1451 A.D. His primary task was to restore the prestige of the Sultan. He began by suppressing the rebellious jagirdars and established the supremacy of the Afghans. His main achievement was the annexation of Sharqi kingdom of Jaunpur. He also brought the entire region of Uttar Pradesh under his control. When he died in 1489 A.D., the Sultanate comprised of the territories from Punjab to Varanasi.

Bahlul was succeeded by his son Sikander Lodhi. He was the most powerful ruler of this dynasty. During his rule the authority of the Lodhis extended upto Bengal. To control the extreme regions of the empire he established his capital at Agra and founded the city in 1504 A.D. He upheld the position of the Sultan and destroyed the power of the nobility. He attacked Tirhut and included it within his empire. Sikander Shah succeeded partially against the Rajput states and conquered Dholpur, Utgir, Narwar and Nagaur. He encouraged agriculture and made roads safe for travel. For measurement of land he introduced Gaz-i-Sikandari. He is also known to have dispensed justice impartially.

The last ruler of the Lodhi dynasty was Sikander's son, Ibrahim Lodhi. He succeeded him after his death. His younger brother Jalal Khan was made the ruler of Jaunpur. The conquest of Gwalior remained his only significant achievement. The most notable feature of his reign was his conflict against the Afghan nobility. The main issue involved in the conflict was the concept of regarding the Sultan as one among equals. He was behaving as an absolute despot. Fed up of his despotic tendencies, Daulat Khan, the governor of Bihar declared independence and invited Babur, the ruler of Kabul to invade Hindustan. In 1525 A.D. Babur came marching towards Delhi. Both the armies met at Panipat in 1526 A.D. Ibrahim Lodhi was decisively defeated by Babur in the first battle of Panipat. Babur occupied Delhi and Agra and laid the foundation of the Mughal Empire in India.

Commerce and Urbanization: It seems that urban activities received an impetus under the Delhi Sultanate. The ruling class of sultanate was based in towns and spent most of their resources in the form of land revenue in buying and procuring various manufactures. The demand created by the nobility made a flourishing market for craft activities and manufacture of skill intensive luxurious items. The other factor that promoted urban industries was the introduction of a number of technological devices that came along with the invaders such as better devices for silk weaving and carpet weaving. The craftsmen worked in the *karkhanas* or factories supervised by the state officials.

Inland trade developed at two levels, short distance village-town trade and long distance trade between towns. The urban centers were dependent for supply of food grains from the rural areas. It was more of a one-way trade between the towns and the villages as most of the villages were self-sufficient. The inter town trade on the other hand was mainly composed of luxury items. The important commodities were wine, muslin, ordinary cloth, ghee and beetle leaf.

The long distance trade constituted an important segment of trade. Multan was the great entry point for overland foreign trade and served as center of exchange for the overseas trade. Delhi Sultans captured the coastal regions of Gujarat and Cambay for controlling the lucrative sea borne trade. Trade relations existed between Gujarat and Red Sea and Persian Gulf. The main export from Gujarat was coloured cloth and spices. Textiles, sugar and silk fabrics were the most important items of trade with the countries of Southeast Asia. Multan was a major trading center for overland trade. The most significant items of import into India were horses from Arabia and Central Asia. Precious metal especially silver that was not mined in India was in great demand. Brocades and other stuffs were imported from Alexandria, Iraq and China. Gujarat was the major center from where the luxury articles from Europe used to enter.

Administration: The Empire was divided into provinces for convenience called *iqtas*. The number of iqtas was not fixed. The head of the iqta was called *wali, nazim* or *naib*. There was no smaller administrative unit than the iqta by the end of the thirteenth century. After that iqtas were divided into smaller units called *shiqqs* that were put under the charge of the *shiqdars*. When the empire decayed the shiqq emerged as a *sarkarand* the officer incharge of a *sarkar* was *shiqqdar-ishiqqdaran*. The shiqqs or sarkars were further divided into *parganas*. The important official of the pargana was the *amil, qanungo* (treasurer) and *karkuns* (clerks). The smallest unit of administration was the village that was administered by local hereditary officers *khut, muqaddam* and *patwari* and the Panchayat.

Eleven

SMALL KINGDOMS

Bengal

Bengal was one of the earliest provinces to assert its independence from Delhi, and in 1338, Fakhruddin Mubarak Shah proclaimed himself the ruler of Sonargaon. Shortly Alauddin Ali, Shah (1339-1345), made himself independent in Northern Bengal. Shamsuddin Ilyas Shah (1345-58) made himself the independent rule of the entire province of Bengal. He founded the Ilyas Shahi dynasty which ruled Bengal up to 1538 with a few breaks in between. Sikandar Shah (1358-89), successfully defied Feroz Tughluq's attempt to subdue him. Ghiasuddin Azam Shah (1389-1409) the next ruler, established diplomatic relations with China and corresponded with Hafiz of Shiraj. He was known for his love of justice. There was a brief spell of Hindu rule under Raja Ganesh who usurped the throne in 1415 A.D. In 1442, the dynasty of Raja Ganesh came to an end and the old Ilyas Shahi dynasty was restored. Rukn-ud-din Barbak Shah (1459-74) was famous for his patronage of Bengali literature. In 1487, Sultan Shahzada Barbak Shah an Ethiopian bodygaurd, usurped the throne. Alauddin Hussain Shah (1493-1519) regarded as the greatest independent Muslim ruler of Bengal eventually deposed the Abyssinians and revived the Ilyas Shahi dynasty. He adopted a liberal policy by offering high offices to the Hindus and it was in his reign that Chaitanya preached Vaishnavism in Bengal and Orissa. Himself a learned man, he patronised learning and the Bengali literature. The Hindus honoured him as an incarnation of Krishna, Nripati Tilak (crown of kings) and the Jagat Bhusan. Nusrat Shah (1519-32) son and successor of Alauddin, was a patron of art, architecture and literature. He constructed two famous mosques, Bara Sona Masjid and Qadam Rasul at Gaur. It was during his reign that the Portuguese made their appearance in Bengal. The rise of Shershah Suri ended the Husain Shahi dynasty of Bengal in 1538.

Assam

There were two warring kingdoms in North Bengal and Assam during this period. Kamata (called Kamrup) was in the west and the Ahom Kingdom in the east. Allauddin Hussain Shah, supported by the Ahoms annexed the Kingdom of Kamata to Bengal. The Ahoms, a Mongoloid tribe from North Burma had become Hinduised in course of time. The greatest Ahom king was Suhungmung (1497-1539) whose reign is marked for the rapid Hinduisation of the Ahoms and the spread of a reformed Vaishnava doctrine under Shankaradeva. Suhungmung changed his name to Svarga Narayana. The Ahom historical chronicles are known are Burangis.

Orissa

The Eastern Ganga rulers ruled Orissa from 1076 to 1435 A.D. Its founder ruler Anantavarman Choda Ganga (1076-1148) built the famous Lingaraja temple at Bhuvaneshwar and the Jagannatha temple at Puri.

Suryavamsi Gajapati Dynasty: Kapilendra (1435-67), a minister of the last Ganga ruler Bhanudeva founded the Gajapati dynasty which ruled Orissa for more than a century. Prataparudra (1497-1540) was the last Hindu ruler of Orissa who suffered defeats at the hand of Allauddin Hussain of Bengal and Krishna Deva Raya of Vijayanagar. He is also remembered for his intimate connection with Chaitanya and his devotion to Vaishnavism.

The Gajapatis were replaced by the Bhoi dynasty whose founder, Govinda Vdyadhara (1542-59) belonged to the writer (Bhoi) caste.

Gujarat

Zafar Khan, appointed as governor of Gujarat in 1391 by one of the later Tughluqs formally assumed independence in 1401. In 1407 A.D. Zafar Khan formally proclaimed himself the ruler, with the title Muzaffar Shah.

The real founder of the Kingdom of Gujarat was, however Ahmad Shah (1411-43). He shifted the capital from Patan to the new city of Ahmedabad, the foundation of which he laid in 1413. As a great builder he built the Jama Masjid in Ahmedabad and the Tin Darwaja. He imposed *jizyah* on the Hindus in Gujarat for the first time.

The greatest sultan of Gujarat was Mahmud Begaraha who ruled over Gujarat for more than 50 years (1459-1511). He was called Begaraha because he captured two of the most powerful forts (garhs) Gimar and Champaner. He is equally famous for his voracious appetite. He also razed the famous Dwarka temple. Under him, the kingdom reached its maximum limit. He joined hands with the Egyptian ruler to check the Portuguese naval power. Later, he granted the Portuguese a site for a factory at Diu.

Bahadur Shah, grandson of Mahmud, was the last energetic sultan of Gujarat (1526-37). He defeated Mahmud II of Malwa and annexed his kingdom in 1531, and after Rana Sanga's death he stormed Chittor in A.D. 1534. He was treacherously drowned by the Portuguese in 1537 while conducting negotiations with the Portugeuese governor Nunho da Cunha.

Malwa

Dilawar Khan Ghuri who had been appointed governor of Malwa by the Tughluqs made himself independent of the Delhi sultanate in 1401 with its capital at Dhar. In 1406, Alp Khan, his son ascended the throne under the title Hushang Shah. He made Mandu his new capital and founded a new town Hoshangabad. He adopted a broad policy of religious toleration.

The Ghuri dynasty was replaced by the Khalji dynasty in 1436. Mahmud Khalji I (1436-

69) minister of Muhammad Shah (who was deposed) the founder of the new dynasty was the most powerful of all the sultans of Malwa. His war with Rana Kumbha of Mewar proved to be indecisive. The Khalifa of Egypt recognised his position and he received a mission from Sultan Abu Said. The last ruler of the Khalji dynasty was Mahmud Khalji II (1511-31) who appointed Medini Rai, the powerful Rajput chief of Chanderi to the office of minister. In 1531, Bahadur Shah of Gujarat captured Mandu and annexed Malwa to his dominions. It was later occupied for a short time by the Mughal ruler Humayun. Malwa was conquered by Mughal generals from Baz Bahadur in 1561.

Mewar

Chittor along with the other portions of Mewar was recovered by Rana Hammir (1314-78) from the Delhi sultans. This Sisodia ruler was a junior branch of the Guhilot dynasty.

Rana Kumbha (1438-68) was one of the greatest rulers of Mewar. He was proficient in the vedas, upanishads, smritis, politics and literature. He wrote a commentary on Jayadeva's *Gita Govinda* and an explanation of the *Chandisatakam.* A literary work, *Ekalinga Mahatmya,* speak eloquently of his military success against neighbouring Rajput princes. He laid the foundation of a new fort at Kumbhalgarh. The greatest architectural monument of his reign was, the Kirti stambha (Tower of victory) built by him at Chittor in commemoration of his victory over Malwa. Rana Sangram Singh (1509-28), popularly known as Sanga took Mewar to the zenith of its glory. He was generally successful in his war against Mahmud Khalji II of Malwa and Muzaffar Shah II of Gujarat. He defeated Ibrahim Lodhi at Ghatoli. Rana Sanga was defeated by Babur in the Battle of Khanwa (1527). Babur places him in his autobiography, next only to the Vijayanagar king among the Hindu rulers of India.

Marwar

The Rathors of Marwar came into prominence after Chunda (1384-1423) established his power at Mandor. His successor, the famous Jodha (1438-89) founded the new city Jodhpur and made it his capital. The greatest ruler of Marwar was Maldeo (1532-62) under whom the power of Rathors reached its height. He came into conflict with Shershah at the Battle of Samel (1544).

Other Rajput States: •The state of Amber was ruled by the Kachhavahas. •Bharmal, one of its ruler voluntarily recognised the overlordship of Akbar. •The state of Bikaner was ruled by a junior branch of the Rathor dynasty of Marwar. Its founder was Rao Bika (1464-1504), Son of Jadha of Marwar who also founded the city of Bikaner which became his capital. •The state of Jaisalmer was ruled by the Bhattis.

Jaunpur

The Sharqi dynasty was founded by Malik Sarwar a eunuch. He was given the title of Malik-us-Sharq (Lord of the East) by Mahmud Tughluq. As governor of Jaunpur, he claimed independence after Timur's invasion. Malik Sarwar was succeeded by Qaranfal under the title of Mubarak Shah (1399-1402). He was the first to assume the title of King. Ibrahim Shah (1402-40) was the greatest ruler of Sharqi dynasty. The Sharqi rulers were eager to conquer Delhi but were unsuccessful in doing so. Mahmud Shah (1440-57) was defeated by Bahlul Lodi. Husain Shah (1458-1505) was the last Sharqi ruler who was defeated by Bahlul Lodi (1483-84). The Sharqi kingdom was effectively annexed to the Delhi sultanate by Sikandar Lodi. Jaunpur was called the 'Shiraz of the East' for its cultural accomplishments. The famous Atala Masjid which stands now as a brilliant specimen of the Jaunpur style of architecture was completed in 1408 A.D.

Kashmir

Shah Mir founded the Shah Miri dynasty in Kashmir after becoming king of Kashmir in 1339 under the title Shamsuddin (1339-1342). This dynasty ruled Kashmir for more than two centuries (1339-1561) without acknowledging the suzerainty of Delhi Sultans. Alauddin (1343-54) transferred his capital from Indrakot to Alauddinpur (Srinagar). During Sikander's reign (1389-1413), Timur invaded India, but he was able to save Kashmir by diplomatic negotations. Sikander's prime-minister Suha Bhatt strove to Islamise the country. Sikander is known as the 'Aurangzeb of Kashmir' for his ruthless persecution of the Hindus. For the first time *jizyah* was imposed on the Hindus.

Zain-ul-Abidin (1420-70), known as the'Akbar of Kashmir', gets the credit for undoing the wrongs done to the Hindus by Sikander. He abolished *jizyah* and cow slaughter and withdrew the ban on sati.

He gave patronage to Sanskrit and Persian scholars, and at his instance the *Mahabharata* and Kalhana's *Rajatarangini*, were translated into Persian. Jonaraja who continued *Rajatarangini* and brought it up to 1458 and Srivara who continued Jonaraja's work enjoyed his patronage. His greatest engineering achievement being Zaina Lake-the artificial island in the Wular Lake. Zaimul-Abidin is still called Bud Shah (The great Sultan) by the Kashmiris.

The Shah Miri dynasty was ultimately overthrown by the Chaks in 1561, which was put to an end by Akbar in 1586.

Khandesh

The principality of Khandesh was founded by Malik Raja Faruqi (1389-99) who declared independence after Firuz Shah Tughluq.

Adil Khan 11 (1457-1503) strengthened Asirgarh and also built the famous citadel of Burhanpur. Akbar annexed it in 1601.

Bahmani Kingdom

The Bahmani kingdom was founded by Alauddin Hasan in 1347. After his coronation, he assumed the title of Alauddin Hasan Bahman Shah (1347-58), it is from this title that the kingdom was called the Bahmani kingdom. He established his capital at Gulbarga which remained till 1424, after which the capital was shifted to Bidar by Ahmad Shah. In the Gulbarga phase, Taj-ud-din Firoz Shah (1397-1422) was the greatest Sultan. The most important step taken by him was the induction of Hindus in the administration on a large scale. Ahmad Shah I was called a saint (wali) on account of his association with the famous saint Gesu Dara. Mahammad Shah III (1463-82) put to death his Vakil and Wazir Mahamud Gawan. Entitled Khwaja-i-Jahan he served three Bahmani rulers, Humayun (1457-61) Nizam Shah (minor) (1461-63) and Muhammad Shah III. As a great scholar and patron of learning he founded a magnificent college and a library at Bidar. After Gawan's execution the Bahamani kingdom began to decline and disintegrate.

Breakup of the Bahmani kingdom

1. The State of Bijapur was founded by Yusuf Adil Shah in 1489 A. D. Ibrahim (1534-58) was the first Bijapuri ruler to replace Persian by Hindvi (Dakhini Urdu) as the official language. Ibrahim II (1580–1627) was affectionately called Jagadguru by his subjects. Muhammad Adil Shah lies buried in the Gol Gumbaz. Bijapur was annexed by Aurangzeb in 1686.
2. Ahmadnagar-The founder of Nizamshahi dynasty was Ahmad Bahri in 1490. This was conquered by Shahjahan in 1633.
3. Berar-The Imad Shahi dynasty at Berar was founded by Fatullah Imad-ul-Mulk in 1490 A.D. This state had the shortest life span as it was annexed by Nizam Shahis in 1574 A.D.
4. Golcunda-The Qutub Shahi dynasty was founded by Auli Qutub Shah in 1518. Muhammad Quli was the founder of the city of Hyderabad. Aurangzeb annexed Golcunda in 1687.
5. Bidar-The Barid Shahi dynasty was founded by Ali Barid in 1518. Bidar was later annexed by the Adil Shahis of Bijapur.

Vijayanagar Kingdom

Its Foundation: The Vijayanagara Kingdom was founded by Harihara and Bukka of the Sangama dynasty in 1336. At the instance of their guru Vidyaranya, they established their kingdom with its capital at Vijayanagar. Harihara became the first ruler, and by 1346 the whole of Hoysala kingdom passed into the hands of the Vijayanagara rulers. Bukka succeeded his brother on the throne of Vijayanagara in 1336 and ruled till 1337. By 1337, the Sultanat of Madurai had been annexed.

The interests of the Vijayanagara rulers and the Bahamani kingdom which had come into existence in 1347, clashed in three separate and distinct areas: in the Tungabhadra doab, in the Krishna-Godavari delta and in the Marathwada country. The beginning of the Vijayanagar-Bahmani conflict started on a large scale during the reign of Bukka I in 1367. He also sent an embassy to the Emperor of China. Under Harihara II (1377-1406) Vijayananara empire embarked upon a policy of eastern expansion. He was able to maintain his position in the face of the Bahmani-Warangal combination. He invaded Ceylon.

Deva Raya I (1406-22) was defeated by the Bahmani ruler Firoz Shah in 1407.

He had to give his daughter in marriage to Firoz Shah. He defeated the Reddis of Kondavidu and recovered Udayagiri. In 1419, he defeated Firoz Shah.

Devaraya II (1422-1446) was the greatest ruler of the Sangama dynasty. He began the practice of employing Muslims in the army. He was called Immadi Deva Raya. In his inscriptions he has the title of Gajabetekara (the elephant hunter). Dindima was his court poet. Abdur Razzak of Persia visited his kingdom. Devaraya II is the author of two Sanskrit works *Mahanataka Sudhanidhi* and a commentary on the Brahmasutras of Badrayana.

There was confusion in the Vijayanagara empire after the death of Deva Raya II. Since the rule of primogeniture was not established, there was a series of civil wars among the contenders. After some time, the throne was usurped by the King's minister Saluva Narsimha and the Saluva dynasty was established.

Saluva Dynasty: Vira Narsimha (1503-04) the regent of Immadi Narasimha, usurped the throne after his assassination and laid the foundation of the Tuluva dynasty in 1505.

Tuluva Dynasty: Vira Narasimha had the title of Bhujabala (1505-09). After his brief reign, he was succeeded by his younger brother Krishna Deva Raya who was the greatest ruler of the Vijayanagar empire. (1509-30) Under him, Vijayanagara emerged as the strongest military power in the south. He defeated the rebellious chiefs of Ummattur, the Gajapatis of Orissa and Sultan Adil Shah of Bijapur. He successfully invaded Gulbarga and Bidar and restored the puppet Sultan Mahmud to the throne. To commemorate this act of restoration he assumed the title of 'Yavanarajya Sthapanacharya' (The restorer of the Yavana kingdom). He conquered almost the whole of Telangana from the Gajapati king Prataprаudra and the Sultan of Golcunda. Krishna Deva Raya maintained friendly relations with Albuquerque, the Portuguese governor whose ambassador Friar Luis resided at Vijayanagar. His relations with Portuguese were governed by two factors (a) common enemity with Bijapur (b) the supply of imported horses by the Portuguese to Vijayanagar.

Krishna Deva Raya was also a great patron of art and literature, and was known as Andhra Bhoja. He was the author of the Telugu work *Amuktamalyada* and one Sanskrit work *Jambavati Kalyanam*. His court was adorned by the Ashtadiggajas (the eight celebrated poets) of whom, Allasani Peddana was the greatest. His important works include *Manucharitam* and *Harikatha Saramsamu*. Krishna Deva Raya also built the famous temples of Krishnaswamy, Hazara Ramaswamy and Vitthalaswamy at his capital. Foreign travellers like Nuniz, Barbosa and Paes speak of his efficient administration and the prosperity of his empire.

After the death of Krishna Deva Raya, the struggle for succession followed among his relations. After the uneventful reigns of Achyuta Raya and Venkata, Sadasiva Raya ascended the throne in 1543. But the real power, was in the hands of Rama Raja the son-in law of Krishna Deva. The Bahmani rulers except Berar combined to inflict a crushing defeat on Vijayanagar in the Battle of Talikota or Rakshasa-Tangadi in 1565. This battle is generally considered to mark the end of the great age of Vijayanagara.

Although the kingdom lingered on for almost one hundred years under the Aravidu dynasty founded by Tirumala Raya with its capital at Penugonda, it came it to an end in 1672.

Central Administration: There was a council of ministers, headed by a Prime Minister to assist and advise the king in administration. The council met in a hall called Venkat Vilas Mantapa. The Pradhani, the fore-runner of Maratha Peshwa was the Prime Minister. The *rayasam* recorded oral orders of the king. The *karanikam* was the accountant.

Provincial and Local Administration: The kingdom was divided into *rajyas* or *mandalam* (provinces) under a governor described as Mandalesvara or Nayaka, Nadus (districts), *sthalas* (sub-districts) and finally into *gramas* (villages). Village self-government were considerably weakened under Vijayanagar ruler. Gauda, Village headman, looked after the village administration. The Ayagar system was an important feature of the village organisation. Every village affair was conducted by a body of 12 functionaries known as *ayagars* who were granted tax free lands (*manyams*).

Military administration: The top grades in the army were the *nayakas* or *palegars* who were granted territory (*amaram*) with fixed revenue in lieu of their salaries. Ordinary soldiers were usually paid in cash. The military department was called *kandachara*.

Revenue administration: Land tax was the most important source of revenue, which after assessment was 1/6th. The Nadalavukul, the Rajavthadankal, the Gandarayagandakol were the names of the' measuring rods. The police tax was known as *arasu svatantram*. The revenue department was known as *asthavana* and was headed by a revenue minister.

Social conditions: Allasani Peddana in his *Manucharitam* mentions the four castes that existed in the Vijayanagar society. 1. Viprulu or Brahmins 2. Rajjulu or rachavaru were generally the ruling class. Kshatriya varna seems to be absent. 3. Matikaratalu were the merchants. 4. Nalavajativaru or Sudras were mainly agriculturists.

Vipravinodins were the artisans, Kaikkolas were the weavers who formed a prominent community. The Tottiyans were the shepherds.

Position of Women: Gangadevi, wife of Kampana, wrote *Maduravijayam*. Hannamma and Tirumalamma were prominent scholars in the reign of Prauda deva and Achyuta Raya, respectively.

From the account of Paes, there was prevalence of Devadasis.

Religion: Early rulers were followers of Saivism. Virupaksha was their family god. Later, they came under the influence of Vaishnavism, but Siva continued to be worshipped.

The Vijayanagara rulers produced a new style called Dravida style in the field of architecture.

Twelve

ADVENT OF MUGHALS

Babur

Zahir-ud-din Muhammad Babur after defeating Ibrahim Lodi at Panipat in 1526 founded the Mughal empire in India. He was a descendent of Timur on his father's side and of Chengiz Khan through his mother. His fifth expedition to India was the Battle of Panipat, the first being the expedition in 1519 when he captured Bhera. He assumed the title of Ghazi, after the Battle of Khanwah (1527) in which he defeated Rana Sangram Singh or Rana Sanga of Mewar the greatest Rajput ruler of the period. Next he captured Chanderi from the Rajput chief Medini Rai. In the Battle of Ghagra 1529, Babur defeated Mahmud Lodi and his ally Nusrat Shah of Bengal. Babur died on December 26, 1530 at Agra and was buried at Kabul.

A scholar of Persian and Turki, he is said to have invented a new style of verse in Persian known as Mubaiyan. Babur wrote his memoirs *Tuzuk-i-Baburi* in Turki.

Humayun

Nasir-ud-din Muhammad surnamed Humayun, the fortunate succeeded Babur in December 1530 at the young age of 23. Following the Timurid legacy, he divided the empire among his three halfbrothers, Kamran, Hindal and Askari. Humayun defeated Mahmud Lodhi at Daurah in 1532 A.D. He laid siege of Chunar in 1532 but could not conquer it. Sher Khan Suri submitted to him. Sher Khan Suri, of the Afghan dynasty proved to be the most formidable enemy of Humayun and in 1539, at the Battle of Chausa, Sher Khan defeated Humayun and assumed the title of Emperor of India under the name Sher Shah. At the Battle of Kannauj in 1540 A.D. Sher Shah routed the Mughal forces under Humayun. After his final defeat, Humayun had to pass nearly fifteen years (1540-55) in exile. But shortly after regaining the empire in 1555 after defeating Sikander Sur, he died in 1556.

Humayun built a new city at Delhi, which he named Dinpanah.

Sur Dynasty

The childhood name of Sher Shah, the founder of the second Afghan dynasty or the Sur Empire was Farid. He began his career with the administration of his father's *iqta* at Sahasram in South Bihar. Later, Farid joined the service of Behar Khan Lohani, the Afghan governor of South Bihar from whom he received the title of Sher Khan. He assumed the reins of government on the death of Queen Dudu Bibi as the independent ruler of South Bihar and styled himself as Hazrat-i-Ala. His first great achievement was the acquisition of the famous fort of Chunar as a consequence of his marriage with Lad Malika. The conquest of Bengal and Bihar enhanced his power and prestige. After the historic victory of Chausa in which he defeated Humayun, Sher Shah Suri was proclaimed Emperor of Northern India at the age of 68. In the Battle of Kannauj (1540) he completely routed the Mughal forces.

As a ruler, Sher Shah ruled the mightiest empire after Muhammad Bin Tughluq. At the Battle of Samel (1544) Sher Shah defeated Maldeo of Marwar. During his last campaign against Kalinjar he died due to a freak accident (1545). He was buried at Sasaram in a tomb which he built for himself.

Sher Shah was succeeded by his second son Islam Shah who ruled till 1553. Mubariz Khan assumed the title of Muhammad Adil Shah and made Hemu the Chief Minister. Humayun defeated Sikandar Suri and occupied Delhi is 1555 and thus the Suri Empire fell.

Administration: Sher Shah Suri established a highly centralised machinery. His administrative works were roughly divided into various departments called Diwans, each headed by a separate minister. The important departments were:

1. Diwan-i-wizarat was headed by a wazir who looked after finance and revenue. 2. Diwan-i-Ariz-headed by Ariz-i-Mammalik (military department). 3. Diwan-i-Rasalat-whose officer-in-charge dealt with foreign affairs and diplomatic corespondence. 4. Diwan-i-Insha-The officer drafted royal proclamation and maintained government records.

Apart from these, the Diwan-i-quaza (justice) headed by chief Qazi, Diwan-i-barid (intelligence) were the other departments.

Provincial and Local Administration: The Empire was divided into province known as lqtas headed by Hakim/faujdar/Monim, which were divided into Sarkars (districts) manned by two officials, Shiqdar-i-Shiqdaran (for law and order) and Munsif-i-Munsifan (for revenue collection). Sarkars were divided into 2 or 3 Parganas, each having a *munsif* or *amin* for measurement of land and collection of land revenue, one Shiqdar (military officer), one fotdar (treasurer) and 2 Karkuns (one Hindi and one Persian writer). Villages were governed by their own Panchayats. Patwari (record keeper), Chaukidar, Muqqadams (headmen) and Qanungo were the village officials.

Justice: Civil cases of Pargana were tried by *amin* and criminal cases by a Qazi or Mir-i-Adil, in Sarkar the Munsif-i-Munsifan tried the civil cases. The chief Qazi or the Imperial Sadr was the chief judicial officer of the capital. Sher Shah introduced the principle of local responsibility for local crimes.

Land revenue system: Land was measured using the Sikandari *gaz,* and a *jarib* of rope was the standard unit of measurement. One-third of the average produce per bigha of land was the state revenue (average of good, bad, and middling lands produce). The peasants was given a *patta* (title deed) and a *qabuliyat* (deed of agreement) which fixed the peasant rights and taxes. Jaribana (surveyor's fee) -2.5% of the land revenue and Muhasilana (Tax collector's fee) at the rate of 5% of the land revenue were paid by the peasants. This land revenue system is called the Ryotwari system as he eliminated the intermediaries and the taxes were directly collected.

Customs: Sher Shah abolished many internal customs and duties. During his reign only two duties were levied on the goods: (a) custom duty-2.5% of the goods price at the entry point, Sikrigali in Bengal and at the Indus on the frontiers. -(b) Sales tax-at their first sale in the market.

Public works: Sher Shah built a new city near Delhi of which the sole survivor is the old Fort (Purana Qila). He built four roads (1) Grand Trunk from Sonargaon (Bengal) to Attock (2) Agra to Mandu (3) Agra to Jodhpur and Chittor. (4) Lahore to Multan. Sarais (rest houses) were built on these roads at a distance of every 2 *kos* which also served the purpose of *dak chaukis*.

Currency: He introduced a radical reform in the currency system. He introduced a new copper *dam*, silver *rupiya* (equal to 64 copper dam) and gold coin-*ashrafi*.

The Portuguese: The Portuguese were the first Europeans to have trading relations with India. Under the leadership of Vasco da Gama the Portuguese landed at Calicut on May 17, 1498 and were received warmly by the Hindu ruler, Zamorin of Calicut. In Portugal, the goods brought by Gama were computed at 60 times the cost of the entire expedition. The arrival of second expedition under Pedro Alvarez Cabral in India in 1500 and the second trip of Vasco da Gama in 1502 led to the establishment of trading stations at Calicut, Cochin and Cannanore.

- Portugal's initial objective was to seize the spice trade but after Cabral's voyage she decided to divert to herself all the trade of the East with Europe. • Francisco de Almeida (1505-1509) the first Portuguese governor in India was invested with full power to wage war, conclude treaties and regulate commerce. • Alfonso de Albuquerque the second governor (1509-15) laid the real foundation of Portuguese power in India. He captured Goa from the Bijapur ruler in 1510. • Other important governors were Nino da Cunha (1529-38) who transferred his capital from Cochin to Goa in 1530 and acquired Diu & Bassein from Bahadur Shah of Gujarat; and Martin Alfonso de Souza (1542—45) The famous Jesuit saint Fransisco Xavior arrived in India with Martin (1542).

The Portuguese monopoly of the Indian Ocean remained unbroken till 1545. The Portuguese maritime empire acquired the name of Estado da India which intended to monopolise the pepper and spice trade of the East. The Portuguese settlements were Daman, Salsette, Chaul and Bombay on the western coast and San Thome near Madras and Hugh in Bengal. The Portuguese introduced the Cartaze system under which the non-Portuguese ships had to obtain passes for trade.

The Portuguese power witnessed a decline by the end of the 16th century and gradually lost many of their settlements to their European counterparts mainly the English. Only Daman, Diu and Goa were retained by them till 1961.

Main causes of Decline of the Portuguese: •Their religious intolerance •Piracy and their clandestine trade practises. •Discovery of Brazil diverted their attention from India. •The Portuguese introduced the cultivation of tobacco in India. The first printing press in India was set up by the Portuguese at Goa in 1556.

Bhakti Movement

The Bhakti movement which stressed mystical union of the individual with God had been at work in India long before the Turks. Its philosophical concept had been fully enunciated in the Upanishads and *Bhagavad Gita*. The concept of Bhakti was placed on a firmer ground in South India when Shankaracharya revived the philosophy of Advaita. After him, the Alvars (Vaishnavite) and Nayanar (Saivite) saints made the concept of Bhakti more popular. Ramananda, the disciple of Ramanuja is regarded as a bridge between the Bhakti movement of South and North India.

Important Features: •The concept of Bhakti means single minded devotion to one god to secure the grace of god for the sake of salvation. •It discarded rituals and sacrifices as modes of worship and instead emphasised the purity of heart and mind, devotion, and humanism. •It was essentially monotheistic which could either have form (*saguna*) or be formless (*nirguna*) The Saguna school again was divided into Krishna margis and Rama margis. •The Bhakti movement completely discarded the discrimination based on caste or creed. Exponents of the Nirguna school were non-sectarian. Kabir and Guru Nanak were two famous exponents of this school.

Kabir: Born near Benaras, he led the life of a normal householder. A disciple of Ramananda, his mission was to preach a religion of love which would unite all castes and creeds. He emphasised the unity of god whom he calls by several names, such as Rama, Hari, Allah, etc. He strongly denounced Hindu and Muslim rituals and denounced the caste system, especially the practice of untouchability. However, he was not a social reformer, his emphasis being reform of the individual under the guidance of a true guru. His *dohas* and *sakhi* (poems) are found in the Bijak. After Kabir's death, his Muslim disciples organised themselves in Maghar, and the Hindu disciples were organised into an order by Surat Gopala, with their centre at Benaras.

Guru Nanak: Guru Nanak, from whose teachings the Sikh religion was derived, was born in the village of Talwandi (now called Nankana) in 1469. Like Kabir, Nanak also preached a casteless, universal, anti-ritualistic, monotheistic and highly spiritual religion. He laid great emphasis on the purity of character and conduct as the first condition of approaching God, and the need of a Guru for guidance. His catholic approach was aimed at bridging distinctions between the Hindus and the Muslims. Janam-Sakhis are hagiographic narratives of his life. He started free community kitchens called Guru Ka Langar. He died at Kartarpur in 1538. Guru Nanak nominated Guru Angad as his successor. After Guru Nanak's death, his followers founded a new religious sect, Sikhism. Guru Angad (1538-52) started the Gurumukhi script. Humayun came to Angad to get his blessings. •Guru Amardas (1552-74), The third Guru reformed the institution of langar. •Guru Ramdas (1575-81), the fourth Guru, was given the site of Har-Mandir at Amritsar by Akbar. •Guru Arjun (1581-1606) compiled the Adi Granth (later called Granth Sahib) and also completed the construction of Har-Mandir at Amritsar. He was executed by Jahangir. •Guru Hargobind, (1606-44) titled himself Saccha Padshah and introduced militancy among the Sikhs. He built the Akal Takht. •Guru Har Rai (1644-61). •Guru Har Kishan (1661-64). •Guru Tegh Bahadur (1664-75) was executed by Aurangzeb at Delhi. •Guru Gobind Singh (1675-1708) the 10th and the last Guru of the sikhs established the Khalsa in 1699 and organised the sikhs into a militancy sect. He was stabbed to death in Deccan at Nanded by a Pathan.

A Sikh is initiated into the religion by a rite known as the *pahul* (khande ka pahul). The orthodox Sikhs are distinguished by the five-Ks Viz., *kesa, kachha, kara, kanga* and *kirpan*. The exponents of the Saguna school were Chaitanya (1486-1533) who spread Vaishnavism in Bengal, Surdas, (popularised Krishna cult) Mirabai (devotee of Krishna) Sankaradeva, (Vaishnava cult) Tulsidas, (worshipped Rama) Vallabhacharya (Krishna cult), etc.

Growth of Regional Literature

During this period, literary works of high quality were produced in many of the regional languages.

Hindi: The Bhakti age was the richest period in the history of Hindi literature. The Saguna saint poets were Tulsidas who wrote *Ramcharitmanas, Vinay patrika* and *Kavitavali*; Surdas who wrote *Sur Sagar, Sur-Sarawali* and *Sahitya Ratna*, Mirabai, etc. Mystic poets such as Malik Muhammad Jaisi wrote *Padmavat*, Nur Muhammad wrote *Indravati*, Uthman wrote *Chitravali*, etc.

Urdu: The earliest available work in Deccani Urdu is a mystical treatise, *Mirat-ul-Ashiqin* by saint Gesu Daraj. Sufi Saint Shah Miran wrote *Khushnama*, Muhammad Nusrat, the outsanding scholar of Urdu throughout the Deccan wrote *Gulshan-i-Ishaq, Alinama,* and *Tarikh-i-Sikanderi.*

Bengali: Kasirama translated *Ramayana*, Maladhar Basu translated *Bhagavata*, Krishnadasa Kaviraja wrote *Chitanya Charitamruta.*

Telugu: Literature developed under the patronage of Vijayanagara rulers. Allasani Peddana wrote *Manucharitam* and *Harikathasaramsamu, Dhurjati-Kalahasti Mahatyam, Timmana-Parijata paharanam* were some of the Telugu works.

Kannada: Narhari, known as Kannada Valmiki, wrote *Taravi Ramayana*, Virupaksha Pandita wrote *Chenna Basava Purana.*

Marathi: Literature emerged due to the contribution made by the saint poets Mukundaraja -(Vivek-sindhu) Jnanadeva (Jnanesvari and Amritanubhava) Eknath, Tukaram (abhangas) Ramdas (Dasbodh), etc.

Punjabi: Masud Farid-ud-din was the pioneer of a new school of poetry in Punjabi. Guru Arjun compiled the *Adi Granth* and wrote *Sukhmani.* Waris Shah wrote *Hir*, a poetic romance.

Art and Culture

The architecture during the period represented a blending of Indian and Islamic styles. The mingling of the Turko-Afghan Islamic styles with the different indigenous styles, according to the needs of religion and personal taste led to the growth of new "Indian" style of architecture distinct in every province like Jaunpur, Bengal, Gujarat, Bijapur, Vijayanagar, etc.

Jaunpur: Sharqi's developed a new style of architecture which shows Hindu influences. Atala Masjid built by Ibrahim Shah Sharqi has no minarets of the usual type.

Bengal: A mixed style of architecture characterised by the use of bricks, Hindu temple style of curvilinear cornices, and designs like lotus. Adina Masjid at Pandua built by Sikandar Shah, Chota Sona Masjid built by Wali Muhammad at Gaur, Bara Sona Masjid and Qadam Rasul by Nusrat Shah at Gaur are some of the important mosques.

Gujarat: The capital city Ahmadabad had a Jami Masjid which was constructed by Ahmad Shah.

Malwa: At Mandu, Jami Masjid Hushang Shah's tomb, Hindola Mahal, Jahaj Mahal and Baz Bahadur's and Rupmati's palaces are some of the architectural monuments.

Bahmani Kingdom: The architecture was a composite mixture of several elements - Indian, Turkish, Egyptian and Persian-the last of which is well marked in some of the buildings like the Jami Masjid at Gulbarga, the Chand Minar at Daulatabad and the college of Mahmud Gawan at Bidar. In the Gol Gumbaz tomb of Muhammad Adil Shah at Bijapur we find the predominant influence of Turkish art.

Thirteen

MUGHAL EMPIRE

Akbar

Akbar was born to Humayun and Hamida Banu Begum on 23rd November 1542 at the palace of Rana Virasal of Amarkot. Humayun reconquered India by defeating the Afghans and entered Delhi on July 23, 1555. After his death on January 26, 1556 at Delhi, Akbar was formally proclaimed as the successor of Humayun on 14th February, 1556 at Kalanaur Akbar was just 13 years and 4 months old at the time of accession. Hemu the general and minister of Adilshah Sur after assuming the title of 'Vikramaditya' was defeated by Akbar in the second battle of Panipat (5 November, 1556). After appointing Abdul Latif as Akbar's tutor, Bairam Khan (guardian of Akbar) consolidated the administration as Akbar's vakil (regent) (1556-60). After his removal from regency, he left for Mecca, however on his way he was assassinated at Patan near Ahmedabad in January 1561. Akbar married his widow Salima Begum and brought up her child as his own son, who later became famous as Abdur-Rahim Khan-i-Khanan. Akbar died after an attack of dysentry on October, 1605 and was buried at Sikandra.

Conquests: During his early phase (1556-67) Akbar successfully contested with the nobility. During 1561 and 1567, the Uzbeks who held important positions in Eastern U.P., Bihar and Malwa broke out in rebellions which were crushed by Akbar. Mirza Hakim, Akbar's half-brother also rebelled by seizing control of Kabul which was also crushed. Malwa was conquered by Adham Khan and Bir Muhammad in 1561 from the musician ruler Sultan Baz Bahadur. In 1562, Raja Bihari Mal tendered his submission to Akbar and cemented the alliance by marrying his younger daughter Harkha bai to Akbar. Her son Salim (later Jahangir) succeeded Akbar. His son Bhagwan Das and grandson entered Akbar's royal service. Man Singh rose to the rank of 3,000 highest among the nobility along with Aziz Khan Kuka. The strong fortress of Merta in Marwar was captured in 1562. The conquest of Gondwana in 1564 under Asaf Khan against Rani Durgavati, the regent of her minor son Vir Narayan was also successful. Akbar himself conducted the siege of Chittor (1567-68) which fell in 1568 after a gallant opposition by the Rajputs under Jaimal and Patta. Rana Udaysingh after the capture of Chittor built a new capital at Udaipur and carried his struggle till his death in 1572. A.D. The fall of Chittor was folowed by the conquest of Ranthambhor (1569) the most powerful fortress of Rajasthan. As a result of these victories, most of the Rajput states including those of Bikaner and Jaisalmer, submitted to Akbar. He also married the princess of Bikaner and Jaisalmer. Raja Ramchand, the chief of Kalinjar in Bundelkhand also submitted to Akbar in 1569.

The conquest of Gujarat (1572-73) was due to its special economic advantage. Akbar himself marched in 1572 against Gujarat and defeated the puppet king Muzaffar Shah III. After this, Akbar turned his attention to Bengal and Bihar (1574-76) ruled by Daud Khan an Afghan. in 1576, Daud Khan was killed which brought to an end the last Afghan ruler in Northern India. In 1576, was fought the famous battle of Haldighati between Akbar and Rana Pratap, the successor to Mewar. The Mughal forces led by Man Singh of Amber and Asaf Khan defeated Rana Pratap who barely escaped with his life.

The Conquest of Kabul in 1581 by Akbar, which was ruled by his half-brother Mirza Hakim was a great triumph for the Mughals. The conquest of Sindh in 1590 opened the trade down the river Indus. Kandhar was incorporated in the empire in 1595. After the first siege of Ahmadnagar by the Mughal forces, the besiegers concluded a treaty with Chand Bibi in 1596, whereby Berar was ceded to the Mughals. In the second siege of Ahmadnagar, Chand Bibi was killed and it was conquered (1600 A.D.). The last campaign of Akbar was against Mian Bahadur Shah of Khandesh in 1601, whereby Asirgarh its strong fortress was captured and Khandesh was annexed to the Mughal Empire

Administrative Measures: Babur brought with him the Timurid traditions that the ruler had the divine right to rule, which was also followed by Humayun. Akbar's concept of suzerainty have been put forward by his biographer, Abul Fazl. According to him "Royalty is a light emanating from god, and a ray from the sun called Farri-izidi (the divine light). Thus, royalty was a divine gift and the ruler endowed with Farr-i-izidi had a paternal love towards the subject. After Akbar had taken the reins of government in his own hand, he took a number of liberal measures. In 1562, he passed a decree that the Hindu prisoners of wars were not to be made slaves or converted to Islam. In 1568, the pilgrim tax was abolished. In 1564, he abolished *jizyah,* which the non-Muslims were required to pay in a Muslim state.

Akbar, next turned his attention to the task of reorganisation of government. He reorganised the central machinery of administration on the basis of the division of power between various departments, and of checks and balances. His important contribution was the development of a provincial administration patterned on the central system of gvernment. Dastur-ul-Amals or Rule books containing detailed rules and regulations for controlling both the provincial and district administration were devised.

Central Administration: The form of Mughal government was despotic monarchy. The king was the head of the state and its chief executive. He was the supreme commander of the imperial forces and the fountain head of justice. Each minister was individually answerable to the monarch.

Provincial and Local Administration: In 1580, the Mughal Empire was divided into 12 Subah or provinces. Later, after the expansion of the empire into the Deccan, three more Subahs-Khandesh, Berar and Ahmadnagar were formed. During Jehangir's reign, the number of Subahs rose to 17, under Shahjahan they rose to 22 and under Aurangzeb to 21.

The head of the administration in the Subah was called Sipahsalar, Subahdaror Nazim. He was the commander of the provincial army and assisted the Diwan in collecting the land revenue and extending cultivation. He was assisted by a diwan, a bakshi, a sadr-cum-qazi, a mir-adl for justice, a kotwal, a mir-bahr and a waqia-navis. These officers were subordinate to the Governor, appointed directly by the Emperor, and were answerable to him and to the head of their ministry at the Centre. Thus, the principle of checks and balances were carried to the provincial government. Akbar introduced the office of the provincial Sadr, particularly with the object of weakening the authority and influence of the imperial Sadr. The Kotwal was primarily a police chief who combined in his office the functions of a municipal commissioner. Posted in provincial capitals and some other big towns, the Kotwal also regulated the market and examined weights and measures. The three Deccan provinces were held by a Viceroy. Prince Daniyal was the first Mughal viceroy of the Deccan.

Thus, the provincial administration of the Mughals was an exact miniature of the imperial government.

District and Local Government: Akbar inherited an excellent system of local administration from Sher Shah. For purpose of administration, the Provinces were divided into Sarkars which were divided into Parganas (tehsil).

Each Sarkar was headed by a Fauzdar or Shiqdar-i-Shiqadaran responsible for law and order. Amalguzar was responsible for the assessment and collection of land revenue.

The Bitikchi or writer was the record keeper of the land revenue establishment and worked under the supervision of Amalguzar. The Khazandar was the treasury officer of the district under the Amalguzar.

Each Pargana had a Shiqdar for general administration, an Amil for assessment and collection of land revenue, a Qanungo who kept local revenue records and clerks or Karkuns. The Fotedar was officer in charge of the tehsil treasury. The Tehsil constituted within its jurisdiction a number of villages. Each village had panchayats of elders headed by a Lambardar. Patwari and Chaukidars were the semiofficial members of village administration.

Land Revenue Administration: Till the 10th year of Akbar's reign (1566) no change was made in Sher Shah's corp rate (ray) which was converted into a cash rate, called *dastur-i-amai* or *dastur,* by using a single price-list. Akbar reverted afterward to a system of annual assessment. In the nineteenth year (1574) officials called *amil,* but popularly known as *karoris* were placed in charge of lands which could yield a crore of tankas. The karori assisted by a treasurer, a surveyor and others was to measure the land of a village and to assess the area under cultivation. In the same year, a new *jarib* or measuring rod consisting of bamboos joined by iron rings was introduced for the measurement of land. This *karori* experiment was introduced in the settled provinces, from Lahore to Allahabad.

In 1580, Akbar instituted a new system called the Dahsala or the Bandobast Arazi or the Zabti system. Under this, the average produce of different crops as well as the average prices prevailing over the last ten years were calculated. One-third of the average produce was the state share, which was however stated in cash.

The credit for developing this system i.e. Ani-i-Dahsala goes to Raja Todarmal. This system did not mean a ten-year settlement but was based on average of the produce and prices during the last ten years. For the measurement of land, *bigha* was adopted as standard unit of area which was 60 x 60 yards. A new *gaz* or yard, *gaz-i-Ilahi* was introduced 41 digits (*anguls*) or 33 inches in length (Sher Shah's *Igaz* 32 digit was discarded).

For purpose of fixing the land revenue, both continuity and productivity of cultivation were taken into account. Lands which were continually under cultivation were called *polaj.* Lands which were fallow (*parauti*) for a year, paid full (polaj) rates when they were brought under cultivation. Chachar was land which had been fallow for 3-4 years. It paid a progressive rate, the full-rate being charged in the third year. Banjar was cultivable wasteland. To encourage its cultivation, it paid full rates only in the 5th year. The lands were further divided into good, bad and middling. One third of the average produce was the state share.

After the assessment of land revenue in kind, it was converted into cash with the help of price schedules (*dastur-ul-aman* prepared at regional level or dastur level in respect of various food crops. For this purpose, the empire was divided into a large number of regions called *dastur* at *pargana* level having the same type of productivity. The government supplied *dastur-ul-amal* at tehsil level which explained the mode of land revenue payment. Each cultivator received a *pafta* or title deed (land holding deed) and *qubuliyat* (deed of aggreement according to which he had to pay state demand).

A number of other systems of assessment were also followed under Akbar. The most common was called *batai* or *ghallabakshi* (crop-sharing) This, again, was of three types: First was *bhaoli* where the crops were reaped and stacked, and divided in the presence of the parties. Second type was *khet batai* where the fields were divided after sowing. Third type was *lang batai* where the grain heaps were divided. In Kashmir, the produce was computed on the basis of ass loads (Kharwar), and then divided. Under Batai, the peasants were given the choice of paying in cash or kind, but in the case of cash crops the state demand was invariably in cash.

Kankut— In Kankut or appraisement, the whole land was measured either by using the *jarib* or pacing it, and the standing crops estimated by inspection.

Nasaq— This system of assessment was widely used in Akbar's time. It meant a rough calculation of the amount payable by the peasant on the basis of past experience.

The peasant was given remission in the land revenue if crops failed on account of drought, floods, etc. The amil was to advance money by way of loans (*taccavi*) to the peasants for seeds, implements, animals, etc., in times of need.

Law and Justice: Judiciary was the weakest part of the Mughal administration. Akbar had struck down the Islamic theory of state in its application to the Mughal empire. Below the Imperial court (Emperor) there was the court of the *qazi-ul-quzat* or the chief justice of the empire appointed by the Emperor, who in turn appointed the provincial qazis. Local courts of justice were manned by three types of judicial officers. Qazi cross-examined the parties, Mufti interpreted the law and Mir-i-adl delivered the judgement. Amils and other officials decided the revenue disputes. Village panchayats enjoyed the sanction of the state to administer justice according to the local tradition customs and personal law of the populace.

The Army: The Mughal army consisted of cavalry, infantry, artillery, elephants and camels. There was no navy in the modern sense except small fleets of boats along the sea-coast or on the river banks which was under an *amir-ul-bahr.*

The organisation of the best cavalry force in Asia was greatest achievement of Akbar and it was the backbone of the Mughal empire. The cavalry was considered the "Flower of the army". (Horsemen mounted and equipped by the state were called Bargirs). The emperor was the head of the army and its commander-in-chief. Akbar revived the practice of *chehra* (descriptive image of each soldier maintained) and *dagh* (branding of horses). The troops were divided into different categories (a) forces supplied by the vassal chieftains. (b) The *mansabdari* contingent (c) *dakhilis-state* directly employed these soldiers and paid from the imperial treasury (d) *ahadi* or gentlemen-troopers-these were individuals who brought their own horses and weapons of war and owed allegiance to the emperor. They had a separate paymaster and were placed under the command of an amir. The ahadis thus formed a special class of prospective mansabdars. The matchlock-men called *banduqchis, ahsams* (first rate warriors), *Shehbandis*-a sort of militia who maintained law and order and apprehended dacoits, *Baraq-Andaz* skilled musketeers, etc., formed the army. Akbar was specially interested in guns. He devised detachable guns which could be carried on an elephant or a camel.

Mansab System: To organise the nobility as well as his army Akbar introduced the Mansabdari system in 1577. Prior to Akbar's reign, this was in use in Central Asia implying rank. In its broadest aspect, the mansab or rank awarded to an individual fixed both his status in the official hierarchy as well as his salary. The lowest rank was 10 and the highest was 5,000 for the nobles. Mansab above 5,000 was reserved for princes of royal blood. The holder could be given any administrative or military appointment, or kept in attendance at the court. Thus, mansabdari was a single service, combining both civil and military responsibilities. Mirza Aziz Koka and Raja Man Singh, were honoured with the rank of 7,000 each. Highest rank of 10,000 was given exclusively to Salim by Akbar, later, it was raised to 12,000. However, during the period the ranks granted to the princes rose to 40,000 zat. The Mansabdars were classified into 66 grades from the mansab of 10 to 10,000, although in practice only 33 grades were constituted. Those holding ranks upto 500 were called *mansabdars,* those from 500—2,500 were called *amirs* and those from 2500 and above *amir-i-umda,* or *amir-i-azam*. Later, all those holding ranks below 1,000 began to be called Mansabdars. The Mansabdars who received pay in cash were known as *naqdi* and those paid through assignment of jagirs were called *jagirdars.*

The mansabdari system had made military service as the basic consideration for the classification of all the imperial service. Accordingly from the beginning, mansabdars of each category were subdivided further into three grades on the basis of the actual number of soldiers commanded by them. An officer whose contingent were equal to their mansab number were placed in the first category. The second category comprised those who maintained half or more than that and the third those whose *sawars* were less than half of their mansab. It was found impossible for the central government to ascertain at anytime, the exact number of soldiers controlled by all imperial mansabdars. This difficulty was solved by Akbar when he introduced the dual rank, the *zat* and the saw", in the 40'" reigned year (1595-96). In the dual Zat and Sawar system, Zat indicated the personal pay and status of a noble, and the Sawar rank the actual number of horseman he was expected to entertain (The mansab was not hereditary but based on merit). There was a possibility of the existence of a Zat rank without a sawar rank, but never a sawar rank without a zat rank. Another feature of this system was the law of escheat (Zabti) according to which after the death of a mansabdar all his property was confiscated. This measure was to curb the exploitation of the people by the mansabdars. The important defects of this system was that it did not give birth to a national army due to non-regimentation of the army.

The reign of Jahangir saw an important addition to the mansabdari system by Jahangir. He introduced the *du-aspah-sihaspa* (2-3 horses) rank, literally meaning troopers having 2 or 3 horses, and hence related to the *sawar* rank. Given to selected nobles, it doubled the ordinary sawar rank and hence doubled the obligation and privileges that went with it to the mansabdars.

Shah Jahan introduced the rule of one-third, one-fourth which scaled down the obligations of the masabdars. A mansabdar serving in a province where his jagir was, should have contingent equal to at least 1/3rd of his sawar rank, if elsewhere then only 1/4th. He also introduced the monthly scale.

By 1595, the number of mansabdars during the reign of Akbar was 180, but towards the close of Aurangzeb's reign their number rose to 14,449, leading to the complaints that no jagirs were left for being granted to them. This led to jagirdari and agrarian crisis which in turn, brought about the collapse of the Mansabdari system after Aurangzeb.

Jagir System: Jagir or tvyul were land revenue assignment to a mansabdar in lieu of his salary. The assignees were known as Jagirdars. The jagirs assigned in lieu of salary were known as *tankhah jagirs*. Besides, there were the *Watan jagirs* (hereditary possessions) of the autonomous chiefs, who were also granted the former type of jagirs if in Mughal service. The jagir lands were different from the Khalisa land, the revenues from the Khalisa lands were earmarked for the maintenance of the imperial court and the personal expenditure of the army. The jagir of the Mughal period was similar to the *iqta* of the Delhi Sultanate. The assignment of a jagir to a mansabdar did not confer any hereditary rights to the jagir. He could enjoy the revenues of the jagir only as long as he held the mansab (rank) and rendered services to the state. For the purpose of assigning jagirs the revenue department had to maintain a register indicating the assessed income (*jama*) in *dams,* calculated at the rate of 40 *dams* to a rupee. This register was called *jams-dami* of an area. The Mughal emperor followed the policy of frequent transfer of jagirs of the jagirdars so as to negate any development of territorial loyalty that would undermine the empire by strengthening the jagirdar.

Thus, the jagir system was closely related to the mansab system. All jagirdars were mansabdars, but not all masabdars were jagirdars, because some were paid in cash.

Policy of Sulh-i-kul: Akbar was the first among the medieval monarchs who raised the policy of religious toleration to the pinnacle of secularism. The evolution of the concept of Sulh-i-kul or peace and harmony among all religions by Akbar was due to the gradual development of his own religious ideas and liberal measures adopted by him. Under him, the state became essentially secular, liberal and enlightened in social matters, and a promoter of cultural integration.

Step towards integration: •Issued a decree in 1562 to stop the practice of enslaving the prisoners of wars and their forcible conversion to Islam. •Abolished the pilgrim tax in 1563. •On March 15,1564, abolished Jiziyah, thus granting religious freedom to the Hindus. •In 1575, he constructed lbadat Khana or the Hall of Prayer at Fatehpur Sikri. He discussed religious and spiritual topics with the Muslim theologians (Sheikh Mubarak, his sons Faizl and Abul Fazl were liberal minded theologians) •Next, he threw open the gates of lbadat Khana to Hindu priests (Purshottam and Debi were prominent), Jainism (Hira Vijaya Suri) Zoroastrianism (Dastur Maharji Rana) and Christianity (Ridolfo Aquaviva, Father Monserrate). [not Buddhism] •Issue of Mahzar in 1579 prepared by Sheikh Mubarak. He read the Khutba in his own name and reserved to himself the function of interpreting the Muslim law (man-i-Adl). V.A. Smith called Mahzar-The Infallibility Decree. •In 1582, he promulgated Tauhid-i-Ilahi or Din-i-Ilahi (Divine monotheism). It has no well-defined philosophy but required belief in one supreme god. It was not a new religion, but a measure adopted by Akbar with a view to establish a national or rather universal creed among the people by providing a common religious-cum-spiritual platform.

Jahangir

After the death of Akbar in 1605, Salim, his eldest son, succeeded to the throne in Agra fort on November 3, 1605 and assumed the title of Jahangir. Two of his younger brothers Murad and Daniyal had died earlier on account of drunkenness. He was married to Man Bai, daughter of Raja Bhagwan Das of Amber (mother of Prince Khusrau). His favourite wife was Jagat Gosai, daughter of Raja Udai Singh of Jodhpur who gave birth to Prince Khurram (later Shahjahan). He issued 12 'ordinances' to mark his coronation, for the general welfare and better governance of the country. Tamgha or Mir-Bahri, a cess was repealed. He forbaded the manufacture and sale of wine and intoxicating drugs throughout the empire. Slaughter of animals were banned on Sunday (day of Akabar's birth) and Thursday (his coronation day). Shortly after Jahangir's accession, his eldest son Khusrau, broke out into rebellion (1606). However, the rebellion by Khusrau proved to be short-lived. Jahangir defeated him at a battle near Lahore and soon afterwards he was captured and blinded. Guru Arjun Dev was executed on May 30, 1606 for blessing the Prince. Later in 1920, Prince Khusrau was killed on Prince Khurram's order at Burhanpur. Khusrau was very popular with the people as well as with the Mughal nobility. For this he was remembered long as the 'martyred saint.'

Jahangir, as Prince Salim was also responsible for the killing of Abul Fazl by the Bundela chief, Bir Singh Deo Bundela in 1602.

Mehrunnisa, later titled Nur Jahan after her marriage with Jahangir in 1611 was made Padshah Begum in 1613. She was the daughter of Ghiyas Beg who was given the title of Itimad-ud-Daulah and prior to her marriage with Jahangir she was married to Ali Quli Istajlu, titled Sher Afghan. She married Jahangir, after the killing of Sher Afghan in Bengal by the gaurds of Qutbuddin Khan, the governor of Bengal.

Some modern historians are of the opinion that along with her father Itimad-ud-daulah brother Asaf Khan and in alliance with Khurram, Nur Jhan formed a group of "Junta" which "managed" Jahangir, so that without its backing and support no one could advance in his career. This led to the division of the court into factions-the Nur Jahan "junta" and its opponents. Nur Jahan's daughter, Ladli Begum, born from her first husband, Sher Afghan was married to Prince Shahryar, the youngest son of Jahangir (political rival of Khurram). Asaf Khan married his daughter, Arjumand Bano, with Khurram.

Conquests: After his accession in 1605, Jahangir himself took up the task of settling the outstanding dispute with Mewar. Three successive campaigns launched proved to be unsuccessful. In 1613, Jahangir, deputed Prince Khurram to invade Mewar. This campaign proved decisive and Rana Amar Singh came to terms with the Mughals. All the territories of Mewar, including Chittor, were restored, but it was stipulated that the fortifications of Chittor would not be repaired. The revolt in Bengal was brought to an end after Jahangir posted to Bengal, Islam Khan in (1608). The principalities of Jessore and Kamrup were annexed. To keep the area under full control, the provincial capital was transferred from Rajmahal to Dacca.

After the fall of Ahmadnagar in 1600 A.D. Malik Ambar, an Abyssinian unleashed a fierce campaign to expel the Mughals from Berar, Balaghat and Ahmadnagar. By 1610, all the gains in the Deccan made by Akbar were lost. From 1603, a number of campaigns were sent by Jahangir against Ahmadnagar and in 1617, Malik Ambar was forced to submit. Jahangir did not try to enlarge the conquest made by Akbar in the Deccan due to deliberate policy. Despite the reverse, Akbar re-conquered large portions of Ahmadnagar and Berar. In 1921, Prince Shah Jahan was deputed to lead the Mughal campaign against the combined Deccani forces under Malik Ambar which again suffered a severe defeat at the hands of the Mughals. Ambar had to restore all the Mughal teritories:

The greatest failure of Jahangir's reign was the loss of Kaṇdahar to Shah Abbas of Persia in 1622. The revolt of Prince Shahjahan (1623-25) was suppressed by Prince Parvez and Mahabat Khan. The defeat of Mahabat Khan who staged a successful coup was the greatest victory attained by Nurjahan. Jahangir died near Lahore and was buried at Shahadra on October 28, 1627.

Shahjahan

Born to Jagat Gosain, daughter of Raja Udai Singh of Jodhpur in 1592, Shahjahan was coronated at Agra in February 1628. Asaf Khan was awarded the official title of uncle and Mahabat Khan was given the title of Khan-i-Khana. Mumtaz Mahal was the wife of Shahjahan. She was the daughter of Asaf Khan and her real name was Arjumand Banu Begum. On his coronation, Shahjahan made her the chief queen with the title of Malika-i-Zamani. She gave birth to 14 children, out of which 8 died in infancy. Only 6 children attained maturity (i) Jahan Ara Begum (ii) Dara Shikoh (iii) Shah Shuja (iv) Roshan Ara Begum (v) Aurangzeb (vi) Murad Baksh. Mumtaz Mahal died in 1631. A.D.

The first three years of his reign were disturbed by a rebellion in Bundelkhand by Jujhar Singh, son of Bir Singh Bundela and another rebellion by Khan-i-Jahan Lodi, governor of the Deccan who joined the Nizam Shahis. The rebellion in Bundelkhand was suppressed by the Mughal army under Aurangzeb, which was his first assignment. Here, Aurangzeb gave the first proof of his religious intolerance by destroying the Hindu temple of Orcha. After suppressing the rebellion of Deccan governor, Shahjahan ousted the Portuguese from Hugli and occupied it in 1632. Even after the death of Malik Ambar, his policy of refusing to recognise the Mughal position was being continued by the Nizam Shahi ruler. Shahjahan, therefore concluded that there could be no peace for the Mughals in the Deccan as long as Ahmadnagar continued as an independent state. This was a major departure from the policy followed by Akbar and Jahangir. In 1633, the Nizam Shahi dynasty came to an end at the hand of Mahabat Khan. Adilshah entered into a treaty with Shahjahan, by which he agreed to recognise Mughal suzerainty (1636). Shahjahan completed the settlement of the Deccan by entering into a treaty with Golcunda (1636) which also recognised Mughal soverignty.

In 1636, Aurangzeb was appointed the Mughal viceroy in the Deccan. This was the first viceroyalty of Aurangzeb (1636-1644). Khandesh, Berar Daulatabad and Telingana were the four Mughal provinces in south. In 1644, he was appointed as Governor of Gujarat. His second viceroyalty of the Deccan was during the period (1652-57). His second term occupies a permanent place in the history of land settlement of Deccan on account of a competent revenue adminstrator Murshid Quli Khan whom he appointed as his diwan. In 1665, the Prime minister of Golcunda joined Aurangzeb and Golcunda was besieged. Consequently, a second treaty was concluded with Golcunda in 1656. Mir Jumla joined the Mughal service. Similarly in 1657, the Adilshahi kingdom of Bijapur was attacked, but peace was made with Bijapur too on the intervention of Shahjahan. By the treaty of 1657, Bijapur was compelled to surrender the Nizam Shahi areas ceded to it by the accord of 1636.

Kandahar and Balkh campaigns: After being free of Deccan affairs in 1636, Shahjahan induced Ali Mardan Khan, the Persian governor of Kandahar to defect to the Mughal side (1638). Thus Kandahar was recovered from Persia (after its loss in 1622) without fighting.

In 1647, Balkh and Badakshan expedition were led by Prince Murad, Sadullah Khan and Aurangzeb, which proved to be a failure. The setback in Balkh also emboldened the Persians to attack and conquer Qandahar in 1649. Three successive campaigns, first and second under Aurangzeb, and the third under Dara in 1653 were launched to recover Kandahar, but all proved to be miserable failures.

War of succession: The last years of Shahjahan's reign were clouded by a bitter war of succession among his sons. At this time, Shah Shuja was governor of Bengal, Prince Murad was Governor of Gujarat, Aurangzeb was the viceroy of Deccan and Dara held the viceroyalty of North-west India. Jahan Ara supported Dara while Roshan Ara supported Aurangzeb. Sulaiman Shikoh, Dara's son aided by Mirza Raja Jai Singh defeated Shah Shuja who had crowned himself near Benaras (February, 1658). Another army under Raja Jaswant Singh faced the combined forces of Aurangzeb and Murad at Dharmat, in which Aurangzeb emerged victorious (April 1658). After this victory, Aurangzeb marched towards Agra and in the ensuing Battle at Samugarh (29 May, 1658) the Mughal forces under Dara were decisively defeated. After the defeat and flight of Dara the fort of Agra was also surrendered by Shahjahan and he was made a prisoner. Living as a captive in Shahburj of Agra Fort he died in 1666. Aurangzeb treacherously imprisoned Murad, after which he was killed. On July 21, 1658 Aurangzeb crowned himself as Emperor in Delhi. Aurangzeb defeated Shah Shuja at Khajwah (December 1658) who fled to Arakan. The Battle of Deorai near Ajmer (March 1659) was the last major battle Dara fought against Aurangzeb. Later, Dara was beheaded in 1658.

Aurangzeb

Aurangzeb, crowned himself as Emperor of Delhi on July 21, 1658 and assumed the title of Alamgir. His formal coronotion took place on June 5, 1659, after the battles of Khajwaha and Deorai.

As a puritan, Aurangzeb was an excellent calligraphist (copist of Quran) and cap maker. He was Viceroy of Deccan (1636-44), Governor of Gujarat in 1645-47 during his early days. After the Balkh expedition, he was appointed Governor of Multan and Sind in (1648-52). He was again appointed as Viceroy of Deccan in (1652-57). His first wife was Dilras Begum, officially styled Rabia-ud-Dauranl. His second wife Nawab Bai was a Kashmiri Rajput lady, mother of Mohammad Muazzam Shah Alam who became Emperor Bahadur Shah in 1707 A. D. His third wife Udaipuri Mahal, was mother of youngest son Kam Baksh. Aurangzeb was also regarded as Zinda piror a living saint on account of his simplicity, orthodox and god-fearing nature. He did away with the Pandari (octroi duties) and *rahadari* tax on (island transport) to alleviate the economic distress of the people. He abolished many unIslamic practices such as practice of engraving Kalima on the coins, stopped the celebration of Nauroz, abolished the solar calender and Arab lunar year was introduced. He also revived the Islamic theory of kingship. The practice of *jharokhadarshan* and the weighing of Emperor on his birthday was also discontinued.

Mir Jumla, the governor of Bengal first annexed Cooch Bihar to the Mughal kingdom in 1661. Next, he invaded the Ahom kingdom and occupied its capital Garhgaon and finally in 1663, he forced the Ahom king to make a humiliating treaty in 1663. In 1667, all the gains made by Mir Jumla were rapidly lost to the Ahoms, following his death. Shaista Khan, who succeeded Mir Jumla as the governor of Bengal conquered Chittagong in 1666.

During the period 1667-75, a series of tribal uprising combined with the religious revivalist movement called Raushanai broke out in the North-west region which was put to an end by Aurangzeb himself. In 1669, the Jats of the Mathura region broke out in rebellion under the leadership of Gokla. In 1672, the Satnamis, a religious body comprising of peasants, artisans and low caste people broke out in an open rebellion. In 1665, there was a second uprising of the Jats under the leadership of Rajaram, which was continued by Churaman, but by 1691, he was compelled to submit. All these rebellions were suppressed, but later it led to the rise of autonomous states.

Aurangzeb annexed Marwar after the death of its chief Maharaja Jaswant Singh (1678) and decided to award the *tika* of Marwar to Inder Singh instead of Jaswant's posthumous son Ajit Singh. It was at this stage that Mewar entered the war on the side of Ajit Singh. Prince Akbar also (Aurangzeb's son) joined Durgadas Rathor the Rajput chief. The war against Mahnrar and Mewar continued till 1698 when at last, Ajit Singh was recognised as the ruler of Merwar. Aurangzeb's policy towards Marwar and Mewar damaged Mughal military prestige.

Expansion in the Deccan: On coming to the throne, Aurangzeb had two problems in the Deccan: the problem posed by the rising power of Shivaji and the Bijapur problem. Jai Singh's Bijapur campaign (1665) proved to be a failure against the united front of the Deccan states. In 1665, treaty of Purandhar was signed between Shivaji and Raja Jai Singh. A desperate effort of Diler Khan, the Mughal viceroy, to capture Bijapur in 1679-80 also failed. Meanwhile Aurangzeb's son, Prince Akbar rebelled in 1681 and sided with the Rajputs. From Marwar, the rebel prince took shetler with the Maratha king Sambhaji. Aurangzeb, marched to Deccan in 1681 in pursuit of his rebel son but never returned to the North. After 18 months of siege, Aurangzeb annexed Bijapur in 1686 and Golcunda was also annexed in 1687. After the downfall of Bijapur and Golcunda Aurangzeb concentrated all his forces against the Marathas. In 1689, Sambhaji, the son and successor of Sivaji was captured at Sangameshwar and executed. Rajaram, the younger brother of Sambhaji, was crowned as king and he continued the fight against the Mughals from Jinji on the eastern coast. Shahu, the son of Sambhaji who was in Mughal captivity along with his mother was given the title of Raja and the Mansab of 7000. In 1703, Aurangzeb opened negotiations with the Marathas and was willing to release Shahu but cancelled it at the last moment. After the death of Rajaram in 1700 at Satara, Tarabai the regent of Shivaji II maintained the pressure on the Mughals.

Aurangzeb died on February 17, 1707 at Ahmadnagar and was buried in a plain grave near the tomb of Sheikh Zainuddin at Khuldabad, now Rauza near Daulatabad.

Religious Policies: Unlike his predecessors, Aurangzeb asserted the fundamentally Islamic character of the state. Regarded as Zinda pir, he abolished all unislamic practices as mentioned earlier, and appointed Muhtasios for regulation of moral conduct. In 1669, Aurangzeb took a number of puritanical measures such as prohibiting singing in the court. (Himself proficient in playing the veena) He ordered that old temples could be repaired but no new temples should be built. In 1669 the Vishwanath temple at Banaras and Keshava Rai temple at Mathura were destroyed and mosques erected in their place. He also ordered the destruction of Somnath temple and many other temples in Gujarat.

Aurangzeb also imposed *jizyah* on Hindus in April 1679, and made a public proclamation of Jeharl (holy war) against all the Hindus with the object of converting the land of infidels into *dar-ul-Islam*. The proportion of Hindu nobility including Marathas was highest in Aurangzeb's reign (33%).

Shivaji

Shivaji was born in the fort of Shivneri on April 10, 1627 to Shahaji Bhonsle and Jijabai. His tutor and guardian was Dadaji Kondadev and his spiritual teacher was Ram Das. With the death of his guardian Dadaji in 1647, Shivaji became his own master and the full control of his father's jagir (Poona) passed under him. Shivaji began his real conquest in 1656 by conquering Javli from the Maratha chief Chandra Rao More. In 1657, Shivaji first confronted the Mughals. On an invitation to Shivaji for a personal interview, Afzal Khan the leading Bijapur noble was killed by Shivaji in 1659. The Mughal governor of Deccan, Shaista Khan occupied Poona in 1669 and made it his headquarter. On the night of 15th April 1663, Shivaji raided Shaista Khan's harem in Poona, whereby Shaista Khan lost a thumb and his son, while Shivaji escaped. He attacked Surat, which was the premier Mughal post and looted (1664) it. In 1665, Aurangzeb sent Mirza Raja Jai Singh of Amber who besieged Purandhar and blockaded Rajgarh, his seat of government. Shivaji negotiated for submission and a treaty was concluded at Purandhar. Shivaji was excused from personal service, hence a mansab of 5,000 was granted in his place to his minor son Sambhaji. Shivaji also promised to join personally in any Mughal campaign in the Deccan. On Jaisingh's persuasion, Shivaji visited the Emperor at Agra where he was imprisoned (1666). Shivaji escaped from the detention in November 1666 and for three years he remained quiet consolidating his hold over his area. Aurangzeb granted the title of Raja on Shivaji. In 1670, Shivaji again sacked Surat. Shivaji was coronated at Raigarh on June 16, 1674 and assumed the title of Maharaja Chatrapati. A formal declaration was made by the priest Ganga Bhatt that Shivaji was a high class Kshatriya. In 1676, Shivaji launched a military campaign for the conquest of Bijapuri Karnataka (modern TN) with the active support of Qutb Shah of Golcunda. The stronghold of Jinji, Vellore and Tanjore along with the territories held be his half-brother, Ekoji, was conquered. The Karnataka expedition being his last one, Shivaji died in 1680.

Administration: Shivaji's system of administration was largely borrowed from the administrative practices of the Deccan states. The Council of Ministers (Ashtapradhan) had eight ministers, each minister being directly responsible to the ruler.

All ministers except Panditrao and the Nyayadish had to perform military duties when necessary. In his departmental duties each minister was aided by eight staff clerks, diwan (secretary), Majumdar (auditor/accountant) Fadnis (deputy auditor), Sabnis (office in charge), Chitnis (correspondence clerk), Jamadar (treasurer), Potnis (cashier), Karkhanis (commissary).

Army: Cavalry was the most important of the Maratha army which was composed of Bargirs (regular state cavalry) and Siladars (brought their own horses and equipments). In the infantry, the smallest unit was of soldiers headed by a Naik. The highest infantry commander was Seven-Hazari. The Commander-in-chief of the army was the Sar-i-Naubat. Shivaji's naval unit was located at Kolaba. Shivaji preferred to give cash salaries to the soldiers, though sometimes the chief's received revenue grants (*saranjam*).

The revenue system was patterned on the system of Malik Ambar. The Swarajya was divided into Mahals (province), Prants (Groups of district), Tarafs (district) and Manzas (groups of villages). The *prant* was headed by *subahdar* who was in charge of revenue collection. Land was measured using the Kathi. The state demand was 40% of the produce in cash or kind. Chauth (1/4th of land revenue) was collected from the reighbouring Mughal territories and Sardeshmukhi was an additional levy of 10% which Shivaji demanded on the basis of his being the (chief headman) hereditary Sardeshmuukh of Maharashtra.

After Shivaji's death Sambhaji (1680-89), Rajaram (1689-1700), and Tarabai (1700-1708) wife of Rajaram carried on the Maratha struggle against the Mughals.

Mughal Painting

The Mughal school of painting represents one of the most significant phases of Indian art, which was largely influenced by the Persian school of painting.

Humayun and his son Akbar took lessons in the art of painting frcm Mir Sayyid Ali, a pupil of the famous Bihzad of Herat who had been styled the Raphael of the East' and Khwaja Abdus Samad. Both these artists helped to prepare the illustrations to the Dastan-i-Amir-Hamzah which had nearly 1200 paintings. Of the 17 leading artists of Akbar's reign, no less than 13 were Hindus, chief among them were Basawan, Lal,

Mukund and Dasawant. Abdus Samad was given the title of 'Shirinqalam'. During Akbar's reign, painting was organised as an imperial establishment or Karkhana. Under Akbar, European painting was introduced at the court by the Portuguese priests. Western influence may be seen in the fables such as *Tuti namah, Anwar-i-Suhaili,* in which animals are shown with detailed realism. Dasawant painted the illustrations of Razm Namah (Persian ṭranslation of Mahabharata).

Under Jahangir, the Mughal painting reached its climax and Persian influence declined. It made way for a style that was essentially Indian. Himself an art connoisseur and an art critic, he could tell the names of individual artists in a composite piece. The famous artists of his court were Aga Reza, Abul Hasan, Muhammad Nadir, Mahammad Murad, Ustad Mansur, Bishan Das, Manohar and Govardhan. Abul Hasan was titled 'Nadir-us-Zaman'. Ustad Mansur specialised in painting rare animals and birds while Bishandas in portraits. Use of halo or divine lights began under Jahangir.

Shahjahan though interested mainly in architecture, continued to patronise paintings. A new technique called Siyahi Qalam, consisting of fine, delicate line drawings with tint of pale colours and gold was introduced during his period. Kalyan Das, Anup Chitr, Muhammad Nadir, etc., were the prominent painters at his court. Dara Shikoh was a patron of art as is proved by his album, now preserved in the India office.

Aurangzeb's age saw a decline in painting and he had many paintings defaced.

Important features: •The Mughal pictures were small in size and hence known as miniature paintings. •The paintings were mostly courtly and aristocratic. •They were a keen appreciation of nature by the artists. •Remarkable excellence achieved in portrait paintings. •Excellence of artists in colour composition.

Architecture

Babur, the founder of the Mughal dynasty had a fine aesthetic taste, though he did not find enough time to build many buildings. However, he built two mosques one at Sambhal in Rohilkhand and the other at Kabulibagh in Panipat. A third mosque in the old Lodhi Fort at Agra has also survived. In the early years of his reign, Humayun built a city at Delhi called Dinpanah.

The real phase of Mughal architecture began with Akbar and he combined the Persian traditions of architecture along with the Indian. Humayun's tomb at Delhi built by his widow Haji Begum, has the first slightly bulbous double domed structure made of marble. Placed in a garden, this is the prototype of the Taj. Akbar built the Agra Fort in red sand-stone. His other forts are at Lahore, Ajmer and Allahabad. During Akbar's reign a palace-cum-fort was built at Sikri, later named Fatehpur after the victory at Gujarat (imperial capital from 1569-1584) The Jami Masjid at Fatehpur-Sikri has been described by Fergusson as a romance in stone. In its courtyard is the tomb of Shaikh Salim Chisti. The massive gateway to the Masjid is the Buland Darwaja started by Akbar in 1573 to commemorate his victory at Gujarat. It stands 176 feet in height. Other important buildings at Fatehpur-Sikri are Jodha Bai's palace (influence of Hindu style) Anup Talao, (Peerless pool) Birbal's house, palace of Mariam, Diwan-e-Am, Diwan-e-Khas and Panch mahal (pyramidal Structure in five storeys, shows influence of Buddhist vihara). Two other remarkable buildings of his period are the Palace of Forty Pillars at Allahabad and Akbar's Mausoleum at Sikandara (started by Akbar himself) which shows influence of Buddhist viharas.

During the reign of Jahangir, his wife Nurjahan built (her father) Itmad-ud-daullah's tomb at Agra. A new technique borrowed from Golmandal temple at Udaipur, Pietra Dura was introduced here (decoration of walls with floral designs made of semi-precious stones. This tomb was entirely made of marble. Jahangir built the Moti Masjid in Lahore and his own tomb at Shahadra near Lahore.

During the reign of Shahjahan, Mughal architecture reached its supreme exuberance. Shahjahan built the famous Taj Mahal in memory of his wife Mumtaj Mahal. Its chief architects were Ustad Ahmad Lahori who was honoured by the title Nadir-ul-Asar, Mir Abdul Karim, Mukarramat Khan, etc. Mosque building also reached its climax under Shahjahan. The noteworthy being the Moti Masjid in the Agra Fort, built entirely in marble and the Jama Masjid at Delhi built in red sandstone (1644). In 1638, Shajahan began at Delhi the construction of a new capital city of Shahjahanabad, which was completed in 1648. The Diwan-e-khas and Rang Mahal are the two most conspicuous buildings inside the Red Fort. Aurangzeb built the Moti Masjid in the Red Fort at Delhi and the Badshahi mosque at Lahore. The tomb of Aurangzeb's queen Rabia-ud-durani at Aurangabad erected in 1679 is a frank imitation of the Taj Mahal. Compared with the Taj, this tomb is a very mediocre production which as Fergusson says "narrowly escapes vulgarity and bad taste."

Culture and Literature

The Mughal age is famous for many-sided cultural developments and has been called the second classical age following the Gupta age. In this cultural development, Indian traditions were amalgamated with the Turko-Iranian culture brought by the Mughals.

The greatest literary development during this period took place not only in the field of Persian literature but also in several regional languages. Persian prose and poetry reached a climax under Akbar's reign. Abul Fazl was the leading Persian poet during Akbar's reign.

Economy

During the 16th and 17th centuties, 85 per cent of India's populaton lived in rural areas. The largest section in the village consisted of peasants or cultivators. There were three main classes of peasants: (1) *Khud-kasht (riyayati):* Those residential peasants living in their own village, owning their own land and implements, paying the land-revenue at a concessional rate, formed the governing body of the village community. Also called mirasdars in Maharashtra and gharu-hala in Rajasthan. (2) *Pahi-kasht:* These peasants were basically outsiders but cultivated the rented land in a village either by staying in the same village (residential Pahi-kasht) or by staying in the neighbouring villages (non-residential Pahi-kasht). (3) *Muzarian (raiyatis):* Those who belonged to the same village but who did not have either land or implements and hence were dependent on the Khud-kasht for their supply. They were divided into two groups; tenants-at-will and those who had hereditary tenant rights, called as paws in Rajastan.

Apart from the cultivators, there were labourers (*majurs*). In addition, there were the ervice people blacksmith, potter, washerman, etc. In Maharashtra these service sectors were welve in number who were called *balutedars* and received a prescribed share (*baluta*) from he village produce.

The Indian peasantry in the Mughal empire was highly stratified and there was onsiderable difference in the size of holdings, produce and resources of peasants within the ame locality. India had a well diversified economy with the cultivation of a large variety of rops. Cotton, indigo, chay (red dye), sugarcane, oil seeds plantations paid land revenue at a igher rate and had to be paid in cash hence, called cash crops or superior crops. The peasants ot only shifted his cultivation from one crop to other but also adopted new crops. Tobacco nd maize were introduced in the 17th century. The adoption of potato and red chillies ollowed during the 18th century. During this period, India also exported foodgrains, especially ce and sugar. The peasant was not disposed from his land as long as he paid the land evenue. Although the life of the peasant was hard, he had enough to eat and meet his simple equirements.

Growth in Trade: Causes for growth in trade • Political and economic unification of ne country and the establishment of law and order over extensive areas. • Improvement of ansport and communications by the Mughals. • Encouragement given by the Mughals to ne growth of money economy. • Arrival of European traders from the early 17th century.

The growth of the rural markets led to the rise of small township or *qasbas*. The demand r all types of luxury goods by the nobles led to the expansion of handicraft production and owth of towns. The Indian trading classes were well organised and highly professional. Those pecialising in long distance, inter-regional trade were called *seth*, *bohra* or *modi* while those in cal retail trade were called *beoparis* or *banik*. There was a special class of traders, the *banjaras* ho specialised in carrying bulk goods. Boat traffic on waterways, and coastal trade was highly eveloped and cheaper than the transport on land. Gujarat was the entry point of foreign oods. It exported fine textiles and silk (*patolas*) to North India. Lahore was an important centre handicraft production. There was a well organised trade network in semi-luxury and luxury oods, with Agra and Burhanpur being the two nodal points in North India. Movement of oods were also facilitated by the growth of a financial system. This was done through the use *hundis* (a letter of credit payable after a period of time at a discount) which often included surance. The *sarrafs* specialised in changing money and *hundis* and thus acted as private nks. The members of the Mughal royal family and prominent nobles were also involved in de. Mir Jumla owned a fleet of ships. According to Ralph Fitch, Agra and Fatehpur Sikri were ger than London.

Inland trade as well as foreign trade, both were well-developed during this period. India d a favourable balance of trade.

Export Items: Textiles, sugar, rice, rawsilk, indigo, salt-petre, pepper, onion, etc.

Imports: Bullion, certain metals such as tin and copper, certain spices for food and edicinal purposes, war horses and luxury items.

Commerce with Europe: Between the middle of the 16th and the middle of the 18th ntury, India's overseas trade steadily expanded. This was due to some extent on account of activities of the various European companies which came to India during the period.

After the Portuguese arrival in India, (May 21, 1998) the Dutch, the English and later the French came to India for purposes of trade. After the decline of Portuguese power the Dutch established themselves at Masulipatam obtaining a *farman* from the ruler of Golcunda in 1606. The spices of the Spice Island (Java & Sumatra) was exchanged for cotton goods from Gujarat and Coromandel. Indigo was exported from Masulipatam. Other commodities exported by the Dutch were salt petre and Bengal raw silk. The credit for making Indian textiles the premier export from India goes to Dutch.

The English set up a factory at Surat in 1612 after defeating the Portuguese fleet. This was confirmed in 1618 by a *farman* from Jahangir, obtained with the help of Sir Thomas Roe, the royal ambassador from King James I. By 1616, the English established four factories at Ahmadnagar Burhanpur, Agra and Surat. In England, there was a growing demand for Bengal goods, especially for silk and salt-petre. In 1633, Mughal governor of Orissa gave English permission to establish factories at Hariharpur, Balasore and Pipli. In 1667, Aurangzeb gave the English a *farman* for trade in Bengal.

The English were permitted to purchase the zamindari of three villages, Sutanuti, Kalikata and Govindpur by the Mughal governor Azimush Shah which later grew up as Calcutta. The English developed the export of Indian textiles caled "Calico" to Europe. For this they sought the cloth produced in Agra and its neighbourhood, and later Coromandal. Indigo produced at Sarkhej in Gujarat and Bayana near Agra were in great demand. The best quality of salt-petre was found in Bihar which supplemented the European sources for gun-powder and ballast for ships.

The French also laid the foundation of French East India Company for trade in India in 1664.

The growth of India's foreign trade, the influx of gold and silver into the country, and the linking of India more closely with the rapidly expanding European markets had a number of important consequences.

- It weakened the old traditional ties in the villages
- Prices almost doubled

Social Stratification: The society looked like a feudal organisation with the king at its apex. Next in rank, were the nobility along with the zamindars. Socially and economically the Mughal nobility formed a privileged class. Below the nobles were a small and frugal middle class comprising of traders, merchants, small mansabdars, etc. The lowest of the society were the peasants. A main feature of rural society in the country was its highly stratified nature. People were divided and grouped on the basis of their resident status, caste and position as office holders. As described earlier the cultivators or peasants were of three types — the Riyayatis or khudkasht, Pahi-kasht and the Muzarian. Generally, those belonging to the higher castes formed the khud-khast, the Muzarian generally belonged to the middle castes Jat, Gujar, Ahir, Mali, etc. The landless and the bulk of the service classes designated as *kamin* or low included a sizeable section of dalits. A higher proportion of the richer section of the peasants including grain dealers (mahajans) and money lenders lived in the villages.

Status of Women: The upper class women were generally educated and lived a life of luxury, though confined to the inmates of the harem some of these played an active part in politics as rulers themselves, such as Rani Durgawati of Gondwana and Chand Bibi of Ahmadnagar or by exercising political powers through their husbands, like Nur Jahan. Jahanara, daughter of Shahjahan was also associated in the political processes.

However, more important than this was the role of women in giving moral and cultural tone to society from behind the curtains. Some of them have many literary works to their credit. Jahan Ara wrote under the pen-name "Makhfi." Roshan Ara set up a literary atalier (bait-ul-ulum) at Delhi.

Many harmful social practices, such as child marriage, denial of share in paretnal property, etc, also continued. There was little impact on Mughal attempt to regulate sati. Divorce was generally not favoured by the Muslim nobles, though there are a few instances of it.

For women belonging to the common fold, life was hard. Women specialised in some vocations. Thus, spinning was widely practised by women of almost all classes. In Bengal, the famous muslin of Dacca and the chikan work of Avadh were the speciality of women.

Fourteen

FALL OF MUGHALS

Later Mughals

The Mughal Empire was vast and extensive in the beginning of the eighteenth century. But by the close of the century it had shrunk to a few kilometres around Delhi. After the death of Aurangzeb in 1707, a war of succession began amongst his three surviving sons, Muazzam - the governor of Kabul, Azam- the governor of Gujarat, and Kam Baksh- the governor of Bijapur. Muazzam crowned himself emperor with the title of Bahadur Shah near Lahore. Azam turned to Ahmednagar and proclaimed himself emperor. Kam Baksh too declared himself the sovereign ruler and conquered important places as Gulbarga and Hyderabad, Muazzam defeated both Azam at Jajau in 1707 and Kam Baksh near Hyderabad in 1708. Muazzam emerged victorious and ascended the Mughal throne. He was also known as Shah Alam I.

Bahadur Shah (1707-12) was the first and the last of the later Mughal rulers to exercise real authority. He was learned, dignified and tried to reverse some of the narrow-minded policies and measures adopted by Aurangzeb.He followed a conciliatory policy towards the Rajputs and Marathas and adopted a strict policy towards the Sikhs.

To have bletter control over Marwar and Amber he forced Ajit Singh of Marwar to submit to the Mughal authority. He made attempts to garrison Amber and replace Jai Singh with his younger brother Vijay Singh. Both Ajit Singh and Jai Singh were later restored but their demand for high mansabs (ranks) and offices of subehdars of important provinces were not accepted.

Shahu, son of Shambhaji who was in Mughal captivity was released in 1707. He granted them the *sardeshmukhi* of the Deccan but not the *chauth.* He also did not recognize Shahu as the rightful Maratha king thus keeping the fight for supremacy going between Tara Bai and Shahu. Marathas thus remained dissatisfied.

Bahadur Shah made reconciliation with Guru Gobind Singh and granted him a high mansab. But after the death of the Guru, the Sikhs once again raised a revolt under the leadership of Banda Bahadur. The Mughal authority defeated Banda-Bahadur at Lohargarh, a fort built by Guru Gobind Singh. That was however recovered in 1712 by the Sikhs.

Bahadur Shah made peace with Chhatrasal, the Bundela chief and the Jat chief Churaman who joined him in the campaign against Banda Bahadur. He adopted a more tolerant attitude towards the Hindus. The *jaziah* imposed by Aurangzeb was withdrawn by him. There was however a deterioration in the field of administration in his reign because he lavishly granted jagirs and promotions. He died in 1712. Henceforth a new element entered Mughal politics and the war of succession. Previously, the contest for power was between the royal princes; the nobles had merely backed and sided with them. Now they became direct aspirants to the throne and began using the princes as pawns to capture authoritarian positions.

In another war of succession following Bahadur Shah's death, his four sons, Jahandar Shah, Raft-us-Shan, Azim-us-Shan and Jahan Shah became involved. Jahandar Shah (1712-13) was more successful in the war than the others. This became a regular practice after Bahadur Shah. But Jahandar Shah was a weak ruler and came to the throne chiefly with the help of Zulfikar Khan, the powerful noble who as a reward was made the wazir (prime minister). He was a clever man and advocated a friendly policy towards the Rajputs, Marathas and the Hindu chieftains not only to strengthen his own position but to ensure the survival of the empire. He quickly abandoned the policies of Aurangzeb and adopted a liberal attitude towards the Hindus. He abolished the jaziah; gave the title of Mirza Raja Sawai to Jai Singh of Amber and appointed him the governor of Malwa. Ajit Singh of Marwar was given the title of Maharaja and appointed the governor of Gujarat. He confirmed the agreement reached between his deputy and Shahu in 1711 whereby the Marathas were given the *chauth* and *sardeshmukhi* of the Deccan on condition that the Mughal officials would make these collections and hand it over to the Maratha officials. He pacified Churaman Jat and Chhatrasal Bundela but continued a strict policy towards the Sikhs.

Zulfikar Khan tried to improve the finances of the empire by checking the reckless growth of jagirs and offices and forced the mansabdars to maintain their official quota of troops. But he also introduced the evil practice of revenue - farming or Ijarah whereby the government established contact with the revenue farmers and middlemen who paid the government a fixed amount while they were free to collect whatever they could from the peasant. This oppressed the peasantry to a great extent. Many nobles were already conspiring against Zulfikar Khan and poisoning the ears of the emperor. However, the inglorious reign of Jahandar Shah soon came to an end in 1713 when he was defeated by his nephew Farrukh Siyar at Agra. Zulfikar Khan was soon executed by the orders of the new emperor.

Farrukh Siyar (1713-19) came to power with the help of Sayyid brothers, Abdullah Khan and Hussain Ali Khan Barha - the kingmakers. They were given the office of the wazir and mir bakshi respectively. The two brothers soon acquired dominant control over the affairs of the state. Farrukh was himself incapable of ruling and was easily influenced by the others. The Sayyid brothers were convinced that if the real authority were in their hands the empire would be safeguarded from perishing. It was during the reign of Farrukh that Banda Bahadur the Sikh chief was captured and killed. However, the struggle for power between the emperor and the Sayyid brothers increased and the efforts of the emperor to overthrow the brothers failed repeatedly. Finally Farrukh was deposed and killed in 1719.

As successors the brothers quickly raised two young princes, Rafi-ud-Darajat and Rafi-ud-Daula (Shah Jahan II) who died within months. Finally Roshan Akhtar, the son of Jahan Shah was placed on the throne under the title of Muhammad Shah. The brothers followed a policy of religious tolerance. They abolished the *jaziah* as well as the pilgrimage tax at many places. In order to maintain harmony. They advocated a policy of associating Hindu chiefs and nobles with Muslim nobles. In their struggle against Farrukh Siyar, the Sayyid brothers sided with the Rajputs and the Marathas. Ajit Sira Singh of Marwar and Jai Singh of Amber were won over by giving them high positions in the administration. Alliance was made with Churaman Jat and later placated Shahu by granting him Shivaji's swarajya and the right to collect the *chauth* and *sardeshmukhi* in six provinces of the Deccan. In return Shahu promised them help in the Deccan with fifteen thousand soldiers.

The efforts made by the Sayyid brothers did not yield great results because they were constantly faced with rival factions and conspiracies in the court. The financial position of the empire was also dwindling as the rebellious elements refused to pay the land tax. This led to increased indiscipline amongst the soldiers. The hostile nobles united themselves under the leadership of Nizam-ul-Mulk of the Deccan. Further the murder of Farrukh Siyar created a wave of terror and repulsion against the Sayyid brothers who were looked down upon as traitors. They were branded as anti-Islamic for their policies. The anti-Sayyid nobles were strongly backed by Muhammad Shah who wanted to free himself from the hold of the brothers. In 1720 Hussain Ali was killed by the rebellious nobles and Abdullah Khan died in 1722 after he was defeated at Agra. This ended the rule of the Sayyid brothers in the Mughal Empire.

After the fall of the Sayyid brothers Muhammad Shah had a long reign (1719-48) to save the empire. The Mughal rule was still held in high esteem by the people. The Mughal army especially the artillery was still the most important force, administration in northern India had deteriorated but not collapsed entirely. The Maratha sardars were still confined to the south and the Rajputs were loyal to the Mughals. But Muhammad Shah was not a good ruler. Nizam-ul-Mulk was appointed the Wazir in 1722. But instead of supporting Nizam, the emperor suspected his own ministers. The attempts to reform the administration proved futile and disgusted with the inability and fickle mindedness of the emperor the Nizam chose to pursue his own ambitions. He gave his office in 1724 and proceeded to the South and found the state of Hyderabad.

The already declining Mughal empire received another fatal blow when the Persian monarch, Nadir Shah invaded India in 1738-39. Nadir Shah was attracted to India by her fabulous wealth for which she was famous. The bankrupt Persian empire found an easy prey in the weak Mughal rule with loose defenses on the north-west frontier and used the golden opportunity. The disunity amongst the nobles too proved an added advantage for the invaders. The two armies met at Karnal in 1739 and the Mughals suffered a crushing defeat at the hands of Nadir Shah. Emperor Muhammad Shah was taken prisoner and Nadir Shah marched on to Delhi. He plundered the royal treasury at his own pleasure and carried back the immense wealth from India. He carried away with him the famous Koh-i-Noor diamond and the jewel studded Peacock throne of Shahjahan. Nadir Shah's invasion inflicted a heavy damage on the Mughal empire and its dwindling image suffered a severe blow. The invasion affected the imperial finances and the economic life of the people adversely. It created indiscipline amongst the nobles who began fighting for better jagirs and high offices.

The death of emperor Muhammad Shah in 1748 saw the beginning of bitter struggle among power hungry nobles of Turani and Irani factions. His successor Ahmed Shah ascended the throne but was unable to cope with the disintegrating forces. The weak defenses of the northwest encouraged Ahmed Shah Abdali, the able general of Nadir Shah to incur repeated invasions in northern India between 1748 and 1761. His most famous victory was that over the Marathas in the third battle of Panipat in 1761.

The invasions of Nadir Shah and Abdali brought the Mughal empire on the verge of collapse. It increased the infighting between the nobles to irreparable limits and the empire from now on was confined to the territory of Delhi. The Marathas too began to make their bid at the imperial mantle. The subsequent descendants of the Great Mughals were no longer interested in saving the empire and merely carried on as nominal heads.

Ali Gauhar under the title of Shah Alam II was crowned the emperor in 1759 after the departure of Abdali but he largely remained a fugitive and spent his time wandering. He made an attempt to capture Bengal with the help of Shuja-ud-Daula. But it was foiled by the English at the battle of Buxar in 1764. The last two rulers of the Mughal dynasty, Akbar II and Bahadur Shah II (1837-58) were at the mercy of the British. The Mughal dynasty after 1761 remained as a symbol of political unity in the minds of the people and served as a political front for the English.

Causes of Decline

On the whole the decline of the Mughal empire can be attributed to many factors. The process of its decay had begun from the time of Aurangzeb whose misguided policies weakened the stability of the Mughal polity. He was ambitious and wanted to increase the geographical limits of his empire even though it cost him heavily in terms of men and money. His hard headed attitude towards the Marathas, Rajputs and the Jats and the refusal to grant them regional autonomy broke the former loyalty that existed between them and the Mughal empire. Further he made the mistake of imposing the centralized system of governance in far flung areas which were beyond his control. Aurangzeb mainly failed to make good alliances to safeguard his empire and went on making more and more enemies. As a fanatic his religious policy alienated the Hindus and the Muslims. This certainly had an adverse effect on the stability of the empire.

The wars of succession that plagued Delhi from 1707 to 1719 too weakened the empire. The trail of weak successors further damaged the integrity of the empire. None of them had the ability to overcome the centrifugal forces and to unite the empire. Most of them were puppets in the hands of powerful nobles who ran the administration on their behalf. One more factor for the disintegration of the Mughal empire was the infighting between the nobles and their internal divisions. The Mughal court consisted of four groups of nobles, the Turanis, the Iranis, the Afghans and the Indian born Muslims. The accession of weak rulers at the center made them strong contenders for power. They fought amongst themselves for more jagirs and high offices which were limited in number. They weakened the military by amassing income from the jagirs for themselves and cutting down the number of troops.

The external invasions by Nadir Shah and Ahmed Shah Abdali broke the remaining strength of the Mughal empire. It took a heavy toll of the imperial treasury and property and laid open the inefficiencies of the military and political administration. It left India vulnerable to disintegrating forces from within and outside. The precarious condition of Mughal rule is evident from the fact that it was the Marathas not the Mughals who fought the third battle of Panipat in1761 with Abdali. The causes for the disintegration of the Mughal empire can be understood in two different terms. One, that the Mughal system of governance depended greatly on the effectiveness of the emperor's personality. It was certainly one of the main imperial pillars especially capable enough to keep the decentralizing forces at bay. The other one is strongly attributed to the so called crisis of the jagirdari system, caused by a shortage of jagirs and the over abundance of the jagirdars. It made the system exploitative and gave way to peasant's revolts disbalancing imperial stability.

Rise of New States

The eighteenth century saw the rise of a large number of autonomous states on the debris of the Mughal empire such as Bengal, Awadh, Hyderabad, Mysore, Marathas, and so on. New centers of power emerged mostly regional in nature.

Hyderabad: The Nizamshahi, the most prominent Muslim state rose to power in the Deccan in the eighteenth century. The Deccan became an autonomous state under Nizam-ul-Mulk. He had served under Aurangzeb both as a soldier and governor. Emperor Farrukh Siyar had appointed him the governor of six subhas. After the death of the Sayyid brothers Nizam-ul-Mulk made himself the master of those six subhas but was recalled to Delhi and appointed wazir by Emperor Muhammad Shah. The intrigues of the Mughal court did not suit him and he left for Aurangabad in 1724. He was countered by Mubariz Khan, the governor who replaced the Nizam. Mubariz was however defeated by the Nizam who kept up his supremacy. Finding himself helpless, the emperor confirmed the Nizam as viceroy of the Deccan in 1725 and gave him the title of Asafjah. The weakening of the imperial rule provided an opportunity to the subehdar of Deccan to lay the foundation of an independent state of Hyderabad. The Nizam established control by removing the officials appointed by the Mughals and installed his own men. Mughal authority was reduced to a symbolic reading of the Khutba. Coins were issued in his name. The Nizam showed nominal allegiance to the emperor and used his right to make treaties, declaring wars, granting mansabs, titles, and so on. He reformed the revenue system and increased religious tolerance as a policy. Nizam-ul-Mulk suffered a humiliating defeat at the hands of Baji Rao in 1737 and died in 1748. His successors Nasir Jang and Muzzaffar Jang were engaged in the second Carnatic war for succession and faced a tough challenge to keep the state autonomous.

Awadh: Saadat Khan Burhan-ul-Mulk was the founder of the autonomous kingdom of Awadh. He gradually secured the independence of Awadh after his appointment as Governor in 1722. The problem was posed by the rebellious zamindars who refused to pay land revenue to the state and acted as autonomous chiefs with forts and armies. Saadat Khan subdued them effectively and introduced a new revenue settlement in 1723 which provided protection to the peasants and the zamindars. It levied equitable land revenue and bettered the lot of the peasants. The jagirdari system was also reformed and jagirs were granted to the local gentry who were also positioned in administration and the army. He discouraged discriminating practices between Hindus and Muslims. He expired in 1739. He had made Awadh independent from central authority and made it a hereditary possession.

He was succeeded by his nephew Safdar Jung as the nawab of Awadh. In 1748 he was also appointed the wazir of the empire and since then his successors came to be known as Nawab-Wazirs. The province of Allahabad was also given to him. The internal administration was no longer dependent on imperial dictates and it was not obligatory to remit revenues regularly to Delhi. Furthermore, the office of the imperial Diwan was abolished and local gentry were encouraged to join the administration. He made alliances with the Maratha chiefs to safeguard his empire and fought wars against the Rohillas. A distinct Lucknowi culture grew around the Awadh court under his patronage and he started administering imperial justice. Awadh prospered in the peaceful and long reign of Safdar Jung and Lucknow soon became a cultural centre.

On his death, his son Shuja-ud-Daula became the subehdar of Awadh. He took a leading part in expanding frontiers of the province and incorporated a part of the Rohiila territory in his dominion. He outmanoeuvered the emperor in his efforts to control north India and secured the position of wazir once again in the imperial court. He sided with Abdali during the third battle of Panipat against the Marathas to check their inroads into his territory. He registered success in internal reorganization especially in the revenue administration and systematization of the army. The next ruler Asaf-ud-Daula and subsequent rulers were manipulated by the English and it became difficuit to maintain the autonomous status of Awadh any furthur.

Bengal: The basis of an independent state in Bengal was first laid by Murshid Kuli Khan. During the time of Aurangzeb he held the office of the Diwan and Deputy Governor of Bengal. In 1713 he was made the Governor of Bengal and in 1719 Orissa was added to his charge. He established the capital at Murshidabad named after him. He is credited with the reforms in the revenue administration whereby he eliminated the intermediary zamindars and encouraged the big zamindars who took responsibility of revenue collection and payment. He converted the majority of jagirs into Khalisa or crown lands. Bengal made great strides during his reign in trade and commerce.

Murshid Khan died in 1727 and was succeeded by Shuja-ud-Din. The governorship of Bihar was added to his charge by Muhammad Shah in 1733. After his death his son Sarfaraz Khan succeed him. In 1740 however Alivardi Khan, the deputy governor of Bihar defeated and killed him to seize power. His reign showed signs towards autonomy. Though the imperial rule was not defied out rightly, the payment of tribute to the emperor and the appointment of officials were both absent from Alivardi's reign. There was no imperial interference in Bengal.

Mysore: The Mysore kingdom was part of the Vijayanagar empire in the beginning and was nominally a part of Mughal empire. Mysore was transformed from a viceroyalty of the Vijaynagar empire into an autonomous state by the Wodeyar dynasty. Two brothers, Nanjraj and Devraj seized power in the eighteenth century and reduced the King Chikka Krishna Raj to a mere puppet. HaiderAli rose to prominence in the Mysore army as a petty officer and became a brilliant commander. In 1761 he overthrew Nanjraj and established authority over Mysore state and suppressed local chieftains. He conquered territories of Bidnur,

Sunda, Sera, Canara and Malabar. He introduced Mughal administrative and revenue system in Mysore and reformed the army. Haider Ali incurred hostilities of the Marathas, the Nizam and the English. In 1769 he defeated the British forces and dictated the Treaty of Madras securing the promise of mutual assistance in case of war. This promise was not kept up later. In 1782 Haider Ali passed away and was succeeded by his able son Tipu Sultan who continued the war.

Tipu was ambitious and attacked Travancore, an ally of the British and in 1789 a third Anglo Mysore war broke out. Tipu made peace with the English at Srirangapatnam conceding many territories from his dominion. He died in 1799 at the hands of the British. He introduced new coinage and weights and measures during his reign.

Maratha Confederacy: Amongst the various provincial states that emerged during this period the most prominent was the Maratha state. The rise of the Marathas was both a regional reaction against Mughal centralization as well as manifestation of the mobility of certain classes and castes internally. They posed the most formidable challenge to the Mughal rule in India from the Deccan. The clash between Shahu, grandson of Shivaji and his aunt, Tara Bai at Kolhapur gave rise to a new system of Maratha government under the leadership of Balaji Vishvanath. That became a period of Peshwa domination in Maratha polity. Now the Maratha state was transformed into the Maratha Empire.

Balaji strengthened hold over most of Maharashtra through sardars except for Kolhapur. Taking full advantage of weakening Mughal authority the Peshwa increased his own power. He used Zulfikar Khan and Sayyid brothers to get the *chauth* and *sardeshmukhi* of the Deccan .The system of *watans* and *saranjams* (jagirs) made the Maratha sardars strong and increased their personal power. In 1740 the Marathas won control over Malwa and Gujarat and parts of Bundelkhand and extended sway over Rajputana too. The third battle of Panipat in 1761 between the Afghan forces under Abdali and the Marathas put a check to their advance in northern India. The aftermath of the defeat was that the British got a tremendous opportunity to extend their influence in Bengal and India.

Punjab: Guru Gobind Singh built the Sikhs into a fighting force. The Sikh movement that was started by Guru Nanak to reform the religious belief and to strengthen Sikh brotherhood, changed into a political movement during the eighteenth century. The numerous Sikh Jatthas posed strong challenge to the Mughal authority under the leadership of Banda Bahadur. The foreign invasions, Maratha incursions and internal rivalry in the provincial administration helped the Sikhs to consolidate their base. In later eighteenth century the Sikhs regrouped into confederacies called *mists*. These were twelve in number under local chieftains. The process towards the establishment of an autonomous state was complete under Ranjit Singh in the nineteenth century. He belonged to the Sukarchakiya misl. He brought the various Sikh principalities into one political entity. In 1799 he made himself the master of Lahore, the political center and in 1802 he captured Amritsar, the religious center. This made him all-powerful and an undisputed monarch. He soon brought all Sikh chiefs west of the Sutlej under his control and established his own kingdom in the Punjab. Ranjit Singh formed a strong enemy to the English and prevented his state from British annexation till his death in 1839.

Rajputs: The Rajputs were alienated by the policies of Aurangzeb and found the weakness in the Mughal empire the perfect opportunity to re-establish their independence. They took advantage of the ongoing tussle between emperor Farrukh Siyar and the Sayyid brothers and followed a policy of opportune aloofness or adherence. They slowly loosened their ties with Delhi and functioned as independent rulers. Their active participation in the court politics of the Mughals helped them to acquire governorships. The Sayyids made Ajit Singh the governor of Ajmer and Gujarat and he held, them till 1721. All the Rajput states followed a policy of constant expansion absorbing weak neighbours whenever possible.

Jat State: The Jats were an agricultural caste inhabiting the Delhi-Agra region. The Mughal Empire faced a tough challenge from the Jats. They took an initiative to establish an autonomous state under Churaman and Badan Singh and revolted against Mughal domination in the seventeenth century establishing the Jat state at Bharatpur. But it was Suraj Mal who consolidated the Jat power from 1756 to 1763. It extended in the east upto the boundary of the Ganges, in the south up to the Chambal, to Delhi in the north and Agra in the west. The administrative and revenue powers were both controlled by the zamindars. However, the death of Suraj Mal in 1763 marked the demise of the Jat state.

Kerala: Kerela was divided into three small principalities of Cochin, Travancore and Calicut. These were controlled by a large number of local chieftains and rajas in the beginning of the eighteenth century. Haider Ali invaded Kerala in 1766 and annexed Malabar and Calicut. Travancore the most prominent of the southern state was spared and Martanda Verma took control of the region.

On the whole the regional polities that emerged in the seventeenth and eighteenth centuries was strong enough to destroy the Mughal power but not capable enough to sustain a stable polity of an all India level. All these states however recognized the Mughals as an umbrella authority. But the internal rivalries existing within these states such as the Rajputs, the southern states, etc, paved the way for their own destruction. Most of the states could not sustain themselves after their founders. These states could not stop the economic stagnation within and their dis-unity paved the way for the British in the Indian political scene.

Fifteen

ARRIVAL OF THE BRITISH

The earliest English settlement in eastern India dates back to 1633 when they established their factories at Hariharpur and Balasore in Orissa. The first English factory in Bengal was established at Hugli in 1651 under permission of Sultan Shuja, the viceroy of Bengal who granted them the privilege of trading in return for a fixed annual payment of duties worth Rs.3000. Soon they established their factories at Qasim Bazar, Patna and other regions nearby. The main items of English trade were silk, cotton piece goods, saltpetre and sugar. Through a series of *farmans* in 1651, 1656 and 1672 the British were exempted from customs duties in return for fixed sums to be paid by the company to the Indian authorities.

In 1698, the English obtained the Zamindari of the villages of Sutanuti, Kalikata and Govindpur on payment of Rs.1200. Here the English built Fort Williams around its factory and Sir Charles Eyre was the first president of the Fort Williams. In 1717, the Company secured valuable privileges under a royal farman by the Mughal Emperor Farrukh Siyar which granted the company the freedom to export and import their goods in Bengal without paying taxes and also the right to issue passes or *dastaks* for free movement of goods. The Company's servants were permitted to trade but were not covered by this farman. As a result they had to pay the same taxes as Indian merchants. This farman became the perpetual source of conflict between the Company and the Nawabs of Bengal. This also meant a loss of revenue to the Bengal government. The officials of the company on the other hand misused the *dastaks* to evade taxes on their private trade. Both Murshid Quli Khan and Alivardi Khan had objected to misuse of the dastaks by the company officials. The company in turn left no opportunity to defy the authority of the nawabs.

Conflict began when Siraj-ud-Daula succeeded Alivardi Khan to the throne of Bengal. The new emperor faced serious challenge from his rivals Ghasti Begum of Dacca and Shaukat Jang of Purnea and was also suspicious of the English. He was strictly against the royal farman and wanted to trade with the English on the same basis as in the times of Murshid Quli Khan without any privileges. The English on the other hand prepared themselves for yet another round of Anglo-French struggle in Europe. The French had established their settlement at Chandernagore. The main causes of dispute between Nawab Siraj-ud-Daula and the English were the misuse of the *dastaks* by the servants of the company, the refusal to pay taxes on their goods to the Nawab and the levying of duties on the Indian goods entering Calcutta which was in their control. Problem arose when the English began to fortify Calcutta as part of the preparations of war with the French without the permission of the Nawab. Siraj-ud-Daula asked both the French and the English to pull down their fortifications as he considered them to be an attack on the Nawab's sovereignty. The French company complied but the English refused to obey the orders.

Siraj-ud-Daula was young and short-tempered and could not tolerate this defiance. He responded by seizing the English factory at Qasim Bazar and subsequently Fort Williams was captured at Calcutta on 20th June 1756. It was during this occupation of Calcutta that the so-called Black-Hole incident occurred. It is known that about 146 English prisoners were confined on one hot summer night in a small room of Fort Williams and only twenty-three of them survived. This is remembered as a tragic episode. Leaving Calcutta in the hands of Manikchand, Siraj-ud-Daula returned to Murshidabad to celebrate his victory, letting the English escape with their ships. He committed the mistake of underestimating the enemy.

Meanwhile the English escaped to Fulta, a small island and awaited aid from Madras. A strong naval and military force arrived from Madras under Col. Clive and Admiral Watson. Hugli was plundered and Calcutta reoccupied in the beginning of 1757.The Nawab was forced to sign the treaty of Alinagar on 9th February 1757 wherein all the demands of the English were conceded. The nawab was asked to restore the rights and immunities of the Company and to compensate them for the losses they had suffered in the war.

By that time the English had decided to remove Siraj from the position of the nawab and place a puppet in his place. They conspired with the leading men of the Nawab's court such as Manikchand, the official in-charge of Calcutta, Aminchand, a rich merchant, Jagat Seth, a well-known banker and Mir Jafar, the Mir Bakshi, and Rai Durlabh, the Nawab's general. It was decided to place Mir Jafar on the throne of Bengal. On 23rd June 1757, the rival forces met each other in the battlefield of Plassey about thirty kilometres from Murshidabad. A major part of the Nawab's army led by the traitors Mir Jafar and Rai Durlabh did not participate in the fighting. A handful of Nawab's forces fought under the leadership of Mir Madan and Mohan Lal and were defeated. The Nawab tried to flee but was captured and put to death. Mir Jafar was proclaimed the Nawab of Bengal.

Mir Jafar rewarded the Company by granting them the undisputed rights to free trade in Bengal, Bihar and Orissa; the Company also got the zamindari of 24 parganas near Calcutta. Besides, Mir Jafar also paid large sums as gifts and bribes to the officials of the company. The battle of Plassey was only a battle in name and it was of immense historical importance because it paved the way for the conquest and mastery of Bengal by the English and subsequently the whole of India. It boosted the morale of the English Company and the rich revenues helped them to organize a strong army for defence. Most importantly it provided an opportunity to the officials of the company to amass untold wealth at the cost of the people of Bengal.

However, the Nawab soon realized that he has struck a bad bargain with the English. His treasury was almost emptied by the demands of the Company. The Company also became greedy and placed more demands to be fulfilled. His incapability to fulfill demands led to his forceful abdication in October 1760 in favour of his son-in-law Mir Qasim. The new Nawab rewarded the Company by granting them the zamindari of the districts of Burdwan, Midnapur and Chittagong. He also paid them huge sums of money as bribes and booty.

Mir Qasim was an efficient and strong ruler determined to improve the affairs of the state and transferred his capital from Murshidabad to Munger. He realized that in order to maintain his independence he must have a full treasury and an efficient army. He also checked the misuse of the farman of 1717 by the company officials to evade internal custom duties. He therefore took the extreme step of abolishing all duties on internal trade and benefiting his own subjects by giving them the concession that the English had forcefully snatched. The problem remained as Mir Qasim regarded himself as an independent ruler while the British wanted him to be a puppet in their hands.

The war between the Company and Mir Qasim began in 1763 and in a series of encounters the Nawab was defeated. He fled to Awadh and formed an alliance with Shuja-ud-Daula, the Nawab of Awadh and the fugitive Mughal emperor Shah Alam II in a final attempt to oust the English from Bengal. The three allies clashed with the Company's army at Buxar on 22"d October 1764 and were completely defeated. It was the most decisive battle in the history of the Indian sub-continent and it established the British firmly in Bengal, Bihar, and Orissa and placed Awadh at their mercy. Never after the battle of Buxar did the Nawabs of Bengal challenge the might of the English.

In 1763 Mir Jafar was restored as the Nawab of Bengal and after his death his second son Nizam-ud-Daula was placed on the throne. He was made to sign a treaty on 20th February, 1765 by which most of the Nawab's army was disbanded and the administration of Bengal was placed in the hands of a Deputy Subehdar who was to be nominated by the Company and could not be removed without their approval. Thus, the Company gained supreme control over the administration of Bengal. The Company also secured a huge war indemnity from the Nawab of Awadh.

The Company became the complete master of Bengal as the Nawab also depended for internal and external security on the English. Moreover, in 1765 the Mughal Emperor granted the diwani of Bengal, Bihar and Orissa to them. It legalized their claim to collect its revenues as the Diwan while through the right to nominate the Deputy Subehdar, it controlled the *nizamat* or the police and judicial powers. This system is known in history as 'Dual Government' and it gave the British power without any responsibility. They reaped the benefits of this system in the form of the rich revenues that they utilized fruitfully for enhancing their trade. As a result of the new system the state was fully impoverished and the people were left to suffer at the hands of fate because neither the Nawab nor the English had any inclination towards the welfare of the province and its people.

Trends of British Expansion. The British expanded in India through a series of encounters and wars with the French and the local rulers. The most important encounters in this regard are the Carnatic Wars, Anglo-Mysore Wars and Anglo-Maratha Wars.

Anglo-French Rivalry

Both the English and the French East India Companies began as trading companies in India. But gradually they were drawn into the internal politics in India. To protect their own trading interests, both the English and the French engaged in opportunities of trade and looked for huge profit margins. These mercantilist companies engaged in competition with each other and wanted to sell their manufactures in India and buy raw material at cheap rates. For achieving their aims they needed political control over the country they traded with. In most of the European conflicts England and France were on opposite sides. India too became the scene of their rivalry.

Carnatic Wars

It was an extension of the Anglo-French War in Europe as the Austrian War of Succession broke out in 1740. English navy under Barnett took the offensive when it captured some French ships. Dupleix, the French Governor-General of Pondicherry sent an urgent appeal for help. In the ensuing battle the English fleet was defeated and Madras was captured by the French.. The first Carnatic war is memorable for the battle of St. Thorne fought between the French and the Indian forces of Anwaruddin, the Nawab of Carnatic (1744-49). Differences had arisen between the Nawab and the French over the custody of Madras. The French won with their superior generalship of Dupleix.

By the Second Carnatic War, the political ambitions of Dupleix had reached high levels. He began to increase his power by interfering in local dynastic politics in Southern India. The much sought after opportunity was provided in the disputed succession to the thrones of Hyderabad and Carnatic. Muzaffar Jang, the grandson of the late Nizam of Hyderabad was contesting the throne with the second son of the Nizam, Nasir Jang. In the Carnatic, right of Nawab Anwaruddin was contested by Chanda Sahib, the son-in-law of the former Nawab. These conflicts were soon merged into one in the following years and several alliances were formed.

Dupleix took this opportunity to support Muzaffar Jang for the subehdarship of the Deccan and Chanda Sahib for the Carnatic. The English supported the other parties. The parties supported by the French won the ensuing battles and secured the throne. French power was thus established in the South. Attempts by Chanda Sahib to capture Trichnapoly failed. Robert Clive in the meanwhile made a surprise attack at Arcot, the capital of Carnatic in order to divert attention from Trichnapoly. Chanda Sahib rushed to save his capital. The English easily captured Arcot. This proved the success of the English and sealed the fate of Dupleix.

The third Carnatic war began with the Seven Years war at Europe. In 1757, the French government sent Count De Lally to India. In the meantime the British had won Bengal by defeating Siraj-ud-Daula at Plassey in 1757. This enhanced their confidence and gave them immense financial resources. Count De Lally attacked Tanjore in 1758. But the campaign damaged French reputation. Next the plan to siege Madras was given up due to strong presence of naval forces of the English. Bussy the French incharge of Hyderabad was called by Lally and doing this he committed the gravest mistake. The French fleet was thoroughly defeated by the English. At the battle of Wandiwash, the French were defeated in 1760. This dropped the curtain on Anglo-French rivalry in India.

Mysore

The English entered into an alliance with Nizam of Hyderabad to help him attack Haider Ali of Mysore. Haider Ali already had territorial disputes with the ruler of Arcot and differences with the Marathas. Haider was in turn able to subdue his enemies through several schemes. He bought the Marathas, allured the Nizam with territorial gains and along with the Nizam launched an attack on Arcot. After playing a game with them for several months Haider suddendy threatened Madras in 1764. Peace was signed with the English on Haider's terms in 1769. Both promised help to each other in case of any attack. However, when the Marathas attacked Haider in 1771, the English did not help him. Thus grew his distrust for the English. This was the first Anglo-Mysore war.

In the occasion of the second Anglo-Mysore war, Haider Ali with his increasing suspicion over the English found the alliance with the French more profitable. Warren Hastings gradually grew more suspicious of Haider Ali and his links with the French. Under these circumstances the English attempt to capture Mahe, that was under the protection of Haider Ali was a direct challenge to him. Haider arranged a joint front with the Nizam and the Marathas against the common enemy, the English. Haider attacked Carnatic and captured Arcot. But in the meanwhile the English broke the alliance and bribed the Nizam out and made peace with the Marathas. Undaunted Haider faced the English and was defeated at Porto Novo in 1781. The following year Haider inflicted a humiliating defeat on the English under Col. Braithwaite. Haider soon died in 1782 leaving the task unfinished to his son Tipu Sultan. Finally the mutual treaty of Mangalore was concluded between both the parties in 1784 on the basis of mutual restitution of each other's territories.

The cause for the third Anglo-Mysore war was an attack on Travancore by Tipu who had differences with the Raja of Travancore in 1790. The English waiting for an opportunity entered the side of the Raja of Travancore. Cornwallis entered into alliance with the Nizam and the Marathas against Tipu. Tipu was defeated and the treaty of Srirangapatnam was signed in 1792. By this treaty Tipu had to surrender half his territory and pay a heavy indemnity. Later Tipu entered into negotiations with France and allegations were levied against him that he was gathering allies against the English. Tipu was again engaged in war with the English in 1799. The war was short but decisive and resulted in the fall of Srirangapatnam.Tipu died fighting bravely and this ended the independence of Mysore.

Anglo-Maratha Struggle

The internal dissensions of the Marathas and the growing ambition of the English brought the beginnings of the Anglo-Maratha struggle. The mutual differences of the Maratha leaders gave the English the much sought after opportunity to establish a kind of dual government as in Bengal. In order to get the *gaddi* of the region, Raghunath Rao, one of the successors of the Peshwa signed with the Bombay government the treaty of Surat. He sought the help of the subsidiary troops of the English. The British attempt to interfere here proved premature and both the parties after engaging in a war signed a peace treaty at Salbai in 1782. Both agreed to respect each other's territories. This was the first Anglo-Maratha war.

The second struggle was created by the presence of the French in India. The English tried to rope in the Marathas through the system of Subsidiary Alliances. Though they refused initially, the Marathas broke down due to their internal differences. With the development of local intrigues, the Scindhias prevailed over and the Peshwa passed under their control. Repeated efforts failed when the Peshwa refused to join the English alliance. Meanwhile the hostilities of the Peshwa and the Holkars increased and the two armies met at Hadapsar in 1802. The Holkars were able to place their protege on the throne replacing the Peshwa. The Peshwa thus fled to Bassein and signed the Subsidiary alliance with the English. Through this treaty the British were placed at an advantageous position and they were firmly placed at Poona.

The third and final struggle between the English and the Marathas began when Lord Hastings move against the Pindaris transgressed the sovereignty of the Maratha chiefs and the two parties were drawn into a war. By careful moves the English forced humiliating treaties on the Raja of Nagpur, the Peshwa and the Scindhia. Desperate, the Peshwa made a last bid to throw off the British yoke. Daulat Rao Scindhia, Appa Sahib, and Malhar Rao Holkar II raised their arms. But the entire Maratha forces were defeated by the superior forces of the Company. Maratha territories were brought under the Bombay presidency and finally in subordination to the Company.

Economic Impact

The primary objective of the British East India Company was to earn through trade. It coupled trading privileges with political hegemony to advance in the final aim of subjugating India. The British rule had a profound impact on the Indian economy. It led to the transformation of India from a self sufficient to a colonial economy.

From 1757 to 1857, the British followed various economic policies to enhance trade privileges and more importantly to exploit Indian economic resources. This duration is usually divided into three phases. The first phase or the Mercantile phase (1757-1813) was one when the East India company completely monopolized trade and used its political power to dictate terms to the artisans of Bengal who were forced to sell their products at cheaper rates. The essence of mercantile capitalism was buying cheap and selling at higher prices, which the company successfully achieved in these years. The second phase was thar of Industrial Capitalism or Free trade (1813-1857). The Industrial revolution in England completely transformed Britain's economy and its relations with India. In this phase, India became the chief exporter of raw materials to British industries and also served as the main market to manufacture British goods. The industrial needs were the basic guide of British commercial policy. The Indian goods faced tough competition from machine made goods in this phase. The third and final phase of British plunder is called the era of Financial Capitalism (1860 onwards). The British introduced roadways, railways, post and telegraph into India for their own commercial and political needs. As a result of the various investments made the burden of public debt on India increased. India became a colony of the British in the true sense. Wealth drained from India played an important role in financing British capitalist development.

Land Revenue Policy: After gaining full control over Bengal, the old revenue system was abolished. In order to implement a durable system the Company carried on a number of experiments in revenue settlement. British agrarian policies were geared towards appropriation of maximum revenue and the growth of more cash crops for exports.

In 1793, the Permanent Settlement was introduced in Bengal, Bihar and Orissa after a series of experiments in revenue collection. It was decided to fix the land revenue permanently. It was to be collected from zamindars of different villages. The zamindar was to pay10/11th to the state and keep 1/11 th of the revenue to himself. Revenue was already fixed at a high rate and promised never to increase in future. However, this did not prove suitable because it gave no scope to increase the revenue in the long run. Also it contained no provision for the flexibility of revenue procurement in times of variable production. Some of these defects in the system led to its abandonment.

The other revenue settlement implemented was the Ryotwari System in 1820. Under this system the cultivator was recognized as the owner of his plot of land subject to the payment of land revenue. The revenue was to be collected directly from the ryot. This settlement was not permanent and was revised every twenty or thirty years. The advantage of this system was the absence of intermediaries in revenue collection. It was implemented in the districts of Madras, Bombay and Sindh. However this system too did not last long for the officials responsible for revenue collection were corrupt and often exacted more revenue from the ryots. Also this settlement did not have any provision for concessions during natural calamities and oppressed the cultivators greatly.

The next was the Mahalwari Settlement. It was introduced in the northern province of Punjab, the Ganga valley and some central provinces between 1801-06. Revenue settlement was to be made by village or estate (mahal). The landlords or heads of families collectively claimed to be the landlords of the village or estate. The revenue demand remained high and this system continued for quite some time.

These policies implemented by the British government had a deep impact on the Indian economy. It completely changed the traditional structure of the economy and made it a colonial economy designed to meet the needs of the newly emergent industrialized economy of Britain. The different sectors of the economy that were affected by the British policies are as follow:

Ruin of Indian handicrafts industry and artisans: The Indian handicrafts that had made the country famous, collapsed under the colonial rule. This was mainly due to the competition posed by the machine made goods that were imported from Britain. The ability of mass production of goods helped Britain to flood the Indian markets with cheap products especially cotton textiles. The railways facilitated the reach of these goods to the remotest parts in India and the procurement of raw materials from these parts. The traditional handicrafts industry faced a tough competition from these goods produced in bulk.

The policy of free trade followed by the East India Company helped them to dictate terms of trade. They compelled the Indian craftsmen to sell their goods below market price and they hired their services at below the prevailing wages. This forced many a craftsman to abandon their ancestral trade. The British exported raw materials from India like cotton. As a result the Indian weaver had to buy these materials at higher prices. This in turn raised the cost of Indian handicrafts as compared to the machine made goods. Indian goods were also subjected to high tariffs in the English market whereas the British goods gained duty free access into the Indian markets.

As a result of these policies Indian handicrafts faced a severe challenge from the foreign goods. India now became the exporter of raw materials to British industries and an importer of ready-made goods from Britain. This phenomenon of the ruination of Indian handicrafts industries is most well known as de-industrialization. This destroyed the self-sufficient village economy as the destruction of the traditional industries led to over crowding in the agrarian sector. De-industrialization had far reaching effects in different sectors of the economy.

Impoverishment of the peasants: Under the British, the condition of the Indian peasants deteriorated steadily. After obtaining the diwani of Bihar, Bengal and Orissa the Englishmen introduced different land revenue policies. Their ultimate aim was the appropriation of maximum revenue from the Indian zamindars and peasants. The exaction of exorbitant rents by the government oppressed the peasants heavily. In order to meet the high demand of revenue, the peasants perpetually remained indebted to the local money-lenders. Many of them lost their lands to these greedy moneylenders for the inability to pay back the borrowed amount.

The policy of commercialization of agriculture by the British encouraged market oriented production of cash crops such as opium, tea, coffee, sugar, jute and indigo. Indian peasants were forced to grow these cash crops that spoiled the fertility of the land and no other crop could be grown on it. The growth of minimum of subsistence crops led to the deterioration and impoverishment of the Indian agriculture and the cultivators. The peasant was suppressed under triple burden of the government, landlord and the moneylender. His subsistence base was completely ruined by the agrarian policies of the British government. The lack of attention in the development of agriculture and in use of new equipments and methods on the part of the British government also ruined Indian agriculture.

Ruin of old zamindars and rise of new landlords: The Permanent Settlement of Lord Cornwallis introduced the policy of auctioning the rights of revenue collection to the highest bidder if the revenue collecting agency failed to fulfill his stipulated task in the given time. This feature ruined most of the old zamindar class who had little consideration for the cultivator. Many of the old zamindars disappeared following demands of heavy land revenue and the rigid methods of collection.

The new zamindar class consisted mostly of merchants and money-lenders who were heartless and least considerate towards the peasants. They grew wealthy at the cost of the small cultivators. Likewise tenants cultivated most of their lands. This class of zamindars encourages tendency of subinfeudation creating hierarchies within the agrarian structure. The distance between the zamindars and the actual tiller grew wider.

Development of modern industry: The Industrial revolution brought forth the need for developing industries on modern lines. In order to develop British industries it was essential to transform Indian infrastructure too. As part of it changes were introduced in agriculture and railways were developed. Railways were developed with the initiative of Lord Dalhousie in 1853. The Company laid the railway lines in the country to export from the interiors to ports and vice versa to reach out the imports to the markets in the remote regions of India. Railways helped in making possible production for a market and opening up the interior to large-scale operations.

The encouragement to cash crops led to the growth of plantation economy wherein profitable crops were especially cultivated for marketing purposes. Among the industries that were made possible by the railways was the cotton mill industry. The first successful Indian cotton mill was started in 1853 in Bombay. Later cotton mills were established at Sholapur, Ahmedabad and Madras. Likewise jute was cultivated as a cash crop and the first jute mill was set up in 1855 in Rishra in Bengal followed by many such mills.

The British also encouraged the infrastructure industries. They were aware that cheap labour was easily available in India and this was a potential they could exploit. Also the procurement of raw materials and mineral resources from India made it necessary to develop these industries in India too. The first iron and steel mill was set up in the Jharia coal mines area in 1873. Similarly other industries such as glass, paper, leather industry were set up by the British government in India for serving their own purpose.

Famines: The most important impact of British rule in India was the occurrence of famines regularly from the second half of the 19th century. The combined effect of the ruin of handicrafts industry and stagnation in agriculture was the complete impoverishment of the common man. The lack of interest in the welfare of the people at large was evident from the repeated occurrence of famines. Two lakh people were killed in the first famine in 1860-61 in western Uttar Pradesh. Five years later, a huge famine occurred in Bengal, Bihar and Orissa and Madras in which lakhs of people perished. All these were in some way effects of the British agricultural policies.

Sixteen

SOCIAL REFORM MOVEMENTS

Nineteenth Century witnessed a remarkable transformation in the social ideas primarily because of the introduction of English education. Liberal ideas of the west flowed through this channel. The new beginning was made by a critical examination of the past and its institutions. Faith and belief were replaced by reason and judgment. People were filled with a new enthusiasm to get rid of social abuses like sati, infanticide, cruel and meaningless rites, and so on. The intellectual currents were geared towards national regeneration in the form of socio-religious movements. Initially the movement was started by a limited number of individuals and later grew in proportion to become institutionalized.

Brahmo Samaj

The chief figure in this reform movement was Raja Rammohun Roy (1772-1833) regarded as the leader of modern India. He was a linguist with the knowledge of different languages such as Sanskrit, Persian, Arabic and western languages like English, French and Latin besides Greek and Hebrew. He made an intensive study of western thought and sought to affect a cultural synthesis between the east and the west. With the support of a few people he started the Atmiya Sabha (Friendly association). Members recited Hindu scriptures, sang hymns and held discussions on religious and social issues. From then on he began a struggle against social and religious evils that had crept into the Indian society. He opposed the practice of sati. He quoted the authority of the Hindu scriptures and demonstrated the hollowness of the customs followed in the society. He distributed pamphlets among the educated Indians to bring awareness regarding the evil custom of burning of widows. With his active persuasion Lord William Bentinck passed the famous Regulation XVII in 1829 that declared sati illegal and punishable by courts.

In 1828 Raja Rammohun Roy founded the Brahmo Samaj. It advocated monotheism and denounced idolatry. Its aim was to clear Hindu religion of all religious evils. He created the Samaj as a strong medium to promote humanism and monotheism and incorporated the best teachings of all religions. The Samaj also opposed polygamy, early marriage and suppression of women in society. Raja Rammohun Roy endeavoured to better the condition of the widows by changing the Hindu laws of inheritance of property. He was a forerunner of women's education and saw a way to bring about changes in society. Rammohun Roy regarded the spread of modern education as the vehicle for dissemination of modern and liberal ideas. In 1817 Rammohun Roy along with David Hare founded the Hindu College at Calcutta and in 1825 set up the Vedanta College in which courses on Indian learning and western social and physical sciences were offered.

Raja Rammohun Roy also took up political and economic issues. Some of the reforms advocated by him were the Indianization of services, trial by court, separation of powers of the executive and judiciary, freedom of the press and judicial equality between Europeans and Indians. He is regarded as the progenitor of national consciousness and ideology in India.

After the death of Rammohun Roy in 1833 Maharishi Devendranath Tagore infused a new life into the Samaj. In 1839 he started the Tatvabodhini Sabha to propagate ideas and brought the Tatvabodhini Patrika for a systematic study of India's past. Under Tagore's influence, the Samaj sought to preserve the best of Hindu religion. The Samaj received a new strength with the joining of Keshab Chandra Sen in 1857. Due to his efforts many new branches of the Samaj were opened outside Bengal. Keshab left the Samaj in 1865 and founded a new organization, the Brahmo Samaj of India. Devendranath's organization came to be known as Adi Brahmo Samaj. In 1878 there was a further split in Keshab's Brahmo Samaj when he married his thirteen-year-old daughter to a minor Hindu Maharaja of CoochBehar. Most of his followers left him and set up a Sadharan Brahmo Samaj. Keshab's Samaj passed into obscurity.

Derozio and Young Bengal

The Young Bengal movement around 1820's and 30's. was inspired by Henry Vivian Derozio who taught in Hindu College. His followers came to be known as Dorozians. He inspired the students to think rationally and freely, to question all authority, to love liberty, equality, freedom and truth. He advocated women's right and demanded education for them. The Dorozians attacked old and decadent customs. They educated the people through newspapers, pamphlets and public speeches.

Ishwar Chandra Vidyasagar

The second half of the 19th century witnessed the emergence of a great Sanskrit scholar, Pandit Ishwar Chandra Vidyasagar. He became the principal of the Sanskrit College in 1851.He promoted the education of non-Brahmins and worked for the growth of the Bengali language. He advocated the education of girls and set up thirty-five schools at his own expense. Vidyasagar was a great advocate of widow remarriage. He proved that Vedic texts sanctioned widow remarriage. He sent a petition to the government urging for legislative action. After the passage of the widow remarriage act in 1856, the first lawful widow remarriage was held at Calcutta under the supervision of Vidyasagar. In 1850, he protested against child marriage. All his life, he campaigned against polygamy. He was deeply involved in encouraging education for women. The Bethune School founded in Calcutta in 1849 was the first fruit of the powerful movement for women's education that arose in.the 1840's and 50's.

Prarthana Samaj

The Prarthana Samaj was an offshoot of Brahmo Samaj. It was founded at Bombay in 1867 by Atmaram Panduranga under the guidance of Keshab Chandra Sen. The Samaj stood for monotheism and social reforms. Its two great leaders were R.G. Bhandarkar and M.G. Ranade. The Samaj started to reform the Hindu religious thought and practice in the light of modern knowledge. It tried to liberate religion from caste-orthodoxy. The greatest service of the Samaj was the organization of social reform movement. It laid stress on the abandonment of caste, introduction of widow remarriage, encouragement of female education, abolition of purdah and child marriage and improvement of the lot of depressed classes. The activities of the Samaj spread to South India due to the efforts of the Telegu reformer Virasalingam. The Prarthana Samaj accepted all religions. It sought truth in all religions.

Arya Samaj

The Arya Samaj was founded in Bombay in 1875 by Swami Dayananda, earlier Mulashankar. Later its headquarter was shifted to Lahore. The movement was an outcome of reaction to western influence and was revivalist in nature. Swami Dayananda believed in the infallibility of the Vedas and looked upon the Vedas as a source of inspiration. His motto was "Go back to the Vedas." Dayananda attacked Hindu orthodoxy and disregarded the authority of the Puranas. He decried polytheism, believed in one God and opposed idolatry and priesthood. He began the Suddhi movement (conversion of non-Hindus to Hinduism). He opposed untouchability and caste discrimination and advocated widow remarriage and high status for women in society.

The most phenomenal achievement of the Arya Samaj was in the field of education. To spread education, DAV College was started at Lahore under the leadership of Lala Hansraj in 1886 while Swami Shradhanand started the Gurukul at Haridwar in 1902 to revive Vedic ideas. The Arya Samajists established a girl's school (the Arya Kanya Pathshala) to provide education not only away from missionary influence but also capable of producing a new ideal Hindu women.

Ramakrishna Mission

Swami Vivekananda, a disciple of Swami Ramakrishna Paramhansa founded the Mission in order to preach the Vedanta philosophy of his guru in the country and abroad. Swamiji realized that truth is in every religion and there are different paths to reach one goal. He founded his conviction on the Vedanta philosophy that God is omnipresent. The Mission was basically revivalist in nature. It upheld pure Vedanta doctrines as its ideal and unlike the Arya Samaj it recognized the value and utility of idol worship. In 1893 he attended the Parliament of Religions at Chicago where he propounded the true meaning of Hinduism. The Irish woman, Margaret Noble popularly known as Sister Nivedita also spread the teachings of the Mission. Swami Vivekananda proclaimed the essential oneness of all religions. He condemned the kind of narrowness in religious matters. The Ramakrishna Mission founded on May 5, 1897 stood not only for religious reform but also for social reform. Its ideal was Vedanta doctrine.

The Theosophical Society

The Theosophical Society was founded in the United States of America in 1875 by Madame H.P. Blavatsky and Col. H.S. Olcott. In 1879 they fixed their headquarters first in Bombay and later shifted to Adyar in Madras. Annie Besant settled in India in 1893 and assumed the leadership of the society. It believed that God had made a definite plan for the progress and development of mankind that had no room for community, religion, race and colour. The chief objectives of the Society were removal of all kinds of discriminations by setting up of universal brotherhood, the sincere study of all religions and creeds and unfold the secrets of the latent powers of men and nature. Annie Besant remained connected to the Society and extended its activities greatly all over the country.

Other Hindu social reformers in the nineteenth century were D.V Karve who was the champion of the cause of Hindu widows in western India, Gopal Hari Deshmukh popularly known as Lokahitawadi. He advocated the reorganization if Indian society on nationalistic, humanistic and secular lines. Jyotiba Phule campaigned against the upper class domination and brahminical supremacy. He founded the Satyashodhak Samaj for the upliftment of the lower caste. In 1851, he founded a girl's school at Poona for education of the children of the depressed classes. Gopal Krishna Gokhale founded the Servants of India Society at Bombay in 1905 for social reform and nationalistic regeneration.

Social Reform among Muslims

The Wahabi Movement was the earliest organized Muslim response to western influence and was revivalist in nature. Its founder was Shah Walliullah. It was aimed at creating a homeland for Muslims. The campaign was initially directed against the Sikhs of Punjab in 1849, The movement was finally crushed in 1870s by British forces.

The Ahmadiya Movement was founded in Punjab by Mirza Ghulam Ahmed in 1869. It was based on liberal principles. It described itself as the torch-bearer of Mohammedan Renaissance and followed the principles of universal religion of all humanity. It opposed the jihad or holy war against non-muslims. The movement spread western liberal education among the Indian Muslims and started numerous schools and colleges for that purpose. This movement was coloured with mysticism.

The Aligarh Movement was a social reform cultural movement with Aligarh as its center. It was based on the liberal interpretation of the Quran and tried to harmonize Islam with modern liberal culture. The greatest leader of the Aligarh movement was Sir Sayyid Ahmed Khan. He was the first Muslim leader to realize the importance of modern scientific and western education for Muslims. In 1864 he founded the Scientific Society and in 1875 the Mohammedan Anglo-Oriental College at Aligarh for spreading western education and modern science among the Muslims.

The second task that Sayyid Ahmed undertook was to introduce social reforms in the Muslim society. He condemned slavery and declared it un-Islamic. He was also against purdah for women. He tried to harmonize western thought and the Quran. Sayyid Ahmed propagated his progressive social ideas through his magazine *Tahzib-al-Akhlaq*.

Social Reform among Sikhs

Some of the movements among the Sikhs were the Singh Sabha Movement, Namdhari movement, Nirankari movement and the Akali movement. They aimed at bringing to the Sikh community the benefits of western enlightenment through modern education; condemned caste system, female infanticide and idol worship.

Movement of the Parsis

The Rehnumai Mazdayasanan Sabha or the Religious Reform Association was started in 1851 by Nauroji Furdoji, Dadabhai Nauroji and S.S. Bangalee. Its main objective was a regeneration of the social condition of the Parsis especially improving the lot of the Parsi women, restoration of Zoroastrian religion to its purity.

Depressed Classes Movement

The socio-religious reformers of the nineteenth century, influenced by rationalist and democratic ideas raised their voice against inhuman treatment meted out to the depressed classes. The Prarthana Samaj of Bombay started the Depressed Classes Mission in 1898. In 1906, V.R. Shinde launched the Depressed Classes Mission Society of Bombay independently in order to organize the educational activities till now carried on by the Prarthana Samaj. Because of this initiative taken by him the government of Bombay had declared a policy of equal rights to educational facilities for the depressed classes. The Gaekwad of Baroda established schools for the children of depressed classes and instituted scholarships for them. The First All India Depressed Classes Conference was held in March 1918. It issued an All India Anti-Untouchability Manifesto to the effect that they would not observe untouchability in their everyday affairs. The Hindu Mahasabha also appealed for the removal of untouchability.

Trade Union Movement

The development of modern industries in India in the second half of the nineteenth century led to the emergence of working class movements. Modern factories brought in their wake several evils of capitalism such as employment of women and children, long excessive hours of work and poor housing and working conditions. Soon after the First World War, the Indian working class realized the effectiveness of strike as a means of obtaining concessions. In 1920, the All-India Trade Union Congress (AITUC) was set up to represent the interests of the workers and also to coordinate the activities of all labour organizations in the country and to help in the extension of the movement. The setting up of the AITUC encouraged the rapid formation of unions throughout the country in big and small industries. The Trade Union Act that was passed in 1926 was a landmark in the history of the trade union movement. The Act gave legal status to the registered trade unions and bestowed some measure of immunity from civil suits and criminal prosecution. The Second World War saw a split in the ideas of the trade union leaders regarding the participation in the war. Trade Union movements acquired a political colour after India's independence and proliferated in numbers.

Peasant Movements

The impact of British rule in India was primarily felt through the rapid changes in the agrarian sector. The high revenue demand, the commercialization of agriculture and the new relations between the landowner and the peasant fostered a process of impoverishment within the Indian peasantry. In the nineteenth century, peasant mobilizations were in the nature of protests, revolts and rebellions aimed at loosening the bonds of feudal exploitation and securing their traditional rights.

The Indigo Revolt (1859-60) was the revolt of the indigo peasants against the British planters. The peasants were forced to grow indigo under oppressing conditions and sell them cheap to the planters. The revolt broke out in 1859 in the Barasat village of Nadia district and soon spread to whole of Bengal. The movement resulted in virtual elimination of indigo plantation in Bengal.

The Pabna Movement (1870-80) started as a reaction against the zamindar's claim to higher landlordism that led to widespread resistance by the ryots in large parts of east Bengal.

The Deccan Riots (1875) were inspired by hardships caused to the peasants by the famine that occurred in 1877-79. V.B. Phadke organized the Ramosi peasant of Maharashtra in 1879 who revolted against the British.

The Bijolia peasants of Rajasthan in 1905 refused to pay the variety of cecses imposed on them and in 1913 the movement was led by Sitaram Das under whom the peasants refused to cultivate their land and migrated to neighbouring areas.The Moplah Uprising of Malabar that occurred in 1921 was both anti-landlord and anti-imperialist.

The Champaran (1917), Kheda (1918) and Bardoli (1928) revolts were a result of oppression of the peasantry by the planters and high revenue demand of the Britishers. These twin factors became the main reason for peasant rebellions throughout the country during the British rule.

Seventeen

THE REVOLTS

Early Uprisings

The century after 1757 witnessed a number of popular mobilizations and revolts against the foreign rule. The infringement of local rights, the innovations in the administrative system, high revenue demands and the disruption of the traditional economy were some of the reasons to give rise to popular insurrections against the alien domination in different parts of India. These revolts and uprisings were mainly local in nature.

The establishment of British rule in Bengal after 1757 and the new economic order spelt ruin on the local zamindars, cultivators and artisans alike. Several revolts in Bengal and Eastern India took place. Religious monks and dispossessed zamindars led the Sanyasi Rebellion in Bengal. It lasted from 1763 to 1800. The Chuarand Ho Risings rose in the tribesmen of Midnapur and Chhotanagpur against the economic distress caused by the British rule. Other uprisings in the region for similar reasons were, Santhal Rebellion among the Santhals of the Rajmahal Hills, Kol Risings, Ahom's Revolt amongst the Ahom nobility in Assam and the Khasi Risings.

In Western India the aboriginal tribes of the Western Ghats with their strongholds in Khandesh revolted against their new masters, the English East India Company in 1817-19. The other risings in this region were the Koli risings, the Kutch rebellion, the Waghera rising, the Kolahapur and Savantvadi revolts against the British. Revolts also took place in South India against the English for mishandling the local customs and traditions.

Revolt of 1857

Political Causes: Lord Dalhousie was the Governor-General of India till 1848-1856. Under him the British followed an expansionist policy in India. Dalhousie through his policies had added considerable territories to the British empire in India. The policy of annexation reacted its climax when he implemented the policy of Doctrine of Lapse and annexed the Indian states on charges of misgovernance and absence of an heir. In the course of eight years Dalhousie annexed Satara (1848), Sambhalpur (1850), Jhansi (1853), Nagpur (1853),

Jaipur (1849) and Bhagat (1850). This policy enraged the Indian rulers against the British government. As part of the Doctrine of Lapse policy, the titles and pensions of some Indian princes were confiscated. The pension of Baji Rao II's son Nana Sahib was discontinued after his father's death and Rani of Jhansi had been deprived of her right to rule in violation of the recognized Hindu law. Dalhousie further proposed to abolish the title of the Mughal emperor after the death of Bahadur Shah II.

Economic Causes: The economic policy of the British adversely affected every section of the Indian society. The British exploited the economic resources of India to their advantage and drained her wealth by crippling the Indian trade and industry. Under the British, India turned into a colonial economy to serve the British capitalist interests. Indian resources were unabashedly exported to London to promote British industries. Consequently the country was reduced to poverty as traditional handicrafts and industries were ruined. Many people were rendered jobless and there was overcrowding in the agrarian sector. Further the high revenue demand crippled the agrarian sector. Both the peasants and the zamindars were pushed by the British to produce more to appropriate the maximum revenue. The various revenue settlements were designed to benefit the government and displayed total disregard for the cultivators. In case of failure to pay the stipulated amount the lands of the zamindar were taken away by the government. A large number of zamindars were thus dispossessed of their lands and estates as part of this policy. These grievances left the Indian people dissatisfied of the British and eventually turned them to be bitter enemies of the British.

Social and Religious Causes: The British looked down upon the Indians as inferior race and discriminated with them racially at every step. Indians were not allowed at many places such as railway compartments and public places as parks and hotels as these were specially reserved for the Englishmen. This racial arrogance of the British hurt the Indian masses most and they began to regard the Englishmen as their worst enemies. The attempt to bring about social reforms in India by the British was not liked by the general public. The social legislations on the evils as sati, infanticide, re-marriage of widows, etc., were considered as interference in the religious matters of Indians about which the Englishmen knew nothing. The introduction of English education, the propagation of the work of the Christian missionaries and the changing of the Hindu law of property with a view to facilitate the conversion of Hindus to Christianity alarmed many orthodox Indians. They feared that these practices would upset the social and religious order of the traditional Indian society.

Military Causes: Dissatisfaction was widespread among the military rank and file under the British. There was great inequality in treatment between the Indian and the British counterparts in terms of salary and other benefits. There was also a disparity in numbers between the Indian and European troops as the latter numbered far less than the Indians. Majority of the Indian soldiers were sent to Crimea, China and Iran to fight wars of the English. The Indian soldiers were considered inferior and were ill-treated by high officers. The high ranks in the army were exclusively reserved for the Englishmen and the Indians were deliberately excluded from responsible positions. What hurt the Indian soldiers most was the prohibition to wear caste and religious marks while serving that amounted to interference in their personal affairs by the British. The immediate cause of the revolt was the introduction of the new Enfield rifle and the greased cartridge. In loading the rifle the sepoy before inserting the cartridge had to bite off its top. It was believed that the grease was made out of the fats of cows and pigs. This was objectionable to the Hindus and Muslims alike. This rumour sparked off fire of discontent against the British in the form of the revolt. The first sign of unrest appeared in 1857 at Barrackpore in Bengal. A sepoy, Mangal Pandey on 29th March 1857, killed senior officers on parade and started the revolt.

Course and Spread of the Revolt: The revolt spread to Berhampur in Bengal. On 24th April 1857. About ninety men of the Native Cavalry stationed at Meerut refused to accept the greased cartridges. Eighty-five of them were dismissed and sentenced to ten years imprisonment. On 10th May the revolt started at Meerut and the mutineers after killing some of their officials marched towards Delhi.

Delhi. On 12th May Delhi was seized and Bahadur Shah II was proclaimed the emperor of India. The real command was in the hands of Bakht Khan who had led the revolt at Bareilly and brought the troops to Delhi.

Kanpur. Here the revolt was led by Nana Saheb who declared himself the Peshwa and governor of Bahadur Shah. Tantya Tope did most of the fighting. Rebels defeated General Windham outside Kanpur.

Lucknow. The revolt was led by Hazrat Mahal, the Begum of Awadh. She had proclaimed her young son Brijis Kadir as the Nawab of Awadh against the wishes of the British. Henry Lawrence, the British resident was killed at Lucknow.

Jhansi. After some initial vacillations, Rani Laxmi Bai assumed the leadership of the mutiny. After being defeated at Jhansi, she captured Gwalior with the help of Tantya Tope and Afghan guards.

Bareilly. Khan Bahadur Khan proclaimed himself as the Nawab and led the revolt there.

The other centers of the revolt were Benaras, Allahabad, Gwalior, Nasirabad in Rajputana, Indore, Aligarh and Kota. At all these places the sepoys killed the senior officers and other Europeans on whom they could lay their hands in many cases not even sparing women and children. They also released prisoners from jail, plundered the treasury and burnt land records at many places.

However, the superior British forces soon suppressed the revolt. Bahadur Shah II proved to be a weak leader. Delhi was recaptured on 20th September 1857 by John Nicholson. Bahadur Shah was arrested and deported to Rangoon where he died in 1862. The rebels were defeated by General Havelock in Kanpur. Nana Saheb after being defeated refused to surrender and escaped to Nepal. At Jhansi Hugh Rose suppressed the revolt and Rani Laxmi Bai died on the battle field. Benaras, Bareilly and Gwalior were also recaptured by British officers.

Causes of the failure: (a) The revolt was highly localized and restricted to north India. Regions beyond the river Narmada in the south remained largely undisturbed. (b) The revolt failed to embrace all the sections of the society. Many of the native rulers and the big zamindars refused to join the revolt against the British. They extended an active support to the British to suppress the revolt. Modern educated Indians were suspicious of the rebels. They feared the opposition of the rebels in bringing about social reforms. (c) The revolt was poorly organized and lacked coordination planning amongst the leaders. (d) The rebels lacked a common cause and had different goals. At most places the rebels were encouraged to revolt against the local zamindars and money-lenders and did not have a larger goal to pursue. They lacked a spirit of nationalism. (e) The British had better resources and succeeded in suppressing the revolt. They had vast resources at their disposal and were helped by the modern means of transport and communications. They also had the services of capable generals as Havelock, Outram, and Lawrence available who could plan the suppression of the revolt well and win back their lost regions.

Nature of the Revolt: Historians have described the nature of the rebellion of 1857 variously. Some call it a sepoy mutiny since the initial thrust of the revolt in the form of the cartridge episode was given by the soldiers. These scholars also contend that the revolt was not related to the general people so much as the sepoys and they formed the bulk of the rebels.

Nationalists as V. D. Savarkar opine that the revolt was the first war of independence. They feel that the revolt sparked off the discontent of the Indians towards the foreign rule and they fought bitterly to drive away the foreigners from their homeland. According to them, the Hindus and Muslims participated equally in the revolt and displayed a new bond of unity against the British.

The Marxists view the revolt as a soldier-peasant struggle against feudal bondage. They contend that the Indian soldier was a peasant in uniform and wanted to throw away the feudal domination infused by the British.

On the whole one may look at the revolt as a product of the accumulated discontent of the people against the foreign government.

Impact of the Revolt: Policy Change. The Queen's Proclamation of November 1858 announced the policy of the British government to be followed from now on in India. It announced that the policy of territorial extension was to be abandoned. The native rulers were assured of the safety of their territory, rights and honour if they cooperated with British. The right of a ruler to adopt a child in the absence of a natural heir was accepted. The government regarded the native rulers as the bulwark against the masses and henceforth followed a policy of protecting this reactionary segment of the Indian society.

A policy of divide and rule was actively pursued to keep the Hindus and Muslims divided.

Administrative Changes. On January 1st 1877 Queen Victoria was proclaimed as the Queen Empress of India and the administration of India was transferred by the East India Company to the British Crown. India was to be administered by the Secretary of State and his fifteen-member council through the Viceroy. The Governor-general became the viceroy and the representative of the Crown in India.

Reorganization of the Army. The army was re-organized to strengthen British control over the country and avert any further rebellions in future. The number of British soldiers was increased and all the higher posts and key positions were filled up,by the British.

Communal and Racial Bitterness. The revolt of 1857 created a big gap between the different religious communities especially the Hindus and the Muslims as each blamed the other for its failure. The Indians, however, developed a deep racial bitterness towards the English and opposed the inferior status granted to them.

Eighteen

MOVEMENT FOR FREEDOM

The year 1885 marked the beginning of a new epoch in Indian history. In that year an All India political organization was formed under the name of the Indian National Congress. The Indians became more and more conscious of their political status. The newly emergent intelligentsia was fed on the radical political thought of the west and soon became the torch-bearers of nationalism in India. It was under the guidance and initiative of A.O. Hume, a retired civil servant that the Indian National Congress was formed. The first meeting of the Congress was held at Bombay in 1885. As an organization of educated Indians it became the main plank of expressing their grievances and communicating with each other.

Moderate Phase

The first phase of the existence of the Congress is known as the moderate phase (1885-1905). During this the Congress worked for limited objectives and concentrated more upon building up its organization. The leadership was confined to a handful of educated middle class Indians who drew inspiration from western, liberal and radical thought. It did not challenge the British authority but adopted a constitutional path. The national leaders like Dadabhai Nauroji, P. N. Mehta, D.E. Wacha, W.C. Banerji, S. N. Banerji, Gopal Krishna Gokhale who dominated Congress policies during this time were staunch believers in liberalism and moderate politics and came to be labelled as moderates. They did not approve of active response policy. They all believed in constitutional method and favoured the policy of protest, prayer and petition.

The basic demands of the Congress at this time were constitutional that stressed on larger share of the Indians in the governance of the country, Indianization of higher grades of service, expansion of the legislative council and its power and Swaraj or self-rule within the British Empire. The early nationalists were very critical of the exploitative economic policy of the British and blamed it for India's economic impoverishment and destruction of its cottage industries. They demanded the promotion of Indian industries through tariff, protection and direct economic aid.

The only achievement of the moderate leaders of the Congress was the exposure of the true nature of British imperialism and creation of a national awakening. However they failed to achieve desired aims largely due to their method of work. They also failed to draw attention of the common masses and were confined mostly to educated middle class and the elite population.

The Congress maintained her attitude of moderation till the end of the nineteenth century. The young leaders like Tilak, Lala Lajpat Rai, Bipin Chandra Pal and Aurobindo Ghose were dissatisfied with the working of the moderate Congressmen. They began to realize the uselessness of the constitutional methods. It became necessary for them to adopt independent and honourable means to force the government. Lajpat Rai believed the Indians should not be content with begging and was sharply critical of the ideology and methods of the older leadership. This attitude marked the beginning of the era of extremism.

Growth of Militant Nationalism

The new leadership of the Congress was opposed to the soft policies of the moderates. They believed that independence could not be begged for but achieved through sacrifice. The main cause for rise of extremism in Indian politics can be attributed to the deteriorating economic condition of India under the British rule. The recurring famines of the nineteenth century coupled with plague that broke out in Maharashtra and the inaction of the British government created a congenial atmosphere for the growth of extremism. Along with these, the contemporary international influences like revolutionary movements in Turkey, Russia, Egypt, etc, had tremendous impact on the Indian youth. The younger generation became convinced of the fact that a united fight by Indians will easily defeat British imperialism.

The extremists aimed at achieving Swaraj that meant complete independence from British rule. They considered that the demand of the moderate leaders for Swaraj was for colonial self-government. Tilak remarked, "Swaraj is my birthright and I shall have it." Aurobindo Ghose said, "Political freedom is the life breath of a nation." The extremists rejected the technique of the moderates and gave up the policy of prayer and preaching. The new leadership sought to create a passionate love for liberty, accompanied by a spirit of sacrifice and a readiness to suffer for the cause of the country.

The revolutionaries advocated boycott of foreign goods, use of Swadeshi goods, national education and passive resistance. The programme of economic boycott of British and other foreign goods and the use of Swadeshi or homemade products were designed to encourage Indian industries. It would provide the people with more opportunities for work and employment. Soon it was discovered that economic boycott might prove a powerful weapon against the economic exploitation by the Britishers. The extremists also used Swadeshi as the most effective weapon for injuring British interests in India. Tilak preached non-cooperation and advocated abstaining from co-operating with the government directly or indirectly. Thus boycott, Swadeshi, passive resistance and national education remained as primary techniques of the extremists to attain independence.

Besides using the press for creating awareness, the extremists made efforts to strike root in the countryside through social work in villages, songs, jatras (theatre), and patriotic festivals. They used religious revivalism for mass contact. Tilak started the Ganpati festival in 1893 and Shivaji festival in 1895 for creating awareness amongst the public.

However, the extremists could attain their goals partially. They failed to develop an effective leadership or sound organization. Also their reach remained confined to urban populace and could not establish effective communication with the rural areas. The extremists too remained divided in their opinion regarding the methods of functioning. Their internal conflicts went a long way in destabilizing their efforts to unify the country against the British rule.

Partition of Bengal

The worst and most hated aspect of Curzon's administration was the partition of Bengal in 1905 into two provinces. The Eastern part of Bengal was dominated by the Muslims. It was separated and merged with Assam to form a new province. The remaining part of Bengal consisting of Hindu dominated areas of present West Bengal, Bihar and Orissa formed another province. The official justification given for the partition was that the province of Bengal was too large to be administered effectively by a single government. Secondly, it was necessary to bring about development of the much-neglected Muslim dominated areas of eastern Bengal.

The nationalists however viewed this as an effort to indulge in divide and rule policy separating the predominantly Muslim dominated eastern part from Hindu dominated western part and create hostility between the two communities. It was an effort to weaken the growth of nationalism in Bengal creating antagonism between Bengali speaking Hindus and Muslims.

The partition of Bengal witnessed sharp reaction from the people of Bengal. Anti-partition movement started in 1905 in Bengal and soon spread to other parts of the country. Hundreds of protest meetings were held and scores of petitions were sent to the government against the partition. On the day of the partition *hartals* were organized in Calcutta. Bande Mataram became the national song. The anti-partition movement developed into the Swadeshi movement with the boycott of British goods. The nationalists initiated the programme of national education. Many educational institutions were opened by the nationalists.

The Swadeshi movement was given a boost by the policy of self-reliance by organizing indigenous enterprises. Many textile mills, jute mills, soap and match factories were opened such as Calcutta Potteries, Bengal Chemicals and Mohini Cotton mills. The boycott of schools and colleges led to the establishment of traditional methods of education. National educational institutions where literary, technical and physical education was imparted were opened by the nationalists. Emphasis was given to vernacular medium of instruction. Amongst the important institutions of this period is the Bengal Technical Institute at Jadavpur. Along with the boycott of British goods, the movement saw full-scale non-cooperation, covering British law courts and other services such as government jobs. Such methods were described as passive resistance or refusal to render any voluntary or honorary service to the government.

Growth of Revolutionary Terrorism

The first decade of the 20th century saw the rise of revolutionary terrorism in Indian politics with active participation from extremists within the Congress. The revolutionaries wanted quicker results and discounted the value of persuasion. The revolutionary terrorists aimed at overthrowing British rule from India.

They were inspired by the Irish terrorists and Russian Nihilists and followed their method of assassinating corrupt and unpopular officials. They also engaged in dacoities to raise funds for the purchase of arms, etc, popularly known as Swadeshi dacoities. The revolutionary terrorists were operating in Bengal, Punjab, Maharashtra, and parts of South India and even in foreign countries. Many secret societies of the terrorist youths also came into existence.

In Bengal, the beginning of revolutionary activities is traced to the Bhadralok class. Secret societies like the Anushilan Samiti came to be established by Pramotha Mitra at Calcutta and by Pulin Das at Dacca. There were other societies as Swadeshi Bandana and Sadhana Samaj. *Yugantar*, a weekly was started by B. Ghose and Bhupindra Nath Datta in 1908. The Bengal revolutionaries namely Khudiram Bose and Prafulla Chaki threw a bomb on the carriage of Kingsford, the unpopular judge of Muzzafarpur in 1908.

In Maharashtra, the first political murder of a European was committed at Poona by the Chapekar Brothers, Damodar and Balkrishna. In 1904, V D. Savarkar organized the Mitra Mala that later merged into the secret society Abhinav Bharat formed on the lines of Mazzini's Young Italy.

In Punjab, the revolutionary movement rose under Lala Lajpat Rai and Ajit Singh. A bomb was thrown at an English official by Rash Behari Bose and Sachindranath Sanyal.

Ghadar Movement

The Ghadar Movement was founded in the United States by Sohan Singh Bhakna and recognized by Hardayal. Some of its prominent leaders were Rehmat Ali Shah, Bhai Paramanand, Mohammed Barkatullah, Ram Chandra, and so on. It aimed at bringing an armed revolution in India and brought out a weekly called *Ghadar*. Under the leadership of Lala Hardayal the Ghadar party operated from Germany and set up an Indian Independence Committee at Berlin. The Committee planned to mobilize Indian settlers abroad to make all efforts, send volunteers to India to incite rebellion among the troops, to send explosives to Indian revolutionaries and even organize an invasion of British India to liberate the country. In reaction to the revolutionary activities the government unleashed repressive measures against the revolutionaries. Many legislations were passed to curb the activities of the revolutionaries.

Surat Split

At the 23rd session of the Congress at Surat, the moderates and extremists came into conflict. The split was caused due to the differences of opinion on the resolution of Swadeshi and boycott passed by the Calcutta Session of the Congress in 1906 under Dadabhai Nauroji.

Home Rule League

In India two Home Rule Leagues were formed in 1916, one by Tilak at Poona in June 1916 and the other by Annie Besant in September 1916 based on the Irish Home Rule League. Tilak's league was to work in Maharashtra while Besant's league was to work on all India basis. Both the leagues were to work in unison and aimed at the achievement of self-government for India. The league's objective was to educate the people and provide the Congress demand for self-government more strongly. The Home Rule League functioned independently from the Congress. They aimed to pressurize the British public for granting self-government to India. The activities of the league consisted of holding public meetings, organizing discussions, distribution of pamphlets, posters, etc.

Lucknow Session

The Lucknow Session of the Congress held in 1916 under the presidentship of A.C. Mazumdar is known for two things. Firstly it marked the reunion of the moderates and the extremists after the Surat split of 1907. Tilak and Annie Besant dominated the proceedings of this session. The Lucknow session is also memorable because the Congress and the Muslim League came together and signed the Lucknow Pact in 1916. This pact accepted a united scheme of constitutional reform.

Gandhi and his Thought

Mohandas Karamchand Gandhi was born on 2nd Oct. 1869 at Porbandar in Gujarat. After getting his legal education in Britian he landed at Durban in 1893 on a one-year contract to sort out the legal problems of Dada Abdullah, a Gujarati. In South Africa, Gandhi protested against the discriminating treatments meted out to the Indians. He formed The Natal Indian Congress and suffered imprisonment. Gandhi soon became the leader of the struggle against these conditions and during 1893-1914 was engaged in a heroic though unequal struggle against the racist authorities of South Africa. Gandhi in South Africa, developed the method of passive resistance or civil disobedience, which he named Satyagraha. His principal mouthpiece was Indian Opinion (1903). He set up Tolstoy farm which was the precursor of the later Gandhian ashrams that were to play important role in the Indian National movement. In 1914, he was awarded Kaisar-i-Hind gold medal for raising an Indian ambulance in England during the Boer war and 1st World War. After his arrival in India in January 1915, he founded the Sabarmati Ashram at Ahmadabad (1916), where his friends and followers were to learn and practise the idea of truth and non-violence. He also set out to experiment with his new method of struggle in the Indian freedom struggle.

Gandhiji was greatly influenced by the works of Leo Tolstoy's essay, 'Civil disobedience' and Ruskin's 'Unto This Last'. Tolstoy's ideal of non-possession was developed by Gandhiji in his concept of Trusteeship. He was also influenced by the life and teachings of Swami Vivekananda. His political guru Gokhale and Dadabhai Naoroji also influenced him.

On Politics: Gandhiji had an experience of moderate phase of the struggle in South Africa (1894-1906) and the 2nd phase of passive resistance or civil disobedience which was named as Satyagraha (1906-1914). He followed moderate techniques of prayers and petitions in the struggle against racial discrimination. He believed in careful training of disciplined cadres. His non-violent Satyagraha involved peaceful violation of specific laws. He resorted to mass courting arrest and occasional *hartals* and spectacular marches. He had readiness for negotiations and compromise at times leading to abrupt unilateral withdrawal. As a politician and not just a saint, Gandhi in practise sometimes settled for less than complete non-violence. Gandhi unified the national struggle against foreign rule.

On Society: Although Gandhiji supported the Varna system without the element of hierarchical occupation, he was against the pernicious caste system including the practice of untouchability. He emphasised on Hindu-Muslim unity and on the equality of man and woman. He was against purdah practice and child marriage. His ideal society was 'Ram-Rajya.'

On Economy: He advocated the concept of swadeshi and was opposed to large scale industries. He stressed the need for reliance on cottage industries as it would make India self-sufficient. He encouraged Khadi for self-reliance and swadeshi, and gave importance to 'Labour and Sweat'. Gandhiji fought for the interest of peasant in Champaran and Kheda, and labourers in Ahmedabad. He was for balanced economic growth and decentralisation of economy. He tried to harmonise the relationship between the labourers and the capitalist by the concept of trusteeship, where the profit of a factory is shared by both the capitalist and the labourers for common good. Thus, he was against capitalism and not the capitalist.

On Religion: Gandhiji was secular in his approach and fought for Hindu-Muslim unity till his death. Religion, is the highest necessity of human life. For him religion was the basis of morality and morality was the guiding factor in politics. Gandhiji said "My religion knows no political limits and my religion does not teach to hate one another." To him religion was the service of the helpless, the meek and the down trodden. According to him, the religion of love and service cannot be practised without Ahimsa or non-violence.

On Education: Gandhiji gave a scheme of basic education, also known as Wardha scheme of education. The aim of true education, in his opinion, should be to make the students self-supporting and self-reliant and to realise the dignity of labour and manual work. He was for the vocationalisation of education by teaching the pupil handicrafts and Hindi to be the medium of education till 7th standard. Education he believed, was the most powerful instrument of human social transformation and should inculcate values like social service, service to the nation and 'humanity.' •Gandhiji's concept of 'sarvodaya' connotes "the greatest good of all." In his view the highest objective of the state and of the individual should be the realization of this ideal. •His concept of Swaraj implied freedom from foreign domination and control of foreign powers. According to Gandhiji, the Government under Swaraj shall be one in which each individual, irrespective of his religion, race, caste, sex and place of birth shall have as his motto the welfare of the people in general. Emphasis on self-restraint and self-rule remained a significant cornerstone of Gandhiji's moral dimension of Swaraj. Gandhiji saw a very close link between nationalism and internationalism, as internationalism could grow only out of true nationalism.

Gandhian Techniques of Mass Mobilisation: Gandhiji's first great experiment in Satyagraha came in 1917 in Champaran (Bihar) where the peasants were forced by the European planters to grow indigo on at least 3/20th of their land and sell it at prices fixed by the planters (*tin-kathia* system). Accompanied by Babu Rajendra Prasad, Mazharul-Huq, J. B. Kripalani, Narhari Parekh and Mahadev Desai, Gandhiji reached Champaran in 1917. In 1918, Gandhiji intervened in a dispute between the workers and owners at Ahmedabad. It was here that he used the weapon of hunger strike and won for the workers a 35 per cent increase in wages. In 1918. the Kheda peasant struggle involved Gandhiji and Sardar Vallabh Bhai Patel. These three significant struggles brought Gandhiji in close contact with the masses.

The 1917 Sedition Committee headed by Justice Sydney Rowlatt led to the passing of Rowlatt Act (1919). whereby the committee made recommendations to arm the government with powers to suppress all unlawful and dangerous activities. Called the Black Act, it was widely opposed. Along with other nationalists, Gandhiji was also aroused and in February 1919, he founded the Satyagraha Sabha whose members took a pledge to disobey the Act and thus to court arrest and imprisonment. March and April 1919 witnessed a remarkable political awakening in India. Gandhiji gave a call for an All-India *hartal* on 6th April 1919. The people responded with great enthusiasm. The Jallianwala Bagh massacre at Amritsar on 13th April 1919, on the order of General Dyer stunned the whole nation. The unarmed crowd had gathered at the Bagh in defiance of the ban on public meeting to protest against the arrest of their popular leaders Dr. Saifuddin Kitchlew and Dr. Satyapal. Tagore renounced his knighthood in protest.

Khilafat and Non-Cooperation Movement: The main object of the Khilafat movement was to force the British government to change its attitude towards Turkey and restore the Turkish Sultan (Khalifa) to his former position. A Khilafat commitee was formed under the leadership of Ali brothers, Maulana Azad, Hakim Ajmal Khan and Hasrat Mohani and a country-wide agitation was organised. In February 1920, Gandhiji suggested to the Khilafat committee to adopt a programme of non-violent non-cooperation to protest at the government's behaviour. On 9 June, 1920 the Khilafat commitee at Allahabad unanimously accepted his suggestion and asked Gandhiji to lead the movement. The Congress leaders, including Gandhiji viewed the Khilafat agitation as a golden opportunity for cementing the Hindu-Muslim unity and bringing the Muslim masses into the national movement. The Congress at its special session in September 1920 at Calcutta supported Gandhi's plan for non-cooperation for three causes-redressal of the Punjab grievances, rectification of the Khilafat wrongs and the establishment of Swaraj. The people were asked to boycott government educational institutions, law courts and legislatures, to give up foreign cloth, to surrender officially conferred titles and honours. Through these negative programmes, the Indians sought to refuse to cooperate with the British government. The positive programmes of the noncooperation movement included establishment of national schools and colleges, setting up of Panchayats, popularisation of Swadeshi and Khadi, development of Hindu-Muslim unity, removal of untouchability, etc. This decision of non-cooperation movement was endorsed at the annual session of the Congress held at Nagpur in December 1920 The Nagpur session also made changes in the constitution of the Congress.

The adoption of the Non-cooperation movement (initiated earlier by the Khilafat conference on 31 August 1920) by the Congress gave it a new energy and from January 1921, it began to register considerable success all over the country. The Tilak Swarajya Fund was started to finance the Noncooperation movement (Earlier, Lokmanya Tilak passed away on 1 August 1920). The visit of the Prince of Wales in November 1921 also led to the observance of *hartal* all over the country on the day the prince landed in Bombay. On February 1, 1922 Mahatma Gandhi announced that he would start mass civil disobedience including non-payment of taxes unless within seven days the political prisoners were released and the press freed from government control. The general mood of the people was also quite rebellious. On 5th February 1922 a Congress procession at Chauri-Chaura in Gorakhpur district of U.P.

was fired upon by the police. The angry crowd attacked and burnt the police station causing death of 22 policemen. Gandhiji was afraid that the movement might take a violent turn and at his insistence the Congress Working Committee on 12 February abruptly called off the movement. Gandhiji was arrested on 10 March 1922 but was released in February 1924.

Significance of Non-cooperation movement: •The Indian Nationalist movement acquired real mass base for the first time with the participation of peasants, workers, students, lawyers, teachers, etc. •The Congress became the organiser and leader of the masses in their freedom struggle. •It marked the height of Hindu-Muslim unity.

Very soon, the Khilafat movement also lost relevance due to the Kemalist revolution in Turkey which made it a secular state.

Swaraj Party

Immediately, after the withdrawal of the Non-cooperation movement the Nationalist ranks were demoralised and serious differences arose among the leaders. One school of thought headed by C.R. Das and Motilal advocated the end of the boycott of the legislative councils, so as to enter the council and expose the government weaknesses. Sardar Patel, Rajendra Prasad and others opposed council entry and were known as no-changers. In December 1922, C.R. Das and Motilal Nehru formed the Congress-Khilafat Swarajya Party with Das as the President. The new party was to function as a group within the Congress. In 1924, the Belgaum Session of Congress which was presided by Gandhiji endorsed the council entry.

Its achievements: •Swarajya Pary won 42 out of 101 elected seats in the Central Assembly with clear majority in Central provinces, and did well in Bengal, Bombay and U.P. •In March 1925, Vithalbhai Patel, a Swarajist was elected as the President of the Central Assembly.

C.R. Das died on 16 June 1925. The Swarajist party was split by communalism. The responsivists group including Madan Mohan Malviya. Lala Lajpat Rai and N.C. Kelkar, offered cooperation to the government so as to safeguard the Hindu interest. In the 1926 council election, Swaraj Party won 40 seats in the centre. It defeated the government on the Public Safety Bill in 1928 and on a number of bills. The Swarajist finally walked out of the legislatures in 1930 as a result of the Lahore Congress resolution and the beginning of civil disobedience.

Other Political Developments

•In 1924, Muddiman Committee was appointed to examine the working of Dyarchy of the Montague-Chelmsford Reforms which recommended minor changes. •In November 1927, the British government appointed the Indian Statutory Commission popularly known as Simon Commission under Sir John Simon, to go into the question of further constitutional reforms. This all-white commission with no Indian representation angered the Indians and it was seen as a violation of the principle of self-determination and an insult to the self-respect of the Indians. It united at least temporarily different groups and parties in the country. •In opposition to the appointment of the Simon Commission the All-Parties Conference at Bombay on May 19, 1928 appointed a committee with Motilal Nehru as its Chairman to consider and determine the principles of the Constitution for India. The Nehru Report submitted in August 1928 at Lucknow, recommended that the country's new Constitution would rest on the solid base of Dominion Status. •Rejecting the Nehru Report, M.A. Jinnah announced the 14-points at the meeting of the Muslim League in Delhi on March 28, 1929. •Butler committee (1927) was set up to inquire into the relationship between the Indian states and the Paramount Power. •At the historic Congress Session at Lahore (1929) which was presided by Jawaharlal Nehru a resolution declaring Poorna Swaraj (complete independence) to be the Congress objective, was passed. •On 31 December 1929 was hoisted the newly adopted Tri -colour flag of freedom. 26 January 1930 was fixed as the first Independence Day which was to be celebrated annually.

Civil Disobedience

Civil disobedience of the laws of the unjust and tyrannical government is a strong and extreme form of political agitation according to Gandhi, which should be adopted only as a last resort.

The Lahore Congress of 1929 had authorised the Working Committee to launch a programme of civil disobedience including non-payment of taxes. The committee also invested Gandhi with full powers to launch the movement. The 11-points ultimatum of Gandhiji to Lord Irwin after being ignored by the British Government made Gandhiji to launch the civil disobedience moment on 12th March 1930 with his famous Dandi March. (From Sabarmati Ashram to Dandi on Gujarat coast). On 6th April, Gandhiji reached Dandi, picked up a handful of salt and broke the salt law as a symbol of the Indian people's refusal to live under British made laws and therefore under British rule.

The movement now spread rapidly. Violation of salt laws all over the country was soon followed by defiance of forest laws in Maharashtra, Karnataka and the Central Provinces and the refusal to pay the rural Chaukidari tax in Eastern India. The people joined *hartals,* demonstrations and the campaign to boycott foreign goods and to refuse to pay-taxes. In many parts of the country, the peasants refused to pay land revenue and rent and had their lands confiscated. A notable feature of the movement was the wide participation of women. In North-western provinces, under the leadership of Khan Abdul Ghaffar Khan, popularly known as 'Frontier Gandhi' the Pathans organised the society of Khudai Khidmatgars (or Servants of God) known popularly as Red Shirts. They were pledged to non-violence and the freedom struggle. In North-East Rani Gaidilieu raised the banner of rebellion against foreign rule. The government resorted to ruthless repression, lathi charges and firing. Over 90,000 Satyagrahis, including Gandhiji and other congress leaders were imprisoned and Congress declared illegal.

Gandhi-Irwin Pact was signed in March 1931 due to the efforts of Sir Tej Bahadur Sapru, Dr. Jayakar and others to bring about a compromise between the government and the Congress. The Government agreed to withdraw all ordinances and end prosecutions, release all political prisoners, restore the confiscated property of the Satyagrahis and permitted the free collection or manufacture of salt. The Congress in turn agreed to suspend the civil disobedience movement and to participate in the Second Round-Table conference.

Significance of Civil disobedience movement: •It had the objective of achieving complete independence •It involved deliberate violation of law and was evidently more militant •There was wide participation of women •It was not marked by the same Hindu-Muslim unity which was witnessed during Non-cooperation movement

First Round Table Conference (Nov. 12, 1930-Jan. 19, 1931)

Congress boycotted the conference while Muslim league was represented by Muhammad Ali, Muhammad Shafi, Jinnah, Aga Khan and Fazlul Haq. Hindu Mahasabha by Moonje and Jayakar, Indian Liberals by Sapru, Chintamani and Srinivas Sastri. Ramsay MacDonald declared the acceptance of the principle of responsibility of the executive and federation.

Second Round Table Conference (Sep. 7-Dec. 1931)

Gandhiji attended as the sole representative of the Congress. There was a deadlock on the minorities issue (Muslim and Depressed classes). The principle of responsible executive and' federation was maintained. Ramsay Mac Donald also announced the formation of two new provinces of Sind and North-West Fronter Province, the setting up of an Indian Consultative Committee and three Expert committes on Finance, Franchise and State and holding out the prospect of unilateral British Communal Award if Indians did not agree on minorities issue.

Third Round Table Conference (Nov. 17-Dec. 24, 1932)

The Congress boycotted and it was attended by only 46 delegates. The session put together the final features of a concrete plan for the Government of India Act, 1935.

Phase II of Civil Disobedience Movement: (1932-34)

On his return to India after the 2nd Round Table Conference Gandhiji resumed the Civil Disobedience movement in January 1932. The Congress was declared illegal by the government and it arrested most of the leading Congress leaders. The movement was gaining strength when it was suddenly sidetracked with the announcement of Communal Award (1932) by the British Prime-minister Ramsay Mac Donald. The movement gradually waned. The Congress officially suspended the movement in May 1933 and withdrew it in May 1934.

The Communal Award (1932)

British Prime Minister Ramsay Mac Donald announced the Communal Award on August 16,1932. According to this Award, the Muslims, European and Sikh voters would elect their candidates by voting in separate communal electorates. Similar provision was also provided for the depressed classes. The provision for depressed classes was strenuously opposed by Gandhiji who decided to go on a fast unto death in the Yervada Prison where he was lodged. This decision brought about negotiations with B. R. Ambedkar culminating in the Poona Pact, (25, September 1932) by which a common electorate of all Hindu was agreed upon with reserved seats for depressed classes in the Central and Provincial legislatures.

The August Offer

The Viceroy Lord Linlithgow, offered a set of proposals on 8th August 1940 to the Congress for securing its cooperation during the war, which are popularly known as 'August Offer'. It turned down the Congress demands for setting up the provisional National government but made alternate proposals (a) a representative Constitution making body to be set up after the war. (b) increase in the number of Indians in the Viceroy's Executive council. (c) a War Advisory Council to be set up. The Congress rejected the August Offer.

Individual Satyagraha (1940-41)

Launched on 17 October 1940, by the Congress, Vinoba Bhave was the first Satyagrahi. It had dual purpose (a) it expressed to the people a strong feeling against joining the war (b) It gave the British government a chance to peacefully accept Indian demands. The movement created little enthusiasm.

Cripps Mission (1942)

As the war situation worsened, President Roosevelt of USA and Chiang Kai Shek of China pressurised Churchill to seek the active cooperation of Indians in the war and a mission headed by Stafford Cripps was sent to India in March 1942. The Draft Declaration promised Indian Dominion status and a constitution making body after the war. The Pakistan demand was accomodated by the provision that any province which was not prepared to accept the new Constitution would have the right to sign a separate aggrement with Britain regarding its future states. Negotations between Cripps and Congress leaders broke down, Gandhiji rejected it by terming it as 'a post-dated cheque on a crashing bank.'

Quit India Movement (1942)

The failure of the Cripps Mission, rising prices and war time shortages and the Japanese threat forced the Congress to take active steps to compel the British for accepting the Indian demand for independence. The All-India Congress Committee met at Bombay on 8 August 1942 and passed the famous 'Quit India' Resolution. It proposed the starting of a non-violent mass struggle under Gandhi's leadership to achieve this aim. But before the Congress could start a movement the government arrested Gandhiji and other Congress leaders on 9th August 1942. Left leaderless and without any organisation, the people reacted in any manner they could. All over the country there were hartals, strikes in factories, schools and colleges and demonstrations which were lathi-charged and fired upon. The people took to violent action and attacked the symbols of British authority-The police stations, postoffices, railway stations, etc. In some areas such as Ballia in eastern UP, Tumluk in Midnapore district of Bengal and Satara district of Maharashtra the revolutionaries set up'parallel government'. In general, the students, workers and peasants provided the backbone of the 'revolt' while the upper classes and the bureaucracy remained loyal to the government. In the end, the govenment succeeded in crushing the movement.

Other National Movements

Revolutionary terrorism was a by-product of the process of the growth of militant nationalism in India. It acquired a more activist form as a fallout of the Swadeshi and boycott movement.

The first revolutionary groups were organised in 1902 in Midnapore under Jnanendranath Basu and the Anushilan Samiti founded by Promotha Mitter and Barindra Kumar Ghosh in Calcutta. The methods adopted by the revolutionaries were propagation of revolutionary ideas through the organisation of secret societies in India and abroad, publication of pamphlets, books and journals, organisation of military conspiracies, assassination of oppressive and unpopular officials, etc. In 1908, Prafuila Chaki and Khudiram Bose threw a bomb at a carriage supposed to be carrying Judge Kingsford in Muzaffarnagar. Two ladies, instead got killed. Khudiram Bose was the first revolutionary to be hanged. In 1908, Barrah Dacoity was organised by Dacca Anushilan under Pulin Das. Rasbehari Bose and Sachin Sanyal staged a spectacular bomb attack on Vicerory Hardinge in 1912. In Maharashtra, the Chapekar brothers, Damodar and Balkrishna murdered the plague cosmmissioner of Poona, Rand and one Lt. Ayerst in 1897. Savarkar and his brother organised Mitra Mela, a secret society in 1899, which merged with Abhinav Bharat in 1904. Madan Lal Dhingra in 1909 asassinated Curzon Wyllie.

During the First World War, the Berlin Committee for Indian Independece was established in 1915 by Virendranath Chattopadhyay, Hardayal and others. Bhaga Jatin organised revolutionary activity in Bengal and died in an encounter at Balasore. Revolutionary terrorism was again revived after the sudden withdrawal of non-cooperation movement. The revolutionaries were influenced by Russian Revolution (1917), Journals such as *Atmasakti, Sarathi, Bijoli,* novels and books such as Bandi Jivan by Sachin Sanyal and *Pather Dabi* by Sarat Chandra Chatterjee were taken out. In 1924, Hindustan Republican Army (HRA) was founded at Kanpur by Sachin Sanyal and Jogesh Chandra Chaterjee with an aim to organise an armed revolution to overthrow the colonial government. The most important action of HRA was the Kakori robbery in which official railway cash was looted (9 August 1925). The participants Bismil, Ashfaqullah, Roshan Singh and Rajendra Lahiri were hanged. In 1928, Hindustan Socialist Republican Association was organised in Delhi under the leadership of Chandra Sekhar Azad. In December 1928 Bhagat Singh, Azad and Rajguru shot dead Saunders, the police official responsible for the lathi charge on Lala Lajpat Rai in Lahore. In 1929, Batukeshwar Dutt and Bhagat Singh were asked to throw a bomb in the Central Assembly against the passage of the Public Safety Bill and Trade Disputes Bill. Azad was killed in a police encounter in Allahabad in February 1931. Bhagat, Sukhdev and Rajguru were hanged on March 23, 1931. In Bengal the famous Chittagong Armouy raid (April 1930) was carried under the leadership of Surya Sen.

Causes for their failures: •The revolutionaries mainly came from the urban middle class intellegentsia out of touch with the peasants and workers. •They lacked a common plan and central leadership. •The British government on its part followed a ruthless and repressive policy towards them.

The Left Movement

The left movements in India developed into two main streams: (a) Communism which functioned as a branch of the International Communist movement and (b) the Congress Socialist Party which functioned as left-wing of the Indian National Congress.

The Communist Party: Towards the end of 1920, M.N. Roy and other Indian emigres at Tashkent announced the formation of the Communist Party of India. Between 1921 and 1925 various formal Communist groups were established in many parts of the country and finally in December 1925, Satyabhakta organised an All-India conference of Communists at Kanpur. The convening of this conference is regarded as the formal beginning of the Communist Party of

India in 1925. The Communist movement during (1922-34) attracted notice by its involvement in Conspiracy Trials viz. The Peshawar Conspiracy Trial (1922-23), The Kanpur Conspiracy Trial (1924) and the Meerut Conspiracy Trial (1929-33). In July 1934, the CPI was declared an illegal organisation. From 1922, Dange published the first Communist weekly *'Socialist'* from Bombay. During the Second World War, the Communists in India supported Allied-Russian war effort and the Government declared it a legal organisation in 1942. In 1942, the CPI adopted a resolution declaring India to be a multinational state and identifying as many as 16 Indian "nations". In 1946, they put forward a plan for division of India into 17 separate sovereign states on the model of the USSR. By 1947, the CPI was in complete disarray,

The Congress Socialist Party: It was formed in 1934 under the leadership of Acharya Narendra Dev and Jai Prakash Narayan. Its propaganda helped considerably in stimulating thinking in Congress ranks and leadership on questions like radical agrarian reform, problems of industrial labour, etc.

Minor Leftist Parties: (1) *The Forward Block:* After losing the leadership contest with Gandhi (at the Tripuri Congress, 1939) Subhas Chandra Bose formed the Forward Block in March 1939. The Block accepted the creed, policy and programme of the Congress. It sought to rally all anti-imperialist, radical and progressive groups under one banner. (2) *Revolutionary Socialist Party:* It was launched in 1940 and stood for violent overthrow of British imperialism and establishment of socialism in India. (3) *Bolshevik Party of India* was formed by N. Dutt Mazumdar in 1939. (4) *Radical Democratic Party* was launched by M. N. Roy in 1940 after his complete disillusionment with Marxism.

Subhash Chandra Bose and the Indian National Army

Born at Cuttack in Orissa in 1897, Subhas Chandra Bose resigned from the Indian Civil Services in 1921, After his resignation, he plunged into the national movement and was unanimously elected President of Haripura Congress session in 1938. He was re-elected for the second term at the Tripuri session in 1939, defeating Pattabhi Sitaramayya who had been backed by Gandhi. On account of his differences with Mahatma Gandhi and the Congress Working Committee he resigned the Presidentship in 1939 and founded the Forward Block. In 1941, Subhash Chandra Bose escaped from India and reached Berlin (Germany), from where he arrived in Singapore in July 1943.

The idea of the Indian National Army (INA) was first conceived in Malaya by Mohan Singh, an Indian officer of the British Indian Army. The first division of the INA with 16,300 soldiers was formed on 1st September 1942 with Japanese help. The more vigorous phase of the INA began with the arrival of Subhash Bose at Singapore on 2nd July 1943. He set up the Azad Hind Government (The Provisional Government of Free India), adopted the Tri-colour flag and gave the slogan of 'Jaihind'. Bose also reorganised the Azad Hind Fauj (INA). To the Indian recruits he offered: "You give me blood and I will give you freedom." His war slogan was "Dilli chalo."The Provisional government then declared war on Britian and the United States; and was recognised by the Axis powers. Subhash Bose set up two INA headquarters at Rangoon and Singapore, even a women's regiment called the Rani Jhansi regiment was formed. He was the first to address Gandhiji as the 'Father of the Nation' in his appeal on the Azad Hind Radio, Singapore. In May 1944, INA captured Mowdok and hoisted the tri-colour flag on Indian soil. The Japanese government handed over the Andaman & Nicobar Islands to him which he renamed Shaheed, and Swaraj Islands, respectively. Unfortunately, the fortunes of the war turned against Japan and forced Japan to retreat from the Indo-Burma border. The retreat of the INA began in middle of 1944 and ended by mid-1945, resulting in surrender of INA troops to the British Army.

Separatist Trends in Indian Nationalist Politics

The British rule and its policy of Divide and Rule bore special responsibility for the growth of separatist trends in Indian Nationalist politics and it could succeed only because of internal social and political conditions. The British government used communalism to counter and weaken the growing national movement and the welding of the Indian people into a nation. The drift from Nationalism to communalism was initiated by Sir Syed Ahmad Khan when in August 1888 he set up the United Indian Patriotic Association with the avowed object of countering the Congress propaganda and policy and to wean away people from the Congress. In 1893, he founded the exclusively sectarian Muhammadan Anglo-Oriental Defence Association of upper India to keep the Muslims aloof from political agitation and strengthen British Rule in India.

Contributory Factors in the growth of Communalism: •Pronounced Hindu tinge in much of nationalist thought and propaganda in the begining of the 20th century. •Communalism in writing of Indian history by the British writers were also initated by Indian scholars. •Patronage in government services used to foster communalism.

Muslim League

The Simla deputation (Muslims) led by the spiritual leader of the Khoja Muslim community, Aga Khan met Lord Minto at Simla on 1, October 1906. The deputationists demanded separate Muslim electorates which was accepted by Lord Minto.

The All-India Muslim League was formerly founded on 30 December 1906 by a group of big zamindars, ex-bureaucrats and other upper class Muslims like the Aga Khan, the Nawab of Dacca Sailimullah and Nawab Mohsin-ul-Mulk with three main objectives: (a) to promote among Indian Muslims feelings of loyalty towards the British government. (b) to protect and advance the political and other rights of the Indian Muslims. (c) so far as possible, without prejudice to the objects (a) (b), to promote friendly relations between Muslims and other communities of India.

For about a decade after 1913, the Muslim League came under the influence of progressive Muslim leaders like Maulana Mohammad Ali, Maulana Mazhar-ul-Haq, Syed Wazir Hussain, Hasan Imam and M.A. Jinnah. The unity between the Congress and the League was brought about by the signing of the Congress-League Pact, known popularly as the Lucknow Pact (1916) and both put forward common political demands before the government. The Pact accepted separate electorates and the system of weightage and reservation of seats for the minorities in the legislatures (the Congress thus formally recognised communal politics). From 1920-1923 the activities of the Muslim League remained suspended. However, the appointment of the Simon Commission (1927-30) and the Round Table Conferences at London (1930-32) that followed again brought the Muslim League into activity by 1934. M.A. Jinnah became the undisputed leader of the Muslim League. In the elections for the provincial legislative councils held in 1937 out of the 485 reserved Muslim seats, the League could capture only 110 seats. In 1988, the Muslim League appointed Pirupur Committee to report on the oppressions of the Muslims by the Hindus in the so-called Hindu Congress Provinces. The Muslim League observed a Day of Deliverance when the Congress Ministries resigned in October 1939 over the war issue.

Two-Nation Theory and Pakistan Movement

Inspired by the spirit of Pan-Islamism poet and political thinker Mohammad Iqbal gave the idea of a separate Muslim State for the Indian Muslims at the Allahabad session of the Muslim League (1930). The idea of a separate homeland for Indian Muslims to be called Pakistan took a definite shape in the mind of a Cambridge student Rahmat Ali in 1933. The most unequivocal declaration of the Hindus and Muslims as separate nationalities was made by M.A. Jinnah at the Lahore session of the League in March 1940. The Muslim League passed the resolution demanding the partition of India. The Pakistan Resolution was drafted by Sikandar Hayat Khan and moved by Fazlul Haq. Henceforth, the demand for Pakistan became as much an article of faith for the Indian Muslims as their holy book, the Quran.

Hindu Mahasabha

The Punjab Hindu Sabha was founded in 1909. Its leader, U.N. Mukerji and Lal Chand laid down the foundations of Hindu communal ideology and politics. In 1990, the leading Hindus of Allahabad decided to organise an All-India Hindu Mahasabha which was held in April 1915, under the Presidentship of the Maharaja of Kasim Bazar. But it remained for many years a rather sickly child compared to the Muslim League. The Hindu Mahasabha was revived in 1923 and openly began to cater to anti-Muslim sentiments. Its proclaimed objective became the maintenance, protection and promotion of Hindu race, Hindu culture and Hindu civilisation for the advancement of Hindu Rashtra. Sangathan and Suddhi movements among Hindus and Tanzeem and Tabligh movements among Muslims, working for communal consolidation and religious conversion, came up. Lala Lajpat Rai, Madan Mohan Malaviya and N.C. Kelkar joined the Hindu Mahasabha and urged for Hindu communal solidarity. Under the leadership of V. D. Savarkar who became the President of the Hindu Mahasabha in 1938 and was re-elected again and again, the Mahasabha developed a political programme. Reacting to the Muslim appeasement policy of the Indian National Congress, Savarkar popularised the concept of Hindu Rashtra. After the death of V.D. Savarkar, Dr. S.P. Mookerji became the leader of the Hindu Mahasabha and imparted a more nationalist outlook.

The Hindu Mahasabha never gained that popularity with the Hindu masses as the Muslim League did with the Muslims in India. At the same time, against the Muslim League's demand for Pakistan, it raised the slogan of Akhand Hindustan.

The Rashtriya Swayamsevak Sangha (RSS) founded by Dr. Keshavarao Hedgewar on 27, Sept. 1925 became the chief ideology and propagator of extreme communalism. M.S. Golwalkar, codified the RSS doctrines in his booklet, We.

Post-Quit India Movement

•The Muslim League observed on March 23, 1943, the "Pakistan Day". •In March 1944, Mr. C. Rajagopalachari evolved a formula for Congress-League cooperation. It was a tacit acceptance of the League's demand for Pakistan. The main points of C.R. Plan were: (a) Muslim League to endorse Congress demand for independence. (b) League to cooperate with Congress in forming a provisional government at Centre. (c) After the end of the war, the entire population of Muslim majority areas in the North-West and North-East of India to decide by a plebiscite, whether or not to form a separate sovereign state. (d) In the event of separation, agreements would be made for defence, communications and other essential matters. (e) These terms were to be binding only in case of transfer of full powers by England. Jinnah rejected the C.R. Plan on the grounds of common Centre and also wanted only the Muslims to vote in the plebiscite instead of the entire population. •The Desai-Liaqat Pact (Jan 1945) proposing for the formation of an Interim government at the Centre consisting of (a) equal numbers of persons nominated by the Congress and the League in Central legislature (b) representatives of minorities and (c) the commander in chief failed to reach a settlement between the Congress and the League.

Wavell Plan (1945)

The essence of the Plan was to reconstruct the Governor-General's Executive Council pending the preparation of a new Constitution. For this purpose, a conference was convened by Lord Wavell the new Viceroy at Simla on 25th June 1945. The main proposals of the Wavell Plan were: (a) With the exception of the Governor-General and the Commander-in-chief all members of the Executive Council were to be Indians. (b) Caste Hindus and Muslims were to have equal representation. (c) The reconstructed Council was to function as an Interim government within the framework of the 1935 Act. (d) Governor-General was to exercise his veto on the advice of Ministers. (e) Representatives of different parties were to submit a joint list to the Viceroy for nominations to the Executive Council, if a joint list was not possible, then separate lists were to be submitted.

The League wanted all the Muslim members to be League nominees and claimed some kind of veto in the Council with decisions opposed to Muslims needing a 2/3rd majority for approval. The Congress objected to the plan as it attempted to reduce the Congress to the status of a purely Hindu party. Lord Wavell ended the Conference by declaring a failure of the talks thus giving the League a virtual veto.

n July 1945, the Conservative Party of Churchill was replaced by the Labour Party in England. Clement Attlee took over as the new Prime-Minister of England and Pethick Lawrence as the new Secretary of State for India.

Elections of 1945-46

On September 19, 1945, the Viceroy's decision to hold elections to the Central and Provincial legislatures in India was announced. In the election (held in India in the winter of 1945-46) the Congress secured 91.3 per cent votes in the General Constituencies (in the Central Assembly) and the Muslim League won every Muslim Seat. In the Provincial Legislature, the Congress won absolute majority in Bombay, Madras, United Provinces, Bihar, Orissa and

Central Provinces and the Muslim League could secure majority only in Bengal and Sind. In the Punjab, a coalition ministry composed of all parties except the Muslim League was formed under Malik Khizr Hyat, leader of the Unionist Party.

Cabinet Mission Plan

The Cabinet Mission had as its members, Pethick Lawarence (Secretary of State for India), Sir Stafford Cripps and A.V Alexander and reached Delhi on March 24, 1946. It had prolonged discussions with Indian leaders of all parties and groups. As the Congress and the League could not come to any agreement on the fundamental issue of the unity or partition of India, the mission put forward its own plan which was issued on May 16, 1946. The main proposals were: (a) Rejection of the League's demand for a full-fledged Pakistan. (b) Grouping of existing provincial Assemblies into three sections. Section A-Madras, Bombay, Central Provinces, United Provinces, Bihar and Orissa; Section B-Punjab, North-West Frontier Province, Sind (Muslim majority provinces); and Section C-Bengal and Assam. The full autonomy of the provinces and the provisions for grouping were meant to give the Muslim League the 'substance' of Pakistan. (c) A Constituent Assembly to be elected by Provincial Assemblies by proportional representation (voting in groups-General, Muslims, Sikhs). This Constituent Assembly was to be a 389-member body with provincial assemblies sending 292, chief commissioner's provinces sending 4 and princely states sending 93 members. (d) In the Constituent Assembly, members from groups A, B and C would sit separately to decide the constitution for provinces and if possible for the groups also, then the whole Constituent Assembly would sit together to formulate the Union Constitution. (e) There would be a common Centre controlling Defence, Communication and External Affairs. (f) Provinces to have full autonomy and residual powers. (g) Princely states to be no longer under paramountcy of British government and would be free to enter into an arrangement with successor governments or the British government. (h) An interim government to be formed from the Constituent Assembly.

The Cabinet Mission Plan was accepted by the Congress and the Muslim League though with mental reservations (The Objection of the Congress to the Plan was mainly its provision of grouping, that of the League to the rejection of its demand for Pakistan).

In the elections to the Constituent Assembly that took place in July 1946, the Congress captured 205 seats and the League 73. The four Sikh seats owed allegiance to the Congress, thus Congress had 209 members in an Assembly of 296. Alarmed at the overwhelming majority of the Congress the Muslim League withdrew its acceptance of the Cabinet Mission Plan on July 29, 1946. August 16, 1946 was fixed 'Direct Action Day' by the Muslim League. From 16 August 1946, the Indian scene was rapidly transformed. There were communal riots on an unprecedented scale, which left 5000 dead. The worst-hit areas were Calcutta, Bombay, Naokhali, Bihar, Garhamukteswar (U.P.).

The Interim Government

The Viceroy invited the President of the Congress Jawaharlal Nehru to form the Interim government which assumed office on September 2, 1946. Initially the Muslim League kept out but later on October 13, it decided to join the Interim government to safeguard the interests of the Muslim and other minorities.

The Constituent Assembly with the Muslim League remaining aloof met for the first time on December 9, 1946 at New Delhi. On December 11, 1946 this Assembly elected Dr. Rajendra Prasad as its President and only two days later Nehru moved his famous "Objectives Resolution".

Attlee's Announcement

On February 20, 1947 the British Prime Minister, Clement Attlee, fixed the deadline of June 1948 by which the British would quit India and envisaged a partition of the country. This was followed by a near chaotic condition in the country as the League resorted to unabashed violence in Calcutta, Assam the Punjab and the North-West Frontier Province. Attlee also announced the appointment of Lord Mountbatten as Viceroy in place of Lord Wavell. Lord Mounbatten, the last British Govenor General and Viceroy arrived in India on March 22, 1947 and immediately began to take measures for the transfer of power.

The Mountbatten Plan-June 3, 1947

The prevailing communal violence in the country led Mountbatten to announce the partition plan or the June 3rd Plan. The Congress leaders too had come to the conclusion that partition was the only choice to check the widespread communal violence and bloodshed that was ravaging the country. The Plan provided for immediate transfer of power on the basis of grant of Dominion Status. The important points of the plan were: (1) The Provincial Assemblies of Punjab and Bengal would meet in two parts, one representing the Muslim majority districts and the other representing the rest of the Province to vote for partition. If a simple majority of either part voted for partition then these provinces would be partitioned. (2) The Legislative Assembly of Sind would take its own decision. (3) Referendum in North-West Frontier Province and Sylhet district of Bengal would decide the fate of these areas. (4) Independence for princely states ruled out, they would either join India or Pakistan. (5) Provision for the setting up of a Boundary Commission to demarcate boundaries in case partition was to be effected.

Partition of India

The Plan of 3rd June was accepted by all political parties in the country. The Legislative Assemblies of Bengal and the Punjab decided in favour of partition of those provinces. East Bengal and West Punjab joined Pakistan; West Bengal and East Punjab remained with the Indian Union. The referendum in the Sylhet resulted in the incorporation of that district in East Bengal. Two Boundary Commissions one in respect of each province were constituted to demarcate the boundaries of the new provinces. The referendum in the N.W.F.P. decided in favour of Pakistan, the provincial Congress refraining from the referendum. Baluchistan and Sind joined Pakistan.

The Indian Independence Act, 1947

The Indian Independence Bill was introduced in the British Parliament on July 4, 1947 and the Indian Independence Act was enacted on July, 18, 1947. This Act merely formalised and gave legal effect to the 3rd June Plan of Lord Mountbatten.

The Act provided for the creation of two independent dominions of India and Pakistan with effect from 15 August 1947. Pending the adoption of a new Constitution for each Dominion, the existing Constituent Assembly would be Dominion Legislature, and either Dominion and every province would be governed by the provisions of the Government of India Act, 1935. Each Dominion was empowered to modify this Act, through its Governor-General upto March 31, 1948, and thereafter by its Constituent Assembly.

As per the provisions of the Indian Independence Act, 1947, Pakistan became independent on 14 August while India got her freedom on 15 August 1947. M.A. Jinnah became the first Governor-General of Pakistan. India, however, decided to continue Lord Mountbatten as the Governor-General of India.

Nineteen

INDIA AFTER INDEPENDENCE

The Constitution

The Indian Constitution was adopted by the Constituent Assembly on November 26, 1949. It is the second longest Constitution of the world. It is a comprehensive document containing 395 articles and several Schedules. As per the Preamble of the Constitution, India has been declared as a Sovereign, Socialist, Secular and Democratic Republic. It is declared that the Constitution has been "given by the people to themselves" showing the republican character of the polity. The framers of the Constitution were eager to preserve the democratic values to which the Constitution attached highest importance. The Government of India Act, 1935, acted as a precedent before the framers. The Constitution has been provided with Fundamental Rights to preserve the basic rights of the people such as right to speech and right to equality besides many more rights. The Preamble declares India to be a socialist country that spells out the aspirations of the people to ensure all the citizens their social, economic and political justice. India being a sovereign state is free from any kind of external control. The Constitution of India also declares India as a secular state. The state has no official religion and guarantees the freedom to practice and propagate any religion of their choice. India is also described as a Union of states with indestructible unity. However its federal form makes it a mixture of the center and states with proper division of power between the two. The Indian Constitution also contains the Directive Principles of State Policy as an essential guideline for the government and these essentially meet the aims and aspirations of the people.

Pt. Jawaharlal Nehru, the first Prime Minister of independent India was born on 14th November 1889. Having toured the country he was extremely attached to the people and was a popular and ideal leader. He dreamt of making India a progressive and modern nation. The five paths laid down by him are peace, democracy, socialism, science and secularism. It is on these ideals that he worked throught his life and strove to inculcate them in his work. Pt. Nehru was a keen believer of democracy and socialism. Democracy to him meant political democracy where each and every citizen would have a right to vote. He showed his trust towards his countrymen by supporting adult franchise. Being a socialist he wanted the citizens to enjoy social, economic and political justice that would end the discrimination in society. In the post independence era too he pursued socialistic goals. His vision of modern India was primarily based on democratic and socialistic ideals. It is because of these ideals that Pt. Nehru is regarded as the true architect of modern India.

Five Year Plans and Industrialization

On 15th August 1947 when India became independent politically, the country stood at the threshold of a new era. The country at this stage was under-developed and its people were on the brink of poverty. Its vast resources, agriculture and minerals were unexploited due to lack of proper direction. Planning offered the only way to achieve a rapid and balanced growth keeping the national priorities in mind. The state was now expected to play an active part in economic and social development. The success of such planned development in both agrarian and industrial sector in the USSR also played a part in popularizing the concept of planned development.

After the adoption of a new constitution, the government of India set up the Planning Commission in March 1950 to assess the country's material, capital and human resources and to formulate a plan for the most effective and balanced utilization. The first Prime Minister, Pt. Jawaharlal Nehru was also its first chairman. The Finance Minister and the Minister for planning were its essential members amongst other ministers in different capacities linked to economic development.

Some of the objectives outlined in these plans were maximization of national income, rapid industrialization, providing full employment and most importantly achieving self-sufficiency. The central purpose identified with the process of development was to raise the standard of living and opening out more opportunities to people. Planning in India needed proper channelling of resources into different developmental activities in accordance with accepted national priorities. While short-term developmental objectives have varied from plan to plan, the planning process was in some ways inspired by certain long-term goals. These are: (a) High growth rate with a view to improve the standard of living. Due to the oppressive policies of the British, the country in the colonial period witnessed a retarded development. The standard of living of the people was very low. The general objective of all the Five year plans has been to raise the standard of living and achieve a much higher growth rate of national income. (b) Achieving social justice. As per the Directive Principles of State Policy laid down in the Constitution, achievement of justice—social, economic and political were proclaimed as a national commitment. The Five Year Plans being an inherent part of state policy, social justice figured as the most important objective in them. Its purview covered the achievement of economic and social equality and regional balance in development and avoidance of concentration of economic power. Special care for the backward classes of the population is one of the targets for attaining social justice. (c) Economic self-reliance. Political independence is never complete without economic independence. Self-reliance in this regard came as a natural objective of the successive Five Year Plans. The emphasis was on achieving financial self-reliance. Its essence lay in the fact that the economy should be able to finance its continued growth at a satisfactory rate largely from domestic resources. Foreign and external help should be kept at minimum level.

However a major policy change occurred in this regard from 1991 when the Government at the Center liberalized the economy and went all the way to attract foreign investments in order to modernize the economy faster. The strategy for development included a comprehensive planning for all round development; a mixed economy approach to keep up the socialistic pattern of development; achieve a balanced development that would develop both agriculture and industry; provide maximum employment; cater to the development of backward areas; to uplift the backward classes and achieve overall social welfare.

First Plan (1951-52 to 1955-56): The first five-year plan had a two-fold objective: (1) To correct the disequilibrium in the economy caused by the Second World War and the partition of the country. (2) To initiate simultaneously a process of all round development which would ensure a rise in national income and a steady improvement in the living standards of the people.

The plan accorded the highest priority to agriculture, including irrigation and power projects. The plan also aimed at increasing the rate of investment from 5 per cent to 7 per cent of the national income. The growth rate achieved in this plan was 3.6 per cent.

Second Plan (1956-57 to 1960-61): In December 1954, the Parliament declared the objective of the Second Plan to achieve the Socialistic Pattern of Society. The basic aim under this was to attain greater equality of income and wealth and not private profit. It promoted a pattern of development that would lead to the establishment of a socialistic society in India. The benefits of the plan were directed towards the betterment of the less privileged than the progressive sections. The main objectives of the second plan were: (a) An increase of 25 per cent in the national income. (b) Rapid industrialization with special emphasis on the development of basic and heavy industries. (c) Large expansion of employment opportunities. (d) Reduction of the inequalities in income and wealth and a more even distribution of economic power.

The Plan aimed at increasing the rate of investment from 7 per cent to 11 per cent of the national income by 1960-61. This plan increased the scope of industrialization by increasing the production of iron and steel, heavy chemicals, development of heavy engineering and machine building industries. For the first time long-term economic policy was formulated and loans were taken from foreign countries. The growth rate achieved was 4 per cent. Rapid industrialization and diversification of the economy were the main course of development. The development of basic industries and allocation of resources among different sectors were also taken carefully.

Third Plan (1961-62 to 1965-66): The Third Five Year Plan aimed at securing a marked advance towards self-sustaining growth. Its objectives were: (a) Increase in the national income of over 5 per cent per annum and at the same time ensure a pattern of investment that would sustain this rate of growth during subsequent plan periods. (b) Achieve self-sufficiency in food grains and increase agricultural production to meet the requirements of the industry and exports. (c) Expand the basic industries like steel, chemicals, fuel and power and to establish machine building ability so that requirement of further industrialization could be met within a period of ten years and that too from the country's own resources. (d) Utilize fully the manpower resources of the country and ensure a substantial expansion in employment opportunities. (e) Bring down disparities of income and wealth and get a more equitable distribution of economic power.

The national income in this plan was to increase by about 30 per cent by 1965-66 and per capita income by about 17 per cent during the period. The growth rate stipulated at 2.2 per cent. The Programmes of the second plan were carried over in the third plan too. The development of basic industries remained a fundamental concern to growth.

Annual Plans (1967, 1968, 1969): The situation created by the Indo-Pak conflict, two successive years of severe drought, 1965-66 and 1966-67, devaluation of the currency in 1966, general rise in prices and erosion of resources available for plan purpose delayed the finalization of the fourth five year plan. Instead three annual plans were formulated within the framework of the draft outline of the fourth plan. The main aim of this plan was to restore normalcy in the economy. The emphasis of these plans was to adopt irrigation projects along with the use of high yielding variety crops in the agricultural sector. In the industrial sector the stress was on the utilization of the existing capacity and on consumer goods industry.

Fourth Plan (1969-70 to 1973-74): The Fourth plan aimed at raising the standard of living of the people through programmes that would promote social justice and equality at the same time. The concentration of the plan was the welfare of the weaker sections of the society especially through employment and education. The rate of growth in national income was 3.3 per cent per annum and the per capita income was 1.2 per cent per annum. The performance in industry as well as agriculture was not satisfactory

Fifth Plan (1974-79): The following objectives were stated under the fifth five-year plan: (a) Removal of poverty. (b) Achievement of economic self-reliance.

To achieve these objectives the procedure thought was to get a 5.5 per cent overall rate of growth; expansion of productive employment; extended programmes of social welfare; emphasis on agriculture and basic industry with special attention to production for mass consumption; export promotion and substitution of imports. The Fifth plan that was to be completed in March 1979 was completed earlier; by March 1978.This was the golden period for rural development as the largest funds were diversified for rural development. The rate of growth achieved was 5.2 per cent.

Sixth Plan (1980-85): This plan accelerated the work for the removal of poverty, generation of gainful employment and technological and economic self-reliance. The plan targeted a growth rate of 5.2 per cent and achieved it. It was successful in achieving the required industrial development and agricultural growth. It also achieved aims of social justice. The plan undertook the development of under developed areas of the country. It also concentrated on the refinement of technology. It was the first perspective plan of the country slated for a long term of fifteen years. It also saw a rapid growth in the service sector. About 94 per cent of the cost of investments was met from the domestic resources projecting the self-reliance of the country.

Seventh Plan (1985-90): The sixth five-year plan provided the background for the next plan. The guiding principles of the plan continued to be growth, equity and social justice, self-reliance, improved efficiency and productivity. The policies to accelerate growth in food grains production, increase employment opportunities and raise productivity were pursued in this plan. The rate of growth of 5.6 per cent was kept for this plan. The strategy in the seventh plan to generate productive employment was to increase cropping intensities and extension of agriculture through use of new technologies. Emphasis was also given on various rural schemes for development.

Eighth Plan (1992-97): The Eighth plan had the following objectives: (a) Generating adequate employment to achieve near full employment level by the turn of the century. (b) Containing population growth through active scheme of incentives. (c) Eradication of illiteracy in the age group of 15 to 35 years. (d) Provision for health and availability of safe drinking water especially in villages. (e) Self-sufficiency in food and generation of agricultural surplus. (f) Strengthening the infrastructure in order to support growth process on a sustained basis.

The strategy for achieving the above mentioned goals was to be a mixture of new investments and correction of imbalances in different sectors and increasing investment efficiency. This plan also aimed at a 5.6 per cent growth per annum. Much of the investments were to be met by capital inflow from abroad in the form of loans.

Ninth Plan (1997-2002): The Ninth plan proposed to achieve a 7 per cent growth rate during the plan period. It introduced fiscal discipline and aimed to control rise in prices through controlling money supply. It aimed at resource mobilization and attract foreign direct investment. The thrust of the plan was to achieve agricultural growth. The proposition was to broaden the direct tax base for raising resources at the center. Some of the objectives outlined in this plan were: (a) Priority to agriculture and rural development and generate productive employment and eradication of poverty. (b) Accelerating the growth rate of the economy and keeping the prices stable. (c) Containing the growth rate of population. (d) Promoting and developing people's participatory institutions like the Panchayati Raj and Cooperatives. (e) Strengthening efforts of building self-reliance.

Agrarian Reforms

Independent India inherited a predominantly agrarian economy from the colonial period. At present 40 per cent of the national income comes from agriculture and allied activities. It has remained the mainstay of the Indian economy and has provided a livelihood to a greater part of the population. Agriculture occupies an important position with regard to industrial development. A steady and sustained agricultural base ensures a self sufficient and adequate industrialization too. Agriculture provides raw materials to industries. The growth of major industries as cotton, textile, jute, sugar, etc, is affected by fluctuations in agriculture. It provides food grains to the industrial population by creating a marketable surplus.

Some of the distinguished features of Indian agriculture are as follows: (a) In spite of being the principal industry, agriculture continues to be backward in character. The yield per hectare of land of all the principal crops produced in India is low. Productivity per worker is equally low. (b) Agriculture in India is largely carried on the basis of subsistence farming. The cultivator produces mainly for himself and his family's consumption. Thus generation of marketable surplus always remained as the focus of the planning for agriculture. (c) Mode of cultivation has always been primitive in India. The cultivator uses the same old techniques of production of the plough. The neglect of modern techniques for production also slowed down productivity in agriculture and it remains labour intensive. (d) Sub-division and fragmentation of land holdings remains a perpetual problem with Indian agriculture. The larger family concept leads to division of family land into several divisions. These lands besides being small and unproductive fail to generate adequate surplus also.

Measures to improve agricultural production and productivity have come to be termed as agrarian reforms. Broadly two sets of measures are adopted. They are linked intricately with land ownership, tenancy and distribution measures. (i) Institutional measures (ii) Technological measures

Institutional Measures. With reference to land reforms, it was necessary to have a land ownership pattern, that is socially just and economically viable. The measures adopted for land reform were: (a) *Abolition of intermediaries.* At the time of independence, three different types of land tenure systems were prevailing in India — Zamindari, Mahalwari and Ryotwari. After independence the first important step that the government took up was the abolition of intermediaries.The state Governments enacted legislations to take over the intermediary rights from zamindars. The abolition of intermediaries was effected by March 1968 and fully implemented in several states. It is said that about 30 million tenants benefited from the zamindari abolition. Tenancy reforms in India had been conferred the benefit of security of land tenure by preventing large-scale eviction of tenants. Resumption of land by the owner for personal cultivation only, assuring a prescribed minimum area of land to the tenants has been provided for in the legislations. Payment of rent by the tenants to the landlord had now been regulated. The rent varied from 1/3rd to 1/5th of the gross produce. Provisions have been made in the tenancy legislation for conferment of ownership rights to tenants. (b) *Ceiling on Land Holdings.* Land holdings, are limited on a minimum as well as a maximum ceiling. The maximum limit has been fixed to do social justice. The minimum has been fixed to prevent uneconomic unit of cultivation. The ceiling on land has been enacted in most of the states in the post independence period. Those possessing land beyond the maximum limit would have to surrender the surplus land to the state. People with uneconomic units, evicted tenants and landless workers are usually distributed these surplus lands. Through this ceiling of land the Government intends to minimize the concentration of economic power and wealth. It would ensure fuller utilization of workforce in agriculture and shall also enhance the social status of the rural poor. (c) *Consolidation of Land Holdings.* In order to solve the problem of fragmented holdings, consolidation is one of the best measures. It means pooling together in one compact block all the plots of land of a farmer that are scattered all over the village. Not only does the cultivator get a compact portion of land but the total land or unit also remains the same. This kind of operation not only makes agricultural production economic but also reduces the area of wasteland. By 1985 about 51.8 million hectares of land had been consolidated. It has led to more productivity and increase in the cultivable area by removal of boundaries. About fifteen states had passed laws on consolidation of land and this has led to the full utilization of agricultural land for cultivation. (d) *Cooperative Farming.* The main problem of agriculture in India is the practice of subsistence farming. Economic farming is far beyond the imagination of the Indian cultivator. A remedy in this regard is cooperative farming. Its essence lies in the retention of the rights of the individual cultivator in his own land, at the same time carrying on the agricultural operations jointly. The main features of this kind of method are the following: (i) Land formed into a single unit. (ii) Land proprietorship remains with the individual cultivator. (iii) Management of land carried on jointly. (iv) Members are paid for their work. (v) Net profits are distributed amongst members but some of it is held back for building up reserves and resources.

In return the state offers its assistance to such a society by advancing loans for purchase of seeds, supply of manures and other necessary implements for cultivation. This has solved the problems of uneconomic farming to a great extent.

Technological Measures. The initial plans did not provide any facility for improvement in farming techniques. Agricultural efficiency depends to a great extent on the input and method of cultivation practiced. The various branches of technological measures are: (a) *Irrigation.* Adequate supply of water is the primary necessity for good agriculture. Geographically India receives substantial rainfall but that is often uncertain in volume, time and place and is not enough to sustain a stable agricultural base. Artificial irrigation thus becomes a necessity to improve agricultural production. Irrigation being a key factor in agriculture helps to extend the net sown area in regions that receive scanty rainfall. It also promotes multi-cropping by making it possible to raise a second crop during dry seasons. It increases the gross cropped area. The main sources of artificial irrigation are canals, wells and tanks. During the seventh plan rapid expansion in irrigation facilities is considered to be a key element in agricultural procedures. (b) *Fertilizers and Manures.* In order to increase agricultural productivity, fertilizers and manures played an important role. Previously animal dung, compost and bones and other organic manures were used to restore the nutrients of the soil. The land was also left fallow to rebuild its nutrients. In recent years the use of chemical fertilizers have greatly added to agricultural productivity. The consumption of fertilizers increased from 69,000 tonnes of nutrients in the first plan to 9.6 million tonnes by the end of the sixth plan. This varied use of improved fertilizers has increased the crop area and led to better productivity. To increase consumption of fertilizer the sixth plan aimed at ensuring equitable and efficient fertilizer distribution and to see that its benefits are received by all sectors of the farming community. To ensure the fuller benefits of such manures adequate measures were taken to protect the crops from rodents and pests. Plant protection measures were also an important component of increasing crop yield. (c) *Improved Seeds.* A great amount of improvement can be brought about by the use of better seeds in agriculture. The yield from better seeds is larger and the crop too sells for a better price. To promote the use of better seeds the Government has set up the National Seeds Corporation. State Farms Corporations have also been established in 1969 to encourage the production and distribution of certified seeds. Thirteen State Seeds Corporations have also been established to supply improved seeds to farmers. Improved varieties of seeds have been discovered for practically all cereal crops and oil seeds, pulses, jute, cotton and sugarcane have been planted in high yielding varieties of seeds. The spread of high yielding technology based on fertilizer and irrigation responsive high yielding varieties of crops since 1960s commonly known as Green Revolution has greatly added to the output of wheat and rice. The high yielding variety programme started as a part of the third plan and the annual plans had a lot of provisions for the improvement in agricultural productivity. The main emphasis under the HYVP was on improved variety of seeds for raising the yield per hectare of land. Total area under HYVP was 54.5 million hectares in 1984-85. These now form a major strategy of agricultural development in India. The introduction of this programme had led to self-sufficiency in food production in India. At a point it was even proposed that such high yielding variety of seeds would be distributed free of cost to cultivators to improve the yield per hectare of land. (d) *Credit and Finance Facilities.* The average farmer in India is very poor. He is unable to improve cultivation on his own. Traditionally his borrowing agencies have been the moneylenders who extorted the maximum out of him to fill their pockets. But in the post independence era, agricultural production came under the supervision of the government and all intermediaries were removed. Besides other assistance in agricultural operations, the average farmer was also advanced credit facilities to improve productivity. The farmer needed financial assistance to buy goods quality seeds, implements and agricultural machinery to carry on operations. The scheme of providing loans was made easy to facilitate the farmer to repay them. Non-traditionally, cooperatives, credit societies and land development banks provide short, medium and long-term credit to the cultivators. These agencies provide loans at reasonable rate of interest. The various agencies providing loans to farmers are the Agricultural Credit Societies. One of the earliest of such agencies are the Primary Agricultural Credit Societies (PACS) while the Land Development Banks were a source of long term loans to the farmers. The former were tied to the Central Cooperative Banks (CCB) and the latter to the State Cooperative Banks (SCB). However the essence of cooperative structures was missing in these agencies. They were not self-sufficient and were dependent on each other for generating credit.

Gradually the Commercial Banks were realized as another source for rural credit. These Commercial Banks too provided loans on direct basis for short as well as long term. They provided loans for distributing fertilizers and other agricultural inputs. A third field agency called the Regional Rural Banks (RRB) was introduced in October in 1975. Their role was to provide credit for agricultural and rural development where the other two agencies were weak. The RRBs were intended to be banks that the average man could afford. Scheduled banks usually public sector banks sponsor the RRBs. The Reserve Bank of India and the State banks help the farmers only through these networks of cooperative institutions. The National Bank for Agriculture and Rural Development (NABARD) has been the apex refinancing institution for agriculture and rural credit. The NABARD functions as a financing institution to the various SCBs and RRBs. Prior to the NABARD these refinancing functions were performed by the RBI. Thus the role of credit institutions in advancing loans crucial to development of agriculture has been immense. It is primarily because of these facilities that agricultural operations have been launched in a big way by various categories of Indian cultivators.

Foreign Policy

India's foreign policy was conducted under the guidance of Pt. Jawaharlal Nehru, the first Prime Minister of independent India. The shaping of India's foreign policy was largely influenced by the international development after the Second World War, the weakening of the forces of imperialism and growth of the forces of democracy and progress. Several countries in the post-war era in Europe and Asia broke away from the capitalist system to form the socialist system. There was an upsurge in the movements for national liberation that resulted in the collapse of the colonial system of imperialism.

The Indian National Congress party had as early as 1920s adopted a resolution expressing a desire to establish cooperation with the neighbouring countries. But at that point the internal situation of India did not permit them to pay attention to international developments. It was mainly due to Nehru's efforts that since the mid-twenties the Congress party began to take interest in international affairs. The Congress resolved to support the peoples and races in their struggle for freedom and equality. They also decided to condemn racial discriminations throughout the world. After 1927 Nehru took an active part in formulating the foreign policy of the Congress that was in effect its first foreign policy statement. It contained a declaration that India should not participate in imperialist and any other war. This position was taken up as the key foreign policy principle in late 1920s and 1930s.

When in 1930s Japan, Italy and Germany engaged themselves in imperialist aggressions, the Congress condemned their brutal imperialist designs and passed resolutions to defend the cause of the nationalist forces in various countries such as China, Ethiopia, etc. The inter-war period shaped a substantial portion of India's foreign policy. India agreed to cooperate with Britain against Nazi Germany but since the cooperation was sought on British terms, the newly constituted Congress ministries resigned.

At no time did India have sympathies for the fascist countries. The Indians consistently criticized the Non-Aggression pact signed between Germany and the USSR in August 1939 and regarded it as an eyewash. The dropping of atom bomb by the Americans on Japanese soil wounded India's feelings and was strongly condemned. Soon after the formation of the interim government in September 1946, India took steps to establish friendly relations with all countries. During the time that the interim government was in office, India established diplomatic relations and exchanged ambassadors with the USA, USSR, China and some other countries. Meanwhile rout of the forces of Nazism and Japanese militarism in World War II altered the correlation of forces in the international arena. It resulted in an upsurge of movements for national liberation in Asia. Nehru on behalf of the Congress participated in several international conferences including the one held at Brussels in 1926 that declared its profound aim of fighting imperialism. The Congress under the leadership of Jawaharlal Nehru constantly supported the newly liberated countries and their struggle against imperialism.

After independence, Nehru became the virtual director of India's foreign policy. And under his guidance India became the first state to have pursued a policy that was new in the history of international relations—the policy of Non-Alignment. He was ably supported by Naser of Egypt, Sukarno of Indonesia and Joseph Broz Tito of Yugoslavia. Early in 1947, at the initiative of India, the Asian Relations Conference at Delhi was convened where the principles of foreign policy of independent India were proclaimed. It was attended by representatives of 29 countries. The Conference helped to strengthen the solidarity of all Asian countries. Nehru also participated in the Afro-Asian Conference held in 1955 in Bandung and popularized the policy of non-alignment there. The agenda contained in these conferences was the economic and cultural cooperation, respect for human rights and self-determination and finally the promotion of world peace and cooperation.

The policy of Non-alignment meant the acceptance of the inevitability of war but on the conviction that war could also be avoided. Non-alignment stood for an independent policy conditioned and controlled by India's own strength. It meant not to entangle oneself with any kind of alliances or commitments that would lead to war and conflict. Non-alignment implied a position to judge each issue without prejudice or bias. It enhanced the chances of effective mediation in bitter conflicts and thereby brighten the prospect of world peace. In the Korean War and the tangle of Indo-China, the role of peacemaker that India played was vital.

The secret of this policy is that India is neither permanently pro-west nor with the east. She was clearly with Communist block on the issues such as disarmament, racial discrimination, colonialism and China's membership of the United Nations. But on major issues of aggression of North Korea, India clearly criticized the Communists. The pro-west move did not prevent India from opposing the US military adventurism in Korea. India was equally vigorous in condemning the Anglo-French action in Suez and Soviet intervention in Hungary. Non-alignment also did not mean isolation because India had established diplomatic relations with almost all independent states. She was a member of the United Nations and also took part in the Commonwealth of Nations. The basis of all this was cooperation but at the same time following an independent course.

The policy of Non-alignment was based on the five principles of Panch Sheela, enumerating international conduct. These were first envisaged and formulated in 1954. These principles were: (a) Mutual respect for each other's territorial integrity and sovereignty. (b) Non-aggression (c) Non interference in each other's military affairs (d) Equality and mutual benefit (e) Peaceful coexistence

By April 1955, Burma, China, Laos, Nepal, Democratic Republic of Vietnam, Yugoslavia and Cambodia had accepted the Panch Sheela.

Non-alignment was a tactic or technique to maintain world peace in such a way that each nation pursues his own interest without disturbing the other. The policy was also in tune with the domestic requirements of democracy and socialism. A major economic factor for the adoption of the policy of non-alignment had been India's economic backwardness. Foreign aid was an important component for developing our underdeveloped economy. Therefore aid was welcome from all quarters — USSR, UK, USA, Germany and Japan. This presupposes non-alignment. India was both tied up with the east and west for economic development.

However, the events on the borders in September-October 1962 threw a serious challenge to the Non-Alignment Movement (NAM). Due to the Chinese aggression on India it was now recognized that non-Alignment must be tied up with the immediate defence requirements in order to serve a useful purpose. Conceived as a struggle against colonialism and growing polarization of international relations resulting from military blocks and cold war, non-aligned India has constantly struggled for allround emancipation of the people of Asia, Africa, Latin America, the Caribbean and other parts of the world. Non-Alignment has achieved success and has continued to play a decisive role in efforts to promote world peace.

Some argue on the relevance of NAM after the end of the cold war. However, the single existence of the United States and its dominating influence today threatens to make the world uni-polar. Instead of territorial imperialist design, the ugly face of economic imperialism has taken its place. The widening gap between the developed and the developing countries is a source of instability in the world. Access to resources and debt burden today threaten the survival of smaller nations. The goal of NAM would now change accordingly to economic needs to face new challenges in terms of new forms of imperialism.

Relations with China. India's relation with China until 1960-62 rested on an age long friendship and contact. The contact developed in the form of Chinese pilgrims coming to India from 221 B.C. to about 101 A.D. Diplomatic as well as commercial relations prevailed through the coast of Arakan and to the Pagan. Sea was also significant for maritime trade between China and India. These routes became points of numerous contacts, religious, trade, diplomatic and cultural. Buddhism was ardently followed from India. Trade contacts between regions of Far East and South India developed amicably during the early Christian centuries.

Contact between India and China though snapped for a while were revived in the 18th and 19th centuries by sharing similar opposition to British imperialism. After 1911 Indian intellectuals became interested in the national movement in China. It was further strengthened by Tagore's visit to China in 1920s. Japanese Aggression on Manchuria was also denounced by India. During the Sino-Japanese war in 1937 the Congress sent a medical mission and supplies to China. In 1942 Chai-Kai-Shek visited India to rally public opinion against Japan. As soon as China became independent in 1949, India established diplomatic relations with her.

The initial problems between India and China started on the question of Tibet. The Government of India in 1947 inherited certain extra territorial rights in Tibet. Delhi now expressed concern to Peking over the unsettled Sino-Tibetan relations that were to be adjusted through peaceful negotiations in 1950. Even when the Chinese troops entered Tibet on October 1950, Delhi followed a policy characterized by forbearance and patient negotiations. Thereafter even in the UN General Assembly India supported the cause of China in the Korean war and condemned US aggression of Indo-China.

On one occasion China for the first time protested against the presence of Indian troops in Barahoti, UP. India refuted the allegation that Indian troops had intruded into Tibet. The attempt to cross into Barahoti by the Chinese troops was also protested by India. But on July 26th, 1956 Peking for the first time claimed that Barahoti was Chinese territory and denied that Tunjun La was a border pass. Towards the end of November Chou-En-lai paid a visit to India. Nehru and Chou discussed the border question in their meeting and Chou assured his Indian counterpart that the Tibet border dispute would be solved through negotiations. The border with Burma was also recognized.

The years between 1957-58 were crucial in relations between India and China. However, Chinese reactions to India's friendly relations were not responded equally. China in turn went on to occupy illegally India's territory on the borders. On July 28th, 1955, they occupied the Barahoti area in south of Ladakh and in September they had intruded ten miles inside India's territory. Gradually they crossed the Shipki pass into India. In April 1958, talks were held on the question of Barahoti. While China agreed to withdraw military personnel their civilian personnel continued to stay in the area. In April 1960 the talks between Chou and Nehru ended in failure amidst violations on the border as well as air space of India.

Besides these border disputes, the relations of China and India were further strained on the question of giving asylum to Dalai Lama. Right from 1959 owing to large-scale demolition of Buddhist monasteries and confiscation of lands, the Chinese had caused discontent among the Tibetans. In the revolt of the Tibetans, certain insurgents together with Dalai Lama fled in the direction of India. Fixed on the question to decide whether he should let the Tibetan refugees into India or refuse them asylum, Nehru was put in a dilemma. On March 30, 1959, Prime Minister Nehru said in the Lok Sabha that should a large group of people attempt to cross the Indian border from Tibet they would not be allowed into India. Nevertheless continuous crossing of the border carried on. Not able to hurt the Indian sentiments especially of the Buddhist community, the entry of Dalai Lama was accepted.

By 10th October 1962 a massive Chinese attack was launched on Indian posts and the next day the Chinese captured the Thagla Ridge, the traditional Indo-Tibetan border. The Chinese refused to recognize the MacMohan line or the accepted eastern border. It took a lot of deliberations before cease-fire was declared and the Chinese agreed to withdraw to the line as it was on September 8th 1962. Meanwhile an intense exchange of notes continued between the two governments and efforts were being made to settle down matters.

The impact of Chinese aggression on India had serious consequences not only on the internal situation of India but also on its foreign policy. Internally the invasion led to economic imbalance and inflation along with mounting taxes. More serious effects of Chinese invasion were on India's foreign policy. First of all it put forward the need for India's defence requirements. Before 1962 the Non-alignment movement was not linked up with defence concerns. After this aggression, top priority was given to defence arrangements. Military assistance was taken from all countries and a clear distinction was maintained between China and other Communist countries. In spite of Chinese aggression non-alignment was not given up. On the international level Soviet Union distanced itself from China.

Section II

OBJECTIVE QUESTIONS WITH ANSWERS

SET I

Questions

1. The Pallava-Dynasty was destroyed by:
(a) The later Chalukyas (b) The Rashtrakutas
(c) The Pandyas (d) Cholas

2. The main contribution of the Pallavas towards the history of South India was
(a) Establishment of a system of administration similar to that of the Mauryas and the Guptas in the North
(b) Emphasis on local-self-government
(c) Patronage to Hinduism
(d) Extension of Aryan culture in the South

3. The highest seat of learning within the kingdom of the Pallavas was:
(a) Madura (b) Kanchi
(c) Mamallapuram (d) Mahabalipuram

4. The language which was patronized by the Pallavas was:
(a) Kannada (b) Tamil
(c) Telugu (d) Sanskrit

5. The finest specimen of Pallava-architecture are
(a) Temples at Madura
(b) Temples at Tanjore
(c) Kailashnath temple at Ellora
(d) Rock-cut Rath temples at Mamallapuram

6. Who, among the following Pallava rulers, defected the Chalukya king, Pulakesan II and occupied his capital, Badami?
(a) Mahendra Varman I (b) Narasinha Varman I
(c) Mahendra Varman II (d) Paramesvara Varman I

7. We do not find republican states in India during
(a) Buddha-age (b) Pre-Mauryan age
(c) Pre-Gupta age (d) Pre-Harshvardhan age

8. Which, among the following methods, was NOT the one adopted by the Republics in Ancient India to elect the representatives of the people?
(a) Only Kshatriya families were given the right to frame laws and elect the members of the executive

(b) Only heads of the joint families were given these rights
(c) All adult males and females were given this right
(d) All adult males were given this right

9. The Republics in Ancient India were finally finished by:
(a) The Mauryas (b) The Kushanas
(c) The Guptas (d) Emperor Harshvardhan

10. Who among the following historians, has contended that the last empire builders in India were Pratiharas?
(a) V A. Smith (b) Iswari Prasad
(c) R.C. Mazumdar (d) Dashratha Sharma

11. Between 8th to 10th century a tripartite contest took place for the capture of Kanauj among the three ruling dynasties of India. Which, among the following, was NOT one of them
(a) The Palas (b) The Chalukyas
(c) The Pratiharas (d) The Rashtrakutas

12. The one distance results of the tripartite contest between the Palas, Pratiharas and the Rashtrakutas was:
(a) The economy of India was shattered
(b) India could not be united politically
(c) It encouraged the Turks to invade India
(d) It led to the rise of regional states in North India

13. Which one of the following was the capital of the Rashtrakutas?
(a) Kanchi (b) Badami
(c) Malbhad (d) Vengi

14. Which, among the following constituted the strongest part of the army of the Pratiharas?
(a) War-elephants (b) War-chariots
(c) Infantry (d) Cavalry

15. Who among the following Pratihara rulers, was defeated by the Rashtrakuta ruler Govind III
(a) Vatsraja (b) Nagabhatta II
(c) Mihirbhoja (d) Mahipala

16. Who, among the following Pratihara rulers, succeeded most against his hereditary enemies the Palas and the Rashtrakutas:
(a) Nagabhatta II (b) Mihirbhoja
(c) Mahendrapala I (d) Mahipala

17. The main contribution of the Pratiharas towards Indian history was:
(a) Progress of Sanskrit literature
(b) Construction of huge temples
(c) Revival of Hinduism
(d) Checking of Arab-invasions beyond Sind

18. Who, among the following rulers, was the founder ruler of the Pala dynasty in Bengal:
(a) Gopala (b) Dharmapala
(c) Devapala (d) Vigrahpala I

19. Who, among the following Pala rulers, established the famous university of Vikramsila:
(a) Dharmapala (b) Devapala
(c) Narayanapala (d) Mahipala 1
20. Who, among the following Pala rulers, succeeded most against his enemies-the Pratiharas and the Rashtrakutas:
(a) Devapala (b) Mahipala I
(c) Nayapala (d) Mahipala II
21. The Palas of Bengal patronized:
(a) Hinduism (b) Jainism
(c) Hinayana Buddhism (d) Tantrika Buddhism
22. The Sena-rulers of Bengal patronized:
(a) Hinduism (b) Jainism
(c) Mahayana Buddhism (d) Tantrika Buddhism
23. The author of Gita-govinda was:
(a) Halayudha (b) Jayadeva
(c) Kalhana (d) Jona-raja
24. The most authentic record of the history of Kashmir has been found in:
(a) Rajatarangini
(b) The description of Al-Beruni
(c) The description of Arab-settlers
(d) Buddhist-text
25. The author of Rajatarangini was:
(a) Kalhana (b) Jona-raja
(c) Halayudha (d) Jayadeva
26. The greatest Paramara ruler of Malwa, Bhoj has been regarded as one of the greatest ruler of medieval India because of:
(a) His conquest only
(b) His contribution towards line arts
(c) His patronage of scholars
(d) Being himself a scholar and author of several books
27. The one unique feature of the polity of Rajput age was:
(a) Centralization of administration
(b) Extensive powers to provincial governors
(c) Local self-government
(d) Extensive use of Jagirdari-system or feudalism
28. The forts were constructed by the rulers of India during the Rajput age primarily for the purpose of
(a) Offence against an enemy
(b) Defence against an enemy
(c) Keeping hold over a territory
(d) Personal and family's Security
29. The one important item of import which was scarce in India was during the Rajput age was:

(a) Gold (b) Silver
(c) Cloth (d) Horse

30. During the Rajput age, interdining and inter-caste marriages were possible among
(a) Brahmins and Kshatriyas (b) Kshatriyas and Vaisays
(c) Vaisyas and Sudras (d) None

31. The author of Hamir Mahakavya was:
(a) Chand Bardai (b) Jayasingha Suri
(c) Nayachanda Sur (d) Hemachandra

32. The famous astrologer of the Rajput age was:
(a) Vagabhatt (b) Vachaspati
(c) Haradatt (d) Bhaskaracharya

33. The Nagar style of architecture developed mostly in:
(a) South India (b) North India
(c) North-West India (d) North-East India

34. The Vesara style of architecture is also known as:
(a) The Chalukyan Style (b) The Chola Style
(c) The Pallava Style (d) The Pandya Style

35. The Sun temple at Konark is in the state of
(a) Orissa (b) Kashmir
(c) Madhya Pradesh (d) Rajasthan

36. Which temple has been described by V.A. Smith as "the most extensive and sumptuous of rock-cut shrines and the most marvellous architectural freak in India?
(a) The Rath temples at Mamallapuram
(b) The Kailash temple at Ellora
(c) The Chaturbhuja-Vishnu temple at Khajuraho
(d) The Kailash-temple at Kanchi

37. The influence of Tantrikism is most prominent on the images of the temples at:
(a) Bhuvanesvara (b) Khajuraho
(c) Tanjore (d) Kanchi

38. The 56 feet high image of Gomtesvara is in:
(a) Tanjore (b) Mysore
(c) Gangaikondacholapuram (d) Belur

39. Which, among the following, was not a reason for the deteriorating condition of the society during the Rajput-age?
(a) Supremacy of the Brahmins
(b) Absence of progressive legislation
(c) Existence of feudalism
(d) Lack of mass-education

40. Which among the following, was NOT a seat of learning during the Rajput age?
(a) Vikramsila (b) Vallabhi
(c) Mathura (d) Kanchi

41. Which, among the following scholarly works, was NOT written by Bhavabhuti?
(a) Venisanhara (b) Mahavir-Charita
(c) Uttar-Ram-Charita (d) Malti-Madhava

42. Which, among the following, scholarly works, was NOT written by Kshemandra
(a) Vrahatakatha-Manjari (b) Dasavatara-charita
(c) Kdla-Vilasa (d) Srikandh-charita
43. Who, among the following, wrote Prithviraja-Raso?
(a) Amara-Singh (b) Yadava
(c) Chandra Baradai (d) Jaya Singh Sura
44. Which, among the following temples, does not exist in South India?
(a) Minakshi temple (b) Sangameswara temple
(c) Rajarajeswara temple (d) Cholesvara temple
45. Which, among the following, temples do NOT exist in north India?
(a) Lingraja (b) Konark Temple
(c) Chaturbhuja Temple (d) Korangnath Temple
46. Which among the following ruling dynasties, became a first rate naval power in South India?
(a) The Pallavas (b) The Hoysalas
(c) Pandyas (d) The Cholas
47. The one conspicuous feature of the social life under the Cholas was:
(a) Absence of Purdah (b) Inter-caste marriages
(c) Devdasi-system (d) Women could own property
48. The language which was patronized by the Chola rulers was:
(a) Sanskrit (b) Tamil
(c) Telugu (d) Kannada
49. The Rajarajeswara temple of Tanjore was constructed by:
(a) Rajaraja the Great (b) Rajendra I
(c) Rajadhiraja I (d) Vikram Chola
50. The chief feature of the temples constructed by the Cholas was their
(a) Gopurams (b) Vimanas
(c) Halls for the devotees (d) Massive pillars
51. Who was the Ghaznavid ruler who fought against Jayapala
(a) Alptigin (b) Ismail
(c) Sabuktigin (d) Mahmud
52. Who among the Brahmana Shahis got converted to Islam and later abjured it?
(a) Anandapala (b) Jayapala
(c) Trilochanapala (d) Sukhpala
53. Which of the following combinations is incorrect?
(a) Samanta -Gurjara Pratiharas
(b) Kallar -Shanis
(c) Govinda III -Rashtrakutas
(d) Yasovarman I -Chandella
54. Who founded the Simha era?
(a) Mularaja (b) Bhimadeva I
(c) Karnadeva (d) Jayasimha Siddharaja
55. Who among the following patronised Hemachandra?
(a) Karnadeva (b) Jayasimha Siddharaja
(c) Mularaja (d) Ajaya

56. What is the meaning of Paramara?
(a) Conqueror of the enemy (b) Slayer of the enemy
(c) A virtuous man (d) An-immortal

57. Who was the founder of the dynasty (Malwa)
(a) Upendra (b) Harsha Siyaka II
(c) Vakpati II (d) Sindhuraja

58. Who among the Paramaras was the hero of any anecdotes narrated in 'Prabandha Chintamani'?
(a) Vakpatiraja II Munjs (b) Harsha Sikya II
(c) Bhoja I (d) Sindhuraja

59. Who established a college for Sanskrit studies at Dhar?
(a) Sindhuraja (b) Bhoja I
(c) Vakpatiraja II (d) Arjunavarman

60. Identify the correct chronological sequence:
(a) Lakshmi-Karna, Vijayasimhadeva, Yasah Karna, Gangeyadeva Vikramaditya
(b) Gangeyadeva Vikramaditya, Lakshmi Karna, Yasah-Kama, Vijyasimhadeva
(c) 'Yasah-Karns, Gangeyadeva Vikramaditya, Vijyasimhadeva, Lakshmi-Karna
(d) Gangeyadeva Vikramaditya, Yasah-Kama, Vijyasimhadeva, Lakshmi-Karna

61. Who founded the Chandella dynasty of Budelkhand?
(a) Jayasakti (b) Yasovarman
(c) Dhanga (d) Nannuka

62. To which of the original clan are the Chandellas of Bundelkhand said to be related?
(a) Gonds (b) Santals
(c) Kols (d) Mundas

63. Name the Pala who made the Pala dynasty a force in north Indian politics.
(a) Dharampala (b) Mahipala
(c) Gopala (d) Vigrahapala

64. Who introduced Kulinism among the Brahmins?
(a) Vijya Sena (b) Hemanta Sena
(c) Samanta Sena (d) Vallala Sena

65. Who said that his name should go down in history not as idol seller but as idol breaker?
(a) Muhammad of Ghur (b) Mahmud of Ghazni
(c) Ala-ud-din Khalji (d) Muhammad bin Qasim

66. Who among the following bore the other name Muiz-ud-din Muhammad bin Sam?
(a) Muhmud of Ghazni (b) Qutub-ud-din
(c) Ghiyas-ud-din (d) Muhammad Ghori

67. Who were the Yaminis?
(a) Khaljis (b) Ghurids
(c) Ghaznavids (d) Tughluqs

68. Who said that the Rashtrakutas were the most feared rulers of India?
(a) Utbi (b) Al-Beruni
(c) Al-Kazwini (d) Sulaiman

69. Which among the following did not contribute significantly for the final disintegration of the Cholas?
(a) Hoysalas (b) Pandyas
(c) Kakatiyas (d) Yadavas

70. Who built the Brihadesvara temple?
(a) Parantaka I (b) Rajaraja I
(c) Rajendra I (d) Rajaraja II

71. Which inscription gives details of election to village assembly?
(a) Tiruvalalgadu plates (b) Uttaramerur inscription
(c) Velvikkudi grant (d) Anbil grant

72. Which one of the following cannot be attributed to the Lingayats?
(a) Worship of Siva
(b) Belief in rebirth
(c) Rejection of the authorities
(d) Aversion to the Brahmanas

73. To which of the following did Kannada literature owe much?
(a) Brahmanism (b) Jainism
(c) Buddhism (d) Virasaivism

74. Which of the following was the capital of Eastern Gangas?
(a) Konarak (b) Mukhalingam
(c) Bhuvaneswar (d) Puri

75. Who were the 'Sevunas'?
(a) Pallavas (b) Western Gangas
(c) Yadavas of Devagiri (d) Eastern Chalukyas of Vengi

76. What is meant by 'the Forty'?
(a) Cream of Afghan nobles (b) Peak of the intellectuals
(c) Body of 'Turkish aristocracy' (d) The Muslim divines

77. Which is the most appropriate way of describing the rulers of Delhi between 1206 and 1290?
(a) Slave dynasty (b) Mamluka
(c) Ilbarites (d) Early Turkish Sultans

78. Who built Quwwat-ul-Islam?
(a) Qutb-ud-din (b) Iltutmish
(c) Balban (d) Raziyya

79. Who among the following, according to the Historian, "shed more innocent blood than a Pharaoh was guilty of"?
(a) Ghazi Malik (b) Balban.
(c) Ala-ud-din Khalji (d) Jalal-ud-din Firuz

80. Who was called the Lakh Baksha?
(a) Iltutmish (b) Qutb-ud-din Aibak
(c) Jalal-ud-din Khalji (d) Aram Shah

81. Who were called the Neo-Muslims?
(a) Hindu converts (b) Mongol converts
(c) Turkish converts (d) Persian converts

82. One of the following cannot be attributed to Ala-ud-din
(a) Siri Fort (b) Hazar Sutun
(c) Hauz-i-Khas (d) Purana Quila
83. Which one of these was built by Ala-ud-din Khalji?
(a) Alai Darwaza (b) Buland Darwaza
(c) Lal Quila (d) Qutb Minar
84. Which of the following cities was renamed Khizrabad?
(a) Ranthambhor (b) Chittor
(c) Jalor (d) Jhain
85. What was the original name of Ala-ud-din Khalji?
(a) Ali Gurshasp (b) Jafar Khan
(c) Alp Khan (d) Chajju
86. What was the religion of Malik Kafur before he entered the service of Ala-ud-din?
(a) Zoroastrianism (b) Hinduism
(c) Buddhism (d) Jainism
87. Which one of the following was NOT the work of Amir Khusrau?
(a) Tarikhi-i-Alai (b) Tarikhi-i-Firuzshahi
(c) Tughlug Nama (d) Ashiqua
88. Ala-ud-din attributed four causes for the rebellion's of the nobles. One of the following is not true. Identify.
(a) Use of wine (b) Sultan's neglect
(c) Intimacy among nobles (d) Poverty
89. "Daulatabad was a monument of misdirection energy". Who said this?
(a) Stanley Lene-Poole (b) Vincent A. Smith
(c) Ishwari Prasad (d) Eliot and Dowson
90. Who, among the following Sultans did not take the royal title?
(a) Khusrav Khan (b) Jalal-ud-din Khalji
(c) Khizr Khan (d) Buhlul Khan Lodi
91. The First Pathan State in Delhi was established by
(a) Al-ud-din Alam Shah (b) Buhlul Lodi
(c) Balban (d) Khizr Khan
92. Who among the following ransacked Delhi in 1398?
(a) Targhi (b) Timur
(c) Chingiz Khan (d) Hulagu Khan
93. Who founded Agra?
(a) Sikander Lodi (b) Khizr Khan
(c) Ala-ud-din (d) Ibrahim Lodi
94. One of the following was NOT a foreign visitor of India.
(a) Albu Abdullah Muhammad (b) Al-Beruni
(c) I'-tsing (d) Al-Qalqashandi
95. The founder of Warangal was
(a) Prola II (b) Pratapparudra I
(c) Mahadeva (d) Rudra I

96. Who is the author of Kathasarita-sagara?
    (a) Ilhana (b) Somadeva
    (c) Kalhana (d) Hemachandra
97. Who is the author of Gaudavadha (Gaudavaho)?
    (a) Vakpatiraja (b) Bhavabhuti
    (c) Bhartrihari (d) Rajasekhara
98. Among the places mentioned below no college existed in the Chola period. Identify.
    (a) Ennayiram (b) Tribhuvanam
    (c) Tiruvaduthurai (d) Tiruchi
99. Pick out the wrong match.
    (a) Guhilas Mewar
    (b) Kachchhapaghatas Gwalior
    (c) Loharas Kashmir
    (d) Pralamba Nepal
100. What is Vesara?
    (a) an art style (b) a literary piece
    (c) a painting (d) a work on music

Answers

1. (d)	21. (d)	41. (a)	61. (d)	81. (a)
2. (d)	22. (a)	42. (d)	62. (a)	82. (d)
3. (c)	23. (b)	43. (c)	63. (a)	83. (a)
4. (d)	24. (a)	44. (b)	64. (d)	84. (b)
5. (d)	25. (a)	45. (d)	65. (b)	85. (a)
6. (b)	26. (d)	46. (d)	66. (d)	86. (b)
7. (d)	27. (d)	47. (d)	67. (c)	87. (b)
8. (c)	28. (b)	48. (b)	68. (d)	88. (d)
9. (c)	29. (d)	49. (a)	69. (d)	89. (a)
10. (c)	30. (d)	50. (b)	70. (b)	90. (c)
11. (b)	31. (b)	51. (c)	71. (b)	91. (b)
12. (d)	32. (d)	52. (d)	72. (b)	92. (b)
13. (c)	33. (b)	53. (a)	73. (d)	93. (a)
14. (d)	34. (a)	54. (d)	74. (b)	94. (d)
15. (b)	35. (a)	55. (b)	75. (c)	95. (b)
16. (b)	36. (b)	56. (b)	76. (c)	96. (b)
17. (d)	37. (a)	57. (a)	77. (d)	97. (a)
18. (a)	38. (b)	58. (a)	78. (a)	98. (d)
19. (a)	39. (d)	59. (b)	79. (c)	99. (d)
20. (a)	40. (c)	60. (b)	80. (d)	100. (a)

SET II

Questions

1. Among the images constructed during the rule of the Cholas, the most famous are:
   (a) Stone images (b) Marble-images
   (c) Images carved out of rocks (d) Images of Nataraja
2. Who, among the following Hoysala rulers, was persuaded to forsake Jainism and instead embrace Vaishnavism by saint Ramanuja:
   (a) Ballal I (b) Ballal II
   (c) Vishnuvardhan (d) Rajadhiraja I
3. "It is the touchstone of Indian architecture as a whole." Who, among the following scholars has opined thus regarding the Rajarajesvara temple at Tanjore"?
   (a) VA. Smith (b) Percy Brown
   (c) Prof Furgusson (d) Dr. K.A. Nilakanta Sastri
4. Which among the following, was NOT one of the administrative measures of Rajaraja?
   (a) Measurement of land (b) Incentive to agriculture
   (c) Incentive to local institutions (d) Centralisation of administration
5. When Rajendra Chola I established his new capital, Gangaikondacholapuram?
   (a) After his conquest over the Pandyas
   (b) After his conquest of Sri Lanka
   (c) After his successful campaign in the North
   (d) After completing his Asvamedha yajna
6. Which, among the following, was not conquered by Rajendra Chola I?
   (a) Pandya and Chera (b) Sri Lanka
   (c) Sailendra-empire (d) Chalukas of Kalyani
7. The primary reason of Rajendra Chola I in attacking north India was:
   (a) To take revenge (b) To bring the water of holy Ganges
   (c) To capture territory in the North (d) To demonstrate his strength
8. What, among the following, was the status of Rajguru in the Chola-administration?
   (a) He was the teacher of royal princes (b) He was the chief-minister
   (c) He was the priest of the king
   (d) He was the advisor of the king in all matters
9. Which, among the following, did not constitute a part of the army of the Cholas?
   (a) Navy (b) War-elephants

(c) Chariots (d) Cavalry

10. Which, among the following, was not the one among the representative assemblies under the rule of the Cholas?
    (a) Ur (b) Mahasabha
    (c) Nagaram (d) Variyam
11. Who, among the following historians, has described that Mahmud invaded India seventeen times?
    (a) Sir Henry Elliot (b) Elphinstone
    (c) V.A. Smith (d) Iswari Prasad
12. Who, among the following scholars, has remarked that "the Hindu believed that there is no country like theirs, no nation like theirs, no king like theirs, no religion like theirs, no science like theirs"?
    (a) Al-Beruni (b) Firdausi
    (c) Firishta (d) Utbi
13. The Most effective achievement of Mahmud's invasions was:
    (a) Plunder of Indian wealth
    (b) Entry of Islam in India
    (c) Destruction of Hindushahi kingdom
    (d) Establishment of Muslim rule in India
14. The famous temple of Somanath on the coast of Kathiawar was attacked by Mahmud of Ghazani in:
    (a) 1021 (b) 1024
    (c) 1026 (d) 1030
15. The first ruler of India who defeated Muhammad of Ghur was:
    (a) Mularaja II (b) Prithviraja Chauhan
    (c) Jayachanda (d) Paramaldeva
16. The 2nd battle of Tarain between Muhammad of Ghur and Prithviraja Chauhan was fought in
    (a) 1190 (b) 1191
    (c) 1192 (d) 1193
17. Among the officers of Muhammad of Ghur, Bihar and part of Bengal were conquered by:
    (a) Qutb-ud-din Aibak (b) Tajuddin Yildiz
    (c) Muhammad Bakhtiyar Khalji (d) Tughril Khan
18. The Capital of Qutb-ud-din Aibak remained:
    (a) Lahore (b) Delhi
    (c) Ajmer (d) Lakknauti
19. Qutb-ud-din Aibak died while:
    (a) Fighting against the Knokhars (b) Fighting against Taj-ud-din Yildiz
    (c) Fighting against Khwarizam Shah Ala-ud-din Muhammad
    (d) Playing Chaugan
20. Iltutmish became the Sultan of Delhi because he was:
    (a) The son of Qutb-ud-din Aibak
    (b) Son-in-law of Qutb-ud-din Aibak
    (c) The nobles at Delhi chose him to be so
    (d) The nobles at Lahore chose him to be so

21. Iltutmish was the first legal Turk-sultan of Delhi because he got the sanction of his title from:
(a) The Sultan of Gur (b) The Caliph
(c) The Sultan of Ghazni (d) All nobles of Delhi

22. The Mongol leader who threatened the safety of the Turkish rule in India during the rule of Iltutmish was:
(a) Chingiz Khan (b) Halaku
(c) Jalaluddin Mangbarni (d) Tajuddin Yildiz

23. Who, among the following historians, has NOT accepted Iltutmish as the greatest ruler of the slave-dynasty?
(a) Dr. A.L. Srivastav (b) Dr. Ishwari Prasad
(c) Sir Woolsely Haig (d) Dr. S.R. Sharma

24. "It was he who gave the country a capital, an independent state, a monarchial form of government and a governing class."
Who, among the following historians, has expressed thus concerning Sultan Iltutmish?
(a) Dr. A.B.M. Habibullah (b) Dr. A.L. Srivastav
(c) Dr K.A. Nizami (d) Dr. Partamtam Saran

25. The group of 'Forty' who contested for state power against the Sultan after the death of Iltutmish were:
(a) Turkish slaves of Sultan Iltutmish
(b) Free Turkish nobles of Sultan Iltutmish
(c) Foreign Muslim nobles belonging to different nationalities
(d) Converted Indian Muslim nobles

26. Raziyya became the Sultana of Delhi after deposing her brother:
(a) Rukn-ud-din Firoz Shah (b) Muizzuddin Bahram Shah
(c) Jala-ud-din Masud Shah (d) Nasir-ud-din Mahmud Shah

27. The group of 'Forty' nobles was finally destroyed by:
(a) Bahram Shah (b) Alauddin Masud Shah
(c) Nasiruddin Mahmud (d) Balban

28. Who, among the following Mamluk Sultans of Delhi, declared himself in favour of divine theory of kingship?
(a) Iltutmish (b) Firuz Shah
(c) Raziyya (d) Balban

29. Who, among the following historians, has opined that Balban ascended the throne of Delhi after getting murdered Sultan Nasir-ud-din Muhmud Shah?
(a) Dr. A.L. Srivastava (b) Dr. A.B.M. Habibullah
(c) Sir Woolsely Haig (d) Dr. K.A.Nizami

30. The dynasty of Balban was replaced by.
(a) The Khaljis (b) the Tughlaqs
(c) The Sayyids (d) The Lodhis

31. 'The accession of Jalaluddin Firoz Shah Khalji ushered a new era in the history of the Delhi Sultanate.' Which, among the following facts, can be given in support of this statement?
(a) The rule of the Khaljis marked the zenith of Muslim imperialism in India during their rule of the Delhi Sultanate

(b) It marked the end of the Turkish rule in India
(c) It marked the beginning of large scale changes in the administrative set up
(d) It marked the beginning of association of the Indian Muslims in the administration

32. The lone conquest during the reign of Jalaluddin Khaliji was that of
(a) Ranthambhor (b) Mandawar
(c) Bhilsa (d) Devagiri

33. Sutan Jalalauddin Firuz Shah Khalji was killed:
(a) In his campaign against Ranthambhor
(b) By his nobles at the court
(c) By his own nephew
(d) By his own son

34. Which, among the following was not the primary aim of Ala-ud-din Khalji in introducing agrarian reforms?
(a) Safeguard the peasants from the oppression of hereditary tax collectors, viz. Chaudhry Khuts, Muqaddam etc.
(b) Eliminate corruption from the revenue department
(c) Welfare of his sub
(d) Enhance the financial resources of the state

35. "The policy was suicidal for it killed the goose that laid the golden egg. It left no incentive for increasing the produce or improving method of cultivation." Who, among the following scholars, has remarked thus concerning the revenue reform of Ala-ud-din Khalji?
(a) Dr. S. Roy (b) Dr. A.L. Srivastav
(c) Dr. Tara Chand (d) Dr. K.S.Lal

36. Which, among the following, was the primary cause in collecting revenue in kind instead of cash?
(a) The revenue could be collected promptly
(b) It provided convenience to the peasants
(c) Revenue was not affected due to fluctuations in prices
(d) It was necessary for the success of his market system

37. The new taxes which were imposed by Ala-ud-din on the peasants were
(a) Jijya and Zakat (b) House-tax and grazing-tax
(c) Irrigation tax and sales-tax (d) Salt tax and Toll tax

38. The abolition of the privileges of the officers like Khuts, Chaudhris and Muqaddamas was NOT with a view:
(a) To enhance the income of the state
(b) To eliminate the causes of the revolt of the Hindus
(c) To get converts to Islam
(d) To reduce the social and economic status of these officers

39. Which, among the following was NOT a part of military-reforms of Alauddin?
(a) Maintaining a standing army at the centre
(b) Cash payment to the soldiers
(c) Abolition of the forces of provincial governors
(d) Branding of the horses and keeping *huliya* of the soldiers

40. Which, among the following was NOT one of the causes of the market-system introduced by Ala-ud-din Khalji?

(a) To reduce the cost of all necessary articles in the capital
(b) To maintain a large standing army at the centre at lower cost
(c) To provide better facilities of life to his subjects at a cheaper cost
(d) To stop speculation and black-marketing in the capital by the traders

41. Who, among the following modern historians, has argued that the primary aim of Ala-ud-din in introducing his market system was not to pay less salary to his soldiers but to reduce the cost of articles?
(a) U.N. Day (b) K.S. Lal
(c) A.L. Srivastava (d) K.A. Nizami

42. The first Muslim commander who attacked South India was:
(a) Ala-ud-din Khalji (b) Malik Kafur
(c) Nusrat Khan (d) Muhammad Tughluq

43. The Commander of Ala-ud-din who subjugated the States of South India was,
(a) Malik Kafur (b) Nusrat Khan
(c) Ulugh Khan (d) Alp Khan

44. The primary aim of Ala-ud-din's policy towards South India was:
(a) Annexation of territory (b) Plunder of wealth
(c) Propagation of Islam (d) Protection of his territory

45. The first kingdom of South India that was attacked by Malik Kafur was:
(a) Devagiri (b) Telingana
(c) Hoysala (d) Pandya

46. The only state of South India which did not accept the sovereignty of Ala-ud-din was:
(a) Devagiri (b) Telingana
(c) Hoysala (d) Pandya

47. Which, among the following causes, was Not responsible for the defeat of the States of the South India against Ala-ud-din Khalji?
(a) The failure of the States of the South to unite among themselves against Ala-ud-din Khalji
(b) Neglect of their frontiers
(c) Ala-ud-din's better military resources
(d) Their weaker economic resources

48. Who, among the notable commanders of Ala-ud-din Khalji, died fighting the Mongols?
(a) Zafar Khan (b) Nusrat Khan
(c) Alp Khan (d) Ulugh Khan

49. The Khalji empire proved short-lived because:
(a) Ala-ud-din was not a good administrator
(b) The army organization of Ala-ud-din suffered from certain inherent defects
(c) Hindu rulers became independent after the death of Ala-ud-din
(d) Ala-ud-din's son, Mubarak Shah, was an unworthy successor to the throne

50. Which among the following causes, was NOT responsible for the failure of the measure of issuing the token currency by Muhammad Tughluq?
(a) The people started minting coins in their own houses
(b) The Sultan issued such coins which could be copied

(c) The people started hoarding silver coins
(d) The measure was not successfully attempted in any part of the world at that time.

51. All measures of Muhammad Tughluq to bring about internal reforms failed because:
(a) The measures were wrong in principle
(b) The people were not prepared to accept his new innovations
(c) The measures were out of date
(d) Lack of practical wisdom of the Sultan

52. Who, among the contemporary historians, described that Muhammad Tughluq had a son whom Firuz got murdered?
(a) Badayuni (b) Barani
(c) Shams-i-Shraj Afif (d) Ibn Batuta

53. The Delhi Sultanate collapsed:
(a) During the reign of Muhammad Tughluq
(b) After the death of Muhammad Tughluq
(c) During the reign of Firuz Tughluq
(d) After the death of Firuz Tughluq

54. Who, among the following historians, has argued that Firuz aspired to captured the throne in league with those sections of influential people who were dissatisfied with the policies of Muhammad Tughluq and desired changes in them?
(a) U. N. Dey (b) A.L. Srivastava
(c) K.S.Lal (d) Iswari Prasad

55. Firuz Tughluq changed the very nature of polity upheld by Ala-ud-din Khalji and Muhammad Tughluq by:
(a) Decentralization of administration
(b) Abandoning the polity of the extension of the empire
(c) Converting the Delhi Sultanate into a theocratic state
(d) Seeking cooperation of all sections of the Muslims in administration

56. The one solid achievement of Firuz Tughluq was:
(a) Restoration of the prestige of Islam
(b) Restoration of the prestige, of the Delhi Sultanate
(c) Recovery of the lost provinces of the Delhi Sultanate
(d) Economic prosperity

57. Who, among the following historians, has commented: "The reign of Firuz closes the most brilliant epoch of Muslim rule in India before the reign of Akbar"?
(a) Sir Woolsely Haiq (b) V.A. Smith
(c) Iswari Prasad (d) R.C. Mazumdar

58. Who, among the following historians, has commented thus about the character of Firuz : "He was a typical product of his age, ambitious and shrewd enough to wear a mask of disinterestedness"?
(a) K.S. Lal (b) U.N. Dey
(c) K.A. Nizami (d) R.P Tripathi

59. The attack of Timur (Tamerlane):
(a) Led to the dismemberment of the Delhi Sultanate
(b) Destroyed the prestige of the Delhi Sultanate

(c) Led to the establishment of the rule of the Sayyid dynasty at Delhi
(d) Destroyed the military power of the Tughluqs

60. The Delhi Sultanate once enjoyed the most extensive territories during the reign of:
(a) Ala-ud-din Khalji (b) Mubarak Shah Khalji
(c) Ghiyasuddin Tughluq (d) Muhammad-bin-Tughluq

61. The dismemberment of the Delhi Sultanate began during the reign of:
(a) Mubarak Shah Khalji (b) Muhammad Bin Tughluq
(c) Firuz Tughluq (d) Successors of Firuz Tughluq

62. Who, among the following historians has remarked: "the Saiyyads (Sayyids) could make no positive contribution to the kingship or to the system of civil administration"?
(a) Khizr Khan (b) Mubarak Khan
(c) Muhammad Shah (d) Alauddin Alam Shah

63. The first battel of Panipat between Ibrahim Lodi and the Mughal ruler Babar took place in the year:
(a) 1525 (b) 1526
(c) 1527 (d) 1528

64. Which, among the following, can NOT be accepted as a consequence of Mongol invasions during the period of the Delhi Sultanate?
(a) Maintenance of large armies by powerful Sultans
(b) Attempt to establish despotic rule by powerful Sultans
(c) Failure to pursue the policy of the extension of the empire by most sultans
(d) Failure to influence Hindu culture by the Muslims

65. The nature of the policy before the period of the Delhi Sultanate differed from that of the Delhi Sultanate primarily in:
(a) Centralisation of administration
(b) Bureaucratic set-up
(c) Powers granted to provincial governors
(d) Non-acceptance of any religion as religion of the State

66. The only Sultan who declared himself Caliph was:
(a) Ala-ud-din Khalji (b) Mubarak Shah Khalji
(c) Khusrav Shah (d) Muhammad Bin Tughluq

67. Who, among the following ministers of the Sultan, looked after the organisation of the army?
(a) The Naib-i-mamlikat (b) The Wazir
(c) The ariz-i-mumalik (d) The Dabir-i-khas

68. Who, among the following officers of the Sultan, was the head of the royal bodyguards?
(a) Vakil-i-dar mahal (b) Barabak
(c) Amir-i-hajib (d) Sar-i-jandar

69. Which, among the following facts is NOT correct about the creation of different departments by various Sultans?
(a) Diwan-i-Arz was created by Balban
(b) Diwan-i-Mustakhraj was created by Alauddin

(c) Diwan-i-kohli was created by Muhammad Tughluq
(d) Diwan-i-Khairat was created by Sikander Lodi

70. The only Sultan of Delhi who exempted his subjects from nearly 24 taxes was:
(a) Mubarak Shah Khalji (b) Ghiyasuddin Tughluq
(c) Firuz Tughluq (d) Sikander Lodi

71. The weakest section of the military organisation of the Sultans of Delhi was their:
(a) Artillery (b) Elephant-force
(c) Cavalry (d) Infantry

72. The ruler of Kashmir who earned the title of But-Shikan or 'idol-breaker' was:
(a) Shamshuddin Shah (b) Shihabuddin Shah
(c) Qutubuddin Shah (d) Sikander Shah

73. The greatest ruler of Kashmir who has also been called 'the Akbar of Kashmir' was:
(a) Ali Shah (b) Zain-ul-Abidin
(c) Haider Shah (d) Mirza Haider

74. The Jaunpuri or the Sharqi style of architecture developed during the reign of:
(a) Mubarak Shah (b) Shamsuddin Ibrahim Shah
(c) Mahmud Shah (d) Husain Shah

75. The kingdom of Jaunpur was annexed to the Delhi Sultanate after the defeat of:
(a) Mubarak Shah Sharqi (b) Ibrahim Shah Sharqi
(c) Mahmud Shah Sharqi (d) Husain Shah Sharqi

76. Among the governors of the Sultan of Delhi at Bengal the one who assumed the title of Sultan first was:
(a) Bakhtiyar Khalji (b) Husamuddin Iwaz Khalji
(c) Ikhtiyaruddin Balka Khalji (d) Malik Alauddin lain

77. Who, among the following historians, has expressed the view that Ala-ud-din Khalji attempted to conquer Bengal but failed?
(a) Dr. K.S. Lai (b) Dr. Iswari Prasad
(c) Dr.A.L.Srivastav (d) Dr. U.N.Dey

78. Who, among the following rulers of Gujarat, first imposed Tizya on his subjects?
(a) Muzaffar Shah (b) Ahmad Shah I
(c) Ahmad Shah II (d) Mahmud I Begarha

79. Bahadur Shah of Gujarat conquered Malwa. Who among the following was the ruler of Malwa at that time?
(a) Ghiyas Shah (b) Nasir Shah
(c) Mahmud Khalji II (d) Qadir Shah

80. Which, among the following kingdoms, was the bitterest enemy of Gujarat?
(a) Khandesh (b) Mewar
(c) Malwa (d) Marwar

81. Sultan Mahmud of Gujarat earned the nick-name of Begarha because he:
(a) Defeated the ruler of Malwa (b) Defeated the Portuguese
(c) Conquered Girnar and Champaner (d) Killed a tiger single-handed

82. Who, among the following, was the founder ruler of the Khalji-rule in Malwa?
(a) Mohammed Shah Khalji (b) Hushang Shah
(c) Ghiyasuddin Shah (d) Nasiruddin Shah

83. The capital city of Malwa, Mandu was established by its ruler:
(a) Hushangtedin Shah (b) Nasiruddin Shah
(c) Bahadur Shah (d) None of these

84. The Vijaya-Stambha or the Tower of Victory at Chittor was constructed by its ruler:
(a) Rana Hamir Deva (b) Rana Khumblia
(c) Rana Sanga (d) Rana Pratap

85. Rana Kumbha constructed the Vijay-Stambha at Chittor in commemoration of his victory against:
(a) Malwa
(b) Gujarat
(c) Combined forces of Gujarat and Malwa
(d) The forces of Delhi

86. Rana Kumbha proved an illustrious ruler of Rajasthan? However, which among the following fads is NOT correct regarding his accomplishment?
(a) He was a scholar and a good musician
(b) He built nearly thirty two forts in Mewar
(c) He built several temples, reservoirs etc. in Mewar
(d) He was not defeated in any of his battles

87. Who among the following rulers of Bahmani Kingdom of the Deccan, was the first who received the formal sanction of the use of Khutba and Sikkah by Abbasid Caliph of Egypt?
(a) Bahman Shah (b) Muhammad I
(c) Daud Shah (d) Muhammad II

88. Who, among the following Muslim-rulers, was the first one who abolished jizya in the Deccan?
(a) Bahman Shah (b) Muhammad I
(c) Alauddin Mujahid (d) Muhammad Shah II

89. Who, Among the following Bahmani kings, shifted the capital from Gulbarga to Bidar?
(a) Muhammad Shah I (b) Ahmad Shah
(c) Nizam Shah (d) Muhammad Shah II

90. Which among the following rulers of Bahamelti kingdom was nick-named Zalim the Tyrant?
(a) Mujahid Shah (b) Tajuddin Firuz Shah
(c) Humayun (d) Mahmud Shah

91. Who, among the following was the first ruling dynasty of the Vijayanagara empire?
(a) Prolaya Verma (b) Bhaktiraja
(c) Harihara I (d) Bukka

92. Which, among the following, was the first ruling dynasty of the Vijayanagara empire?
(a) The Sangama dynasty (b) The Saluva dynasty
(c) The Taluva dynasty (d) The Aravidu dynasty

93. The Vijyanagar and the Bahamani rulers fought against each other constantly for the possession of:
(a) The kingdom of Madras (b) Konkan
(c) Goa (d) Raichur-doab

94. Abdur Razzak remained as the Persian ambassador at the court of Vijyanagara during the reign of:
(a) Devaraya II (b) Virupaksha II
(c) Sulva Narasingha (d) Krishnadevaraya

95. Who, among the following rulers of Vijayanagra, entered into a treaty with the Portuguese, Almedia for purchasing all the horses imported by him?
(a) Saluva Narsingha (b) Vir Narsingha
(c) Krishnadevarya (d) Achyuta Raya

96. Which, among the following foreigners, described in detail the fortification of the city of Vijayanagara?
(a) Abdur Razzak (b) Nicolo Conti
(c) Duarte Barbosa (d) Domingos Paes

97. Krishnadevaraya, under whom the Vijayanagara empire reached its zenith of power and prosperity belonged to:
(a) Sangama dynasty (b) The Saluva dynasty
(c) Taluva dynasty (d) The Aravidu dynasty

98. The battle of Talikota which led to the destruction of the Vijayanagara empire by the combined armies of Bijapur, Ahmadnagar, Golkonda and Bidar was fought in:
(a) 1555 (b) 1560
(c) 1565 (d) 1570

99. Who, among the following, was the ruler of Vijayanagara-empire when the battle of Talikota was fought?
(a) Sadasivo Raya (b) Rama Raya
(c) Achyuta Raya (d) Tirumala

100. The rule of the kings of Vijayanagara was:
(a) Rule by Council (b) Irresponsible despotism
(c) Benevolent despotism (d) Oligarchical rule

Answers

1. (d)	21. (b)	41. (a)	61. (b)	81. (c)
2. (c)	22. (a)	42. (a)	62. (a)	82. (a)
3. (b)	23. (b)	43. (a)	63. (b)	83. (a)
4. (d)	24. (c)	44. (b)	64. (d)	84. (b)
5. (c)	25. (a)	45. (a)	65. (d)	85. (a)
6. (c)	26. (a)	46. (d)	66. (b)	86. (d)
7. (d)	27. (d)	47. (d)	67. (c)	87. (b)
8. (d)	28. (d)	48. (a)	68. (d)	88. (a)
9. (c)	29. (d)	49. (d)	69. (d)	89. (b)
10. (d)	30. (a)	50. (d)	70. (c)	90. (c)
11. (a)	31. (c)	51. (d)	71. (a)	91. (c)
12. (a)	32. (b)	52. (a)	72. (b)	92. (a)
13. (c)	33. (c)	53. (d)	73. (b)	93. (d)
14. (b)	34. (d)	54. (a)	74. (b)	94. (a)
15. (a)	35. (c)	55. (c)	75. (d)	95. (b)
16. (c)	36. (d)	56. (d)	76. (b)	96. (a)
17. (c)	37. (b)	57. (a)	77. (a)	97. (c)
18. (a)	38. (c)	58. (b)	78. (b)	98. (c)
19. (b)	39. (c)	59. (b)	79. (c)	99. (a)
20. (c)	40. (c)	60. (d)	80. (c)	100. (c)

SET III

Questions

1. The number of the provinces of the Vijayanagara empire was:
(a) Three (b) Four
(c) Five (d) Six

2. Which, among the following was the duty of Mahanayakacharya, in the administration of Vijayanagara?
(a) To supervise the observance of Dharma
(b) To supervise the work of Nayakas
(c) To supervise the village-administration
(d) None of the above

3. For what does the term Athavana stand for?
(a) Land-revenue department (b) Land-revenue
(c) Custom-duties (d) Trade-tax

4. The revenue collected by the rulers of the Vijayanagara empire was:
(a) 1/2 of the produce (b) 1/3 of the produce
(c) 1/4 of the produce (d) 1/5 of the produce

5. Which, among the following, is not correct concerning the administration of justice in the state of Vijayanagara?
(a) Laws were mostly based on tradition and customs
(b) Sometimes disputes were settled by the state officials with the help of local bodies
(c) There were regular courts for administering, justice
(d) Punishment was mostly in form of fines

6. For what did Varam stand for in the Vijayanagara empire?
(a) Dowry given in marriage
(b) A tax imposed by the state
(c) Land-revenue
(d) System of sharing of agriculture-income between the landlord and the tenant

7. The one remarkable change which the Hindus introduced in their society during the later period of the Delhi Sultanate was:
(a) Relaxed observance of casteism
(b) Non-acceptance of slavery

(c) Acceptance of military service under Muslim rulers
(d) Acceptance of conversion of Muslims to Hinduism

8. The social evil which grew among the Hindus concerning women because of the establishment of the Muslim rule in India was:
(a) Sati system (b) Child-marriages
(c) Purdah-system (d) Polygamy

9. The most remarkable feature of Indian foreign sea-trade during the period of the Delhi Sultanate was:
(a) Monopoly over it by the state
(b) Incentive provided to it by the Sultans
(c) Heavy taxes on it
(d) Monopoly of the Arabs and the Persians over transportation of the goods.

10. Who, among the following, were responsible for change in miniature paintings by introducing paper in India by the fifteenth century?
(a) The Turks (b) The Arabs
(c) The Chinese (d) The Portuguese

11. Who, among the following, did not help in the formation of Indo-Islamic music?
(a) Ala-ud-din Khalji (b) Firuz Shah Tughluq
(c) Sikandar Lodi (d) Raja Man Singh

12. The rulers of Delhi Sultanate patronized.
(a) Arabik language (b) Turki language
(c) Persian language (d) Urdu language

13. 'Several Muslim rulers encouraged translation of Sanskrit-texts in Persian' Who, among the following, was not one of them?
(a) Ala-ud-din Khalji (b) Firuz Shah Tughluq
(c) Zain-ul-Abidin of Kashmir (d) Husain Shah of Bengal

14. Which, among the following branches of learning, got impetus by the coming of the Turks in India?
(a) Logic (b) Literature
(c) Astrology (d) History

15. The first notable writer who helped in the growth of Maithili literature was:
(a) Vidyapati Thakur (b) Chand Bardai
(c) Sarangdhar (d) Raghunandan Misra

16. One of the notables and earliest writers of Hindu was:
(a) Chand Bardai (b) Amir Khusrau
(c) Namadeva (d) Nanak

17. Who, among the following scholars at the court of Sultan Iltutmish wrote Lubato-ul-Albab?
(a) Khawaja Abu Nasr (b) Abu Babar bin Muhammad
(c) Taj-ud-din Dabir (d) Nur-ud-din Muhammad Aufi

18. Who, among the following, was the author of "Tabqati-i-Nasiri"?
(a) Minhaj-ud-din Siraz (b) Rafi-ud-din Shiraz
(c) Shaikh Abdulla (d) Yahiya-bin-Ahmad

19. Who, among the following, was the author of Tarikh-i-Mubarakshahi?
(a) Shaikh Azizulla (b) Shaikh Jamal-ud-din
(c) Fazlullah Zain-ul-Abidin (d) Yahiya-bin-Ahmad
20. Who, among the following, was the author of Fatwah-i-Jahangiri
(a) Sayyid Muin-ul-huq (b) Ibrahim Farukhi
(c) Khawaja Abu Malik Isami (d) Zia-ud-din Barani
21. Prataprudradeva-Yashabhusan, describing the glory of Prataprudradeva, ruler of Telingana was written in Sanskrit language by:
(a) Agastaya (b) Vidya Chakravartin
(c) Madhan (d) Uaman Bhatt Bana
22. Who, among the following , was the author of Narayana Vilas:
(a) King Virupakya (b) King Krishnadeva Raya
(c) Vidyapati (d) Divakara
23. Who, among the following, was the author of Jambavati Kalyan:
(a) King Virupakya (b) King Krishnadeva Raya
(c) Kirtiraja (d) Srivara
24. Jai Singh Suri was the author of:
(a) Hammir-Mad-Mordana (b) Parvati-Parinaya
(c) Durga Bhakti Tarangini (d) Krishna-Charita
25. One of the most famous works on Hindu law, the Mitakshara was written by:
(a) Vidyaranya (b) Nayachandra
(c) Gangadhar (d) Vijnanesvara
26. One among the following factors may be regarded as the most decisive one in the choice of the Sultan. Identify.
(a) Priority of birth (b) Efficiency
(c) Nomination by the dead king (d) Nobility
27. One of the following army divisions was not important in the Delhi Sultanate period. Identify.
(a) cavalry (b) archers
(c) artillery (d) elephants
28. At times, Ala-ud-din defied the Quranic Law. Which among the following reasons can be considered the most important?
(a) He was not a pious Musalman
(b) Quranic law clashed with his personal interests
(c) He had the support of a powerful army
(d) He wanted to establish a secular state
29. Who among the following sultans of Delhi called himself the Khalifa?
(a) Balban (b) Muhammad bin Tughluq
(c) Mubarak Khalji (d) Iltutmish
30. One among the following did NOT receive a letter of investiture from the Khalifa. Identify
(a) Iltutmish (b) Muhammad bin Khalji
(c) Firuz Tughluq (d) Ala-ud-din Khalji

31. Pick out the correct sequence from among the groups of officers arranged in descending order.
(a) Sultan, naib, wazir, qazi (b) Sultan, wazir, naib, qazi
(c) Sultan, qazi, naib, wazir (d) Sultan, qazi, wazir, naib
32. One of the following was not an officer of the royal household
(a) Vakil-i-dar (b) Barbak
(c) Amir-i-shikar (d) Sadr-us-sudur
33. What was the salary of a well-equipped trooper with one horse in the time of Ala-ud-din Khalji?
(a) 500 tankas (b) 234 tankas
(c) 434 tankas (d) 300 tankas
34. What was the religious tax collected from the Muslims?
(a) Ushr (b) Khams
(c) Jizya (d) Zakat
35. Who among the following interpreted law?
(a) mufti (b) muqti
(c) qazi (d) sadr
36. Who was the first ruler of India who dug canals for promoting agriculture?
(a) Ghiyas-ud-din Tughluq (b) Firuz Tughluq
(c) Muhammad bin Tughluq (d) Buhlul Lodi
37. Who among the following has created the biggest network of canals known in India until the 19th century?
(a) Balban (b) Ala-ud-din Khalji
(c) Firuz Tughluq (d) Sikander Lodi
38. When could sericulture have been introduced into India?
(a) 12th century (b) 13th century
(c) 14th century (d) 16th century
39. What is Charai?
(a) Land revenue (b) House Tax
(c) Poll tax (d) Cattle tax
40. What does the term Chaudhri indicate?
(a) Village headman
(b) Knights or the rais
(c) Governor
(d) Local magnate held answerable for collection of revenue in each Pargana?
41. What is biswa?
(a) a unit of area (b) a tax
(c) a tax collector (d) measuring rod
42. By what name was the main instrument of transferring agrarian surplus called?
(a) milk (b) inam
(c) waqf (d) iqta
43. What was the main source of wealth of India during the Sultanate period?
(a) industry (b) trade
(c) agriculture (d) colonies

44. In whose time was the department of agriculture createt l?
(a) Muhammad bin Tughluq (b) Balban
(c) Ghiyas-ud-din Tughluq (d) Firuz Tughluq

45. Where was ginger of the best quality produced during the period of the Sultanate?
(a) Malabar (b) Konkan
(c) Carnatic (d) Gujarat

46. What was the percentage of the state demand during the reign of Ala-ud-din Khalji?
(a) $33\ ^1/_3$ (b) 25
(c) $16\ ^2/_3$ (d) 50

47. Under whose orders a Bengali version of the Mahabharata was written?
(a) Hussain Shah (b) Jalal-ud-din Muhammad
(c) Nusrat Shah (d) Haji Iliyas

48. Pick out the wrong match

(a) Nusrat Shah	Qadam Rasul
(b) Raja Ganesh	Danujamardana Deva
(c) Ala-ud-din Husain	Ikdala Shah
(d) Indil Khan	Bengali version of the Mahabharata

49. Pick out the wrong match.

(a) Bengal	Haji Iliyas
(b) Jaunpur	Khwaja Jahan
(c) Malwa	Dilawar Khan Ghuri
(d) Gujarat	Tatar Khan

50. Who is the founder of the cult of Satyapir?
(a) Husain Shah (b) Sikander II
(c) Nasir-ud-din (d) Haji Iliyas

51. Pick out the wrong match.

(a) Atala Masjid	Jaunpur
(b) Bara Sona Masjid	Gaur
(c) Adina Masjid	Pandua
(d) Gol Gumbaz	Ajmer

52. Which one of the following is described as the Shiraz of India
(a) Gaur (b) Agra
(c) Jaunpur (d) Ikdala

53. Jaunpur was hailed as the Shiraz of India. What could be the most important reason for such a description?
(a) Some of the Sharqi-rulers were themselves men of culture
(b) The Sharqi rule was marked by prosperity
(c) It was not involved in any war with its neighbour
(d) It was nearer to Delhi

54. Pick out the correct match.

(a) Tower of victory	Chittor
(b) Shiraz of India	Delhi
(c) Gol Gumbaz	Bijapur
(d) Vithalasvami Temple	Belur

55. Whom do you regard the ablest of the Muslim rulers of Malwa?
(a) Hushang Shah (b) Mahmud I
(c) Mahmud II (d) Nasiruddin

56. Medini Rai was appointed minister of Malwa because
(a) Mahmud wanted to destroy the influence of the Muslim oligarchy
(b) Medini Rai helped Mahmud against his enemies
(c) Medini Rai was a great administrator
(d) Medini Rai was a great general

57. Name the ruler who assisted Mahmud II to oust Medini Rai
(a) Rana Sanga (b) Ratan Singh
(c) Muzaflar Shah (d) Chand Khan

58. One of the following may not be regarded as the cause of external invasions of Gujarat. Identify.
(a) fertility (b) wealth due to active commerce
(c) natural resources (d) strategic importance

59. Who was the real founder of the independent sultanate of Gujarat?
(a) Zafar Khan (b) Tatar Khan
(c) Shams Khan (d) Ahmad Khan

60. What was the name of the old town near which Ahmedabad was built?
(a) Junagarh (b) Siri
(c) Asawal (d) Mandu

61. Who was called the Zar Baksha?
(a) Ahmad Shah (b) Qutb-ud-din Ahmad
(c) Muhammad Shah II (d) Mahmud Begarha

62. Where did Mahmud Begarha register a naval victory over the Portuguese?
(a) Diu (b) Daman
(c) Goa (d) Chaul

63. Who has been described as the pattern of excellence?
(a) Ahmad Shah (b) Muhammad Shah
(c) Bahadur Shah (d) Mahmud Begarha

64. Who had put an end to the independence of Sind in about 1514?
(a) Babur (b) Shah Beg Arghun
(c) Mahmud Begarha (d) Mahmud of Ghazni

65. Who was Gangu?
(a) founder of the Bahmani kingdom
(b) astrologer of Delhi
(c) descendent of the Persian hero Bahman
(d) Governor of Daulatabad

66. "With him departed all the cohesion and power of the Bahmani kingdom" - about whom was thus said?
(a) Mahmud Gawan (b) Alimad Shah
(c) Muhammad Shah III (d) Humayun

67. Pick out the wrong match:
(a) Nizam Shahi Ahmadnagar
(b) Qutb Shahi Golkunda

(c) Barid Shahi — Berar
(d) Adil Shahi — Bijapur

68. Which among the following may be regarded as the most significant achievement of Vijayanagar empire?
(a) Building up a vast empire
(b) Efficient administration
(c) Economic prosperity
(d) Saving the Hindu religion and culture from being engulfed by the rush of new forces

69. This is the best provided city in the world. Who has said this about Vijyanagar?
(a) Domingos Paes (b) Nuniz
(c) Nicolo Conti (d) Edoardo Barbosa

70. Who was the founder of the city Zainabad?
(a) Malik Nasir (b) Adil Khan
(c) Malik Raja (d) Muzaffar Shah

71. One of the following was not regarded as one of the four pillars of the state:
(a) Diwan-i-wizarat (b) Diwan-i-insha
(c) Diwan-i-arz (d) Diwan-i-khairat

72. From whom did the Turks know the association of divinity with kingship?
(a) The Hindus (b) The Chinese
(c) The Sassanians (d) The Arabs

73. Who among the following has described himself as the second Alexander on his coins?
(a) Ala-ud-din Khalji (b) Ahmad Shah
(c) Muhammad Shah II (d) Firuz Shah

74. Which one of the following defects of Vijyanagar empire may be regarded as the most serious one?
(a) Independence enjoyed by the provincial governors
(b) Failure to develop a sustained commercial activity in spite of the facilities available
(c) Permission given to the Portuguese to settle on the west coast
(d) Failure to develop a disciplined army

75. Bhaskaracharya wrote his treatise on:
(a) Hindu law (b) Brahmasutra
(c) Astronomy (d) Karma-mimamsa

76. Rajatarangini, written by Kalhan describes the history of:
(a) Bengal (b) Gujarat
(c) Kashmir (d) Malwa

77. Among fine arts, the art which flourished most during the period of the Delhi Sultanate was:
(a) Architecture (b) Sculpture
(c) Music (d) Painting

78. The architecture which flourished during the period of the Delhi Sultanate has been called:
(a) Early Muslim architecture (b) Turk-Afghan architecture
(c) Hindu-Muslim architecture (d) Indo-Islamic architecture

79. Who, among the following Sultans, constructed the Alai Darwaza?
(a) Balban (b) Ala-ud-din Khalji
(c) Mubarak Shah Khalji (d) Firuz Tughluq

80. Alai Darwaza built by Ala-ud-din Khalji is a gateway giving passage into the extension of:
(a) Qutub Minar (b) Dhai-din-ka-jaunpara
(c) Tomb of Iltutmish (d) Quat-ul-Islam

81. Which, among the features of architecture, was absent in the buildings constructed by the Sharqi rulers of Jaunpur?
(a) The dome (b) Square pillars
(c) Small galleries (d) Minarets

82. The Jama Masjid of Jaunpur was constructed by:
(a) Mubarak Shah Sharqi (b) Ibrahim Shah Sharqi
(c) Muhammad Shah Sharqi (d) Husain Shah Sarqi

83. Who, among the following kings of Vjayanagara constructed the Vatthalswami temple?
(a) Vijaya I (b) Devaraya II
(c) Vir Narsingha (d) Krishnadevaraya

84. Which, among the following did not constitute a chief characteristic of the temples in South India?
(a) Gopuram (b) Vimana
(c) Mandapa (d) Assembly hall for the devotees

85. Which, among the following did not constitute a distinctive feature of the, buildings constructed by the Sultans of Delhi?
(a) The dome (b) Minarets
(c) The Arch (d) Attached gardens

86. Among the buildings constructed by the Sultans of Delhi, the following constructions are remarkably absent:
(a) Mosques (b) Tombs
(c) Minarets (d) Forts

87. The precursors of the Bhakti movement, Jnanadeva and Namadeva belonged to:
(a) Maharashtra (b) Uttar-Pradesh
(c) Mysore (d) Kerala

88. The pioneer' saint of Bhakti-movement in Vaishnava sect of Hinduism was:
(a) Ramanuja (b) Nimbekara
(c) Madhavacharya (d) Namadeva

89. Who, among the following saints, had twelve famous disciples including a barber and a weaver?
(a) Ramanuja (b) Nanak
(c) Kabir (d) Ramananda

90. Ramananda, the first saint who popularized the Bhakti movement among the masses believed in the worship of:
(a) Sita-Rama (b) Radha-Krishna
(c) Vishnu (d) Siva

91. Vallabhacharya believed in the worship of:
(a) Sita-Rama (b) Radha-Krishna
(c) Vishnu (d) Siva

92. The novelty which was added to Bhakti movement by Chaitanya was:
(a) Idol worship
(b) Recitation of prayers to God
(c) Acceptance of both men and women as devotees
(d) Kirtan (recitation of God's name in group or assembly of the people)

93. The novelty which Kabir added to the Bhakti movement was:
(a) Emphasis on Bhakti to Rama
(b) Tradition of family-saints
(c) Neglect of Sanskrit language
(d) Efforts to bring about unity among the Hindus and the Muslims

94. Babur captured Samarqand thrice but failed to keep it under his control because of the resistance of the:
(a) Persians (b) Uzbeqs
(c) Turks (d) Afghans

95. Who, among the following, did not assure of his help to Babar against Ibrahim Lodi?
(a) Alam Khan Lodi (b) Daulat Khan Lodi
(c) Diawar Khan Lodi (d) Rana Sangram Singh

96. Which, among the following, did not constitute one of the results of the first battle of Panipat?
(a) It sealed the fate of the Lodi dynasty in India
(b) The power of the Afghans was weakened though not destroyed
(c) Babar captured Delhi and Agra and, thus, laid down the foundation of the Mughal dynasty in India
(d) No power was left in North India to contest with Babar for the sovereignty of Delhi

97. The most decisive battle which Babar fought in India was:
(a) The battle of Panipat (b) The battle of Khanna
(c) The battle of Chanderi (d) The battle of Ghaghara

98. Which, among the following, was not one of the causes of the battle of Khanna?
(a) Babur's decision to stay in India
(b) Boundary disputes between Babar and Rana Sangram Singh
(c) Rana Sangram Singh's desire to capture Delhi
(d) Babur's desire to capture Rajasthan

99. The battle of Khanna was fought in:
(a) 1526 (b) 1527
(c) 1228 (d) 1529

100. Which, among the following, was not one of the results of the battle of Khanna?
(a) It weakened the Rajput power
(b) It reduced the power of resistance of the Afghans against the Mughals
(c) The conquest of Rajasthan by the Mughals became easy
(d) It secured the position of Babar in India

Answers

1. (d)	21. (a)	41. (a)	61. (c)	81. (d)
2. (c)	22. (a)	42. (d)	62. (d)	82. (d)
3. (a)	23. (d)	43. (c)	63. (d)	83. (d)
4. (d)	24. (a)	44. (a)	64. (d)	84. (d)
5. (d)	25. (d)	45. (a)	65. (b)	85. (d)
6. (d)	26. (4)	46. (d)	66. (a)	86. (d)
7. (d)	27. (d)	47. (c)	67. (c)	87. (a)
8. (c)	28. (b)	48. (d)	68. (d)	88. (a)
9. (d)	29. (c)	49. (d)	69. (a)	89. (d)
10. (b)	30. (d)	50. (a)	70. (a)	90. (a)
11. (a)	31. (a)	51. (d)	71. (d)	91. (b)
12. (c)	32. (d)	52. (c)	72. (c)	92. (d)
13. (a)	33. (b)	53. (a)	73. (a)	93. (d)
14. (d)	34. (d)	54. (a)	74. (b)	94. (b)
15. (a)	35. (a)	55. (b)	75. (c)	95. (c)
16. (a)	36. (a)	56. (a)	76. (c)	96. (d)
17. (d)	37. (c)	57. (c)	77. (a)	97. (b)
18. (a)	38. (c)	58. (d)	78. (d)	98. (d)
19. (d)	39. (d)	59. (d)	79. (b)	99. (b)
20. (d)	40. (d)	60. (c)	80. (d)	100. (c)

SET IV

Questions

1. Which, among the following, was not one of the early difficulties of Humayun?
   (a) Brothers of Humayun (b) Humayun's own character
   (c) The Afghans (d) The Rajputs
2. When Humayun proceeded to fight against Bahadur Shah, the ruler of Gujarat, he was engaged in fighting against?
   (a) Malwa (b) Mewar
   (c) Marwar (d) Bundelkhand
3. When Humayun ascended the throne of Delhi, Sher Khan, who ultimately drove him out of India, was?
   (a) In the Mughal service
   (b) In the service of Jalal Khan, ruler of Bihar
   (c) Master of South Bihar only
   (d) Master of Bihar & Bengal
4. Humayun fought his decisive battle against Sher Khan at:
   (a) Chunargarh (b) Chausa
   (c) Bilgram (near Kanauj) (d) Delhi
5. Which, among the following, has not been accepted as one of the reasons of the defeat of Humayun against Sher Shah?
   (a) Humayun was weak as a commander as compared to Sher Shah
   (b) Humayun was not a determined fighter
   (c) Sher Shah possessed an equally powerful artillery
   (d) Humayun failed to get the cooperation of his brother, Kamran before the battle of Kannauj
6. Humayun recaptured Delhi in 1555 A.D. from the hands of:
   (a) Islam Shah (b) Muhammad Adil Shah
   (c) Ibrahim Shah (d) Sikander Shah
7. Who, among the following historians, has remarked that "Humayun tumbled through the life and tumbled out of it?"
   (a) Lane-Poole (b) Malleson
   (c) S.R. Sharma (d) A.L. Srivastava

8. Where did Farid (Sher Shah), after running away from the house of his father, receive education?
(a) Jaunpur (b) Patna
(c) Kannauj (d) Sahasram
9. Sher Shah died while attacking:
(a) Mandu (b) Raisin
(c) Marwar (d) Kalinjar
10. Who, among the following historians described Sher Shah as a greater constructive genius and a better nation-builder than Akbar the Great?
(a) K.R. Qanungo (b) R.P. Tripathi
(c) P. Saran (d) S.R. Sharma
11. The one province where Sher Shah did not appoint a Subedar to check the possibilities of revolt was:
(a) Multan (b) Malwa
(c) Bihar (d) Bengal
12. The most notable work of public welfare done by Sher Shah was:
(a) Construction of new roads
(b) Construction of nearly 1, 700 Caravan-sarais
(c) Plantation of fruit-gardens
(d) Construction of Charitable-hospitals
13. Who, among the following historians, gives no credit to the religious policy of Sher Shah and contends that in this field he did not rise above the Turko-Afghan rulers of the Delhi Sultanate?
(a) S.R.Sharma (b) K.R. Qanungo
(c) A.L. Srivastava (d) R.P. Tripathi
14. Who, among the following, was half inclined to prefer the mausoleum of Sher Shah at Sasaram in Bihar to even the Taj Mahal?
(a) Cunningham (b) K.R. Qanungo
(c) Havel (d) Percy Brown
15. Which, among the following, did not constitute part of army-reforms of Sher Shah?
(a) Keeping a large army at the centre
(b) Cash payment to the soldiers
(c) Introduction of the practices of keeping Huliya of soldiers and of branding horses
(d) Keeping of a swiftly-moving artillery
16. Who, among the following rulers, began the policy of bringing Rajput rulers of Rajasthan under the suzerainty of Delhi?
(a) Babar (b) Humayun
(c) Sher Shah (d) Akbar
17. Who, among the following, succeeded Sher Shah?
(a) Islam Shah (b) Firoz Shah
(c) Muhammad Adil Shah (d) Ibrahim Shah
18. The best novelty of the administration of Islam Shah, son of Sher Shah, was:
(a) Passing a large number of administrative laws and freeing them from religion
(b) Construction of a number of sarais

(c) Keeping his nobles under his strict control
(d) Safeguarding of royal privileges

19. Bairam Khan worked as regent of emperor Akbar between the period:
(a) 1555-1556 (b) 1556-1558
(c) 1555-1558 (d) 1556-1560

20. The first reform introduced by Akbar was the:
(a) Abolition of the practice of Sati
(b) Abolition of the practice of enslaving the prisoners of war
(c) Abolition of pilgrims' tax
(d) Abolition of Jizya

21. Jizya, the tax most hated by the Hindus, was abolished by Akbar in:
(a) 1562 (b) 1563
(c) 1564 (d) 1565

22. The only state in Northern India which Akbar failed to annexe or reduce to submission was:
(a) Gondwana (b) Malwa
(c) Marwar (d) Mewar

23. The one state of Southern India which was completely annexed by Akbar was:
(a) Khandesh (b) Ahmadnagar
(c) Bijapur (d) Golkonda

24. Which, among the following was not one of the reasons for accepting Akbar as a national king?
(a) He gave up Islam
(b) His administrative unity and universality of laws
(c) His encouragement to the formation of a common culture
(d) His religious policy

25. Mewar accepted the suzerainty of the Mughals during the reign of Emperor:
(a) Akbar (b) Jahangir
(c) Shah Jahan (d) Aurangzeb

26. Which among the following was NOT a term of treaty between Rana Amar Singh of Mewar and emperor Jahangir?
(a) The Rana recognised Jahangir as his suzerainty
(b) All territory of Mewar including Chittor, was restored to the Rana
(c) The fort of Chittor was not to be fortified or repaired
(d) Rana agreed to enter into a matrimonial alliance with the emperor and attend the imperial darbar

27. No fresh conquest was made in Southern India during the reign of Jahangir because:
(a) Jahangir did not try to conquer South India
(b) The States of South India unitedly resisted the imperial forces
(c) Malik Ambar, the Prime Minister of Ahmadnagar, put up a very stiff resistance
(d) The military resistance of the Marathas

28. In the war of succession which was fought among the sons of Shah Jahan, his daughter Roshan Ara supported the cause of:

(a) Dara Shukoh (b) Shah Shuja
(c) Aurangzeb (d) Murad Baksh

29. In the war of succession which was fought the sons of Shah Jahan, his daughter Gauhan Ara supported the cause of:
(a) Dara Shikoh (b) Shah Shuja
(c) Aurangzeb (d) Murad Baksh

30. Several tribal-revolts-occurred during the reign of Aurangzeb in the North-West which, among them, proved most furious?
(a) Revolt of the Afghans (b) Revolt of the Yusufzais
(c) Revolt of the Afridis (d) Revolt of the Khataks

31. Which, among the following methods, formed the core of the policy of Aurangzeb while dealing with the revolts of the tribal chiefs in the North-West?
(a) Conciliating them (b) Crushing them bitterly by force
(c) Bribing them by money (d) Setting up one clan against another

32. Aurangzeb's highest ideal of kingship was that a monarch should rule in the:
(a) Co-religionists (b) Ulema
(c) Islam (d) Subjects

33. The best means by which Aurangzeb tried to serve the best interests of his subjects was:
(a) Service to Ulema
(b) Attempt to bring about economic prosperity
(c) Attempt to bring about political unity of the country
(d) To spread the Islam throughout the length and breadth of India

34. Aurangzeb:
(a) Increased the land-revenue
(b) Enhanced the rate of all taxes
(c) Imposed many taxes on all subjects
(d) Abolished many taxes

35. The cause of the revolt of the Satnamis during the reign of Aurangzeb was:
(a) Aurangzeb destroyed their temples
(b) Aurangzeb imposed religious tax on them
(c) Aurangzeb enhanced land-revenue in their district
(d) A quarrel arose between a Satnami peasant and a Mughal soldier

36. Which, among the following, was the cause of the revolt of the Rathors of Marwar against Aurangzeb?
(a) The Rathors opposed the imposition of Jazya by Aurangzeb
(b) Aurangzeb ordered the destruction of the temples of the capital-city, Jodhpur
(c) Rathors stood in support of the state of Mewar
(d) Aurangzeb refused to accept the posthumous son of Jaswant Singh viz. Ajit Singh as the ruler of Marwar and, instead, occupied Marwar

37. Who, among the following princes, revolted against his father, Aurangzeb?
(a) Akbar (b) Mauzzam
(c) Azam (d) Shahriyar

38. The one Rajput State which persisted in its attempt to regain independence till the death of Aurangzeb was:

(a) Marwar (b) Mewar
(c) Jaipur (d) Bikaner

39. Who, among the following Rajput chiefs fighting against Aurangzeb, has been described as 'the flower of the Rajput chivalry'?
(a) Raja Singh of Mewar (b) Jaya Singh of Mewar
(c) Durga Das of Mewar (d) Ajit Singh of Mewar

40. The kingdom of Bijapur and Golkonda were annexed to the Mughal empire during the reign of:
(a) Akbar (b) Jahangir
(c) Shah Jahan (d) Aurangzeb

41. "Deccan ulcer ruined Aurangzeb". It is true because of the fierce resistance put up by:
(a) State of Bijapur (b) State of Golkonda
(c) Shivaji (d) Marathas after the death of Sambhuji

42. Who, among the following Mughul emperors, was the most pious in his personal life?
(a) Akbar (b) Jahangir
(c) Shah Jahan (d) Aurangzeb

43. Who, among the following Mughal emperors, was NOT a lovable head of the family?
(a) Akbar (b) Jahangir
(c) Shah Jahan (d) Aurangzeb

44. Who, among the following historians, has expressed the opinion that Akbar indulged in anti Islamic activities?
(a) Woolseley Haig (b) A.L. Srivastava
(c) S.R. Sharma (d) R.S. Tripathi

45. Akbar introduced Din-e-Ilahi in the year:
(a) 1578 (b) 1579
(c) 1582 (d) 1585

46. Akbar introduced Din-e-Ilahi because he:
(a) Had lost faith in Islam
(b) Desired to become 'Pope as well as king'
(c) Desired to corrupt Hinduism
(d) Desired a synthesis of all religions known to him

47. Who, among the following historians, has commanded that "the divine faith (Din-e-Ilahi) was a monument of Akbar's folly, not of his wisdom"?
(a) Woolseley Haig (b) V.A. Smith
(c) A.L. Srivastava (d) S.R. Sharma

48. The religious policy of Akbar has been regarded successful because it:
(a) Brought about religious harmony between the Hindus and the Muslims
(b) Brought about synthesis of all religions
(c) Liberalised Islam
(d) The majority of his subjects became loyal to the throne

49. 'Akbar tried to bring about certain social reforms'. Which, among the following, was NOT included in them?

(a) Abolition of the practice of sati by force
(b) Permission to Hindu-widows to remarry
(c) Fixation of marriageable age for the boys and girls as 16 and 14 years respectively
(d) Restrictions on observance of casteism

50. Who, among the following Gurus of the Sikhs, was the first tortured to death by one of the Mughal emperors?
(a) Arjun (b) Har Govind
(c) Har Rai (d) Har Kishan

51. The office of the Guru of the Sikhs became hereditary from the period of Guru:
(a) Amar Das (b) Ram Das
(c) Arjun (d) Har Govind

52. Who, among the following Gurus of the Sikhs, first constructed the golden temple of Amritsar?
(a) Ram Das (b) Arjun
(c) Har Govind (d) Teg Bahadur

53. Who, among the following Gurus of the Sikhs, compiled teachings of all previous Gurus in the Guru Granth Sahib?
(a) Arjun (b) Har Govind
(c) Har Rai (d) Har Kishan

54. Who, among the following Gurus of the Sikhs, made a beginning to convert the Sikhs into a military sect?
(a) Har Govind (b) Har Rai
(c) Har Kishan (d) Teg Bahadur

55. The credit of organising the Sikhs into a strong military sect, the Khalsa, went to the Sikh Guru:
(a) Har Rai (b) Har Kishan
(c) Teg Bahadur (d) Govind Singh,

56. The Sikh Guru who was put to death by the order off Aurangzeb was:
(a) Har Rai (b) Har Kishan
(c) Teg Bahadur (d) Govind Singh

57. After Babar, the first Mughal emperor who attempted to conquer Central Asia was
(a) Akbar (b) Jahangir
(c) Shah Jahan (d) Aurangzeb

58. Kandhar was finally lost to the Mughal empire during the reign of:
(a) Akbar (b) Jahangir
(c) Shah Jahan (d) Aurangzeb

59. The Mughals failed to recapture Kandhar because, primarily, as compared to Persians they proved weaker in:
(a) Financial resources (b) Numerical strength of the army
(c) Military strategy (d) Artillery

60. 'As compared to the rulers of the Delhi Sultanate the Mughal emperors brought a fundamental change in the policy of the State.' The change was:
(a) The rulers claimed divinity
(b) The administration was highly centralized

(c) There was no interference in the working of village-assemblies
(d) The state no more remained theocratic

61. Who, among the following historians, first described the rule of the Mughals as the 'Rule by Aristocracy'?
(a) Tara Chand (b) J.N. Sarkar
(c) A.L. Srivastava (d) S.R. Sharma

62. The rule of the Mughals has been described as the 'Rule by Aristocracy' because the Mughal-nobility wielded large influence in matters of state by virtue of its:
(a) Extensive powers (b) Extensive jagirs
(c) Large armies (d) Hereditary status in most cases

63. The Mir Bakhshi of the Mughal-emperors was head of the department of: .
(a) Finance (b) Army-organisation
(c) Foreign affairs (d) Intelligence

64. Who, among the following was the head of the administration in a Paragana?
(a) Shiqdar (b) Amil
(c) Amal-Guzar (d) Fotadar

65. Kotwal was the head of the administration of a city. However, which among the following, was NOT one of his duties?
(a) Maintaining peace and order
(b) Regulating prices and checking weight and measures
(c) Supervising the system of slaves
(d) Supervising the dak-chaukies

66. The origin of the Mansabdari-system introduced by Akbar in the Mughal army can be traced back to:
(a) Khalifa Abba Said (b) Changiz Khan
(c) Amir Timur (d) Ala-ud-din Khalji

67. Mansabs were allotted to:
(a) Only nobles (b) Only the members of the army
(c) Whomsoever the Emperor desired (d) All officers of the state

68. The highest mansab assigned to an officer other than the royal princes during the reign of Akbar was that of:
(a) 5000 (b) 7000
(c) 10000 (d) 12000

69. Which, among the following texts, is most useful for obtaining information on agrarian conditions during the period of the Mughals?
(a) Akbarnama (b) Ain-i-Akbari
(c) Tabkat-i-Akbari (d) Taufa-i-Akbarshahi

70. Who, among the following revenue officers of Akbar, was responsible for his major revenue reforms?
(a) Aitmad Khan (b) Muzaffar Khan
(c) Shihabuddin Ahmad (d) Todar Mal

71. Land was classified into varied categories during the reign of Akbar. The basis of this classification was:
(a) Kind of land

(b) Fertility of land
(c) Means of irrigation
(d) Continuity or otherwise of its cultivation

72. Which, among the following, was regarded as the first-quality land during the rule of the Mughals?
(a) Polaj (b) Parauti
(c) Chachar (d) Banjar

73. Who, among the following, was responsible for the collection of the land-revenue in a Paragana during the period of the Mughals?
(a) Amal-Gujar (b) Amil
(c) Potadar (d) Qanungo

74. The revenue charged during the reign of Shah Jahan was:
(a) 1/3 of the produce (b) 2/3 of the produce
(c) 1/2 of the produce (d) 2/5 of the produce

75. The practice of collecting revenue through contractors during the Mughal period started during the reign of:
(a) Jahangir (b) Shah Jahan
(c) Aurangzeb (d) Later Mughals

76. Who, among the following Mughal emperors, hung a chain with bells outside his palace for people to call him for grant of justice?
(a) Akbar (b) Jahangir
(c) Shah Jahan (d) Aurangzeb

77. The laws of Islam were compiled in a book titled Fatwa-i-Alamgiri during the reign of the great Mughals. Who, among the following emperors was responsible for it?
(a) Akbar (b) Jahangir
(c) Shah Jahan (d) Aurangzeb

78. During the Mughal period, sugarcane was mostly produced in:
(a) Western Uttar-Pradesh (b) Punjab & North-West provinces
(c) Madhya Pradesh (d) Bengal & Bihar

79. The famous Kohi-noor diamond was produced from one of the mines in:
(a) Bijapur (b) Gotkonda
(c) Chotta Nagpur (d) Orissa

80. The top-most industry of India during the Mughal period was:
(a) Cotton-cloth (b) Ivory-products
(c) Pearls-Production (d) Silk-cotton

81. Which, among the following, did NOT constitute a handicap in the industrial progress during the Mughal period:
(a) Absence of Joint-stock companies
(b) Insecurity of property and its inheritance
(c) Mughal-emperors themselves established many Karkkanas (industries)
(d) Shortage of capital-money for investment

82. During the rule of Mughals, wealth was mostly concentrated in:
(a) Temples & Mosques (b) Industrialists & Traders
(c) Emperors and nobility (d) Brokers & speculators

83. The most popular sect within Hinduism during the Mughal rule was:
(a) Vaishnavism (b) Saivism
(c) Tantrik cults (the Saktas) (d) Adi-vedantism
84. During the Mughul period the basic feature of Hindu Tantrik cults was:
(a) Further emphasis on sensual enjoyment
(b) Emphasis on use of intoxicants
(c) Worship of idols
(d) Attempt to purge it of baser elements
85. Which, among the following schools of Sufism lost its image during the period of the Mughals?
(a) Chistiya School (b) Suhrawardi School
(c) Naqsbandiya School (d) Qadiriya School
86. Abu-Fazl and Faizi Sarhindi gave same title to one of their works
(a) Akbarnama (b) Ain-i-Akbari
(c) Tabaqat-i-Akbari (d) Tofah-i-Akbarshahi
87. The Razmnamah compiled by several Persian scholars was a translation of:
(a) Bhagavat-Gita (b) Ramayana
(b) Mahabharata (d) Rig-Veda
88. Who, among the following, wrote Muntkhab-ut-Tawarikh?
(a) Abdul Rahim Khan-i-Khana (b) Abbas Sarwani
(c) Ahmad Yadagara Mirza (d) Badyuni
89. Who, among the following sons of Shah Jahan, was the author of Majmaul Bahrain?
(a) Dara Shukoh (b) Shah Shuja
(c) Aurangzeb (d) Murad
90. 'Several Sanskrit-texts were translated into Persian under the patronage of Dara Shukoh'. However, which, among the following was NOT one of them?
(a) The Upanishads (b) The Bhagavat-Gita
(c) The Bhagavat-Purana (d) The Yoga-Vashist
91. Farhang-i-Jahangiri, compiled by Jamaluddin Hussain is a
(a) Historical work (b) Collection of poems
(c) Literary work in prose (d) Dictionary of Persian words
92. The best and most important historical work in Aurangzeb's reign was written by Muhammad Hashim Khafi Khan. The title of his work was:
(a) Alamgir-nama (b) Malhnavi-i-Alamgiri
(c) Miratual Alam (d) Muntakhab-ul-Lubab
93. 'One important feature of the literary progress during the period of the Mughals was the translation of many important Sanskrit texts in Persian, viz, Ramayana, Mahabharat, Rajatarangini etc.' Who, among the following scholars, translated Ramayana into Persian?
(a) Abu-i-Fazl (b) Abdur Rahim Khan-i-Khana
(c) Badayuni (d) Faizi
94. Among the following Muslim-scholars, one who made a valuable contribution towards Hindi literature was:

(a) Abul-Fazl (b) Faizi
(c) Abdur Rahim-i-Khana (d) Prince Dara Shukoh

95. Who, among the following, was the author of the Vinaypatrika?
(a) Tulsi Das (b) Raskhana
(c) Parmanand Das (d) Vitthal Nath

96. The Hindi-poet, Bihari Lai was patronized by:
(a) Jaswant Singh (b) Jaya Singh
(c) Emperor Akbar (d) Chhatrasal

97. Which, among the following forts, was NOT constructed by Akbar?
(a) The fort at Lahore (b) The fort at Agra
(c) The fort at Delhi (d) The fort at Allahabad

98. The most magnificent buildings constructed by Akbar are found at:
(a) The fort at Agra (b) The fort at Lahore
(c) The fort at Allahabad (d) Fatehpur Sikri

99. Who, among the following, has described the buildings at Fatehpur Sikri "a romance in stone"
(a) V.A. Smith (b) Fergusson
(c) E.B. Havell (d) Percy Brown

100. Akbar built Bulanda-Darwaza at Fatehpur Sikri to commemorate his conquest of:
(a) Malwa (b) Gujarat
(c) Bengal (d) Kashmir

Answers

1. (d)	21. (c)	41. (d)	61. (a)	81. (d)
2. (b)	22. (d)	42. (d)	62. (d)	82. (c)
3. (c)	23. (a)	43. (d)	63. (b)	83. (a)
4. (c)	24. (a)	44. (a)	64. (a)	94. (d)
5. (b)	25. (b)	45. (c)	65. (d)	85. (a)
6. (d)	26. (d)	46. (d)	66. (a)	86. (a)
7. (a)	27. (c)	47. (b)	67. (b)	87. (c)
8. (a)	28. (c)	48. (d)	68. (b)	88. (d)
9. (d)	29. (d)	49. (d)	69. (b)	89. (a)
10. (d)	30. (c)	50. (a)	70. (d)	90. (c)
11. (d)	31. (d)	51. (c)	71. (d)	91. (d)
12. (b)	32. (d)	52. (b)	72. (a)	92. (d)
13. (a)	33. (d)	53. (a)	73. (b)	93. (c)
14. (a)	34. (d)	54. (a)	74. (c)	94. (c)
15. (d)	35. (d)	55. (d)	75. (b)	95. (a)
16. (c)	36. (d)	56. (c)	76. (b)	96. (c)
17. (a)	37. (a)	57. (c)	77. (d)	97. (c)
18. (a)	38. (a)	58. (c)	78. (d)	98. (d)
19. (d)	39. (c)	59. (d)	79. (b)	99. (a)
20. (b)	40. (d)	60. (d)	80. (a)	100. (b)

SET V

Questions

1. Which among the following was the immediate cause of attack of Nawab Siraj-ud-daula on Calcutta in 1756?
   (a) Refusal of the English company to pay the overdue trade tax
   (b) English conspired against the Nawab with a view to depose him from the throne and that became known to him
   (c) Siraj-ud-daula desired to turn out the English from Bengal
   (d) Refusal of the English to demolish the fortifications of Calcutta
2. 'When a strong British force under the command of Clive and Watson reached Bengal from Madras, Nawab Siraj-ud-daula agreed for peace.' Where, among the following places, that peace treaty was signed?
   (a) Alinagar (b) Dacca
   (c) Murshidabad (d) Patna
3. Who among the following Indians was NOT a party to the conspiracy of the English against Nawab Siraj-ud-daula with a view to depose him from the throne?
   (a) Amichand (A Sikh merchant)
   (b) Jagat-Seth Fateh Chand (A very rich trader)
   (c) Mir Zafar (Mir-bakshi of the Nawab)
   (d) Ghasiti Begum (Widow of one of the son-in-laws of Alivardi Khan)
4. Who among the following threatened English to inform Siraj-ud-daula about the conspiracy against him if his terms were not accepted?
   (a) Mir Jafar (b) Amichand
   (c) Jagat-Seth Fateh Chand (d) Rai Durlabh
5. Which among the following began the first Anglo-Mysore war?
   (a) The attack of Haider Ali on Travancore which was a friendly state to the British
   (b) The attack of the British on Mahe which was in possession of the French who were friendly to Haider Ali
   (c) The treaty between the Nizam, the English and the Marathas against Haider Ali and the attack of the Marathas on Mysore
   (d) The attack of Haider Ali on Madras

6. Which among the following was the immediate cause of the second Anglo-Mysore war?
 (a) The treaty between the Nizam, the Marathas and Haider Ali against the British and the attack of Haider Ali on Karnataka
 (b) The attack of the English on Mysore
 (c) The attack of the combined armies of the Nizam and the English on Mysore
 (d) The attack of the Nizam and Haider Ali on Karnataka when the English captured Guntur which was in possession of a relative of Nizam
7. The immediate cause of the third Anglo-Mysore war (1790-92 A.D) was:
 (a) The boundary dispute between Tipu and Nizam of Hyderabad who was an ally of the English
 (b) Tipu's attack on Madras
 (c) Cornwallis's desire to annihilate the French who were allies of Tipu
 (d) Tipu's attack on the State of Travancore, which was a friendly state of the English
8. Which, among the following was the primary cause of the 4th Anglo-Mysore war?
 (a) The attack of the English on Mysore to finish the power of Tipu for once and all
 (b) The attack of Tipu on English territory in Madras
 (c) The support of the English to the Nizam who had started hostilities with Tipu
 (d) The attack of Tipu on Hyderabad which was a friendly state to the British
9. Which, among the following factors, was not responsible for the fall of the state of Mysore established by Haider Ali?
 (a) The animosity of the Nizam and the Marathas against Mysore
 (b) The English were certainly more powerful economically and military than the State of Mysore
 (c) Neither Haider Ali nor Tipu sought assistance of either the Nizam or the Marathas against the English
 (d) The incapable leadership of Haider Ali and Tipu Sultan
10. After the defeat and death of Tipu in the Fourth Anglo-Mysore War in 1799 A.D. a part of the Mysore State was restored back to:
 (a) The descendents of Tipu
 (b) The descendent of the previous Hindu ruler of Mysore
 (c) The Hindu Raja of Travancore
 (d) The Nawab of Karnataka
11. 'Haider Ali possessed several good qualities.' However, which, among the following, was not one of them?
 (a) He was a good commander
 (b) He was a determined soldier
 (c) He possessed keen intellect and sound memory
 (d) He was well-educated
12. 'Tipu brought about several innovations in administration.' However, which, among the following, was NOT one of them?
 (a) Survey and measurement of land for the purpose of revenue
 (b) Started a new calendar
 (c) Started new coinage-system
 (d) Introduced new weights and measures

13. Which, among the following was NOT one of the causes of the first Anglo-Maratha war (1775-1782 A.D.)?
 (a) The treaty of Surat (1775 A.D) between Raghunath Rao and the Bombay Government of the English
 (b) The treaty of Purandhar (1776 A.D.) between the Calcutta Council and the Poona-darbar
 (c) The refusal of Warren Hastings to observe the treaty of Purandhar
 (d) The ambition of Nana Phadnavis to become Peshwa himself and expulsion of Raghunath Rao from the Poona-Darbar

14. Ruhelkhand was occupied by Avadh with the help of the English Company on payment of Rs. 40, 00, 000/- in:
 (a) 1773 (b) 1774
 (c) 1775 (d) 1776

15. Sir Johan Shore interfered in Avadh to:
 (a) Settle its financial affairs (b) Settle succession issue
 (c) Settle terms of a new treaty (d) Settle the strength of its army

16. Wellesley (1798-1805) forced Avadh to accept the subsidiary alliance and occupied Ruhelkhand in the year:
 (a) 1798 (b) 1800
 (c) 1801 (d) 1804

17. Who, among the following, was the last Nawab of Avadh?
 (a) Nasiruddin (b) Nasiruddaulah
 (c) Muhammad Ali Shah (d) Wajid Ali Shah

18. Which among the following, was the primary cause of the 2nd Anglo-Maratha War (1803-1805 A.D.)?
 (a) Interference of the English in the mutual conflicts of the Marathas
 (b) Wellesley's desire to uproot the Maratha Power
 (c) English intrigues with Peshwa Baji Rao
 (d) Interference of the English in the conflict between the Marathas and the Nizam of Hyderabad

19. The first Maratha-Chief who accepted the subsidiary of Lord Wellesley was:
 (a) Peshwa Baji Rao II (b) Raghuji Bhonsle
 (c) Daulat Rao Sindia (d) Yashwant Rao Holkar

20. Who, among the following, has remarked about the consequences of the subsidiary alliance that "our policy and our aim have reduced all the power of India to the State of Sifars".
 (a) Lord Wellesley (b) Arthur Wellesley
 (c) General Lake (d) Lt. Col. Ochterlony

21. Yashwant Rao Holkar signed with English:
 (a) The treaty of Bassein (b) The treaty of Deogaon
 (c) The treaty of Surji-Arjangaon (d) The treaty of Rajpurghat

22. Which, among the following, was not one of the causes of the 3rd Anglo-Maratha war (1817-1818 A.D.)
 (a) The Maratha Chiefs, particularly, the Peshwa desired to throw off the restrictions imposed on them by the treaties with the English

(b) The determination of Lord Hastings to give a final blow to the Maratha-power
(c) The United effort and desire of the Marathas to turn the English from India
(d) The attack of Peshwa Baji Rao on the residency at Khirki

23. Which, among the following was not one of the causes of the failure of the Marathas against the English?
(a) Inept leadership
(b) Absence of unity among the Marathas
(c) Absence of stable economic policy of the Marathas
(d) The support of native-rulers, other than the Marathas, to the English

24. 'The English fought only one war with Nepal (1814-1816).' Who, among the following, was the governor-general of the English Company at that time?
(a) Lord Wellesely (b) Marquess (Lord) Hastings
(c) Lord Amherst (d) Lord Dalhousie

25. Which, among the following, was not a term of the treaty of Sigauli accepted by the Nepal-Darbar with the British in 1816 A.D.:
(a) The English got the districts of Gharwal and Kumayun and also larger part of Tarai region.
(b) The boundary of the state of Nepal and the territory of the English was settled
(c) Nepal withdrew its sovereign status form the state of Sikkim
(d) The English got the right to trade, free of tax, within the territories of the state of Nepal

26. Who, among the following governor-generals, suppressed the Pathans the Pindaris?
(a) Marques (Lord) Hastings (b) Lord William Bentinck
(c) Lord Amherst (d) Lord Dalhousie

27. Which, among the following, was not conquered by Ranjit Singh?
(a) Kashmir (b) Multan
(c) Peshawar (d) Cis-Sutlej-territory

28. The treaty of Amritsar (1809 A.D.) established permanent friendship between Ranjit Singh and the English. Which, among the following, was NOT a term of this treaty?
(a) The English accepted 'the sovereign right of Ranjit Singh over 45 Paraganas North of the River Sutlej
(b) The river Sutlej was accepted as the dividing line of each other's territories by the English and Ranjit Singh
(c) The English and Ranjit Singh agreed to remain friends to each other
(d) The English agreed not to interfere in the affairs of Sind

29. From whom among the following, Ranjit Singh acquired the famous Koh-i-noor diamond?
(a) Shah Shuja (b) Zamen Shah
(c) Dost Muhammad (d) Sher Ali

30. Who, among the following officers of Ranjit Singh, had direct contact with the peasants as a revenue, executive and judicial officer?
(a) Kardar (b) Diwan
(c) Nazim (d) Qanungo

31. Ranjit Singh's ideas concerning religious-policy were
(a) Bigot (b) Tolerant towards the Hindus
(c) Tolerant towards the Muslims (d) Liberal to all

32. Who, among the following, has remarked that "But in almost all cases, as Bismarck has put it, a political alliance means a rider and a horse. In this Anglo-Sikh alliance, the British Government was the rider and Ranjit Singh was the horse":
(a) Cunningham (b) Sarkar and Datta
(c) N.K. Sinha (d) B.C. Mazumdar

33. 'The English obstructed the expansion of the kingdom of Ranjit Singh at several places' but they did not interfere in:
(a) Sindh (b) Cis-Sutlej States
(c) Firozepur (d) Kashmir

34. Which, among the following, was made a pretext by the English for the beginning of the 2nd Anglo-Sikh War (1849-49 A.D.):
(a) The conspiracy of Rani Jindan against the English
(b) The revolt of the Sikh-Darbar against the English
(c) The revolt of Mulraj, the Governor of Multan
(d) The revolt of the Khalsa-army

35. Which, among the following, was not the place where major battles between the Sikh and the English took place during the course of the 2nd Anglo-Sikh War?
(a) Ramnagar (b) Chillianwala
(c) Gujarat (d) Sobraon

36. Who, among the following, was the Governor General of the English Company when Punjab was annexed to the empire of the English after the 2nd Anglo-Sikh War?
(a) Lord Auckland (b) Lord Ellenborough
(c) Lord Hardinge (d) Lord Dalhousie

37. Before the annexation of Sindh by the English, its Sovereign power was shared by three Chiefs. Which, among the following, was not one of those chiefs of Sindh?
(a) The Amir of Hyderabad (b) The Amir of Khairpur
(c) The Amir of Mirpur (d) The Amir of Shikarpur

38. Which, among the following, was made a pretext by the English to annex Sindh to their empire:
(a) The Amirs refused to fulfil the terms of the treaties imposed on them from time to time
(b) The insubordinate and non-cooperative behaviour of the Amirs towards the English during the course of Ist Afghan War
(c) The revolt of the soldiers of Amirs
(d) The refusal of the Amir of Khairpur to determine its issue of succession with the consent of the English

39. Sindh was occupied by the English in:
(a) 1840 (b) 1841
(c) 1842 (d) 1843

40. The Anglo-Afghan relations in the 19th century were mostly determined because of the fear of expansion towards India by:
(a) France (b) Russia
(c) Persia (d) Afghanistan

41. Dalhousie divided native States into three categories for the enforcement of the Doctrine of Lapse. Which, among the following, was NOT one of those categories?
(a) States which were created or revived by the English
(b) States which had accepted the English as their paramount power
(c) States which had handed over their administration to English officials
(d) States which were accepted as independent States by the English

42. The right of every native ruler to freely adopt a child as his successor was restored to them by:
(a) Lord Canning, the Governor-General of India
(b) The Government of India Act, 1858
(c) The Queen's proclamation of 1858
(d) Sir Charles Wood in 1860 the then Secretary of State for India

43. Which, among the following, was NOT a condition of the Permanent Settlement of Bengal?
(a) The Zamindars (landlords) were recognised hereditary owners of land
(b) They could not be displaced from their land so long they paid the revenue to the Govt
(c) The revenue was fixed permanently with the landlords by the Govt
(d) The share of the landlords out of the produce of the land was also fixed permanently

44. Which, among the following, was not an advantage which the English Company drew by the Permanent Settlement of Bengal?
(a) It created a class of loyal people (landlords) to the English
(b) The Company's annual income out of the revenue was fixed and it had to take no trouble for it
(c) The settlement brought about general prosperity in the provinces of Bengal, Bihar and Orissa and the dividends were shared by the Company as well
(d) The Company gained the loyalty of the peasants as well

45. The worst feature of the Permanent Settlement of Bengal was:
(a) The Company could not increase the revenue in case there was increased production in agriculture
(b) The landlord, could be evicted from their lands in case of non-payment of revenue
(c) The landlords who were actually the, farmers or collectors of the revenue were given hereditary ownership of the lands
(d) The share of the landlord and the peasant, out of agriculture-produce, was not fixed up by the Government

46. Cornwallis increased the number of courts for the dispension of justice'. Which, among the following courts, were in existence prior to his reforms?
(a) Munsif's Courts to Settle the Civil disputes involving an amount upto Rs. 50/- only

(b) Indian Registrar's Courts to settle the Civil disputes involving an amount upto Rs. 200/ - only
(c) District Courts for Civil & Criminal cases separately
(d) Provincial, Civil & Criminal Courts at Calcutta, Dacca, Murshidabad & Patna

47. Which, among the following, was not a cause of introducing the Ryotwari revenue settlement in south-west India by the Company
(a) Absence of big landlords in these territories
(b) Expectation of better financial gain to the Company
(c) Perusal of past tradition in these territories
(d) Failure of Mahalwari-revenue system

48. The driving force behind the introduction of the English as official language of India was:
(a) Efforts of William Bentinck
(b) Minutes of Macaulay
(c) Design of the British to make the Indians only fit for clerks
(d) The philosophy of the Evangelicals, Humanitarians and Liberals, strongly prevalent in Britain at that time.

49. Who, among the following, argued in favour of introducing English language in India thus: "If it had been intended to keep the British Nation in ignorance of real knowledge, the Baconian philosophy would not have been allowed to displace the system of schoolmen .... In the same manner the Sanskrit system of education would be the best calculated to keep this country in darkness."?
(a) Charles Trevelyan (b) Macaulay
(c) R. Heber (d) Raja Ram Mohan Roy

50. Who, among the following, described that one aim of imparting English education in India was "to produce a class of persons who would be Indians in blood and colour but English in taste, in opinions, in orals and in intellect"
(a) Sir Charals Trevelyan (b) Macaulay
(c) William Bentinck (d) Raja Ram Mohan Roy

51. 'William Bentinck attempted to reform Hindu Society by legally abolishing a few social evils'. Which, among the following was not included in them.
(a) Sati-system (b) Infanticide
(c) Thugi (d) Widow remarriage

52. The remarriage of Hindu-widows was first legalised during the Governor Generalship of
(a) William Bentinck (b) Lord Dalhousie
(c) Lord Canning (d) Lord Ripon

53. 'Dalhousie has been regarded as the maker of modern India because he brought about reforms and made a beginning in many fields.' Which, among the following was not included in his scheme of reforms?
(a) Educational reforms based on 'Charles Wood's despatch' and the establishment of examining universities at Madras, Bombay & Calcutta and the Engineering College at Roorkee
(b) Construction of Railways & Telegraph and provision of postal facilities to citizens
(c) Establishment of a separate public works department

(d) 'Factory Act' to improve the working conditions of Indian labour

54. 'Lord Lytton brought about certain measures with a view to strengthen the British rule in India'. Which, among the following, was not helpful to fulfil his aim?
(a) The Royal Titles Act (1876 A.D.)
(b) The Vernacular Press Act (1878 A.D.)
(c) The Arms Act (1878 A.D.)
(d) The establishment of "Statutory Civil Services". (1879A.D.)

55. Which, among the following measures of Lord Ripon, was regarded as the best measure in the interest of the Indians but was made defunct because of a change in it?
(a) Repeal of Vernacular Press Act (1882)
(b) Factory Act (1881)
(c) Resolution on Local Self-Government (1882)
(d) The Ilbert Act (1884)

56. 'Curzon brought about certain measures which were despised by the Indians.' Which, among the following, was not one of them?
(a) The Indian Universities Act (b) The Calcutta Corporation Act
(c) The Ancient Monument Act (d) The partition of Bengal

57. The partition of Bengal was revoked by the British Government in the year:
(a) 1911 (b) 1914
(c) 1917 (d) 1919

58. Which, among the following was not one of the measures which Lord Curzon adopted to bring about improvement in the Police-system
(a) Direct recruitment of officers of the police and establishment of a training school from them
(b) Establishment of Criminal Investigation Department (C.I.D) at the centre and provinces
(c) Increase in salaries of all ranks of police
(d) Recruitment of Indians to high police-posts

59. Which, among the following, was the reason of discontentment of Nana Sahib, the adopted son of the deceased Peshwa Baji Rao against the British?
(a) Nana Sahib was not allowed to assume the title of Peshwa
(b) His jagir was taken over by the British
(c) His hereditary treasure was taken over by the British
(d) The British refused to pay him the pension which was given to his father

60. The Taluqdars of Avadh were annoyed by the British because:
(a) They were asked to pay higher revenue to the company
(b) Their hereditary privileges were abolished by the British
(c) Their share in the land-revenue was fixed
(d) They were asked to prove their claims over their respective jagirs and those who could not prove it were deprived of their Jagirs

61. Which, among the following, was not the one which exhibited racial arrogance of the British in India?
(a) In several hotels and clubs the entry of the Indians was banned

(b) The English misbehaved with their Indian servants
(c) The English indulged in disrespecting Indian women
(d) The entry of the Indians was banned in Britain

62. Which, among the following, was not a measure which created doubt among the Indian that the English were trying to convert them to Christianity?
(a) Introduction of Female education
(b) Reading of the Bible was compulsory in Government and missionary schools
(c) Official support to missionaries
(d) Forceful conversions to Christianity

63. 'Certain measures of Dalhousie created serious discontentment in India which was also responsible for the revolt of 1857'. However, which among the following measures, was not one of them?
(a) 'Doctrine of lapse' and annexation of several states
(b) Introduction of Railways and Telegraph
(c) Abolition of titles and pensions of several rulers
(d) Educational reforms

64. The primary cause of the revolt of 1857 was:
(a) Indian soldier's loyalty to their country
(b) The economic hardships imposed by the British on Indian masses
(c) The desire of the Indians to throw of the British rule
(d) The insistence of the English to use greased cartridges by the Indian soldiers

65. Which, among the following, was the charge against Mangal Pandey who became the first martyr in the revolt of 1857?
(a) He refused to use greased cartridges
(b) He disobeyed his officers
(c) He incited other soldiers for revolt
(d) He attacked his officers

66. Mangal Pandey who mutinied first single handed in 1857 belonged to:
(a) 19th N.I. (b) 22nd N.I.
(c) 34th N.I. (d) 38th N.I.

67. The revolt of 1857 started with the revolt of the , Third Cavalry at Meerut on:
(a) 10th February (b) 10th March
(c) 10th April (d) 10th May

68. Who, among the following, was responsible for the massacres of the English at Kanpur?
(a) Nana Sahib (b) Nana Sahib's soldiers
(c) Tantia Tope (d) Rani Laxmi Bai

69. Which, among the following important centres of the Revolt, was captured first by the English
(a) Jhansi (b) Lucknow
(c) Kanpur (d) Delhi

70. Who, among the following leaders of the Revolt, was the last one subdued by the British
(a) Rani Laxmi Bai (b) Begum Hazrat Mahal
(c) Tantia Tope (d) Azimullah

71. Besides the Indian rulers, which, among the following classes, did not participate in the Revolt
(a) The Zamindars (b) The peasants
(c) The artisans (d) The educated middle class

72. Who, among the following, was in command of the forces at Delhi under Bahadur Shah?
(a) Bakht Khan (b) Azimullah
(c) Khan Bahadur Khan (d) Kanwar Singh

73. Who, among the following, was the leader of the revolt at Kanpur?
(a) Nawab Wazid Ali Shah (b) Begum Hazrat Mahal
(c) Azimullah (d) Birjis Qadar, son of Wazid Ali Shah

74. Who, among the following was the most popular leader of the Revolt in Bihar?
(a) Kanwar Singh (b) Azimullah
(c) Khan Bahadur Khan (d) Amar Singh

75. Who, among the following, has denied to accept the revolt of 1857 as the first war of Indian independence?
(a) Ashoka Mehta (b) Vir Savarkar
(c) S.M. Sen (d) R.C. Mazumdar

76. 'Dr. S.N. Sen has accepted that the revolt of 1857 was a war of independence. Which, among the following reasons, has not been given by him to support his conclusion?
(a) The revolt got the sympathy of the people, may be, that of a minority
(b) The mutineer's ultimate object was to free India from the rule of the foreigners
(c) The Mughal emperor was declared as the leader of the revolt
(d) The leaders of the revolt were national leaders

77. Who, among the following, organised the movement against the oppression of the Indigo- planters in Bengal in 1858-60:
(a) Dinabandhu Mitra
(b) Harish Chandra Mukherji
(c) Sisir Kumar Ghosh
(d) Bishnu Charan Biswas and Digamber Biswas

78. The movement of Indigo-peasants in Bengal took shape of:
(a) Non-payment of revenue to planters
(b) Litigation against the planters
(c) Non-cultivation of Indigo
(d) Passive resistance against the oppression of planters

79. The net result of the movement of Indigo peasants in Bengal was:
(a) Reduction in the revenue
(b) Higher wages to peasant-labour
(c) Passing of an Act removing gross injustices perpetrated to peasants
(d) Elimination of Indigo plantation in Bengal

80. Which, among the following items of Indian export, found the best market in Europe through the efforts of British East India Company?

(a) Cotton textiles (b) Silk-cloth
(c) Spices and pepper (d) Medicinal herbs

81. The main item of import in Britain through the British East India Company in the late 17th century was cotton calicoes. Which, among the following, was the primary reason of it?
(a) France and Holland had prohibited its import in their country
(b) There were no import duties on it in Britain by that time
(c) Improvement in the quality of calicoes by the Indians
(d) Change in fashions in Britain

82. The British started economic exploitation of the Indians when:
(a) There remained no fear of the Mughal emperor
(b) There remained no fear of the might of the Marathas after the 3rd battle of Panipat
(c) There remained no European rival after the 3rd Anglo-French war
(d) They captured political power in the provinces of Bengal, Bihar, and Orissa after the battle of Plassey

83. After the occupation of Bengal, Bihar and Orissa, the English used their power by several means for the betterment of their trade resulting in destruction of rafts: However, which among the following means, was not adopted by them for the purpose?
(a) They monopolished the trade of Bengal by several legislations
(b) The English Company engaged Indian representatives gomashtas who registered Indian artisans particularly cloth weavers to work only for the company
(c) The weavers registered with the company were assigned fixed quantity and quality of work while they were paid arbitrarily
(d) The English manipulated the prices of raw materials much against the interest of the artisans

84. Which, among the following, was NOT the consequence of the destruction of Indian handicrafts?
(a) It destroyed the self-sufficient economy of the villages
(b) It put pressure on land because artisans were also forced to take up agriculture
(c) Several towns famous for different handicrafts were ruined
(d) Indian economy, as a whole, suffered a serious set-back

85. Which, among the following measures of the English, was primarily responsible for moulding the Indian economy in the colonial pattern?
(a) Buying Indian raw material for the industries of Britain selling their manufactured products in India
(b) Pursuing bilateral trade in the interest of their mother-country
(c) Restricting Indian trade with countries other than Britain
(d) Imposing heavy taxes on Indian goods entering Britain

86. Prior to 1813 A.D. which, among the following measures, was NOT adopted by the British to exploit the Indians economically?
(a) Forcing Indian craftsmen to produce quality products in fixed quantity and at fixed price
(b) Elimination of Indian traders from competition by every means i.e., privilege of trade free of tax

(c) Monopolising the trade of raw goods wherever possible and selling them at higher rates
(d) Free-trade policy

87. East India Company lost its monopoly over the trade in India in the year:
(a) 1798 (b) 1813
(c) 1833 (d) 1853

88. Which, among the following, was not the result of exporting raw-materials from India to Britain?
(a) India lost its surplus agriculture produce which, in case of emergency, could be utilised for home-consumption
(b) It resulted in several famines in India
(c) It raised the prices of agriculture products
(d) It led to black-marketing in agriculture products

89. Which, among the following, conveys the correct nature of the policy of 'free trade' pursued by the English in India?
(a) Both Britain and India charged protective duties on the export and import of each others products
(b) Both Britain and India abolished all duties on the export and import of each other's products
(c) India charged no tax or only nominal tax on products of export and import to and from Britain respectively while Britain charged protective duties on its exports and imports to and from India respectively
(d) India charged no tax or only nominal tax on British goods entering India while Britain charged no tax on Indian goods of all sorts

90. 'In the 20th century several other countries other than Britain, entered the Indian market' which, among the following, was, however, NOT one of them?
(a) Germany (b) U.S.A.
(c) Japan (d) U. S. S. R.

91. Besides the policy-measures of the British the one cause which resulted in the economic exploitation of India by the British in the 19th century was:
(a) Industrialization of Britain by modern means
(b) Deterioration in the quality of Indian products
(c) Absence of quality raw-material in India
(d) Lack of capital in India.

92. Which, among the following was NOT one of policy-measures of British which resulted in the economic exploitation of India by the British
(a) Savings of all Britishers in India were transferred to Britain
(b) India was forced to accept unfavourable balance of trade
(c) The income from Indian revenue and other sources was utilised for the purchase of Indian raw-goods and transferred to Britain as 'Investments'
(d) Indian traders were encouraged to invest their capital with English trading companies

93. Which, among the following typical problems of Indian agriculture during the 19th and 20th centuries was not a direct result of British agrarian policy?

(a) Fragmentation of land holdings
(b) Rural indebtedness
(c) Disparity of prices between agricultural and non-agricultural products
(d) Increase in the number of landless agriculturists

94. Which, among the following, was not a cause of fragmentation of holdings of the Indian peasants?
(a) Hindu law of succession which gave equal share in the property of the father to all his sons
(b) Increase in population
(c) Right of selling their lands by the peasants
(d) Destruction of Indian handicrafts.

95. Which among the following agricultural products, was NOT commercialized during the British rule:
(a) Cotton (b) Silk
(c) Indigo (d) Tea
(e) Coffee (f) Jute

96. Which, among the following, was not a pioneer industry in India during the British rule?
(a) Cotton (b) Jute
(c) Coal (d) Iron

97. Which, among the following, was primarily responsible for initiating Industrial progress in India?
(a) The initiative of Indian enterprises
(b) The desire of the British government to start certain auxiliary industries in India
(c) The necessity to absorb the surplus production of raw materials in industries
(d) The British capitalists found it profitable to invest their capital in India as compared to Britain when Industrial growth reached a stage of optimum in Britain

98. 'The British capitalists found it profitable to invest their capital in India due to several reasons.' However, which, among the following, was NOT one of those reasons?
(a) Labour was cheap in India
(b) Indian government was prepared to give them every possible facility
(c) India and nearby countries provided a good market for their finished goods
(d) The Indians felt shy of entering into competition with them

99. Which, among the following agricultural products, was NOT the one which attracted British capital?
(a) Indigo (b) Tea
(c) Coffee (d) Cotton

100. Heavy industries could not develop in India during the 19th century primarily because of:
(a) Shortage of capital
(b) Absence of skilled labour
(c) Inadequate production of coal
(d) None

Answers

1. (d)	21. (d)	41. (c)	61. (d)	81. (b)
2. (a)	22. (c)	42. (c)	62. (d)	82. (d)
3. (d)	23. (d)	43. (d)	63. (d)	83. (a)
4. (b)	24. (b)	44. (d)	64. (d)	84. (c)
5. (c)	25. (d)	45. (d)	65. (d)	85. (a)
6. (b)	26. (a)	46. (c)	66. (c)	86. (d)
7. (c)	27. (d)	47. (d)	67. (d)	87. (b)
8. (a)	28. (d)	48. (d)	68. (b)	88. (d)
9. (d)	29. (a)	49. (d)	69. (d)	89. (c)
10. (b)	30. (a)	50. (b)	70. (c)	90. (d)
11. (d)	31. (d)	51. (d)	71. (d)	91. (a)
12. (d)	32. (c)	52. (b)	72. (a)	92. (d)
13. (d)	33. (d)	53. (d)	73. (b)	93. (c)
14. (b)	34. (c)	54. (a)	74. (a)	94. (c)
15. (b)	35. (d)	55. (d)	75. (d)	95. (b)
16. (c)	36. (d)	56. (c)	76. (d)	96. (d)
17. (d)	37. (d)	57. (d)	77. (d)	97. (d)
18. (a)	38. (d)	58. (d)	78. (c)	98. (d)
19. (a)	39. (d)	59. (d)	79. (c)	99. (d)
20. (b)	40. (b)	60. (d)	80. (a)	100. (c)

SET VI

Questions

1. The industrial progress of India received impetus in the second decade of the 20th century due to:
   (a) Rise in demand of Indian Industrial goods abroad
   (b) The British industrial progress reached an optimum point
   (c) Heavy investments were made in India by foreigners
   (d) First World War which created the necessity of production of certain goods in India
2. Which, among the following statements, is NOT correct concerning the growth of Industries in India?
   (a) There was regional disparity in industrial growth
   (b) The growth was extremely slow
   (c) All the industries were owned or controlled by British Capital
   (d) The government provided no help to them
3. 'British capital entered Indian industries extensively.' However, which among the following industries, was largely managed by the Indian capital?
   (a) Jute (b) Coal
   (c) Cotton-textiles (d) Sugar
4. Which, among the following, was NOT one of the handicaps in the industrial growth of India?
   (a) The government favoured foreign investors than the Indians
   (b) Most of the banks were managed by the Britishers which did not finance Indian industrialists
   (c) Heavy industries like coal and iron were not well-developed in India
   (d) Indian capital was in shortage
5. 'Several plantation-industries owned by the Britishers grew up in India in the 19th century. However, which among the following was NOT one of them ?
   (a) Coffee (b) Tea
   (c) Rubber (d) Indigo
6. The British undertook the development of the means of communication in India. Which among the following, was NOT a cause of it?

(a) Procurement of raw material from distant place
(b) Supply of manufactured goods even to remote areas
(c) Welfare of the people in case of famines or epidemics
(d) Transportation of military personnel and supplies

7. 'The industrial development of India, however meagre it was during the British rule affected the social framework of India.' Which among the following, however, was NOT a consequence of it?
(a) It led to the consolidation of the unified national economy
(b) It brought into existence modern cities which became the centres of modern culture and increasing democratic social life
(c) It created a new class i.e., the industrial working class
(d) It opened avenues for the employment of the educated middle class

8. The drain of the wealth of India began after the year
(a) 1757 (b) 1764
(c) 1783 (d) 1813

9. Which, among the following , was the means by which the English could manage the drain of wealth of India after 1747?
(a) Sent the revenue of Bengal, Bihar and Orissa to Britain
(b) Sent their salaries, pensions, etc, to Britain
(c) Purchased trade goods from the revenue of Bengal, Bihar and Orissa instead of the money from Britain and thus, traded without their own investment.
(d) None

10. Which, among the following urban classes, emerged as a direct result of modern education during the British rule? '
(a) Capitalist class (b) The professional classes
(c) The modern working class (d) The class of petty traders

11. 'One striking characteristic of the new social classes which emerged during the British rule was their national character 'Which among the following was NOT one of the causes of that:
(a) Emergence of national leadership
(b) All classes were integral parts of a single national economy
(c) All classes under a single state regime
(d) Uniform system of education

12. 'Various social and religious reform movements took place in India during the 19th century' Which among the following was NOT one of the sources of inspiration for them?
(a) Nationalism (b) Democracy
(c) Individualism (d) Socialism

13. Who, among the following, was the pioneer of the social and religion movements of the 19th century in India?
(a) Raja Ram Mohan Roy (b) Swami Dayanand Saraswati
(c) Swami Vivekananda (d) Aurobindo Ghosh

14. 'Raja Ram Mohan Roy wrote several books and articles for the enlightenment of the people'. Which, among the following, was NOT conveyed by him to the people through his writings?

(a) Social and religious reform
(b) Development of national outlook
(c) Certain grievances of the people to be looked into by the government
(d) Administration lapses of the government

15. 'Raja Ram Mohan desired to improve the lot of the peasants and for that suggested several means.' Which among the following, was NOT suggested by him?
(a) Employment of Indians in the revenue department which would have reduced the cost of administration
(b) Reduction in the revenue
(c) Fixation of the revenue which was to be paid by the peasants to the Zamindars
(d) Abolition of the Zamindari system

16. The Prarthana Samaj was inspired by the Bhartiya Brahmo Samaj and its founder Keshab Chandra Sen. It mostly accepted the social and religious reforms ideas of it: But which, among the following, was NOT accepted by it?
(a) Inter-dining and inter-caste marriages
(b) Remarriages of windows
(c) Improvement of the lot of Depressed classes
(d) Unity of God

17. Who, among the following, was the chief architect of the Prarthana Samaj in Maharashtra?
(a) Mahadev Govinda Ranade (b) Bal Gangadhar Tilak
(c) R.G. Bhandarkar (d) Atmaram Panduranga

18. The pioneer of the 'Young Bengal Movement' was:
(a) Keshab Chandra Sen (b) Henry Vivian Derozio
(c) Surendra Nath Banerjee (d) None

19. Which, among the following, was the primary reason because of which the Young Bengal Movement could not become popular in Bengal?
(a) It did not appeal to educated people
(b) It was too revolutionary
(c) Its economic programme was not appealing
(d) Theoretically it had an ideal appeal but, being based too much on reason it lacked emotional appeal

20. Primarily, Ishwar Chandra Vidyasagar was an educationist and did much for female-education but his name is attached with a social reform which, among the following, was that social reform?
(a) Widow remarriages (b) Abolition of Sati
(c) Prohibition of polygamy (d) Prohibition of child marriages

21. Swami Dayanand Saraswati established Arya Samaj in 1875 at:
(a) Lahore (b) Nagpur
(c) Ahmadnagar (d) Bombay

22. Which, among the following, was the distinguishing feature concerning religion between Brahmo Samaj and Arya Samaj?
(a) Anti idolatry (b) Separation of social evils from religion
(c) Anti ritualism (d) Equal status to all religion

23. Who, among the following was the founder of Ramakrishan mission?
(a) Ramakrishan Paramahansa (b) Devendra Nath Tagore
(c) Swami Vivekananda (d) Keshav Chandra Sen

24. 'The teachings of Ramakrishna constitute the soul of the Ramakrishna mission' and he emphasized on three things. Which among the following, was NOT one of his principal teachings
(a) Spiritualism (b) Parity to all religion
(c) Service to humanity (d) Suppression of worldly desires

25. Who among the following said that 'so long as the millions live in hunger and ignorance, I hold every man a traitor who, having been educated at their expense, pay not the least heed to them?'
(a) Raja Ram Mohan Roy (b) Swami Dayanand
(c) Sri Ramakrishna (d) Swami Vivekanand

26. Swami Vivekanand went to U. S. A. and participated in the World Religions Conference held in 1893 at:
(a) New York (b) Chicago
(c) Philadelphia (d) Washington

27. Who, among the following, first used the word 'Swarajya' and accepted Hindi as the national language of India?
(a) Raja Ram Mohan Roy (b) Swami Dayanand
(c) Swami Vivekananda (d) Bal Gangadhar Tilak

28. Where, among the following places, the Theosophical Society was established first in India?
(a) Bombay (b) Thana near Bombay
(c) Adyar near Madras (d) Calcutta

29. The Anglo Oriental College, which later on grew up as the University of Aligarh, was started by Sir Syed Ahmad Khan in
(a) 1875 (b) 1876
(c) 1877 (d) 1888

30. Who, among the following was NOT a leader of the justice movements in Tamil Nadu aiming to destroy the supremacy of Brahmins in services, education and politics?
(a) C.N. Mudaliar (b) T.M. Nair
(c) C. Rajagopalachari (d) P Tyagaraja

31. Who, among the following, was the founder of the 'Satya-Shodak-Samaj' in Maharashtra in 1873 primarily claiming the status of the Kshatriyas for the Marathas?
(a) Jyotiba Phule (b) Keshavaro Jedhe
(c) Dinkarroa Javalkar (d) Mukandrao Patil

32. Class concept is against Casteism because the concept of class is:
(a) Opposed to religion (b) Opposed to social divisions
(c) A Western concept (d) An economic concept which directly attacks social distinctions based on heredity

33. The All-India Depressed Classes Federation was founded by:
(a) A.V. Thakkur (b) Dr. Ambedkar
(c) M.K. Gandhi (d) Sir Narayan Chandavarkar

34. 'A few states under the native rulers initiated reforms of the Hindu society by legislation. Which, among the following states, was NOT one of them?
(a) Mysore (b) Baroda
(c) Travancore (d) Nagpur

35. The practice of hook-swinging at Charak puja and other acts of self torture in public were first made illegal in:
(a) 1856 (b) 1860
(c) 1865 (d) 1870

36. 'The passing of the Age of Consent Act, forbidding the consummation of marriage before the wife had reached the age of twelve in 1891 A.D. was opposed by one of the national leaders on the plea that a foreign government had no right to interfere in the social reform of the Hindus'. Who, among the following, was that leader?
(a) M.G. Ranade (b) S.N.Banerjee
(c) B.G. Tilak (d) Lala Lajpat Rai

37. Which among the following, was NOT one of the causes which helped much in the emancipation of women during the British rule?
(a) Female-education
(b) Social and religious movements and reforms societies
(c) Participation of women in national movement
(d) Legalisation concerning rights of women by the government

38. Who, among the following, found the All India Harijan Sangh in 1932?
(a) Dr. B.R. Ambedkar (b) A.V. Thakkar
(c) M.K. Gandhi (d) B.G. Tilak

39. 'Dr. B.R. Ambedkar, throughout his life, fought for the rights of the depressed classes.' To what conclusion, among the following, he reached as the final solution for the protection of their rights after Indian Independence?
(a) Representation of the Depressed classes according to their population
(b) Reservation of seats for them in Services, Assemblies and Parliament
(c) Acceptance of Islam by them
(d) Acceptance of Buddhism by them

40. 'The first Factory Act was passed in 1881'. With what, among the following, it was concerned?
(a) Female labour
(b) Child labour
(c) Fixation of working hours of adult male labour
(d) Compensation to workers in case of accidents

41. 'Factory laws were passed in 1881, 1891, 1911, 1922 and 1930 well'. Which, among the following, was the cause of their beginning?
(a) Government felt that justice should be provided to the labour
(b) The Factory owners were too much oppressive towards the labour
(c) Organisations of the labour had become strong

(d) Competition between British and India-made goods started and, therefore, these laws were used as levers to discourage that competition.

42. Which, among the following, was NOT one of the reasons of intensification of labour-movement after the First World war?
(a) Rise in cost of living
(b) Russian Revolution 1971
(c) Non-cooperation Movement inspired the labour
(d) The labour-movement of Britain inspired the Indian labour

43. The All India Trade Union Congress to further the interests of the Indian labour in matters economic, social and political was first established in:
(a) 1915 (b) 1920
(c) 1925 (d) 1930

44. Who, among the following, was NOT among the founder members of A.I.T.U.C.(All India Trade Union Congress)?
(a) V.V. Giri (b) N.M. Joshi
(c) Lala Lajpat Rai (d) Joseph Baptista

45. Which, among the following, was Not one of the objectives of the A.I.TU.C. ?
(a) Every industry should have the right to form its own union
(b) To socialise and nationalise the means of production and distribution
(c) To establish a social state in India
(d) To reach economic justice for the labour

46. Who, among the following, was the founder of the I.TU.F. (Indian Trade Union Federation)?
(a) V.V. Giri (b) N.M. Joshi
(c) Lala Lajpat Rai (d) Joseph Baptista

47. The first Trade Union Act was passed in:
(a) 1918 (b) 1920
(c) 1926 (d) 1930

48. Which, among the following was NOT the demand of the peasants during the period of economic depression in the late 1920s and early 1930s?
(a) Relief from indebtedness (b) Reduction of land-revenue
(c) Abolition of Zamindari (d) Support price for agricultural goods

49. 'The British changed the patterns of their policy towards the native-rulers at different times. The policy has been divided primarily into four categories. Which, among the following categories, was pursued by the British during the period 1858-1935?
(a) Policy of Ring Fence
(b) Policy of Subordinate Isolation
(c) Policy of Subordiante co-operation and Union
(d) Policy of Equal Federation

50. Which, among the following was the primary aim of the British in pursuing the policy of Ring fence (1765-1183) with native rulers?
(a) Maintenance of good relations with neighbouring states
(b) Seeking military help from neighbouring states against enemy rulers

(c) Keeping neighbouring states divided among themselves
(d) Defence of neighbour's frontiers for safeguarding their own territories

51. Which, among the following was the primary aim of the British in pursuing the policy of subordinate union and cooperation (1858-1935) with native rulers?
(a) Acceptance of British paramountcy by native rulers
(b) Seeking cooperation of Indian rulers in all Indian matters
(c) Recognition of their claim as hereditary rulers of their states and obligation to keep their territories and respect intact
(d) Reducing native states to the status of feudatories and vessels and pursuance of the "Theory of one charge, in administration"

52. Which, among the following, was the primary aim of the British in pursuing the 'policy of equal federation' (1935-1947) with native rulers?
(a) Providing status equal to the British governed-provinces to Indian States
(b) Encouraging native-rulers to assert their independent status as rulers of distinct states
(c) Encouraging native-rulers to develop extra territorial loyalties
(d) Seeking co-operation of native rulers in an 'All India Federation scheme' envisaged in the Act of 1935

53. Which, among the following native states, was forced to merge itself into Indian union after Independence of India?
(a) Mysore (b) Kashmir
(c) Patiala (d) Hyderabad

54. Who, among the following members, was the chairman of Reorganization Commission of States?
(a) K.M. Pannikar (b) Fazal Ali
(c) Hridayanath Kunzru (d) V.B. Patel

55. The 'States Reorganization Act' was passed in the year
(a) 1948 A.D. (b) 1950 A.D.
(c) 1954 A.D. (d) 1956 A.D.

56. The first newspaper which was published in India was titled,
(a) The Bengal Gazette (b) The Calcutta Gazette
(c) The Oriental Magazine (d) The Calcutta Chronicle

57. The censorship of the press started during the period of Governor-general ship of:
(a) Lord Welesley (b) Lord Hastings
(c) Lord Elianborough (d) Lord Lytton

58. The Vernacular Press Act passed during the Viceroyalty of Lord Lytton was repealed by:
(a) William Bentinck (b) Lord Canning
(c) Lord Ripon (d) Lord Dufferin

59. The most comprehensive Act limitin the liberty of the Indian Press was:
(a) The Newspaper Act, 1908
(b) Indian Press Act 1910
(c) The Indian Press (Emergency Power Act, 1931)
(d) The Press (Objectionable Matters Act, 1951)

60. In which, among the following presidency towns, the local body came into existence first?
(a) Calcutta (b) Madras
(c) Bombay (d) Delhi

61. Which among the following provinces made a beginning of Municipal Institutions outside the presidency towns?
(a) Bengal (b) Madras
(c) Bombay (d) Uttar Pradesh

62. Which among the following, was NOT included in Ripon's Resolution of 1882 concerning local self-government?
(a) Local boards viz. Municipalities, Taluka Boards, District Boards were to be developed throughout the country
(b) Local bodies were to have non official majorities coupled with a general system of election wherever possible
(c) Local bodies were provided freedom to raise financial resources within their geographical limits
(d) Official interference was to be reduced to the minimum

63. Which, among the following, was NOT one of the recommendations of the Decentralization Commission, 1908?
(a) Larger powers to village Panchayats and establishments of Sub-District Boards with independent powers
(b) Withdrawals of restrictions on the powers of taxation of local bodies
(c) Unrestricted powers to raise loans by local bodies on their own credit
(d) All of the above were recommended

64. Who, among the following, was the author of the novel Gora?
(a) Bankim Chandra Chatterjee (b) Rabindranath Tagore
(c) Sarat Chandra (d) Sanjib Chandra

65. Sarat Chandra, the Bengali scholar-writer is famous because of his:
(a) Poems (b) Novels
(c) Dramas (d) Essays

66. Modern Punjabi literature begins with the work of:
(a) Bhai Vir Singh (b) Puran Singh
(c) Kirpa Singh (d) Khushwant Singh

67. Who, among the following writers of Urdu, has the poems, titled Shikwa (complaint) and Jawab Shikwa (Reply to the complaint)?
(a) Muhammad Iqbal (b) Akbar Ilahabadi
(c) Shabbir Hussain Josh Malihabadi (d) Upindar Nath Ashq

68. Which, among the following Acts, first made the provision of an Indian High Commissioner in England
(a) Indian Council's Act (b) Government of India Act
(c) Government of India Act (d) India Independence Act

69. Who, among the following leaders, was NOT among the Moderates?
(a) Gopal Krishan Gokhale (b) Firoz Shah Mehta
(c) Dada Bhai Naoroji (d) S.N. Banerjee

70. The planned venue for holding the first session of the All India Congress was:
(a) Madras (b) Poona
(c) Bombay (d) Ahmedabad

71. 'The resolutions which were passed by the Congress in its Calcutta session in 1906 A.D. formed, the genesis of the split of the Congress at Surat in 1907 A.D. However which, among the following, was NOT the topic on which the resolutions were passed in 1906 A.D.?
(a) Self-government (b) Swadeshi
(c) Boycott of foreign goods (d) Economy of the country

72. Who, among the following was elected President of the Congress in 1907 A.D. ?
(a) Dadabhai Naoroji (b) Rashbihari Ghosh
(c) Moti Lai Nehru (d) Surendra Nath Banerjee

73. Which, among the following, was the first step of M.K. Gandhi when be started the Civil Disobedience Movement?
(a) He gave a call for a country-wide Hartal
(b) He gave a call to the people to stop payment of taxes to the government
(c) He marched from Sabarmati ashram to Dandi and picked up some salt left by the waves
(d) He gave a call to the people to disobey the laws of the government

74. Which, among the following, was the objective of Gandhi in starting the Dandi-March to prepare salt from sea-water?
(a) To gain sympathy of the masses
(b) To propagate the ideology of the Congress among the masses
(c) To defy the salt-law
(d) To defy the prohibitory orders of the local officers of Dandi against mass-meeting

75. 'All India States' Peoples' Conference was formed in 1927 to strengthen the political movement in Indian states'. Who, among the following Congress leaders, was the first one to accept its Presidentship in 1929?
(a) Sardar Vallabh Bhai Patel (b) Acharya Kriplani
(c) Maulana Azad (d) Pt. Jawahar Lai Nehru

76. Who, among the following, modern Assamese Writers, has- translated the Rubaiyat of Omar Khayyam from Fitzgerald's English version:
(a) Sarat Chandra Goswami (b) Jatindranath Durga
(c) Nalinibala Devi (d) Mafizuddin Ahmad

77. Who, among the following, group of writers formed the 'illustrious trio' of Oriya literature in its beginning:
(a) Phakir Mohan Senapati, Radha Nath Reya and Madhu Sudan Rao
(b) Asvini Kumara Ghosa, Godavarisa Misra and Chandra Shekhara Pani
(c) Madhu Sudana Das, Visva Nath Kora and Basudeva Mahapatra
(d) Prof Girija Shankar Raya, Pandit Binayaka Misra and Pandit Nilakantha Dasa

78. Who, among the following, is acknowledged as one of the makers of modern Hindi?
(a) Ram Prasad Niranjani (b) Pandit Daulatram
(c) Munshi Sadasukh Lai Niyaz (d) Bharatendu Harish Chandra

79. Who, among the following, was the pioneer in making Hindi a standard literary language?
(a) Munshi Prem Chand (b) Mahavir Prasad Dwivedi
(c) Jitendra Kumar (d) Brindaban Lal Verma

80. Who among the following Hindi poets, is the author of Kamayan?
(a) Sumitra Nandan Pant (b) Mahadevi Verma
(c) Jayasartkar Prasad (d) Suryakanta Tripathi Nirala

81. Who, among the following Marathi scholars, has been regarded as the Panini of Marathi?
(a) Sadashiv Kashinath (b) Bapu Chhatra
(c) Hari Keshavji (d) Dadoba Pandurang

82. The outstanding novel of Marathi Ranangam Apte is by
(a) Hari Narayan Apte (b) Prof N. S. Phadke
(c) P. V. Deshpande (d) Vishram Badekar

83. Who, among the following poets, has been called the Tagore of Punjabi?
(a) Puran Singh (b) Mohan Singh
(c) Amrita Pritam (d) Kartar Singh Duggal

84. Who, among the Gujarati scholars, was the author of the novel, Sarasvatichandra?
(a) Narmada Shankar (b) Govardhanram Madhavram Tripathi
(c) Manilal Nabhubhai Dvivedi (d) K.M. Munshi

85. Who, among the following, scholars in the beginning of the 20th century, has been described as the pioneer of modern Tamil literature?
(a) Subramania Bharati (b) C. Rajagopalachari
(c) Bharati Dasar (d) Namakkal Ramalingam Pillai

86. Who, among the following modern poets of Telgu literature, has been compared with poet Shelley of English literature?
(a) Visvanatha Satyanarayana (b) Devulapalli Krishnasastri
(c) Krishnamurti Sastri (d) D.R. Reddi

87. Who, among the following, translated a few works of Bankim Chandra into Kannada language?
(a) B. Venkatachar (b) Galga Nath
(c) A.N. Krishan Rao (d) Kattimani

88. Who, among the following writers, has been regarded as the most eminent writer of Urdu in the 19th century?
(a) Pallathu Raman (b) Kuttippurath Kesavan
(c) C. Sankara Kurup (d) Changampuzha Krishna Pillai

89. Who, among the following writers, has been regarded as the most eminent writer of Urdu in the 19th century?
(a) Muhammad Ibrahim Zauq (b) Asadullah Khan Ghalib
(c) Amir Ahmad Minai (d) Nawab Mirza Khan Dagh

90. Who among the following wrote Gitanjali?
(a) Rabindra Nath Tagore (b) Aurobindo Ghosh
(c) Sarojini Naidu (d) Harindra Nath Chattopadhyaya

91. Who, among the following, is the author of the novel, Coolie?
(a) Raja Rao (b) Mulk Raj Anand
(c) R.K.Narayanan (d) Bhabani Bhattacharya

92. The Victoria Memorial Hall in Calcutta constructed in 1921, has been built of:
(a) White stone (b) White Makrana marble
(c) Red Stone (d) Bricks and stone

93. The city of New Delhi was opened for public habitation in:
(a) 1920 (b) 1925
(c) 1930 (d) 1935

94. 'The paintings executed by the British artists in India fall into three categories. Which, among the following, was NOT one of them:
(a) Large-size oil paintings (b) Miniature paintings
(c) Water colour drawings (d) Frescoes

95. Which, among the following, constituted the novelty of the art of painting of Ravi Varma?
(a) Portraits (b) Frescoes
(c) Use of oil colours (d) Water colour drawings

96. Who, among the following, was the leader of the neo-Bengal school of painting:
(a) Rabindra Nath Tagore (b) Gajendra Nath Tagore
(c) Rabindra Nath Tagore (d) Nand Lai Bose

97. Pitt's India Act, which was meant to remove the defects of the Regulating Act was passed in the year:
(a) 1781 (b) 1782
(c) 1784 (d) 1786

98. Which, among the following Acts of the British Parliament, abolished the monopoly over the trade of India of the Company?
(a) Company's Charter Act 1793 (b) Company's Charter Act 1831
(c) Company's Charter Act 1833 (d) Company's Charter Act 1853

99. Which, among the following was the most distinguished and despised provision of the Indian Councils Act, 1909 or the Minto-Morley Reforms?
(a) Enlargement of the Legislative Councils both at the Centre and provinces
(b) Provisions of the majority of non-official members in provincial legislatures
(c) Provision of separate electorates
(d) Increased powers of the members of Legislative Councils both at the Centre and Provinces

100. Where was Brahmo Samaj first established?
(a) Bengal (b) The Punjab
(c) Bombay (d) Madras

Answers

1. (d)	21. (a)	41. (b)	61. (a)	81. (b)
2. (c)	22. (d)	42. (d)	62. (c)	82. (d)
3. (c)	23. (c)	43. (b)	63. (d)	83. (a)
4. (d)	24. (a)	44. (a)	64. (b)	84. (b)
5. (c)	25. (d)	45. (a)	65. (b)	85. (a)
6. (c)	26. (b)	46. (b)	66. (a)	86. (b)
7. (d)	27. (d)	47. (c)	67. (a)	87. (a)
8. (a)	28. (c)	48. (d)	68. (b)	88. (c)
9. (c)	29. (c)	49. (c)	69. (c)	89. (b)
10. (b)	30. (c)	50. (d)	70. (b)	90. (a)
11. (a)	31. (a)	51. (d)	71. (d)	91. (b)
12. (b)	32. (d)	52. (d)	72. (b)	92. (b)
13. (a)	33. (b)	53. (d)	73. (c)	93. (c)
14. (d)	34. (d)	54. (b)	74. (c)	94. (d)
15. (d)	35. (c)	55. (d)	75. (d)	95. (c)
16. (d)	36. (c)	56. (a)	76. (b)	96. (a)
17. (a)	37. (d)	57. (a)	77. (a)	97. (c)
18. (a)	38. (d)	58. (c)	78. (d)	98. (b)
19. (d)	39. (d)	59. (d)	79. (a)	99. (c)
20. (d)	40. (b)	60. (b)	80. (c)	100. (a)

SET VII

Questions

1. Where was the purdah system not practised in the 18th century?
   (a) South India (b) Rajasthan
   (c) The Punjab (d) Gujarat
2. Among the language known to Raja Rammohan Roy, one of the following was not known to him. Identify.
   (a) Sanskrit (b) Persian
   (c) Hebrew (d) Malayalam
3. In what language did Rammohan write his Gift to Monotheists?
   (a) Sanskrit (b) Bengali
   (c) Persian (d) Hindi
4. Pick out the correct statement about Rammohan Roy:
   (a) Raja Rammohan relied blindly on India's
   (b) Rammohan aped blindly the western system
   (c) He wanted that new India should acquire all that was best in the East and the West
   (d) He did not want India to learn from the West.
5. Against which of the following social evils Rammohan organised the historic agitation?
   (a) Sati (b) Female infantaticide
   (c) Early marriage (d) Untouchability
6. Who founded the Hindu College?
   (a) David Hare (b) William Jones
   (c) Rammohan Roy (d) Dayananda
7. Henry Vivian Derozio was a/an:
   (a) Irish man (b) Anglo-Indian
   (c) Englishman (d) Frenchman
8. Derozio was removed from the Hindu College because of one of the following reasons. Identify.
   (a) He was a Christian (b) He hated Hinduism
   (c) He was racial (d) He was a bad teacher

9. Who are described by Surendranath Banerjea as pioneers of the modern civilisation of Bengal, the co-script fathers of our race?
(a) Brahma Samajists (b) Asiatic society of Bengal
(c) Derozians (d) Arya Samajists
10. Outside Bengal, Where did Brahmo Samaj take a firm root?
(a) Rajasthan (b) Andhra
(c) Orissa (d) Maharashtra
11. Who founded the Deccan Education Society?
(a) R.G.Bhandarkar (b) Professor Kelkar
(c) Jotiba Phule (d) M.G. Ranade
12. Who was known in early life as Mula Sankara?
(a) Dayananda (b) Ramakrishan
(c) Vivekananda (d) Rabindranath Tagore
13. Which among the following started a crusade against other religions?
(a) Brahmo Samaj (b) Prarthana Samaj
(c) Theosophical Society (d) Arya Samaj
14. Which of the following is said to have contributed to the growth of communalism in India in the 20th century?
(a) Brahmo Samaj (b) Arya Samaj
(c) Prarthana Samaj (d) Ramakrishan Mission
15. Who was the Parmahansa Mandali started by?
(a) C.F. Andrews (b) Rammohan Roy
(c) H.V. Derozio (d) Dayananda
16. Who gave the call 'Back to the Vedas'?
(a) Vivekananda (b) Ramakrishna Paramahansa
(c) Dayananda (d) Raja Rammohan Roy
17. Which of the following statements cannot to attributed to Dayananda?
(a) Every person had the right of direct access to God
(b) He led a revolt against Hindu orthodoxy
(c) He favoured the study of western sciences
(d) He considered the priests as highly learned and selfless
18. Who said that the different creeds are but different paths to reach the same God (yat mat tata path)?
(a) Ramakrishna (b) Annie Besant
(c) Vivekananda (d) Dayananda
19. Among the teachings of Ramakrishana one of the following cannot be attributed to him. Identify.
(a) Service to humanity is service to divinity
(b) Women should be treated with honour
(c) Renunciation of worldly life is essential for realisation of God
(d) The worship of images is not incompatible with the highest spiritual development
20. Who wrote 'Ramakrishana-His Life and Sayings'?
(a) Swami Vivekananda (b) Max Muller
(c) Rasmani (d) Keshab Chandra Sen

21. One of the following was not a follower of Dayananda
(a) Lala Hansraj (b). Pandit Guru Dutt
(c) Lala Lajpat Rai (d) M.G. Ranade
22. When was the Parliament of Religions held?
(a) 1893 (b) 1902
(c) 1883 (d) 1913
23. Where did the Theosophists establish their headquarters?
(a) Calcutta (b) Lahore
(c) Poona (d) Adyar
24. Who formed Aligarh school? The followers of:
(a) Sayyid Ahmad Khan (b) Muhammad lqbal
(c) Abul Kalam Azad (d) Muhammad Ali Jinnah
25. Who coined the word Pakistan?
(a) Muhammad Iqbal (b) Sayyid Ahmad Khan
(c) M.A. Jinnah (d) Ch. Rahmat Ali
26. Who founded the Servants of India Society?
(a) G.K. Gokhale (b) Surendranath Banerjee
(c) B. G. Tilak (d) M.G. Ranade
27. Who among the following favoured Indian Women's University?
(a) D.K. Karve (b) M.G. Ranade
(c) B.G. Tilak (d) G.K. Gokhale
28. Who among the following was not a discoverer?
(a) J.C. Bose (b) C.V. Raman
(c) B.N. Seal (d) Meghnad Saha
29. Who founded a Sanskrit College at Benares?
(a) William Jones (b) Jonathan Duncan
(c) Charles Grant (d) Warren Hastings
30. One of the following did not establish an English school. Identify.
(a) William Carey (b) David Hare
(c) Rammohan Roy (d) Jonathan Duncan
31. Who made a powerful plea in favour of western education in his Minute of 2nd February, 1835?
(a) Alexander Duff (b) T. B. Macaulay
(c) William Bentinck (d) Jonathan Duncan
32. Who organised the Non-Brahmin movement in Maharashtra?
(a) Jotiba Govind Phule (b) M.G. Ranade
(c) B.G.Tilak (d) G.H. Deshmukh
33. When was the non-Brahmin movement started in Tamil Nadu?
(a) 1914 (b) 1916
(c) 1928 (d) 1939
34. Who started the Dravida Kazhagam?
(a) E.X. Ramasami (Periyar) (b) C.N. Annadurai
(c) T.M. Nair (d) K. Veeramani
35. Who among the following people launched a spirited depressed classes' fight against caste tyranny?

(a) B.R. Ambedkar (b) M.C. Rajah
(c) Jagjivan Ram (d) Rao Bahadur Srinivasan

36. What made B. R. Ambedkar lead the movement of mass conversion of the depressed classes to Buddhism?
(a) No great efforts were taken to abolish caste system
(b) Buddhism was easy to follow
(c) Buddhism was against doing harm to others
(d) Buddhism was popular in India

37. When was the All India Union Congress set up?
(a) 1920 (b) 1914
(c) 1926 (d) 1885

38. What is the most serious of the defects of the Trade Union Movement in India?
(a) Predominance of small-sized unions
(b) Poor finance
(c) Absence of whole time paid officials of the union
(d) Leadership is provided by outsiders especially professional politicians

39. Whom do you consider as a major curse of the rural people?
(a) Zamindars (b) Government
(c) Money-lenders (d) Robbers

40. Why did M.K. Gandhi go to Champaran?
(a) To launch salt satyagraha
(b) To launch non-cooperation movement
(c) To inquire personally into the grievances of the indigo cultivators
(d) To fight against the zamindars

41. Who said the following words? "Long years ago we made a tryst with destiny, and now the time comes when we shall redeem our pledge ...."
(a) M.K. Gandhi (b) Subhas Chandra Bose
(c) Jawaharlal Nehru (d) M.A. Jinnah

42. What was the important cause of the boycott of Simon Commission?
(a) It was sent after the due date
(b) It came at a time when famine ravaged the country
(c) All its members were English - men
(d) It offered to study further constitutional reform instead of complete independence

43. What method did the British adopt to deal with the boycott of the Simon Commission?
(a) brutal suppression (b) talks with Congress
(c) concession (d) persuasions

44. How many kms. did M.K. Gandhi walk to reach Dandi?
(a) about 320 kms (b) about 200 kms
(c) about 400 kms (d) about 250 kms

45. Who was the first Prime Minister of Pakistan?
(a) Qaid-i-Azam M.A. Jinnah (b) Liaquat Ali Khan
(c) Khwaja Nazim-ud-din (d) Z.A. Bhutto

46. What was the chief aim of Ghadar Party?
(a) To free India from British rule through an armed insurrection
(b) To give financial assistance to the Indians
(c) To persuade the British government to give independence to India
(d) To end communal strike in India

47. Who formed Khudai Khidmatgars in 1929?
(a) M.A. Jinnah (b) Ali brothers
(c) Khan Abdul Ghaffar Khan (d) Maulana Azad

48. Jawaharlal Nehru wrote in 1937 that a day would come when India would remember and cherish her. About whom did Nehru write?
(a) Rani Gaidinliu (b) Rani of Jhansi
(c) Capt. Laxmi (d) Aruna Asaf Ali

49. One of the following princely states did not hesitate to accede to India. Identify
(a) Junagadh (b) Jammu and Kashmir
(c) Hyderabad (d) Baroda

50. Which, among the following, was NOT one of the causes of the failure of the system of Dyarachy in provinces established by the Act of 1919?
(a) Neither the system was sound in principle nor the divisions of the subjects into 'Transferred' and 'Reserved' was made on a logical principle
(b) Indian Ministers were dependent on the governor for many things, particularly for finance
(c) The Senior Civil Servants were under no obligation to obey the Indian ministers
(d) There was too much interference by governor-general in provincial administration

51. Which, among the following, was NOT a provision under the Government of India Act, 1935?
(a) Federal structure at the Centre
(b) Provision of the system of Dyarchy at the Centre
(c) Autonomy of administration to the province
(d) The governors were to act as constitutional heads

52. Which, among the following, was the reason of resignations of Indian ministers in all provinces in 1939 A.D.?
(a) The governors did not act as constitutional heads
(b) The centre did not provide the required financial help to provinces
(c) The governor general converted Indian administration from Federal to Unitary one because of the beginning of the Second World War
(d) India was declared a party to the Second World War without the consent of Indian ministers

53. Who, among the following, was the founder of the Indian National Conference in 1876?
(a) Surendranath Banerjee (b) Dwarkanath Tagore
(c) Dadabhai Naoroji (d) Ram Gopal Ghosh

54. Which, among the following facts, proves that the All India Congress was established as 'a safety valve' for the escape of great and growing forces?
(a) It was started by a retired British Civil servant, A.O. Hume

(b) The plan of such an organisation had the blessings of the then governor-general, Lord Dufferin
(c) In the beginning the Congress had no objective of securing representative government in India
(d) The first session of the All India Congress was held in the same week of the year 1885 A.D. which was decided over by the Indian National Conference, a more politically conscious organisation , to hold its All India Session at Calcutta

55. Who, among the following, was the first president of the All India Congress?
(a) A.O. Hume (b) W.C. Banerjee
(c) B. C. Pal (d) Ferozeshah Mehta

56. 'Under the leadership of the Moderates or the 'Old Guards, the Congress having implicit faith in British sense of justice and fair play demanded expansion of legislative councils with enlarged powers and more representation of Indians in them, representation of Indian in the Secretary of State's council, Viceroy's and Governor's executive, etc, but not self-government. In which year it demanded representation of Indians in the British House of Commons?
(a) 1900 (b) 1901
(c) 1902 (d) 1904

57. Who, among the following national leaders, commented regarding the activities of the Congress under the Moderates that "It was at best an opportunist movement. It opened opportunities for treacheries and hypocracies. It enabled some people to trade in the name of patriotism".
(a) S.N. Banerjee (b) Lala Lajpat Rai
(c) Aurobindo Ghosh (d) Mrs. Annie Besant

58. The British Committee of the Indian National Congress was started in 1889 in England to serve as a forum of the Congress there. Who, among the following was its Chairman?
(a) Sir W Wedderburn (b) Mr. Digby
(c) Dada Bhai Naoroji (d) W.C. Bannerjee

59. Who, among the following historians has remarked that 'their failure lay in not breaking through the twin beliefs that British rule was invincible and that the capitalist mode of production was the only one possible', concerning the failure of the Moderates?
(a) Dr. R.C. Majumdar (b) Dr. Bipan Chandra
(c) Dr. Sunil Sarkar (d) Dr. S.Gopal

60. Which, among the following, was NOT a motive of the government in partitioning Bengal in 1905:
(a) Disruption of the economy of Bengal
(b) Administrative convenience
(c) To curb the growth of national feeling in Bengal by driving a wedge between the Bengali speaking Hindus and Muslims
(d) To curb Indian nationalism as a whole

61. When was the partition of Bengal annulled by the government?
(a) In 1910 (b) In 1911
(c) In 1912 (d) In 1913

62. Which, among the following, was NOT advocated by the Extremists as a means of fulfilling their demands?
(a) Boycott of foreign goods (b) Use of Swadeshi
(c) National Education (d) Disobedience to laws

63. Which, among the following, separated the Extremists from the Revolutionaries?
(a) Lack of faith in the British
(b) Faith in self-efforts
(c) Attainment or freedom as an ultimate goal
(d) Non-violent means to attain Swaraj

64. 'The activities of Birendra Kumar Ghosh, younger brother of Aurobindo Ghosh and Pulin Bahari Das led to the establishment of a secret revolutionary society in Bengal. Which, among the following societies, was that?
(a) Anusilan Samiti (b) Swadesh Bandhava Samiti
(c) Brati Samiti (d) Sadhana Samaj

65. Who, among the following revolutionaries, threw a bomb on Lord Hardinge, the governor-general in 1912?
(a) Prafulla Chalsi (b) Khudiram Bose
(c) Rash Behari Bose (d) Madan Lal Dhingra

66. 'The Ghadar party was formed in U.S.A. in 1913 and it settled to start a revolt in February 1915 in India.' Which among the following provinces, the Ghadar party chose to begin its armed revolt?
(a) Punjab (b) Bengal
(c) Uttar Pradesh (d) Bihar

67. Who, among the following revolutionaries formed the Ghadar Party in America?
(a) Bhupendra Nath Datt (b) Sardar Ajit Singh
(c) Lal Hardayal (d) Ganesha Sarvarkar

68. 'The terrorist movement again got momentum in late 20's and early 30's of the 20th century and several organisations were formed, one of them being the Hindustan Republican party whose members were involved in a well-known terrorist activity.' Which, among the following activities, they were involved?
(a) Meerut conspiracy case (b) Kanpur conspiracy case
(c) Kakori case (d) Chittagaon Armoury Raid

69. Who, among the following, was the leader of the Chittagaon Armoury Raid?
(a) Surya Sen (b) Jatin Das
(c) Chandra Shekhar Azad (d) Sukhdeva

70. 'Because of the influence of socialist ideas, the Hindustan Republican Association became Socialist Republican Association.' Who, among the following revolutionary leaders was responsible for it?
(a) Chandra Shekhar Azad (b) Sardar Bhagat Singh
(c) Rajguru (d) Sukhdeva

71. Did the policy of undiluted opposition to the government pursued by the 'Swaraj Party' succeed?
(a) Yes (b) No
(c) N.A. (d) Question invalid

72. 'B.R. Dutt and Sardar Bhagat Singh threw a bomb in the legislative Assembly in April 1929. 'Which, among the following, was their primary objective?
(a) To destroy the Legislative Assembly Hall
(b) To terrorise the British
(c) Exhibit protest against non-withdrawl of the Rowlatt Act
(d) To protest against the passage of the Public Safety Bill which would have curbed the civil liberties

73. Who, among the following revolutionaries was shot dead in an encounter by the British?
(a) Sardar Bhagat Singh (b) Chandra Shekhar Azad
(c) Rajguru (d) Sukhdev

74. Who, among the following, first declared that 'Swaraj' is my birth-right?
(a) Swami Dayanand (b) Aurobindo Ghosh
(c) Bal Gangadhar Tilak (d) Gopal Krishan Gokhale

75. Who, among the following, was NOT an Extremist?
(a) Aurobindo Ghosh (b) M.G. Ranade
(c) Bal Gangadhar Tilak (d) Lala Lajpat Rai

76. Which, among the following, was NOT adopted by B.G. Tilak as a means to infuse militant nationalism among Indians?
(a) Revival of the glory and greatness of Indian culture in the past through his newspaper Kesari
(b) Inauguration of Ganapati and Shivaji festivals
(c) Emphasis on self help and faith in the masses
(d) Encouragement to youths for revolutionary activities

77. The Swadeshi movement and boycott of foreign goods were accepted by the Indians first when:
(a) Bengal was partitioned in 1905
(b) The Congress was divided in 1907
(c) The Home Rule League was established by Mrs. Annie Besant in 1915
(d) M.K. Gandhi entered into Indian politics

78. The Congress was united at its Lucknow session in 1916. Who, among the following, was primarily responsible for it?
(a) B.G.Tilak (b) Mrs. Annie Besant
(c) Moti Lai Nehru (d) Lala Lajpat Rai

79. Both Mrs. Annie Besant and B.G. Tilak founded separate Home Rule League but both Leagues were soon united in:
(a) 1914 (b) 1915
(c) 1916 (d) 1918

80. Which among the following was the aim of Indian Home Rule League?
(a) Complete Swaraj (b) Self-government
(c) Independence (d) None

81. The extremists got hold over the Congress when Mrs. Annie Besant was elected President of the Congress in:
(a) 1916 (b) 1917
(c) 1918 (d) 1919

82. 'The Lucknow Pact was agreed upon by the Congress and the Muslim League in 1916 A.D.' However, which among the following, was NOT one of the terms of the Pact?
(a) Acceptance of communal weightage (proportionately more representation to the Muslims in Legislative Assemblies than their numerical strength) by the Congress
(b) Acceptance of communal Veto (A bill concerning with affairs of a particular community would not be passed unless it was approved by elected representatives of that community in Assemblies)
(c) Acceptance of separate electorates (communal-franchise) by the Congress
(d) Muslim League's acceptance to allow its members to join the Congress

83. 'A historical declaration was made by Mr. Montague, the Secretary of State for India. It declared that 'the policy of his Majesty's Government, with which the Government of India are in complete accord, is that of increasing associations of Indians .... and gradual development of self-governing institutions' Which, among the following was the year of its declaration?
(a) 1917 (b) 1918
(c) 1919 (d) 1920

84. M.K.Gandhi appeared on the political scene of India and became popular very soon because his first Satyagraha movement (1919 A.D.) which he started as a protest against:
(a) Inadequate reforms introduced by the Act of 1919
(b) The passing of Rowlatt Act
(c) The British policy towards Turkey
(d) Non-fulfilment of the assurances given by the government during the First World War to the Congress in return of its cooperation in war efforts

85. Which among the following, was the reason of surrendering of his title of 'Sir' by Rabindra Nath Tagore and of the resignation of Shankar Ram ` Nagar from the executive council of the viceroy?
(a) The passing of the Rowlatt Act
(b) Protest against the Act of 1919
(c) To support M.K.Gandhi in his Satyagraha movement
(d) To protest against the event at Jallianwalabagh and the martial-law imposed in Punjab

86. Who, among the following, was chosen the President when the All-India Khilafat conference met at Delhi in 1919?
(a) Muhammad Ali (b) Shukat Ali
(c) Muhammad Ali Jinnah (d) M.K.Gandhi

87. Which, among the following, was the reason of M.K. Gandhi to support the Khilafat movement whole-heartedly with a view to keep intact the position and honour of the Khalifa of Turkey?
(a) It was another experiment of non-violent movement in India
(b) He wanted to form the base for his noncooperation movement which he started just after it
(c) He wanted to become the leader of the Indian Muslims also
(d) He found in it the best opportunity to bring the Hindu and the Muslims of India closer to each other

88. In which year, among the following, the Congress decided to launch the Non-Cooperation movement?
(a) 1919 (b) 1920
(c) 1921 (d) 1922

89. Which, among the following, was NOT a programme adopted by the Congress while launching the non-cooperation movement?
(a) Surrender of titles and honorary offices, registration, from nominated seats in local bodies and refused to attend the official and semi-official functions
(b) Withdrawal of children from government schools and colleges
(c) Boycott of elections to the Reformed councils, foreign goods and government courts and refusal to offer as recruits for service in Mesopotamia
(d) Refusal to pay the revenue to the government

90. Which, among the following, was NOT a demand of M.K.Gandhi to the Government as a condition of settlement before he launched the Non-cooperation movement?
(a) The Government should withdraw the Rowlatt Act
(b) The Government should express regret at the massacre at Jallianwala Bagh
(c) The British government should behave leniently with Turkey
(d) The government should put a better scheme of reforms than that of the Act of 1919

91. The Non-Cooperation was stopped by M.K.Gandhi and the Congress in the year
(a) 1921 (b) 1922
(c) 1923 (d) 1924

92. Which, among the following, was the cause of withdrawal of the Non-Cooperation movement?
(a) It received no response from the people
(b) The government agreed to fulfil the demand of then Congress
(c) A violent incident at Chauri Chaura provoked M.K.Gandhi to stop it
(d) The leaders of the Congress felt disheartened because of the repressive measures of the government

93. 'The Non-Coopertion movement failed to achieve any of its objects, yet it brought about certain useful results.' However, which, among the following was NOT one of its useful results?
(a) The Hindus and the Muslims became closer to each other with a view to enhance the national cause
(b) The Congress-movement became a mass movement for the first time
(c) The Congress left the constitutional path to attain Swaraj and entered on the path of struggle against the government
(d) Removed the fear of the British from the minds of the people

94. Which, among the following, was NOT one of the causes of the armed Mopiah rebellions of 1921?
(a) It was an offshoot to the Non-Cooperation
(b) It was an offshoot of the Khilafat movement
(c) It was the result of discontentment at the failure of non-cooperation and Khilafat movements
(d) It was the result of the violent speeches of Ali Brothers

95. 'Gandhi succeeded in mobilising the Indian masses for achieving national independence.' Which, among the following, was NOT helpful for his success:
   (a) His appeal for Hindu-Muslim unity and emancipation of depressed classes and women
   (b) His insistence on truth and non-violence
   (c) He Indianised his personal life and made himself one among the masses
   (d) His support to the British during World War
96. Who, among the following, never remained a leader of the Swarajya Party
   (a) C.R. Das (b) Moti Lai Nehru
   (c) C.Rajagopalachari (d) Lala Lajpat Rai
97. Which, among the following, was the primary aim of the Swarajya Party?
   (a) To cooperate with the government in implementing the reforms of 1919
   (b) To gain experience of the functioning of representative government
   (c) To wreck the scheme of the reform of 1919 by a policy of uniform continuous and consistent obstruction
   (d) To exhibit the displeasure over the failure of Non-Cooperation movement
98. The Swarajya party succeeded in winning election in several provinces and did quite useful job in certain fields but it ceased to be a united and effective party after:
   (a) 1925 (b) 1926
   (c) 1928 (d) 1950
99. 'The Swarajists failed to gain something concrete.' Which, among the following causes, was NOT responsible for it:
   (a) The policy of Swarajists of entering into the Councils but not to cooperate with the government was self contradictory
   (b) The All India Congress withdrew its support to Swarajists
   (c) Their policy was unrealistic
   (d) They talked of extremism and yet were resolved to easy parliamentarism
100. 'The Swarajya Party failed to achieve its goal, yet it served the cause of national struggle in several ways.' Which, among the following, was NOT one of its successes?
   (a) After the failure of the Non-cooperation Movement, it alone helped in keeping up the spirit of resistance among the people against the foreign rule
   (b) It exposed the autocratic functioning of the government.
   (c) The Round Table Conferences called afterwards were because of its demand
   (d) It brought nearer the goal of Swaraj

Answers

1. (a)	21. (d)	41. (c)	61. (b)	81. (b)
2. (d)	22. (a)	42. (c)	62. (d)	82. (d)
3. (c)	23. (d)	43. (a)	63. (d)	83. (a)
4. (c)	24. (a)	44. (a)	64. (a)	84. (b)
5. (a)	25. (d)	45. (b)	65. (c)	85. (d)
6. (a)	26. (a)	46. (a)	66. (a)	86. (d)
7. (b)	27. (a)	47. (c)	67. (c)	87. (d)
8. (c)	28. (e)	48. (a)	68. (c)	88. (b)
9. (c)	29. (6)	49. (d)	69. (a)	89. (d)
10. (d)	30. (d)	50. (d)	70. (a)	90. (a)
11. (d)	31. (b)	51. (d)	71. (b)	91. (b)
12. (a)	32. (a)	52. (d)	72. (d)	92. (c)
13. (d)	33. (b)	53. (a)	73. (b)	93. (a)
14. (b)	34. (a)	54. (d)	74. (c)	94. (c)
15. (c)	35. (a)	55. (b)	75. (b)	95. (d)
16. (c)	36. (a)	56. (d)	76. (d)	96. (c)
17. (d)	37. (a)	57. (b)	77. (a)	97. (c)
19. (a)	38. (d)	58. (a)	78. (b)	98. (b)
19. (c)	39. (c)	59. (b)	79. (c)	99. (b)
20. (b)	40. (c)	60. (a)	80. (b)	100. (d)

SET VIII

Questions

1. Which, among the following Indian political parties decided to cooperate with the working of the Simon Commission?
(a) The Hindu Maha Sabha (b) All-India Muslim League
(c) National Liberal Federation (d) None

2. Which, among the following was the cause of the boycott of the Simon Commission?
(a) Not a single member of the commission was an Indian
(b) No member of the British Labour Party was appointed a member of the Commission
(c) The scope of inquiry of the Commission was limited
(d) M.K.Gandhi has already given a call for Civil Disobedience movement

3. 'An all party conference, was held at Delhi in February, 1928, ' to frame a constitution for India acceptable to all Indians. Who, among the following, was elected its Chairman?
(a) Moti Lal Nehru (b) Lala Lajpat Rai
(c) M.A. Ansari (d) M.K. Gandhi

4. Which, among the following was decided by the Nehru Report of 1928?
(a) A draft constitution for India
(b) Means of boycott of Simon Commission
(c) Working of the reforms of 1919 A.D.
(d) Proposals to be discussed with Simon Commission

5. In which year the Congress decided to place the Nehru report before the government for its acceptance?
(a) 1927 (b) 1928
(c) 1929 (d) 1930

6. The Congress declared complete independence as its goal in its session at:
(a) Madras in 1927 A.D. (b) Calcutta in 1928 A.D.
(c) Lahore in 1929 A.D. (d) Allahabad(A.I.C.C.)in 1930 A.D.

7. Who, among the following was elected the President of the Congress at its Lahore Session in 1929?
(a) Moti Lal Nehru (b) Jawaharlal Nehru
(c) Subhash Chandra Bose (d) Pandit Govind Ballabh Pant

8. The Civil Disobedience Movement was started by M.K. Gandhi in the year
(a) 1929 (b) 1930

(c) 1931 (d) 1932

9. 'Before the start of the Civil Disobedience Movement, M.K. Gandhi had put up a charter of demands before the Viceroy.' The number of those demands was:
(a) Six (b) Eight
(c) Eleven (d) Twelve

10. Which, among the following, was the agenda for the Round Table Conferences held in London between 1930-32?
(a) To discuss the report of the Simon Commission
(b) To form a Constitution for India
(c) To find a solution of the communal problem in India.
(d) To find a solution of the Depressed classes in India

11. Which, among the following-Round Table Conferences held in London, was attended by M.K. Gandhi as the sole representative of the Congress?
(a) 1st in 1930 (b) 2nd in 1931
(c) 3rd in 1932 (d) None

12. Which, among the following, was NOT a term of Gandhi-Irwin Pact in 1931?
(a) Civil Disobedience Movement be suspended
(b) The Congress would participate in the Round Table Conference to find out some political settlement of India
(c) The government would discuss the demand of the Congress to grant Dominion status to India
(d) All non-violent political prisoners would be released and special ordinances withdrawn

13. Ramsay Macdonald, the British Minister announced his 'Communal Award' in the year:
(a) 1931 (b) 1932
(c) 1933 (d) 1934

14. Which, among the following, was NOT one of the provisions of the 'Communal Award'?
(a) Separate electorates for the Muslims, Europeans and the Sikhs
(b) Members of the Depressed Classes were assigned reserved seats and separate electorates
(c) Distinction was being drawn between Depressed classes and higher caste Hindus
(d) None of the above

15. 'M.K. Gandhi declared 'fast unto death' as a mark of protest against the Communal Award'. Which, among the following, was the reason to give up that fast by him?
(a) The British government withdrew the offer of Communal Award
(b) The Depressed Classes refused to accept the concessions awarded to them by the Government
(c) The Congress agreed to fight against the 'Award' till it was withdrawn by the government
(d) The Poona Pact, ratified by the Hindu Mahasabha and accepted by the government

16. The Civil Disobedience Movement and even the 'Individual Civil Disobedience virtually ended by the year:
(a) 1930 (b) 1932

(c) 1934 (d) 1936

17. The Congress participated in the election of 1937 A.D. and won an absolute majority in:
(a) Three Provinces (b) Four Provinces
(c) Five Provinces (d) Six Provinces

18. Who, among the following leaders, has been described as the 'Frontier Gandhi'?
(a) Badshah Khan (b) Khan Abdul Ghaffar Khan
(c) Maulana Azad (d) M.A. Jinnah

19. Subash Chandra Bose was elected as the President of the Congress in the year:
(a) 1938 (b) 1939
(c) 1940 (d) 1941

20. Who, among the following, formed the party named the Forward Block?
(a) Subash Chandra Bose (b) Sardar Bhagat Singh
(c) Chandra Shekhar Azad (d) Jawaharlal Nehru

21. The primary difference between the Quit India Movement and other previous movements led by the Congress was that:
(a) It was without leadership (b) It was more widespread
(c) It started spontaneously (d) It was a violent movement

22. The Quit India Movement of 1942 collapsed within:
(a) A year (b) Within Eight months
(c) Within Six months (d) Within Two months

23. Which, among the following political parties opposed the Quit India Movement of 1942?
(a) Muslim League and CPI (b) Muslim League
(c) Communist Party of India (d) Forward Block

24. Who, among the following was the first commander-in-chief of the Indian National Army (I.N.A)?
(a) Captain Mohan Singh (b) Giani Pitam Singh
(c) Subash Chander Bose (d) Shah Nawaz Khan

25. Subash Chandra Bose escaped from India in the year:
(a) 1940 (b) 1941
(c) 1942 (d) 1943

26. The Indian Independence League and the Indian National Army (I.N.A.) were found primarily due to the efforts of
(a) Rash Behari Bose (b) Subash Chandra Bose
(c) Captain Mohan Singh (d) Pitam Singh

27. Subhash Chandra Bose took over the leadership of Indian Independence movement in the East Asia and supreme command of the Indian National Army at Singapore in the year:
(a) 1942 (b) 1943
(c) 1944 (d) 1945

28. Which, among the following was the cause of the failure of Wavell's plan and the Simla Conference held in 1945 A.D.?
(a) Refusal of M.A. Jinnah to participate in the Simla Conference
(b) Insistence of M.A. Jinnah that all Muslim members of the Vicerory's Council would be the members of Muslim League only

(c) Exclusion of the Hindu Mahasabha from the deliberation of the Simla Conference
(d) Soft attitude of the Congress towards M.A. Jinnah

29. The Cabinet Mission Plan was proposed in:
(a) 1944 (b) 1945
(c) 1946 (d) 1947

30. Which, among the following, was NOT one of the demands of the mutineers of Navy in 1946,
(a) Issue of better food
(b) Equal pay for the English and Indian soldiers
(c) Release of I.N.A. officers and soldiers and also that of political prisoners
(d) Acceptance of the demand of Swaraj by the Congress

31. Which, among the following was NOT a cause of the Naval Mutiny of 1946:
(a) Supply of bad food to sailors
(b) Racist insults to Indian sailors
(c) I.N.A. Trials
(d) None of these

32. Who, among the following political parties gave a call for strike in Bombay in sympathy of Naval Strikers:
(a) The Muslim League (b) The Communist Party of India
(c) The Congress (d) None of these

33. The Naval Mutineers surrendered themselves at the call of:
(a) The Communist Party of India
(b) The Muslim League
(c) The Muslim League and the Congress
(d) The Communist Party and the Congress

34. The election for the Constituent Assembly of India were held in the year:
(a) 1946 (b) 1947
(c) 1948 (d) 1949

35. The Muslim League refused to accept the Cabinet Mission Plan because:
(a) It refused to accept the Constituent Assembly as a Sovereign body
(b) It was not asked to participate in the formation of Interim-government formed in 1946
(c) It could capture very few seats in the Constituent Assembly
(d) The attitude of Wavell, the Governor-General was cooperative with the Muslim League

36. The British Government declared to leave India in every case before June, 1948 in:
(a) 1946 (b) February, 1947
(c) April, 1947 (d) June, 1947

37. The Mountbatten Plan which proposed the partition of India was declared in
(a) April, 1947 (b) May, 1947
(c) June, 1947 (d) July, 1947

38. The All India Muslim League was founded in the year:
(a) 1906 (b) 1909
(c) 1912 (d) 1914

39. Who, among the following founded the All India Muslim League?
(a) Sir Syyad Ahmad Khan (b) Sir Muhammad Iqbal
(c) Sir Agha Khan (d) Nawab Salimullah Khan

40. Which, among the following was NOT one of the early aims of the Muslim League?
(a) Support to the British Government
(b) Demand of a Separate home-land for the Indian Muslims
(c) Protection of the rights of the Indian Muslims
(d) Put check to the growing influence of the Indian National Congress

41. Which, among the following, was NOT conducive to the Lucknow Pact (1916) between the Muslim League and the Congress?
(a) The growing weakness of Turkey against its European rivals created sympathy of the Indian Muslims towards its cause
(b) Turkey became an enemy-country of Britian in the First World War
(c) Britain showed least sympathy towards the cause of Turkey and the Khalifa
(d) M. A. Jinnah, the then President of the Muslim League, desired cooperation with the Congress to enhance the national cause

42. Whether the Moplah rebellion of Malabar in 1921 A. D. became communal in character and led to communal riots between the Hindus and the Muslims in many places of the country?
(a) Yes (b) No.
(c) N.A. (d) Question invalid

43. Who among the following first used the word Pakistan for the home-land of the Indian Muslims?
(a) Sir Muhammad Iqbal (b) Sir Agha Khan
(c) M. A. Jinnah (d) Chaudhary Rahmat Ali and his friends

44. The Muslim League once celebrated The Deliverance Day. It celebrated it in:
(a) 1926 A.D. when Swarajya Party lost its majority in the provinces
(b) 1929 A.D. after the declaration of the demand of complete Independence by the Congress
(c) 1932 A.D. when the Congress was declared illegal by the government.
(d) 1939 A.D. when the Congress ministers in the provinces resigned as a protest against the inclusion of India in the Second World War

45. The Muslim League demanded a separate home land for the Indian Muslims openly for the first time at its annual session held in Lahore in the year:
(a) 1938 (b) 1939
(c) 1940 (d) 1941

46. 'The word Pakistan for a separate homeland for the Indian Muslims was in vogue in many British and Indian newspapers prior to its use by the Muslim League'. The Muslim League accepted it only in the year:
(a) 1940 (b) 1941
(c) 1942 (d) 1943

47. The Constitution of Independent India was put in practise on:
(a) 15th August, 1947 (b) 26th January, 1949
(c) 26th January, 1950 (d) 26th January, 1951

48. All native states who afterwards became part of the Indian Union had agreed to accede to it by the end of the year:
(a) 1947 (b) 1948
(c) 1949 (d) 1950

49. Who, among the following, was primarily responsible for the passing of the Hindu Code Bill?
(a) Pt. Jawaharlal Nehru (b) Sardar Vallabh bhai Patel
(c) Rajendra Prasad (d) Radhakrishnan

50. The earliest coins of India were:
(a) made of gold
(b) made of silver
(c) punch-marked only on one side
(d) punch-marked on both sides

51. Who was the Hindu king shown playing on the Veena on ancient coins?
(a) Shivaji (b) Vikramaditya
(c) Samudragupta (d) Ashoka

52. Who among the following is credited with the invention of Algebra?
(a) Medhatithi (b) Bhaskara
(c) Apastamba (d) Aryabhatta

53. Evidence of maritime trade during the period of Harappan culture came from the site of
(a) Mohenjo-daro (b) Lothal
(c) Ropar (d) Kalibangan

54. Chandragupta Maurya's empire extended in the North-West up to
(a) Hindukush (b) Indus
(c) Ravi (d) Sutlej

55. The best-known example of the Hoyasala style of temple is found at:
(a) Ajanta (b) Madurai
(c) Karle (d) Halebid

56. The poet Hansena was the courtier of:
(a) Skandagupta (b) Lakshmanasena
(c) Chandragupta (d) Samudragupta

57. The capital of Sasanka was:
(a) Toshali (b) Karnasuvarna
(c) Mahasthangarh (d) Suvamagiri

58. Pushyabhuti dynasty ruled over:
(a) Ujjain (b) Patliputra
(c) Sakal (d) Thaneshwar

59. The Huna leader Mihirkula was defeated by:
(a) Yeshodharman (b) Rajyavardhana
(c) Buddhagupta (d) Chandragupta

60. Who, amongst the following brothers of Aurangzeb was condemned to death, and his body was paraded in Delhi?
(a) Dara Shikoh (b) Murad Baksh
(c) Shah Shuja (d) None of these

61. Who amongst the following were a maritime power?
(a) Bahmanis (b) Chalukyas
(c) Cholas (d) Rashtrakutas
62. Which of the choices gives the correct chronological order of the following events (1) War of Succession (2) Death of Mumtaz (3) Coronation of Aurangzeb (4) Shahajahan's captivity for about 8 years before his death?
(a) 1, 3, 4, 2 (b) 2, 4, 1, 3
(c) 2, 1, 4, 3 (d) 1, 4, 3, 2
63. Who amongst the following Mughal rulers reimposed 'Jaziya'?
(a) Akbar (b) Aurangzeb
(c) Jahangir (d) Humayun
64. Which of the following statements about Aurangzeb is not correct?
(a) In expanse, the Mughal Empire was the largest during his reign
(b) By his antagonistic attitude, he alienated the Rajputs
(c) His Deccan policy in the end proved to be ruinous for the Mughal Empire
(d) Only (b) and (c) are correct
65. Ibn Batutah visited India during the reign of:
(a) Ala-ud-din Khilji (b) Ghiyas-ud-din Tughlaq
(c) Sher Shah Suri (d) Muhammad-bin Tughlaq
66. During the reign of which of the following rulers did Tulsidas, the author of Ramcharitamanas, flourish?
(a) Akbar (b) Humayun
(c) Shahajahan (d) Sher Shah Suri
67. Who was the author of Padmavat?
(a) Abdur Rahim (b) Jayqsi
(c) Kabir (d) Surdas
68. The rulers of which of the following dynasties established the largest dominion in Southern India
(a) Chalukyas (b) Cholas
(c) Pallavas (d) None of these
69. Two of the great Mughals wrote their own memoirs. They were:
(a) Babur and Humayun (b) Humayun and Jahangir
(c) Babur and Jahangir (d) Jahangir and Shahjahan
70. Who amongst the following was the first to make use of artillery in warfare during the medieval period in India?
(a) Babur (b) Ibrahim Lodhi
(c) Sher Shah Suri (d) Akbar
71. Which of the following is the correct chronological order of the Slave dynasty rulers?
(a) Iltutmish, Qutub-ud-din Aibak, Raziya Sultan, Balban
(b) Qutub-ud-din Aibak, Iltutmish, Balban, Raziya Sultan
(c) Qutub-ud-din Aibak, Iltutmish, Raziya Sultan, Balban
(d) Iltutmish, Balban, Qutub-ud din Aibak, Raziya Sultan
72. Which of the following is not true about the administration of Ala-ud-din Khilji?
(a) He issued edicts regulating the prices of all articles and goods

(b) He introduced new currency notes
(c) He forbade intoxicating drinks
(d) He required all grains to be stored in the royal granaries in Delhi

73. Ala-ud-din Khilji became the Sultan of Delhi in A.D. 1296 after treacherously murdering his uncle and patron. Who was this patron?
(a) Jalal-ud-din Firuz (b) Nasir-ud-din Khusrau Shah
(c) Ghiyas-ud-din Balban (d) Qutub-ud-din Mubarak

74. Who amongst the following is believed to have been the benefactor of the Khilji dynasty
(a) Khusrau Shah (b) Malik Kafur
(c) Ghazi Malik (d) Qutub-ud-din

75. Who amongst the following was the first Sultan of Tughlaq dynasty?
(a) Firuz Shah Tughlaq (b) Muhammad-bin Tughlaq
(c) Ghiyas-ud-din Tughlaq (d) Nasir-ud-din Muhammad

76. When Timur invaded India at about the close of the 14th century, the dynasty that ruled the Sultanate of Delhi was:
(a) Lodhi (b) Sayyid
(c) Tughlaq (d) Khilji

77. Who amongst the following Bhakti-cult saints was the product of the 15th century?
(a) Chaitanya (b) Nanak
(c) Wallabhacharya (d) All of these

78. Who wrote the biography of Harshavardhana in the 7th century A.D.?
(a) Sandhyakara (b) Banabhatta
(c) Bilhana (d) Kalhana

79. The first expedition of Muhammad of Ghor in 1175 was directed against:
(a) the Raja of Gujarat
(b) his co-religionists, the Ismailian heretics of Multan
(c) Khusrau Malik, the last representative of the dynasty of Subuktgin and Sultan Mahmud
(d) the powerful Rajput king, Prithviraj Chauhan

80. Who amongst the following was responsible for the total extinction of the kingdom of Ghazni in 12th century
(a) Ala-ud-din Husain (b) Ghuzz Turkmans
(c) Ghiyas-ud-din (d) Muhammad

81. Who founded the so-called Slave Dynasty in India?
(a) Balban (b) Ghiyas-ud-din Tughlaq
(c) Iltutmish (d) Qutub-ud-din Aibak

82. Who amongst the following Delhi Sultans died of a fall from his horse while playing Chaugan or Polo?
(a) Muhammad of Ghor (b) Qutub-ud-din Aibak
(c) Iltutmish (d) Ghiyas-ud-din Balban

83. The famous poet Amir Khusrau, surnamed the "Parrot of India" was the contemporary of all of the following except:
(a) Ghiyas-ud-din Balban (b) Ghiyas-ud-din Tughlaq

(c) Ala-ud-din Khilji (d) Iltutmish

84. When was Ashoka born?
(a) 232 B.C. (b) 269 B.C.
(c) 273 B.C. (d) 291 B.C.

85. Of which of the following Kingdoms was Krishnadeva Raya one of the famous rulers?
(a) Bahmani (b) Chola
(c) Pallava (d) Vijayanagar

86. In essence, the Varna system of the Aryans was based on
(a) caste (b) colour
(c) occupation (d) sex

87. On breaking up of the Mauryan Empire, the Satavahanas rose to power in the North-western Deccan in the:
(a) second century B.C. (b) first century B.C.
(c) first century A.D. (d) second century A.D.

88. Which of the following is the correct chronological order of the following imperial Guptas?
(a) Chandragupta I, Kumaragupta I, Samudragupta, Skandagupta
(b) Chandragupta I, Skandagupta, Samudragupta, Kumaragupta I
(c) Chandragupta I, Samudragupta, Kumaragupta I, Skandagupta
(d) Samudragupta, Chandragupta I, Kumaragupta I, Skandagupta

89. Chandragupta Vikramaditya was the:
(a) Son of Chandragupta I
(b) Father of Skandagupta
(c) Grandfather of Kumaragupta I
(d) Son of Samudragupta

90. The first sermon of Gautama Buddha was called the:
(a) Turning of the Wheel of Law
(b) Salvation through Meditation
(c) Asceticism was not the path to Salvation
(d) God was not essential to the Universe

91. Which of the following was not common between Buddhism and Jainism:
(a) Both denied the authority of the Vedas
(b) Both regarded rigid penance and austerity as essential for salvation
(c) Both were antagonistic to the practice of animal sacrifices
(d) Both were started by members of the Kshatriya caste

92. Who amongst the Chalukyas was the most famous king of the line
(a) Pulakesin I (b) Kirtivarman I
(c) Vikramaditya I (d) Pulakesin II

93. Medical encyclopaedias and pharmacopoeias were composed in ancient India, the most famous being that of Charaka, who was a contemporary of:
(a) Chandragupta Maurya (b) Ashoka
(c) Kanishka (d) Samudragupta

94. Kanishka's capital was at Purushapura. Which of the following places in his large kingdom had the status almost of a second capital?

(a) Banaras (b) Mathura
(c) Sanchi (d) Taxila

95. Who were the immediate successors of the imperial Mauryas in Magadha?
(a) Kushanas (b) Pandyas
(c) Satavahanas (d) Sungas

96. Gita Govinda by Jayadeva was written in:
(a) Pali (b) Magadhi
(c) Sanskrit (d) Brahmi

97. Who invented the decimal- notation in Arithmetic?
(a) The Indians (b) The Greeks
(c) The Arabs (d) The Romans

98. The twenty-third Jaina teacher, Parsva, the immediate predecessor of Mahavira, enjoined on his disciples four great vows. To these Mahavira added which of the following as the fifth vow
(a) Abstention from stealing (b) Non-injury
(c) Brahmacharya or continence (d) Non-attachment

99. A Jaina Council was held in the fifth or sixth century A.D., which made a final collection of the scriptures and reduced them to writing. This Council was held at:
(a) Kundapura (b) Nalanda
(c) Valabhi (d) Vaishali

100. If tradition is to be believed, it was a Taxilian Brahmin who raised to power a youngman as a mighty king of India in the fourth century B.C. This person was:
(a) Chanakya (b) Manu
(c) Patanjali (d) Pushyamitra

Answers

1. (d)	21. (d)	41. (d)	61. (d)	81. (d)
2. (a)	22. (d)	42. (a)	62. (c)	82. (b)
3. (c)	23. (a)	43. (d)	63. (b)	83. (d)
4. (a)	24. (a)	44. (d)	64. (a)	84. (b)
5. (b)	25. (b)	45. (c)	65. (d)	85. (d)
6. (c)	26. (a)	46. (d)	66. (a)	86. (b)
7. (b)	27. (b)	47. (c)	67. (b)	87. (b)
8. (b)	28. (b)	48. (b)	68. (b)	88. (c)
9. (c)	29. (c)	49. (a)	69. (c)	89. (d)
10. (a)	30. (d)	50. (d)	70. (a)	90. (a)
11. (b)	31. (c)	51. (c)	71. (c)	91. (b)
12. (c)	32. (b)	52. (d)	72. (b)	92. (b)
13. (b)	33. (c)	53. (b)	73. (a)	93. (c)
14. (d)	34. (a)	54. (a)	74. (b)	94. (b)
15. (d)	35. (a)	55. (d)	75. (c)	95. (d)
16. (c)	36. (b)	56. (d)	76. (c)	96. (c)
17. (d)	37. (c)	57. (b)	77. (d)	97. (a)
18. (b)	38. (a)	58. (d)	78. (b)	98. (c)
19. (b)	39. (d)	59. (a)	79. (b)	99. (c)
20. (a)	40. (b)	60. (a)	80. (a)	100. (a)

SET IX

Questions

1. The Buddhists shared with their fellow countrymen, including the Brahminical Hindus and Jainas, the belief
   (a) in the existence of a supreme creative spirit
   (b) in Samsara (transmigration) and Karma
   (c) in the immortality of soul
   (d) that rigid penance is as useless as indulgence in sensual pleasure
2. Who amongst the following Rajputs offered uncompromising resistance to the Mughals in the sixteenth century and never accepted their over lordship?
   (a) Rana Fateh Singh (b) Rana Kumbha
   (c) Rana Pratap (d) Rana Sanga
3. Who amongst the following, after succeeding to the throne, came to be known as Emperor Shahjahan?
   (a) Jalal-ud-din (b) Khurram Shihab-ud-din
   (c) Nur-ud-din Muhammad (d) Muhi-ud-din Muhammad
4. Who amongst the following, after succeeding to the throne, came to be known as Emperor Aurangzeb?
   (a) Jalal-ud-din (b) Muhi-ud-din Muhammad
   (c) Nur-ud-din Muhammad (d) Zahir-ud-din
5. Who amongst the following was opposed to the accession of Shahjahan to the throne?
   (a) Asaf Khan (b) NurJahan
   (c) Mahabat Khan (d) Jahangir
6. At which of the following battles was artillery used for the first time by one of the two parties to the battle?
   (a) First Battle of Panipat (b) Battle of Chandwar
   (c) Second Battle of Panipat (d) Battle of Khanua
7. Who amongst the following were the first to invade India?
   (a) Afghans (b) Arabs
   (c) Mongols (d) Turks
8. Who amongst the following first prohibited the practice of Sati?
   (a) Aurangzeb (b) Jahangir
   (c) Sher Shah Suri (d) Akbar

9. Shahjahan ascended the Mughal throne in
   (a) 1625 (b) 1626
   (c) 1627 (d) 1628
10. Who built the mausoleum of Jahangir and where?
   (a) Nur Jahan at Lahore (b) Shahjahan at Agra
   (c) Nur Jahan at Fatehpur Sikri (d) Shahjahan at Delhi
11. Which of the following was the chief cause of Dara Shikoh's failure in the war of succession and his ultimate destruction by Aurangzeb?
   (a) His father's excessive fondness for him and his constant presence at court had made his brothers jealous of him
   (b) Lack of qualities of an astute politician or of a brave general
   (c) Excessive sense of pride made him contemptuous of advice
   (d) He incurred the displeasure of the orthodox members among his co-religionists because of his eclectic views, liberal disposition and of scholarly instincts
12. Which of the following statements about Krishnadeva Raya is not correct?
   (a) He was a great warrior and an able administrator
   (b) He was the last great Hindu king of Southern India
   (c) He was a very learned person
   (d) He was the founder of the Vijayanagar Kingdom
13. Who was the Nawab of Bengal at the time of the Battle of Plassey
   (a) Mir Jafar (b) Mir Jumla
   (c) Mir Qasim (d) Siraj-ud-daula
14. The buildings constructed by which of the following Mughal rulers represent the climax in the evolution of Mughal architecture?
   (a) Akbar (b) Shahjahan
   (c) Jahangir (d) Aurangzeb
15. Harshavardhana, who was one of the greatest kings of ancient India, died in the:
   (a) second half of sixth century (b) first half of seventh century
   (c) second half of seventh century (d) first half of eighth century
16. Who amongst the following was the guardian and Regent of Akbar when he succeeded to the dominion of his father?
   (a) Asad Khan (b) Adam Khan
   (c) Asaf Khan (d) Bairam Khan
17. Which of the following battles marked the real beginning of the Mughal Empire in India?
   (a) First Battle of Panipat (b) Second Battle of Panipat
   (c) Battle of Talikota (d) Battle of Haldighati
18. When Akbar besieged the fort of Chittor in October 1567, the Rana of Mewar was:
   (a) Fateh Singh (b) Kumbhakaran
   (c) Udai Singh (d) Sanga
19. Which of the following is the correct chronological order of the following Maurya rulers?
   (a) Bindusara, Ashoka, Chandragupta
   (b) Chandragupta, Bindusara, Ashoka
   (c) Bindusara, Chandragupta, Ashoka
   (d) Chandragupta, Ashoka. Bindusara

20. The last king of the line of imperial Mauryas was
(a) Brihadratha (b) Kunala
(c) Sampadi or Samprati (d) Salisuka
21. The Great King, Seleucus I Nicator, was a contemporary of
(a) Ashoka (b) Chandragupta Maurya
(c) Pushyamitra (d) Salisuka
22. Nalanda University was associated with:
(a) Ashoka (b) Chandragupta Vikramaditya
(c) Harshavardhana (d) Kanishka
23. The paintings in the famous Ajanta Caves belong to the period:
(a) 500 B.C. to 100 B.C. (b) 100 B.C. to A.D. 30
(c) A.D. 300 to A.D. 700 (d) A.D. 700 to A.D. 1100
24. Who amongst the following was associated with ancient system of medicine?
(a) Bhaskara (b) Charaka
(c) Kalhana (d) Somadeva
25. The Buddhist monument of Borobodur is in:
(a) Bumna (b) Indonesia
(c) Korea (d) Thailand
26. The Italian traveller, who left very praiseworthy account of the Vijayanagar Empire, was:
(a) E. Barbosa (b) Manucci
(c) Marco Polo (d) Nicolo Conti
27. At which of the following places was a large Buddhist monastery established during the reign of Harshavardhana?
(a) Nalanda (b) Pataliputra
(c) Valabhi (d) Vaishali
28. Which of the following is the correct chronological order of the following dynasties?
(a) Mauryas, Nandas, Kushanas, Guptas
(b) Guptas, Kushanas, Nandas, Mauryas
(c) Nandas, Mauryas, Kushanas, Guptas
(d) Kushanas, Guptas, Mauryas, Nandas
29. Who amongst the following was also a poet and musician, and took delight in the title of "Kaviraja" or "King of Poets"
(a) Chandragupta I (b) Samudragupta
(c) Skandagupta (d) None of the above
30. The celebrated astronomers of ancient India, Aryabhatta and Varahamihira, lived during the:
(a) Maurya period (b) Kushana period
(c) Gupta period (d) Nanda period
31. In the domain of historical literature, the post-Gupta period produced works, the like of which had not been seen in the earlier ages. Which of the following is not one of those works?
(a) Arthashastra (b) Harshacharita
(c) Ramacharita (d) Rajatarangini
32. The end of the Gupta Empire is attributed to the invasions of Huns. Who amongst the following played the part of 'a lion to the Hun deer' and routed them out?
(a) Prabhakaravardhana (b) Harshavardhana

(c) Rajyavardhana (d) Bhaskaravarman

33. The famous Pala dynasty, whose rule of Bengal commenced in the second half of the eighth century, began with:
(a) Dharmapala (b) Devapala
(c) Gopala I (d) Jayapala

34. The great Mauryan Emperor of India, Ashoka was:
(a) the grandson of Bindusara
(b) the son of Chandragupta Maurya
(c) the grandson of Chandragupta Maurya
(d) the great grandson of Bindusara

35. What approximately is the period that intervened between the fall of the Mauryas and the rise of the Gupta Empire
(a) 200 years (b) 300 years
(c) 400 years (d) 500 years

36. The dynasty to which Harshavardhana belonged, claimed descent from:
(a) Madhava Gupta (b) Pushyabhuti
(c) Yashodharman (d) Pratiharas

37. In whose reign was the Fourth Buddhist Council held?
(a) Ashoka (b) Harsha
(c) Kanishka (d) Menander

38. Panini, a famous personality of ancient India, was
(a) an astronomer (b) a grammarian
(c) a mathematician (d) a philosopher

39. Who was the founder of the Sunga dynasty which succeeded the Imperial Mauryas?
(a) Agnimitra (b) Divakzramitra
(c) Pushyamitra (d) Vasumitra

40. The two principal monuments of Ala-ud-din Khilji's reign-the Jama'at Khana Masjid and Alai Darwaza-were constructed at
(a) Agra (b) Delhi
(c) Dhar (d) Gulbarga

41. The head of the University of Nalanda was the great Bengali scholar
(a) Nagarjuna (b) Basubandhu
(c) Sheelabhadra (d) Shreejnan Atisha

42. The Kaulinya System was introduced in Bengal by
(a) Lakshmana Sena (b) Ballala Sena
(c) Vijaya Sena (d) Hemanta Sena

43. The Ashokan inscription which gives an account of the Kalinga War and its effects is
(a) Minor Rock Edict IV (b) Minor Rock Edict III
(c) Minor Rock Edict XIII (d) Girnar Rock Edict

44. Which of the following rulers built some of the famous Dilwara temples at Mount Abu (1) Vimala (2) Tejpala (3) Sidharaja (4) Udayaditya?
(a) 1 and 2 (b) 1, 3 and 4
(c) 2, 3 and 4 (d) 1, 2 and 3

45. To conquer and annex Peshwar and Punjab, Mahmud of Ghazni defeated
(a) Ghurids (b) Arabs
(c) Karkotakas (d) Hindushahis

46. Which one of the following rulers granted land to high officials for their maintenance?
(a) Bimbisara (b) Chandragupta Maurya
(c) Ashoka (d) Harshavardhana

47. The Harappan deity not found in later Hindu pantheon is
(a) Pasupati Siva (b) Seven Mothers (Sapta Matrikas)
(c) Compound Creatures (d) Unicorn

48. What kind of evidence supports the view of the original home of Aryans in South Russia/ Central Asia?
(a) Archaeological (b) Anthropological
(c) Philological' (d) Climatic.

49. Which of the following pairs in respect of the later Vedic officials is not correct?
(a) Sangrahitri - Treasurer (b) Bhagadugha - Collector of Taxes
(c) Kshattri - Chamberlain (d) Adhikrita - Superintendent of Police.

50. Which of the following was not one of the ideas of Sanskrit Literature incorporated into Sangam Literature?
(a) Worship of Indira as the principal deity
(b) Arundhati as the ideal of chastity
(c) The concept of three-fold debt
(d) Utrtar-Karu (Northern Country) as a land of perpetual enjoyment.

51. Small village assemblies during the Sangam Age were known as
(a) Manaram (b) Ambalan
(c) Avai (d) Podiyil

52. From the point of view of places of Buddhist pilgrimage/interest/which of the following is the latest archaeological discovery?
(a) Discovery of Buddha's tooth relic at Bharut in Madhya Pradesh
(b) Sanghol - a Kushana Buddhist site
(c) Discovery of a pillar indicating the actual birth place of Buddha at Lumbini
(d) Discovery and identification of Kapilvastu with Piprahawa, a village in Basti District of Uttar Pradesh.

53. The Indian Buddhists monk, who went to China in the first century A.D. and translated the Buddhist works in the Chinese language, was
(a) Dharmakirti (b) Asanga
(c) Kashyapa Matanga (d) Nagarjuna

54. The concept of Trimurti-the Supreme God manifested in the form of Brahma, Vishnu and Siva was the expression of
(a) the spirit of reconciliation and harmony between orthodox and sectarian forms
(b) adoption of Vedic and non-Vedic deities into a unified deity
(c) Both (a) and (b)
(d) None of the above

55. The latest inscriptions of Ashoka were discovered from
(a) Kandhar bilingual inscriptions (b) Sannatai inscriptions
(c) Maski inscriptions (d) Bhabru edict

56. Which Indus city lay underneath a Buddhist monastery belonging to the Kushana Period?
(a) Harappa (b) Mohenjo-Daro
(c) Chanhudaro (d) Alimurad

57. How many blocks are there in the granary of Mohenjo-Daro?
(a) 16 (b) 19
(c) 23 (d) 27

58. Toy carts have been discovered from
I. Harappa II. Amri
III. Lothal IV. Chanhudaro
Select the correct answer from the codes given below Codes:
(a) I, II (b) I, II, III
(c) I, IV (d) I, II, III, IV

59. Which site produces the earliest evidence for the emergence of agricultural communities?
(a) Mehergarh (b) Kiligul Muhammad
(c) Balakot (d) Ranaghundai

60. From which month would the Mauryan fiscal year begin?
(a) Phalgun (b) Asadha
(c) Jyestha (d) Pausa-Magha

61. The general designation applied by Megasthenes to the Mauryan officials in the rural administration was
(a) Astyomonoi (b) Agronomoi
(c) Agrammes (d) Arappian

62. Exchange of merchandise led inevitably to an exchange of ideas during the pre-Gupta and Gupta Periods. Which of the following was not the result of this interaction with the West:
(a) The borrowing of words, largely of a technical kind, on both sides
(b) Conversion of foreigners to Hinduism and Indians to Christianity
(c) The emergence of hybrid Indo-Greek style of Gandhara Art
(d) Adoption of Indian folk tales and fables in European Literature

63. Which of the following towns was not an important commercial centre in early Ancient India?
(a) Bharukachcha (b) Patala in the Indus Delta
(c) Pushkalavati in the North West (d) Malaimandalam in South India

64. Which of the following statements about the agrahara land grant is not correct?
(a) The king could give it to anyone he pleased
(b) It was a village granted tax-free to the Brahmins
(c) The king had the power to confiscate it
(d) It underlined the privileged position of the donees.

65. Udranga-uparikara, mentioned in several post-Gupta epigraphs, has been interpreted as a tax
(a) levied for the maintenance of police
(b) on fish and other water products
(c) on cultivators not having proprietary rights
(d) All of the above

66. In ancient India, Punarbhu was a
(a) mixed caste (b) remarried widow
(c) child born of a widow (d) divorced widow

67. The first epigraphic reference to committing sati (510 A.D.) has been found from
(a) Eran (b) Prayaga

(c) Bhitari (d) Mandasor

68. Which of the following authorities permits a young man to apply himself to win the girl of his choice by courtship or even by trickery and violence under special circumstances?
(a) Manu (b) Kautilya
(c) Vatsyayana (d) Baudhayana

69. The Sanskrit poet Sri Harsa, author of Naisadhiyacharitam, lived in the court
(a) Jai chandra (b) Vijai chandra
(c) Govind chandra (d) Harish chandra

70. The Rashtrakuta king, who defeated the Pratihara ruler Nagabhatta, was
(a) Amoghavarsha-I (b) Govinda-III
(c) Indra-III (d) Krishna-III

71. Who among the following foreign travellers pays tribute to the efficiency of Bhoja's administration and his forces?
(a) Al Beruni (b) Firdausi
(c) Sulaiman (d) Abdur Razaq

72. Who among the following Pratihara rulers conquered greater part of Magadha and North Bengal?
(a) Mihir Bhoja (b) Mahendrapula I
(c) Mahendrapala 11 (d) Rajyapala

73. Who was the last Pratihara ruler when Mahmud of Ghazni invaded Kanauj into 18 A.D.?
(a) Rajyapala (b) Mahipala I
(c) Mahendrapala III (d) Mahipala II

74. Who was the greatest Gahadavala ruler?
(a) Chandradeva (b) Govinda Chandra
(c) Vijaya Chandra (d) Jaya Chandra

75. Who was the patron of famous Sanskrit poet Sri Harsa?
(a) Chandradeva (b) Govinda Chandra
(c) Vijay Chandra (d) Jaya Chandra

76. Who wrote Naisadhacharita?
(a) Harsha (b) Sri Harsha
(c) Harshavardhan (d) Hala

77. Who wrote Karpuramanjari?
(a) Rajashekhara (b) Kshameshvara
(c) Sri Harsha (d) None of these

78. Who was the last great Pala ruler in Bengal
(a) Mahendrapala (b) Dharampala
(c) Mahipala I (d) Devapala

79. During whose reign the Chola ruler Rajendra I invaded Bengal
(a) Gopala (b) Devapala
(c) Dharampala (d) Mahipala I

80. Who among the following had their capital at Mudgagiri?
(a) The Palas (b) The Senas
(c) The Kalabhras (d) The early Khalji rulers

81. Who introduced Kalimism in Bengal in 12th century A.D.?
(a) Ballal Sena (b) Jaydeva
(c) Dhoyi (d) Lakshmanasena

82. Match the following
(A) Jejaka Bhukti (B) Khajuraho
(C) Kalanjara (D) Mahotsavanagar
(I) Fort (II) Temple
(III) Palace and Capital (IV) Region ruled by the Chandelas
(a) A-I, B-II, C-III, D-IV (b) A-II, B-III, C-IV, D-I
(c) A-IV, B-III, C-I, D-II (d) A-IV, B-II, C-I, D-III

83. The greatest Pannar ruler of Malwa was
(a) Vakpati Munja (b) Bhoja
(c) Both of these (d) None of these

84. Who was popularly known as Kaviraja?
(a) Bhoja (b) Harsha
(c) Sri Harsha (d) Mihir Bhoja

85. Who was the greatest Chalukyan king of Anhilwara?
(a) Jayasinha Siddharaja (b) Bhima I
(c) Bhima II (d) Mularaja

86. The celebrated Jain scholar, Hemachandra was patronised by the Chalukyan ruler
(a) Mularaja (b) Bhima I
(c) Bhima II (d) Jayasimha Siddharaja

87. Who of the following did not rule over the Kashmir
(a) The Kaxkotas (b) The Utpalas
(c) The Loharas (d) The Ismailis

88. Kalhana was patronised by
(a) The Loharas (b) The Kaxkotas
(c) The Utpalas (d) The Ismailis

89. Who founded the Lohara dynasty
(a) Didda (b) Vinayaditya
(c) Vigraharaja (d) Zain-ul-Abidin

90. Who built the famous city of Puri in Orissa
(a) Chodaganga (b) Sri Ganga
(c) Gangadeva (d) Chodagupta

91. Mahmud of Ghazi invaded India
(a) 17 times (b) 15 times
(c) 18 times (d) 19 times

92. Who among the following Rashtrakuta kings did not invade north India?
(a) Dhruva (b) Govinda III
(c) Indra III (d) Amoghavarsha

93. Taila II, a feudatory of Krishna III who overthrew the Rashtrakuta, belonged to or claimed descent from
(a) Early western Chalukyas of Badami
(b) Later western Chalukyas of Kalyani
(c) Eastern Chalukyas of Vengi
(d) All of these

94. In which of the following years Mahmud led the first invasion against India?
(a) 998 (b) 999
(c) 1000 (d) 1001

95. Where was the capital of Hindu Shahi Kingdom located at the time of Mahmud's attack?
(a) Kabul (b) Peshwar
(c) Attock (d) Uch

96. Who burnt himself on a funeral pyre after being defeated by Mahmud of Ghazni?
(a) Anandapala (b) Jayapala
(c) Trilopchanapala (d) Bhima

97. Tomars of Dhillika were overthrown by
(a) Chauhans (b) Chandellas
(c) Gahadavalas (d) Solankis

98. Who started a new era in place of the old Saka era?
(a) Taila II (b) Someshvara III
(c) Vikramaditya VI (d) Vikramaditya V

99. The Yadava kingdom of Deogiri was founded by
(a) Prolaraja II (b) Bhillama
(c) Singhana (d) Ganapati

100. Which one of the following Kakatiya rulers is mentioned in glowing terms by the Venetian traveller Marco Polo
(a) Rudmmma (b) Ganapati
(c) Bhillama (d) Harihara

Answers

1. (b)	21. (b)	41. (c)	61. (b)	81. (a)
2. (c)	22. (c)	42. (b)	62. (b)	82. (d)
3. (b)	23. (b)	43. (c)	63. (d)	83. (b)
4. (b)	24. (b)	44. (a)	64. (a)	84. (a)
5. (b)	25. (b)	45. (d)	65. (a)	85. (a)
6. (a)	26. (d)	46. (d)	66. (b)	86. (d)
7. (b)	27. (a)	47. (d)	67. (a)	87. (d)
8. (d)	28. (c)	48. (c)	68. (c)	88. (a)
9. (c)	29. (b)	49. (d)	69. (a)	89. (c)
10. (a)	30. (c)	50. (a)	70. (b)	90. (a)
11. (d)	31. (a)	51. (c)	71. (c)	91. (a)
12. (d)	32. (a)	52. (b)	72. (b)	92. (d)
13. (d)	33. (c)	53. (d)	73. (a)	93. (a)
14. (b)	34. (c)	54. (c)	74. (b)	94. (c)
15. (b)	35. (d)	55. (b)	75. (a)	95. (d)
16. (d)	36. (b)	56. (b)	76. (b)	96. (b)
17. (b)	37. (c)	57. (d)	77. (a)	97. (a)
18. (c)	38. (b)	58. (c)	78. (c)	98. (c)
19. (b)	39. (c)	59. (a)	79. (d)	99. (b)
20. (a)	40. (b)	60. (b)	80. (a)	100. (a)

SET X

Questions

1. The Pandyas of Madurai were finally absorbed into
   (a) Delhi Sultanate (b) Vijayanagar
   (c) The Cholas (d) Bahmani
2. What was the system of Mandala?
   (a) provincial administration (b) art of diplomacy
   (c) interstate politics (d) interstate irrigational system
3. Which one of the following authorises the husband to beat his erring wife with a rope or a split bamboo but not on the head or the breasts?
   (a) Vishnu Purana (b) Vayu Purana
   (c) Matsya Purana (d) Manusmiriti
4. Who among the following were not 'antyajas'?
   (a) Sailors (b) Fisherman
   (c) Oilmen (d) Weavers
5. Which one of the following was the centre of general education in a village?
   (a) Mathas (b) Viharas
   (c) Guilds (d) Temples
6. Which one of the following was the most famous seat of learning during this period?
   (a) Vikramshila (b) Nalanda
   (c) Valabhi (d) Jagadalla
7. The Lingayats openly opposed
   (a) Buddhists (b) Jainas
   (c) Alvars (d) Nayanars
8. The first historical document referring the Cholas was
   (a) II and XIII rock edicts of Ashoka (b) V and XIII rock edicts of Ashoka
   (c) I and XIII rock edicts of Ashoka (d) IV and XIII rock edicts of Ashoka
9. Who assumed the title Mummadi Chola?
   (a) Vijayalaya (b) Karikala
   (c) Uttama (d) Rajamja
10. Which one of the following was not one of the titles assumed by Rajendra?

(a) Tyagasamudra (b) Gangaikonda
(c) Mudikonda (d) Kadarangond G

11. Give the correct descending order
(a) Mandalam, Valanadu, Kurram (b) Mandalam, Nadu, Kottam
(c) Kurram, Nadu, Kottam (d) Nadu, Kurram, Taniyur

12. A very large village administered as a single unit was called
(a) Taniyur (b) Kottam
(c) Kurram (d) Nadu

13. Which of the following was not one of the sub-committees of Variyum?
(a) Annual Committee (b) Gold Committee
(c) Garden Committee (d) Tank Committee

14. Which one of the following committees was responsible for maintenance of village road?
(a) Five fold Committee (b) Garden Committee
(c) Annual Committee (d) Tank Committee

15. The tenure meant for educational purposes was known as
(a) Brahmendeya (b) Agrahara
(c) Devadana (d) Askara

16. What was the main feature of Dravida style temple architecture?
(a) Shikhara (b) Gopuran
(c) Vimana (d) Mandapam

17. Who wrote Ramayana in Tamil?
(a) Pugalendi (b) Kamban
(c) Jayangondur (d) Ranna

18. Which one of the following years did Chola kings send an embassy to China is incorrect
(a) 1016 A.D. (b) 1033 A.D.
(c) 1077 AD. (d) 1125 A.D.

19. Which one of the following important Chola ports was situated on the Malabar Coast?
(a) Korkai (b) Shahyar
(c) Quilon (d) Kaveripattinam

20. Who were the balahars
(a) ordinary peasants (b) big peasants
(c) middle peasants (d) bonded labour

21. The Mustakhavar were appointed to supervise the
(a) land revenue assessment
(b) measurement of land
(c) maintenance of actual revenue realised
(d) all the above

22. Of which one of the following sources did the Naib-i-diwan-i-Vizarat not verify the accounts of revenue assessed
(a) Patwari's record (b) Imperial officer's record
(c) Local government official's record (d) Local governor's record

23. Sera-i-Adl was erected near
(a) Kashmiri gate (b) Delhi Gate
(c) Ajmeri Gate (d) Badaun gate
24. Who built a great mosque at Deogiri?
(a) Malik Kafur (b) Malik Yaklaki
(c) Ala-ud-din Khalji (d) Mubarak Shah
25. Who assumed the tile of al-wasiq billah?
(a) Iltutmish (b) Balban
(c) Nasiruddin Mahmud (d) Mubarak Shah
26. Who of the following contemporary historians did not mention that Khusrav Shah favoured the Hindus?
(a) Ziauddin Barani (b) Sirhindi
(c) Ibn Batutah (d) Afif
27. Who was the second most responsible person after Zafar Khan in defending the foundries of Delhi sultanate from the onslaughts of the Mongols?
(a) Malik Ghazi (b) Malik Yaklaki
(c) Malik Kafur (d) Malik Sarwar
28. Who among the following contemporary historians did not suspect a conspiracy in the death of Ghiyasuddin Tughluq?
(a) Abul Fazl (b) Nizamuddin Ahmad
(c) Badauni (d) Sirhindi
29. Who among the following rulers did not introduce token currency in their respective empire?
(a) Qublai Khan (b) Gai Khatu
(c) Ghazau Khan (d) Chengiz Khan
30. Muhammad bin Tughluq obtained a patent of investitute from
(a) Abbasid Califate of Egypt (b) Khalifah of Baghdad
(c) Afrasiyab (d) Asfandiyar
31. Who was the official historian of Firuz Shah Tughluq?
(a) Shams-i-Siraj-Afif (b) Ziauddin Barani
(c) Yahiya Ahmed bin Sirhindi (d) Amir Khusrau
32. What was the main achievement of Firuz Shah Tughluq in his campaign against Nagarkot?
(a) destruction of the temple (b) punishment to the ruler
(c) captured females slaves (d) Dalail-i-Firuz Shahi
33. Who was the author of Dalail-i Firuz-Shahi?
(a) Afif (b) Sirhandi
(c) Ziauddin Barani (d) Khalid Khani
34. Who declared himself the Deputy of Khalifah of Egypt?
(a) Iltutmish (b) Alauddin Khalji
(c) Mubarak Shah (d) Firuz Shah
35. Who revived the Jagir System which was abolished by Ala-ud-din Khalji?
(a) Muhammad bin Tughluq (b) Firuz Shah
(c) Bahlul Lodi (d) Sher Shah

36. Timur invaded India during the reign of
(a) Nasiruddin Mahmud (b) Khizr Khan Sayyid
(c) Alauddin Alam Shah (d) Mubarak Shah

37. Who of the following Delhi Sultans abducted his throne and retired to his favourite place, Badaun?
(a) Nasiruddin Mahmud (b) Khizr Khan Sayyid
(c) Alauddin Alain Shah (d) Mubarak Shah

38. Who founded a new town in 1504 A.D. on the site where Agra stands?
(a) Mubarak Shah (b) Bahlul Lodi
(c) Sikander Shah Lodi (d) Ibrahim Lodi

39. Who annexed Jaunpur effectively to Delhi Sultanate?
(a) Delhi Sultanate (b) Bahol Lodi
(c) Barbak Shah (d) Sikandar Shah

40. Who of the following held the highest and an extraordinary position in the Central Government?
(a) Qaa (b) Waldl
(c) Wazir (d) Naib-ul-Mulk

41. Akbar conquered Malwa from
(a) Mahmud Khalji I (b) Mahmud Khalji II
(c) Sujaat Khan (d) Baz Bahadur

42. Who was regarded as the greatest independent Muslim ruler of Bengal?
(a) Ghiyasaddin Azam Shah (b) Raja Ganesh
(c) Alauddin Hussain Shah (d) Nusrat Shah

43. Which one among the following rulers was the contemporary of Great Vaishnava saint Chaitanya in Bengal?
(a) Shamsuddin Ilyas Shah (b) Sikandar Shah
(c) Ghiyasuddin Azam Shah (d) Alauddin Hussain Shah

44. Which one among the following sultans of Bahmani empire encouraged the influx of Afaqis or West Asians to settle down in Deccan
(a) Tajuddin Firuz (b) Alauddin Hasan
(c) Ahmad Shah I (d) Md. Shah

45. The capital of Bahmani empire was shifted from Gulbarga to Bidar during the reign of
(a) Alauddin Hussain Shah (b) Ahmad Shah I
(c) Muhammad Shah (d) Ibrahim Adil Shah

46. Match the following:

I		II
(A) Adil Shahi	(I)	Bijapur
(B) Qutbshahi	(II)	Golconda
(C) Nizam Shahi	(III)	Ahmad Nagar
(D) Barid Shahi	(IV)	Bidar
(E) Imad Shahi	(V)	Berar

(a) A-I, B-II, C-III, D-IV, E-V (b) A-II, B-III, C-IV, D-V E-I
(c) A-II, B-I, C-IV, D-III, E-V (d) A-IV, B-III, C-V D-I, E-II

47. Which one of the following finally annexed Bengal and brought about the decline and fall of the dynasty of Ilyas Khan?
(a) Babur (b) Humayun
(c) Sher Shah (d) Akbar

48. Which of the following ruler of Bengal did not promote communal harmony?
(a) Shamsuddin Ilyas Shah (b) Shamusuddin Ahmed
(c) Raja Ganesh (d) Alauddin Hussain Shah

49. Which one of the following dynasties of Orissa constructed the temple of Jagannath at Puri and the temple of the Sun-God at Konark
(a) Bhoj (b) Gajapati
(c) Choda Ganga (d) All of these

50. Who annexed Khandesh to his empire?
(a) Sikander Lodi (b) Akbar
(c) Shah Jahan (d) Aurangzeb

51. The capital city of Ahmedabad was built by Ahmadshah on the site of the old town of:
(a) Sabarmati (b) Sidhpur
(c) Idar (d) Asawal

52. Mahmud Begarha founded the new town of Mustafabad after his victory over
(a) The fort of Champaner (b) The fort of Gimar
(c) The fort of Asirgarh (d) The fort of Burhanpur

53. Mahmud Begarha founded another town named Muhammadabad after capturing the fort of
(a) Burhanpur (b) Dhar
(c) Mandu (d) Champaner

54. Which one of the following, wars seems to have been indecisive with both sides building monuments to commemorate the victory
(a) Rana Kumbha of Chittor-Ahmed Shah of Gujarat
(b) Rana Kumbha-Mahmud Khalji of Malwa
(c) Rana Kumbha-Rao Jodha of Marwar
(d) Rana Kumbha-Humayun

55. Zain-e-Abidin's greatest engineering achievement, Zaina Lanha, was an artificial island in
(a) Dal Lake (b) Woolur Lake
(c) Sukhna Lake (d) Mansalal Lake

56. Bidar was absorbed into
(a) Bijapur (b) Ahmednagar
(c) Golconda (d) Berar

57. Berar was absorbed by
(a) Bijapur (b) Ahmednagar
(c) Golconda (d) Bidar

58. Which one of the following travellers visited Bahmani Kingdom and observed that the common people led a miserable life while the nobles lived in luxury?
(a) Abdur Razzaq (b) Nicolo Conti

(c) Nuniz (d) Nikitin

59. Which of the following rulers was infamous and got the epithet of zalim or tyrant?
(a) Md. Shah (b) Humayun
(c) Md. Shah III (d) Tajuddin Firuz Shah

60. Adina mosque in Bengal was built by Sikandar Shah and it had
(a) 100 domes (b) 200 domes
(c) 300 domes (d) 400 domes

61. Which one of the following groups did not form part of imperial council
(a) The Prime Minister, Ministers and Deputy Ministers
(b) Selected blood relations of the king
(c) Amarnayakas
(d) Heads of departments

62. Which one of the following statements about the Nayankara System is not correct?
(a) The king granted a maram or territory with a fixed revenue to the nayaks
(b) They formed a very powerful group and occasionally it was difficult to control them
(c) The hereditary Nayankara system tended to curb the freedom and the initiative of the kings
(d) This office was hereditary from the very beginning

63. Which one of the following rulers conducted a detailed land survey and assessment?
(a) Bukka I (b) Devaraya II
(c) Krishnadeva Raya (d) Achyuta Raya

64. The Dandanayaka was the head of
(a) Kandachara department (b) Ayagars
(c) Athavana (d) none of these

65. Match the following

I

(A) Kudi (B) Kaivinaikuddi
(C) Varam (D) Kuttagai

II

(I) Lease system of cultivation
(II) Hired labour
(III) Sharing of agricultural income between landlord and tenant
(IV) farm lands

(a) A-I, B-II, C-III, D-IV (b) A-II, B-III, C-IV, D-IV
(c) A-IV, B-II, C-III, D-I (d) A-II, B-IV, C-III, D-I

66. Which of the following places had a flourishing business of ship building?
(a) Nagapattanam (b) Quilon
(c) Calicut (d) Maldive Islands

67. Which one of the following types of marriages was the most popular in Vijaynagara?
(a) Brahma (b) Daiva
(c) Arsa (d) Prajapatya

68. The most important musical instrument was
(a) Vina (b) Sitar
(c) Mridungam (d) Cymbals

69. The Vaishnavism became the personal religion of the rulers of Vijaynagar during the reign of
(a) Tirumala (b) Venkata I
(c) Venkata II (d) Krishnadeva Raya

70. Which one of the following rulers followed a policy of religious toleration and granted the permission to Portuguese to establish churches at Vellore?
(a) Venkata I (b) Venkata II
(c) Deva Raya II (d) Achyutadeva Raya

71. Which one of the following travellers to Vijaynagar was an envoy?
(a) Nuniz (b) Paes
(c) Nicolo Conti (d) Abdur Razzaq

72. Which one of the following travellers did not visit during the reign of Krishnadeva Raya
(a) Conti (b) Paes
(c) Nuniz (d) Barbosa

73. The Hazura temple was built during the reign of Krishnadeva Raya and was dedicated to
(a) Lord Rama (b) Lord Siva
(c) Lord Vishnu (d) Lord Murugam

74. Which one of the following territories was not the bone of contention between the Vijaynagar and the Bahmani Empire?
(a) Raichur doab (b) Krishna-Godavari basin
(c) Konkan region (d) Eastern Vengi

75. Who was the last important ruler of Vijaynagar Empire?
(a) Venkata I (b) Venkata II
(c) Venkata III (d) Ranga II

76. Who tells us that the empire possessed 300 sea ports?
(a) Abdul Razzaq (b) Nicolo Conti
(c) Paes (d) Nikitin

77. Which one of the following gives the information that on the last day of famous nine days festival 250 buffaloes and 4500 sheep were slaughtered?
(a) Abdul Razzaq (b) Domingos Paes
(c) Barbosa (d) Nuniz

78. Which one of the following rulers of Vijay Nagar was accomplished in music?
(a) Deva Raya I (b) Vanket I
(c) Harihara II (d) Rama Raya

79. Who tells "every thing has to be sold alive so that each may know what he buys..."
(a) Barbosa (b) Paes
(c) Conti (d) Nuniz

80. The fiscal sources of Akbar's empire were divided into two main divisions-central and local. The most lucrative and important source of revenue was
(a) commerce
(b) customs duties
(c) land
(d) religious taxes, such as Zakat, pilgrims tax, Jizya and inheritance tax, etc.

81. "In short, the system (assessment and collection of land revenue) was an admirable one. The principles were sound and the practical instructions to officials were all that could be desired".
The above statement best sums up the land revenue assessment and collection system prevalent in the reign of
(a) Ala-ud-din Khilji (b) Mughal Emperor Akbar
(c) Sher Shah Suri (d) Mughal Emperor Shah Jahan

82. For purposes of determination of land revenue, the basis of classification of land during Akbar's reign was
(a) kind of land
(b) continuity or otherwise of cultivation of land
(c) fertility of the soil
(d) all of the above

83. During Akbar's reign the most common gold coin was Ilahi, which in value was equal to
(a) 10 rupee silver coins (b) 12 rupee silver coins
(c) 15 rupee silver coins (d) 20 rupee silver coins

84. In the field of art and architecture, biographer of one of the great Mughals wrote that his sovereign "planned splendid edifices and dressed the work of his mind and heart in the garment of stone and clay". This great Mughal Emperor was:
(a) Babar (b) Akbar
(c) Jahangir (d) Shah Jahan

85. Jahangiri Mahal, built according to Hindu design, is located inside the
(a) Agra Fort (b) Allahabad Fort
(c) Lahore Fort (d) None of these

86. The lovely Moti Masjid or Pearl Mosque at Agra, an example of true art for its purity and elegance, was built by
(a) Akbar (b) Jahangir
(c) Shah Jahan (d) Aurangzeb

87. Who, amongst the following, took away to Persia the 'Peacock Throne' of Shah Jahan in the first half of 18th century?
(a) Ahmed Shah Abdali (b) Nadir Shah
(c) Chin Qilich Khan (d) Mir Mannu, Abdali's Governor in Lahore

88. To express it in modern terms, the Mughal forces were composed of
(a) cavalry and infantry (b) cavalry and artillery
(c) infantry, artillery and navy (d) infantry, cavalry, artillery and navy

89. The Diwani of Bengal, Bihar and Orissa was granted by Shah Alam II to the English East India Company in the
(a) Second half of 17th century (b) First half of 18th century
(c) Second half of 18th century (d) Soon after the end of 18th century

90. The Vijayanagara and Bahmani kingdoms in southern India emerged during the concluding years of the reign of
(a) Ala-ud-din Khilji (b) Ghias-ud-din Tughlaq
(c) Muhammad-bin Tughlaq (d) Bahlol Lodi

91. Which of the following rulers' duration of their reign was very nearly the same and the longest?
 (a) Humayun and Sher Shah (b) Babar and Muhammad-bin Tughlaq
 (c) Jahangir and Shah Jahan (d) Akbar and Aurangzeb
92. The Maratha movement developed into a challenging power under Shivaji during the reign of
 (a) Jahangir (b) Shah Jahan
 (c) Aurangzeb Alamgir I (d) Bahadur Shah 1
93. Who, among the following functionaries during Akbar's reign, was responsible for payment of salaries of officers, including Mansabdars?
 (a) Diwan or Wazir (b) Mir Bakshi
 (c) Sadr-us-Sadr (d) Vakil
94. By which of the following designations was the Prime Minister known during the reign of Akbar?
 (a) Diwan or Wazir (b) Mir Bakshi
 (c) Sadr-us-Sadr (d) Vakil
95. When offered the choice between death and conversion by Aurangzeb, the Sikh Guru chose the former and was executed. Who was this Guru?
 (a) Guru Arjan Dev (b) Guru Har Gobind
 (c) Guru Teg Bahadur (d) Guru Gobind Singh
96. Who, amongst the following Generals or Commanders, carried out coup d'etat against Jahangir in 1626?
 (a) Asaf Khan (b) Malik Ambar
 (c) Mahabat Khan (d) None of these
97. Who, amongst the following, was the last ruler of the Timurid dynasty in India?
 (a) Aziz-ud-din Alamgir II (b) Akbar Shah II
 (c) Bahadur Shah II (d) Shah Alam II
98. Who, amongst the following Sikh Gurus, was tortured to death by Jahangir on a charge of treason?
 (a) Guru Amardas (b) Guru Arjan Dev
 (c) Guru Har Gobind (d) Guru Har Kishan
99. Soon after his coronation, Aurangzeb gave the much needed relief to the people by abolishing
 (a) inland duty (Rahdari) (b) octroi (Pandari)
 (c) both the above taxes (d) none of the above
100. Fergusson aptly remarked that Fatehdur "was a reflex of the mind of a great man". This tribute is in the field of architecture to the genius of
 (a) Akbar (b) Jahangir
 (c) Shah Jahan (d) Aurangzeb

Answers

1. (b)	21. (d)	41. (d)	61. (c)	81. (b)
2. (c)	22. (c)	42. (c)	62. (d)	82. (b)
3. (c)	23. (d)	43. (d)	63. (c)	83. (a)
4. (c)	24. (d)	44. (a)	64. (a)	84. (b)
5. (d)	25. (d)	45. (b)	65. (a)	85. (a)
6. (b)	26. (d)	46. (a)	66. (d)	86. (c)
7. (b)	27. (a)	47. (c)	67. (a)	87. (b)
8. (a)	28. (d)	48. (b)	68. (a)	88. (d)
9. (d)	29. (d)	49. (c)	69. (c)	89. (c)
10. (a)	30. (a)	50. (b)	70. (b)	90. (c)
11. (a)	31. (a)	51. (d)	71. (d)	91. (d)
12. (a)	32. (d)	52. (d)	72. (a)	92. (c)
13. (b)	33. (d)	53. (d)	73. (a)	93. (b)
14. (b)	34. (d)	54. (d)	74. (d)	94. (d)
15. (c)	35. (b)	55. (b)	75. (c)	95. (c)
16. (c)	36. (a)	56. (a)	76. (a)	96. (c)
17. (b)	37. (c)	57. (b)	77. (b)	97. (c)
18. (d)	38. (c)	58. (d)	78. (d)	98. (b)
19. (c)	39. (c)	59. (b)	79. (d)	99. (c)
20. (a)	40. (d)	60. (d)	80. (c)	100. (a)

SET XI

Questions

1. Who, amongst the following Muslim rulers imposed all sorts of disabilities, including use of force on Hindus with a view to converting India into a Muslim country?
   (a) Qutab-ud-din Aibak (b) Sher Shah Suri
   (c) Aurangzeb (d) Muhammad-bin Tughlaq
2. Which of the following Sikh gurus rose against Shah Jahan and defeated an imperial army at Sangrama near Amritsar in the first half of 17th century?
   (a) Guru Arjan Dev (b) Guru Har Gobind
   (c) Guru Har Rai (d) Guru Har Kishan
3. The battle of Buxar, which enabled the English to acquire a firm hold of Bengal, was fought between them and the combined forces of?
   (a) French and Mir Qasim
   (b) Siraj-ud-daula and Mir Qasim
   (c) Shah Alam II and Nawab of Oudh
   (d) Shah Alam II, Mir Qasim and Nawab of Oudh
4. Consequent upon Humayun's sudden death as a result of an accident, Akbar was enthroned and proclaimed Emperor by his guardian at
   (a) Amarkot (b) Kalanaur
   (c) Lahore (d) Mankot Fort
5. Jalal-ud-din Muhammad Akbar was proclaimed Emperor in
   (a) 1556 (b) 1557
   (c) 1558 (d) 1560
6. Who, amongst the following, is regarded as responsible for the firm re-establishment of the Mughal rule in Hindustan in the latter half of 16th century?
   (a) Ali Qulikhan (b) Bairam Khan
   (c) Mir Abdul Latif (d) None of these
7. Which of the following reforms was carried out by Akbar in the first ten years of his rule?
   (a) Abolition of the practice of enslaving prisoners of war
   (b) Abolition of the tax levied on the pilgrims who visited Hindu places of pilgrimage
   (c) Abolition of the most hated tax, called Jizya, on non-Muslims
   (d) All of the above

8. Which of the following coins of Akbar's reign carried the highest value?
(a) Illahi (b) Jalah
(c) Jital (d) Shansab

9. Which of the following is not true of Emperor Akbar's administration?
(a) The Mughal ministers did not constitute a cabinet in the modern sense of the word
(b) The ministers worked as secretaries rather than ministers
(c) The initiation of policy was in the hands of ministers
(d) The Emperor appointed or dismissed his ministers, including the Prime Minister, as he liked

10. The reign of which of the following is usually considered to have been the golden period of Mughal rule in India
(a) Akbar (b) Aurangzeb
(c) Jahangir (d) Shah Jahan

11. Who, amongst the following Muslim rulers, was venerated by Muslims as a Zinda Pir or living saint?
(a) Ghias-ud-din (Ghazi Malik) Tughlaq Shah I
(b) Sher Shah Suri
(c) Haji Shamsuddin Ilyas
(d) Muih-ud-din Muhammad Aurangzeb

12. Who, amongst the following, was the accredited ambassador of the king of England, James I, to the Mughal Emperor Jahangir's court?
(a) James Lancaster (b) Sir Henry Middleton
(c) Sir Thomas Roe (d) None of the above

13. The most accomplished writer (Persian) of Akbar's reign-a man of letters, a poet, an essayist, a critic, and a historian-was
(a) Abul Fazl (b) Badauni
(c) Faizi (d) None of these

14. Who built the tomb of Itimad-ud daula at Agra?
(a) Akbar (b) Jahangir
(c) Nur Jahan (d) Sher Shah

15. Who amongst the following sons of Emperor Jahangir, was married to the daughter of Nur Jahan (by Sher Afghan)?
(a) Khurram (b) Khusrau
(c) Parwez (d) Shahryar

16. The battle of Sanugarh, which resulted in the defeat of Dara Shikoh and paved the way for Aurangzeb to the Mughal throne, took place in
(a) 1657 (b) 1658
(c) 1659 (d) 1660

17. Emperor Shah Jahan died in
(a) 1658 (b) 1659
(c) 1666 (d) 1667

18. The English East India Company laid the foundation of Fort St. George at Madras during the reign of
(a) Akbar (b) Aurangzeb
(c) Jahangir (d) Shah Jahan

19. Who led the people of Bundelkhand and Malwa against Aurangzeb and succeeded in carving out an independent principality in eastern Malwa with its capital at Panna?
(a) Champat Rai (b) Chhatrasal
(c) Churaman (d) Raja Ram

20. Where did the English East India Company set up its first factory in India during the reign of Jahangir
(a) Agra (b) Ahmedabad
(c) Broach (d) Surat

21. Who, amongst the following, was in-charge of land revenue system during the reign of Akbar?
(a) Abul Fazal (b) Birbal
(c) Man Singh (d) Todar Mal

22. Who, amongst the following after marriage, became known as Nur Jahan, wife of Emperor Jahangir
(a) Arjumand Banu Begam (b) Asmat Begam
(c) Ladli Begam (d) Mehr-un Nisa

23. Whose daughter was Mumtaz Mahal?
(a) Kha-e-Khanan (b) Sher Afgan
(c) Abul Fazal (d) Asif Jah

24. Who, amongst the following after marriage, became known as Mumtaz Mahal, the beloved wife of Shah Jahan?
(a) Arjumand Banu Begam (b) Asmat Begam
(c) Ladli Begam (d) Mehr-un-Nisa

25. The Indian design of the colossal structure of Akbar's mausoleum at Sikandara was inspired by
(a) Jaina temple architecture (b) Buddhist Viharas
(c) Rajput architecture (d) None of the above

26. In the latter half of the 17th century, which of the following Deccan kingdoms capitulated to the onslaught of Aurangzeb?
(a) Adil Shahi kingdom of Bijapur (b) Qutb Shahi kingdom of Golkunda
(c) Maratha kingdom of Shivaji (d) Nizam Shah kingdom

27. All of the following Muslim scholars of Akbar's court rendered the epic Mahabharata into Persian, except
(a) Abdul Qadir Badauni (b) Haji Ibrahim Sarhindi
(c) Naqib khan (d) Shaikh Sultan of Thaneshwar

28. Who, amongst the following Muslim scholars of Akbar's court, translated Atharva Veda into Persian?
(a) Abdul Qadir Badauni (b) Haji Ibrahim Sarhindi
(c) Naqib Khan (d) Shaikh Sultan of Thaneshwar

29. Rajatarangini of Kalhan, a Sanskrit history of Kashmir, was translated into Persian by
(a) Abdul Qadir Badauni
(b) Haji Ibrahim Sarhindi
(c) Mulla Shah Muhammad of Shahabad
(d) Shaikh Sultan of Thaneshwar

30. Ain-i-Akbari and Akbarnama were written by Abul Fazl in
(a) Arabic (b) Persian
(c) Urdu (d) Turkish

31. Which of the following statements about the style of architecture from the Turko-Afghan kings to the Mughal period is not correct?
(a) The buildings erected by the Sultans of Delhi were mainly foreign, in design and workmanship
(b) The buildings erected during the time of Akbar reveal a mixed style, which is partly Muslim and mainly Hindu in character
(c) Decorative carvings were an important feature of Mughal architecture
(d) All the above statements are correct

32. Once free from the tutelage of Bairam Khan and Maham Anaga, Akbar formed an ambitious design of conquering northern India. Which one of the following was the first to be annexed to his empire in 1561 A.D.?
(a) Chunar (b) Jaipur
(c) Jaunpur (d) Malwa

33. In the matter of succession to the Mughal throne Roshanara-one of the two daughters of Shah Jahan sided with and supported the cause of
(a) Dara Shikoh (b) Murad Baksh
(c) Aurangzeb (d) Shujah

34. The Muslim state in India during the Sultanate period was?
(a) a theocratic state, the Sultans owing complete allegiance to the Khalifas of Baghdad and Egypt
(b) essentially military in character
(c) by and large democratic in character
(d) none of the above

35. Abdur Rahim Khan-e-Khana was a?
(a) diplomat of high calibre of king of Persia
(b) wise counsellor of Aurangzeb
(c) great military leader of Shivaji
(d) versatile genius and writer in Hindi, Persian and Arabic in the reign of Akbar

36. The Mughal public service during the reign of Akbar suffered from all of the following drawbacks, except
(a) there were no regular rules of appointment, promotion or dismissal
(b) it was the emperor's pleasure to appoint or promote any one he liked
(c) fixity of tenure often resulted in complacency among the services
(d) the imperial officials of the upper grades were expected to be extravagant

37. Which of the following was the official court language during Akbar's reign
(a) Arabic (b) Persian
(c) Urdu (d) Turkish

38. Which of the following religions influenced Akbar much more than any single religion, all of which were meticulously examined by him
(a) Christianity (b) Jainism
(c) Hinduism (d) Zoroastrianism

39. According to his memoirs, what lured Babar to come to India and establish an empire?
   (a) Its fruit and flowers (b) Its religions and rituals
   (c) Its art and architecture (d) Its abundance of gold and silver
40. Which of the following statements about the religious policy of Akbar is not correct?
   (a) He gave the highest place to Islam among the various religions prevalent at the time
   (b) His religious policy was based on the principle of universal toleration
   (c) In general the policy commanded the adoption of good points of all the religions
   (d) Unlike during the time of his forebears, the state as such was no longer an Islamic theocracy, i.e., he abolished Islam as the state religion
41. Who built the mausoleum of Jahangir and where?
   (a) Shah Jahan at Agra (b) Nur Jahan at Fatehpur
   (c) Nur Jahan at Lahore (d) Shah Jahan at Delhi
42. Which of the following was the chief cause of Dara Shikoh's failure in the war of succession and his ultimate destruction by Aurangzeb?
   (a) His father's excessive fondness for him and his constant presence at court had made his other brothers jealous of him
   (b) Lack of qualities of an astute politician or of a brave general
   (c) Excessive sense of pride made him contemptuous of advice
   (d) He incurred the displeasure of the orthodox members among his co-religionists because of his eclectic views, liberal disposition and of scholarly instincts
43. The Infallibility Decree was issued by Akbar in the year
   (a) 1575 (b) 1579
   (c) 1581 (d) 1595
44. Which of the following historians contends that "Taj is the product of a combination of European and Asiatic genius"?
   (a) Fergusson (b) Percy Brown
   (c) V.A. Smith (d) Stanlay Lanepoole
45. Which of the two following kingdoms were conquered by Akbar?
   (a) Bijapur and Khandesh (b) Ahmednagar and Golkunda
   (c) Khandesh and Ahmednagar (d) Khandesh and Golkunda
46. Which one of the following names is famous for association with music during the Mughal period?
   (a) Faizi (b) Abdul Fazl
   (c) Baz Bahadur (d) Abdur Rahim Khan-i-Khanan
47. Who was the last Mughal emperor of India?
   (a) Akbar II (b) Bahadur Shah II
   (c) Alamgir II (d) Shah Alam II
48. Which of the following emperors was deposed by the Sayyid brothers with the help of the Marathas?
   (a) Raft-Ud-Darjat (b) Jahandar Shah
   (c) Farrukhsiyar (d) Shah Jahan II

49. The Third Battle of Panipat was between the
(a) Afghans and the Marathas
(b) Afghans and the Sikhs
(c) Marathas and the Mughals under Shah Alam II
(d) None of the above

50. The Deccan Subah of the Mughal empire of Aurangzeb became independent in 1724 under
(a) Najib-ud-daulah (b) Nizam-ul-mulk
(c) Mubariz Khan (d) Alivardi Khan

51. The establishment of the Mughal administration, on ideas and principles different from Sultans of Delhi, was mainly the work of
(a) Akbar (b) Jahangir
(c) Shah Jahan (d) Aurangzeb

52. Of the following Mughal rulers, the credit of bringing about the fusion of two diverse systems of music (Hindu and Muslim music) belongs to
(a) Babar (b) Akbar
(c) Jahangir (d) Shah Jahan

53. Which of the following factors caused the disintegration of the Mughal empire?
(a) Attacks of Nadir Shah and Ahmed Shah Abdali
(b) War of succession among the sons of Aurangzeb
(c) Revolts of various sections of population, like Jats, Rajputs, Sikhs etc.
(d) All of the above together caused the disintegration

54. Which of the following battles maked the real beginning of the Mughal Empire in India?
(a) Battle of Talikota (b) Battle of Haldighati
(c) First Battle of Panipat (d) Second Battle of Panipat

55. The reign of which of the following Mughal emperors is believed to have seen a distinct decline of pictorial art?
(a) Akbar (b) Jahangir
(c) Aurangzeb (d) Shah Jahan

56. The principal purpose of Akbar in following the strategy of befriending Rajputs and seeking their cooperation was to
(a) Secure matrimonial alliances
(b) Strengthen the foundations of Mughal empire in India
(c) Wipe out Afghan power from the land
(d) Check the inflow of foreign invaders of India

57. As a result of extensive reforms, Akbar centralised the control and functioning of the various mints in
(a) 1570 (b) 1577
(c) 1584 (d) 1591

58. Which of the following is not true of Akbar's judicial system?
(a) He restricted the scope of the Islamic law
(b) The king's court was highest court of appeal but sometimes initial cases were heard by him

(c) Hindu judges were appointed to decide cases of both Hindus and Muslims
(d) Hindu law was administered in deciding civil and religious disputes of which the parties were Hindus

59. All of the following were contemporaries of Emperor Akbar, except
(a) Abbas the Great of Persia (b) Henry VIII of England
(c) Elizabeth I of England (d) Henry IV of France

60. Who, amongst the following, after succeeding to the throne was known as Emperor Shah Jahan?
(a) Jalal-ud-din (b) Nur-ud-din Muhammad
(c) Muhi-ud-din Muhammad (d) Khurram Shihab-ud-din

61. What was the early settlement of the Portuguese on the Southeast coast?
(a) San Thorne (b) Amargaon
(c) Karikal (d) Pulicat

62. Who established the factory at Sultanate in 1690?
(a) Job Chamock (b) Sir John Child
(c) Sir William Courten (d) Eyre Coote

63. When did the Danes form an East India Company after their arrival in India?
(a) 1614 (b) 1615
(c) 1616 (d) 1617

64. Which region in India provided the best quality saltpetre and opium to the Europeans?
(a) Coromandal (b) Gujarat
(c) Bihar (d) Malabar

65. Who among the following was the religious guru of Shivaji?
(a) Tukaram (b) Ramdas
(c) Eknath (d) Jnanadeva

66. Silappadikaram, a Tamil epic deals with
(a) nature worship (b) a human story
(c) the exploits of the Pandyas (d) the philosophy of life

67. Which of the following Mughal Emperors was himself a painter?
(a) Akbar (b) Jahangir
(c) Shah Jahan (d) Aurangzeb

68. Which building marks the beginning of the Indo-Islamic 'baroque' style?
(a) Humayun's Tomb (b) Musamman Burj
(c) Tomb of Salim Chishti (d) Tomb of Itmad-ud-aullah

69. Tafta variety of cloth during the Mughal period, was made of
(a) Cotton (b) Silk
(c) Wool (d) Linen

70. The Chief Officer of harbours during the Mughal period was:
(a) Musharif (b) Tahawildar
(c) Balutedar (d) Mutasaddi

71. Which of the following paintings greatly influenced the Akbari School of Paintings
(a) Pahari (b) Bundi
(c) Rajasthani (d) Kishangarhi

72. Which of the following types of cavalrymen were also known as gentleman-troopers during the Mughal period?
(a) Barwardis (b) Ahadis
(c) Dakhilis (d) Sawars
73. The army of the nobles during the Mughal Period was known as
(a) Mashrut (b) Khanazad
(c) Barawardi (d) Tabinan
74. Which of the following statements is wrong regarding the Treaty of Purander of 1665 between Shivaji and the Mughals?
(a) Shivaji surrendered 23 of the 35 forts in the Nizamshahi region
(b) Shivaji came closer to the Mughals through this treaty
(c) The Mughals tried to isolate Shivaji and the Bijapur rulers
(d) The treaty laid the seeds of struggle between Shivaji and the Bijapur rulers
75. Under the aegis of which of the following kings was the third Buddhist Council held?
(a) Ashoka (b) Kanishka
(c) Menander(Milinda) (d) Harsha
76. Who among the following got the title of Sena Karte?
(a) Balaji Vishwanath (b) Balaji Baji Rao
(c) Baji Rao-I (d) Mahadji Scindia
77. What made Shivaji temporarily suspend hostile activities against the Adil Shahis of Bijapur for a brief period of six years (1649-55)?
(a) Internal problems created by the other Maratha chief's
(b) His arrest and imprisonment by the Adil Shahi ruler
(c) Arrest and imprisonment of Shivaji's father by the Adil Shahi ruler
(d) Shivaji's engagements against the Mughal forces
78. Nagarjuna is known as the Einstein of India because
(a) like Einstein he had a rare insight into the nature of the universe
(b) he was one of the greatest Physicists of all time
(c) he propounded the theory of Shunyavada similar to Einstein's theory of relativity
(d) he was a great dialectician
79. Arrange the following successors of Maharaja Ranjit Singh in a chronological order
(I) Sher Singh (II) Kharak Singh
(III) Dalip Singh (IV) Naunihal Singh
Select the correct answer from the codes given below Codes
(a) II, IV, I, III (b) II, I, IV, III
(c) I, III, II, IV (d) I, IV, III, II
80. Which of the following was not one of the reasons for the popularity of Buddhism in China?
(a) There were no rival religions at the time of introduction of Buddhism in China
(b) The writing of such people as Mou-tse created confidence in the minds of the educated Chinese

(c) The life of purity followed by the immigrant Indian Buddhists and their Chinese disciples attracted the Chinese to Buddhism
(d) The patronage of reigning dynasties in China (e.g. Wei dynasty) helped the cause of Buddhism

81. Murshid Quli Khan transferred his capital from Dacca to
(a) Karimnagar (b) Monghyr
(c) Murshidabad (d) Gaur

82. Who was the Maratha chieftain to whom Alivardi Khan, the Nawab of Bengal, ceded the revenues of a part of Orissa?
(a) Raghuji Bhonsle (b) Trimbak Rao Dhabade
(c) Ranoji Scindia (d) Malhar Rao Holkar

83. Who established the College of Fort William at Calcutta to train the young civil servants of the East India Company
(a) Wellesley (b) Dalhousie
(c) William Bentinck (d) Cornwallis

84. Match list I with list II and select your answer from the codes given below
List I
I. Battle of Khed II. Battle of Sidhkhed
III. Treaty of Mungi-Sirgaon IV Treaty of Warne
List II
(A) Between Peshwa and Sambhaji
(B) Between Tarabai and Shahuji
(C) Between Peshwa and Salabat Jang
(D) Between Raghuji and Alivardi Khan
(E) Between Peshwar and Nizamul Mulk
Codes:
(a) I-A, II-C, III-D, IV-E (b) I-B, II-C, III-E, IV-A
(c) I-C, II-D, III-A, IV-B (d) I-D, II-B, III-C, IV-E

85. For the exercise of Diwani functions in Bengal, the East India Company appointed two Deputy Diwans. One of them was Mohammaed Reza Khan. The other was
(a) Rai Durlabh (b) Jagat Seth
(c) Manick Chand (d) Raja Shitab Roy

86. Which one of the following pairs is incorrectly matched
(a) First Anglo-Mysore War — Defeat of Madras Government by Haider Ali
(b) Second Anglo-Mysore War — Treaty of Mangalore
(c) Third Anglo-Mysore War — Defeat of Tipu Sultan
(d) Fourth Anglo-Mysore War — Subsidiary Alliance Treaty imposed on Mysore

87. What was Asafi Turki during the reign of Tipu Sultan?
(a) A branch of army (b) A province
(c) A military officer (d) A district

88. During whose Viceroyalty was the Widow Remarriage Act passed?
(a) Lord Canning (b) Lord Dalhousie
(c) Lord Auckland (d) Lord William Bentinck

89. Who was the President of the Indian Education Commission of 1882?
(a) Thomas Raleigh (b) W. W. Hunter
(c) Sandherst (d) Sadler

90. Who was the first to attempt decentralisation of financial administration
(a) Rippon (b) Mayo
(c) Curzon (d) Lytton

91. Which of the following Acts created the first official legislature in India?
(a) Indian Councils Act, 1861 (b) Mayo
(c) Curzon (d) Lytton

92. Which of the following Acts created the first official legislature in India?
(a) Indian Councils Act, 1861 (b) Indian Councils Act, 1892
(c) Charter Act, 1853 (d) Charter Act, 1833

93. Arrange the following events of Warren Hasting's period in their chronological sequence.
I. Begums of Oudh Affair II. Nand Kumar Episode
III. Chait Singh Affairs IV. Rohilla War
V. Founding of Asiatic Society of Bengal
Codes
(a) IV, II, III, I, V (b) II, I, III, V, IV
(c) III, II, V, I, IV (d) V, II, IV, I

94. Which of the following is correctly matched?
(a) Wood's Despatch - Primary Education
(b) Hunter Commission-Pay Commission
(c) Raleigh Commission-Religious Education
(d) Sadler Commission-Rejection of Filtration Theory

95. The Treaty of Allahabad was concluded by
(a) Rober Clive, Mir Jafar and Raja Balwant Singh
(b) Robert Clive, Najm-ud-Daula and Shuja-ud-Daula
(c) Robert Clive, Siraj-ud-Daula and Mir Kasim
(d) Shah Alam, Mir Jafar and Shuja-ud Daula

96. The first native state to introduce military training on the European model was
(a) Golconda (b) Mysore
(c) Oudh (d) Kashmir

97. Mangalore, Parambakkam and Porto Novo were places where major battles took place during the
(a) First Anglo-Mysore war (b) Second Anglo-Mysore war
(c) Third Anglo-Mysore war (d) Fourth Anglo-Mysore war

98. The East India Company began to use the term 'investments in India' for
(a) their bullion imports to purchase Indian goods
(b) the loot from Buxar for purchasing Indian goods
(c) the profits made from duty free inland trade and the surplus from Diwani revenue
(d) the borrowed money from Indian moneylenders or purchases in India

99. Madras was restored to the English by the French by
(a) the Treaty of Aix-la-Chapelle (1749)

(b) the Treaty of Pondicherry (1754)
(c) the Treaty of Salbai (1782)
(d) the Treaty of Mangalore (1784)

100. The remittance problems from India was initially tackled by the East India Company Government through the
(a) development of more exports of grains from India
(b) exports of more cotton and silk goods to Europe
(c) development of indigo and export of opium to China
(d) development of jute and promotion of its export to Europe

Answers

1. (c)	21. (d)	41. (c)	61. (a)	81. (c)
2. (b)	22. (d)	42. (b)	62. (a)	82. (a)
3. (d)	23. (d)	43. (b)	63. (c)	83. (a)
4. (d)	24. (a)	44. (c)	64. (c)	84. (b)
5. (a)	25. (b)	45. (c)	65. (b)	85. (d)
6. (b)	26. (a)	46. (c)	66. (b)	86. (c)
7. (d)	27. (b)	47. (b)	67. (b)	87. (b)
8. (c)	28. (b)	48. (c)	68. (d)	88. (a)
9. (d)	29. (c)	49. (a)	69. (b)	89. (b)
10. (d)	30. (b)	50. (b)	70. (d)	90. (b)
11. (d)	31. (d)	51. (a)	71. (c)	91. (c)
12. (c)	32. (d)	52. (b)	72. (b)	92. (a)
13. (a)	33. (c)	53. (d)	73. (d)	93. (c)
14. (c)	34. (b)	54. (d)	74. (b)	94. (b)
15. (d)	35. (d)	55. (c)	75. (a)	95. (b)
16. (b)	36. (c)	56. (b)	76. (a)	96. (b)
17. (c)	37. (b)	57. (a)	77. (c)	97. (c)
18. (d)	38. (c)	58. (c)	78. (c)	98. (a)
19. (b)	39. (d)	59. (b)	79. (a)	99. (c)
20. (d)	40. (a)	60. (d)	80. (a)	100. (c)

SET XII

Questions

1. Which, among the following was NOT a new feature of buildings constructed by Shah Jahan?
   (a) Substitution of red sandstone by marble of a pure white texture
   (b) Preference for curved lines in place of rectangular aspect in the buildings
   (c) Addition of certain sensuousness to the building
   (d) Creative design or form
2. The red fort at Delhi was constructed by:
   (a) Akbar (b) Jahangir
   (c) Shah Jahan (d) Aurangzeb
3. The Jama Masjid at Delhi, the largest and most well known masjid in the whole of India was constructed by:
   (a) Akbar (b) Jahangir
   (c) Shah Jahan (d) Aurangzeb
4. Which, among the following, can be accepted as a novelty introduced by Mughal emperors to their buildings:
   (a) Domes (b) Minarets
   (c) Arches (d) Attached gardens
5. The Mughal-painting reached its zenith during the reign of:
   (a) Akbar (b) Jahangir
   (c) Shah Jahan (d) Aurangzeb
6. Who, among the following Mughal emperors, possessed keen knowledge of painting?
   (a) Babar (b) Humayun
   (c) Akbar (d) Shah Jahan
7. Which, among the following articles, was in great demand in Europe because of which the Europeans desired to keep trade relations with India and other countries of the East?
   (a) Cotton Textiles (b) Wool
   (c) Spices and Pepper (d) Ivory

8. Vasco-da-Gama, who discovered first the direct sea-route from Europe to India reached the Coast of Calicut in the year:
   (a) 1495 (b) 1496
   (c) 1497 (d) 1498
9. Who, among the following Europeans, established their trade and influence in India first:
   (a) Portuguese (b) Dutch
   (c) French (d) British
10. Goa, which put 'the seal on Portuguese naval supremacy along the South West Coast of India was conquered in 1510 A.D. by the Portuguese Governor
    (a) Almeida (b) Albuquerque
    (c) Lopo Soaues (d) Nuno-da-Cunha
11. Which, among the following, was the reason of handing over Bombay by the Portuguese to the British?
    (a) The Portuguese surrendered it to the British after their defeat in a naval battle in the Arabian sea.
    (b) The Portuguese handed it over to the British after a peace-treaty in Europe
    (c) The Portuguese gave it to Britain as dowry when princess Catherine of Braganza was married to Charles II of Britain
    (d) None of the above
12. Which, among the following places, was NOT the one which the Portuguese lost to the Dutch?
    (a) Malacca (b) Sri Lanka
    (c) Cochin (d) Hugh
13. The British missions under William Hawkins and Sir Thomas Roe at the court of Jahangir failed because:
    (a) Jahangir did not like the presence of the Europeans in India
    (b) Jahangir feared their navel power
    (c) The terms offered by the British for the purpose of their trade was not acceptable to Jahangir
    (d) The Portuguese at the court of Jahangir made him hostile to the British
14. 'In 1613 A.D., Jahangir agreed for the establishment of a British factory in Surat.' Why?
    (a) The defeat of the Portuguese at sea by the British convinced Jahangir of the desirability of granting trade-rights to the British
    (b) The Portuguese being reconciled to the British stopped their hostility to them at the court of the Emperor
    (c) The British could gain the favour of Begum Nur Jahan
    (d) His Minister advised him to do so
15. Who, among the following Mughal emperors, granted permission to trade free of tax within the territories of Bengal, Hyderabad and Gujarat to the British?
    (a) Bahadur Shah (b) Jahandar Shah
    (c) Farrukhsiyar (d) Muhammad Shah

16. The first fort which the British constructed in India was the fort:
(a) St. George (b) At Calcutta
(c) At Bombay (d) St. David

17. 'The first British company to trade with India was established in 1600 A.D. and the 2nd one in 1698'. But, both companies were united in the year:
(a) 1702 (b) 1712
(c) 1715 (d) 1722

18. The first French Company to trade with India was established in the year:
(a) 1664 (b) 1680
(c) 1700 (d) 1720

19. Which, among the following was NOT one of the settlements of the French in India:
(a) Masulipatam (b) Chandra Nagar
(c) Pondicherry (d) Chinsurah

20. The first French Governor who received the title of Nawab from the Mughal emperor was:
(a) Caron (b) Francois Martin
(c) Benoist Dumas (d) Joseph Francoin Dupleix

21. 'The Geographical features of Maharashtra, particularly it being the plateau, helped in the rise of the Marathas in several ways.' However, which among the following, was one which was NOT conducive to their rise?
(a) It was a fit place for guerilla warfare
(b) Forts could be built easily which could be defended well but were not easily accessible by the enemy
(c) It made the Marathas simple, sturdy and courageous
(d) It provided good sea-ports which helped in foreign trade and made the Marathas economically self-sufficient

22. Who, among the following nobles of one of the Deccan Muslim states first trained the Marathas in guerilla warfare?
(a) Malik Amber of Ahmadnagar (b) Mir Zumla of Golkunda
(c) Madanna of Golkunda (d) Afzal Khan of Bijapur

23. Shivaji was born in the year?
(a) 1617 (b) 1627
(c) 1637 (d) 1647

24. The Mughal Subedar Shayista Khan was attacked and forced to run away by Shivaji when he was camped at:
(a) Poona (b) Surat
(c) Ahmadnagar (d) Kalyan

25. Who, among the following Mughal-commanders, forced Shivaji to sign the treaty of Purandar in 1665 A.D.
(a) Shayista Khan (b) Bahadur Khan
(c) Raja Jay Singh (d) Raja Jaswant Singh

26. When, among the following occasions, Shivaji came in conflict with the Mughals?
(a) When he attacked 'the Mughul districts of Ahmadnagar and Junnar while assisting Bajipur
(b) When Shayista Khan attacked him
(c) When he attacked Surat
(d) When he advanced to Agra

27. Which, among the following, was the cause of the attack of Shivaji on Surat twice?
(a) To annex it to his territory (b) To enhance his prestige
(c) To avenge the British (d) To plunder it

28. Shivaji visited Agra and was imprisoned there in the year:
(a) 1664 (b) 1665
(c) 1668 (d) 1670

29. Which, among the following, was the Capital of Shivaji?
(a) Singha Garh (b) Rai Garb
(c) Panhala (d) Poona

30. The coronation of Shivaji was carried out in the year:
(a) 1670 (b) 1672
(c) 1674 (d) 1678

31. Which, among the following, was NOT one of the advantages which Shivaji drew because of his coronation?
(a) It helped him in the growth of Maratha nationalism around his personality
(b) It placed him above all other Maratha-chiefs,
(c) It provided him equal status with the Muslim states of the Deccan
(d) It gave him better bargaining capacity with the Mughals

32. Shivaji was helped by his father when:
(a) He was beginning his career
(b) He was attacked by Afzal Khan
(c) He was attacked by Shayista Khan
(d) He came in first conflict with the Mughals

33. Shivaji was helped by his father in the beginning of his career by:
(a) Supply of a park of artillery
(b) Supply of a good contingent of Cavalry
(c) Encouragement to carve out an independent kingdom for himself
(d) Deputation of some of his capable officers like Shyamji Nirkantha, Balkrishna Didit, Sonajipant etc., under his service

34. Shivaji died in the year:
(a) 1680 (b) 1684
(c) 1686 (d) 1690

35. 'Shivaji had divided his kingdom into provinces'. Their number was:
(a) Two (b) Three
(c) Four (d) Five

36. Which, among the following, was NOT important in the army of Shivaji?

(a) Cavalry (b) Infantry
(c) Large number of war elephants (d) Navy

37. 'Bargirs and Silahdars were two types of cavalrymen in the army of Shivaji'. Which, among the following, was the basic distinction between them?
(a) Each Bargir kept two horses while a Silahdar possessed only one horse
(b) Bargirs were regular soldiers while Silahdars were employed only at the occasion of war temporarily
(c) Bargirs were Maratha soldiers while Silahdars belonged to other castes
(d) Bargirs were provided houses by the state while Silahdars purchased their own horses

38. 'In the infantry of Shivaji, a soldier was called 'Paik' and his immediate officer was called 'Nayak.' How many paiks, among the following numbers, were kept under a Nayak?
(a) Nine (b) Ten
(c) Fifteen (d) Twenty

39. In the infantry of Shivaji a Havaldar commanded:
(a) Nine Nayaks (b) Ten Nayaks
(c) Fifteen Nayaks (d) Twenty Nayaks

40. 'Shivaji paid special attention towards the security of his forts and all officers of a fort had joint responsibility.' Who, among the following, was NOT one of the officers in a fort?
(a) Havaldar (b) Jumladar
(c) Sabnis (d) Sar-i-Naubat

41. 'Shivaji used to collect taxes from the citizens of his neighbouring kingdoms as well'. These taxes were:
(a) Revenue and irrigation tax (b) Custom duties
(c) Grazing tax and road-tax (d) Chauth and Sardeshmukhi

42. Chauth was a tax which Shivaji collected from the citizens of neighbouring kingdoms and it was:
(a) 1/5th of annual income of a territory
(b) 1/4 of the annual income of a territory
(c) 1/3 of the annual income of a territory
(d) 1/2 of the annual income of a territory

43. 'Sardeshmukhi was a tax which Shivaji collected from the citizens of neighbouring kingdoms and it was:
(a) 1/5th of the annual income of a territory
(b) 1/6th of the annual income of a territory
(c) 1/8th of the annual income of a territory
(d) 1/10th of the annual income of a territory

44. Shivaji collected revenue from the peasants through:
(a) Jagirdars (b) Contractors or farmers of the land
(c) Landlords (d) His own officers

45. Shivaji collected as revenue:
(a) 1/5 of the produce (b) 1/4 of the produce
(c) 1/3 of the produce (d) 1/2 of the produce

46. Who, among the following, were mirasdars in the kingdom of Shivaji?
(a) Who owned land free of revenue
(b) Whose lands were attached to temples
(c) Jagirdars
(d) Who possessed hereditary rights over their lands

47. Which, among the following, is correct regarding Shivaji's treatment towards Dehmukhas (Zamindars)?
(a) Shivaji abolished the Deshmukhi-system
(b) Shivaji left them as before
(c) Shivaji increased their powers
(d) Shivaji curbed their powers

48. Which, among the following, was observed by Shivaji in his treatment with Islam:
(a) Disrespect to mosques
(b) Disrespect to Islam
(c) Dishonour to Muslim women
(d) Complete respect to Islam and its followers

49. Who, among the following, has remarked that "I regard him (Shivaji) as the last constructive genius and nation builder that the Hindu race has produced"?
(a) G.S. Sardesai (b) J.N. Sarkar
(c) S.N. Sen (d) M.G. Ranade

50. Shivaji had:
(a) Only one wife (b) Four wives
(c) Six wives (d) Seven wives

51. Shambhuji, the son and successor of Shivaji was captured and put to death by Aurangzeb in the year:
(a) 1686 A.D. (b) 1689 A.D.
(c) 1690 A.D. (d) 1693 A.D.

52. Which, among the following was NOT one of the causes of the rise of Peshwas?
(a) Shahu's incapacity as an administrator and military commander
(b) The capability of the first three Peshwas of Shahu
(c) The military conquests of Peshwa Baji Rao I
(d) The personal ambition of the first three Peshwas to grab the power of the Chattrapati Shahu

53. Who, among the following, was the first Peshwa of Shahu?
(a) Balaji Vishwanath (b) Baji Rao
(c) Balaji Baji Rao (d) Madhava Rao

54. Which, among the following, was NOT one of the achievements of Peshwa Balaji Vishwanath?
(a) Establishment of Shahu's power in Maharashtra
(b) A favourable treaty with the Muslims in 1719 A.D.

(c) Treaty with Kanhoji Angria
(d) Improvement in the finances of the State

55. Who, among the following, aspired for an independent kingdom of the Marathas like Shivaji?
(a) Tara Bai (b) Shahu
(c) Peshwa Baji Rao (d) None

56. The expansion of the Maratha-power in Northern India began when the Peshwa of Chattrapati Shahu was:
(a) Balaji Vishwanath (b) Baji Rao
(c) Balaji Baji Rao (d) None of the above

57. Mastani was the beloved of:
(a) Chattrapati Shahu (b) Peshwa Balaji Vishwanath
(c) Peshwa Baji Rao (d) Peshwa Balaji Baji Rao

58. 'Bahadur Shah I the successor of Auragnzeb instead of improving the finances of the state, deteriorated them further which, among the following was the reason for it ?
(a) Constant fighting against the rivals, the Rajputs and the Sikhs
(b) Licentious life of the Emperor
(c) Foreign invasions
(d) Reckless distribution of jagirs

59. Who among the following succeeded Bahadur Shah I as the Mughal Emperor ?
(a) Jahandar Shah (b) Farrukhsiyar
(c) Muhammad Shah (d) Ahmad Shah

60. Who among the following was primarily responsible for the capture of the Mughal throne by Jahandar Shah?
(a) Asad Khan (b) Sarfaraj Khan
(c) Zulfigar Khan (d) Chin Qilich Khan

61. Who, among the following, helped Farrukhsiyar in snatching the throne of Delhi from the hands of Jahandar Shah?
(a) Sayyid brothers (b) Chin Qilich Khan
(c) Murshid Quli Khan (d) Sarfaraz Khan

62. The first Mughal emperor who was put to death by the order of a nobel was:
(a) Bahadur Shah I (b) JahandarShah
(c) Farruk siyar (d) Raft-ud-darjat

63. Who, among the following nobels, was/were regarded as King-maker during the period of the later Mughuls?
(a) The Sayyid brothers (b) Sarbuland Khan
(c) Nizam-ul-Mulk Asaf Jah (d) Itikhuab Khan

64. Which, among the following, was the primary reason of the failure of the Sayyid brothers in managing the affairs of the Mughal empire?
(a) Neglect towards administration
(b) Policy of reconciliation towards the Hindus

(c) Political rivalry and intrigues by the nobles at the court
(d) Seeking support of the Marathas

65. Which, among the following was NOT the result of the faulty policies of Sayyid brothers?
(a) The weakness of the Empire was exposed to the Marathas
(b) The Jats and the Bundelas could dare to take up anti-empire activities
(c) The immoral precedent of insulting and humiliating the members of the royal house was set up
(d) Nadir Shah dared to attack India

66. Who among the following emperors was responsible for the fall of the Sayyid brothers?
(a) Farrukhsiyar (b) Rafi-ud-darjat
(c) Rafi-ud-daula (d) Muhammad Shah Rangila

67. The Mughal empire began to disintegrate
(a) Just after the death of Aurangzeb
(b) After the death of Bahadur Shah I
(c) During the reign of Farrukhsiyar
(d) During the reign of Muhammad Shah Rangila

68. Which among the following was the primary cause of the attack of Nadir Shah on Delhi?
(a) Support of the 'Mughals to his enemies, the Afghan rebels
(b) Invitation to him by several Mughal nobles at the courts
(c) Boundry Disputes
(d) To loot the wealth of Delhi

69. 'Nadir Shah attacked India and looted Delhi in 1739'. Who among the following was the Mughal Emperor at that time?
(a) Rafi-ud-darjat (b) Muhammad Shah
(c) Ahmad Shah (d) Alamgir II

70. 'Nadir Shah ordered a general massacre at Delhi'. Which among the following, was the reason of it?
(a) Refusal of the Mughal emperor to part with Takht-i-Taauj (Peacock-throne) and the diamond, Kohinoor
(b) To terrorise the Mughal emperor and the nobles with a view to extract maximum wealth from them
(c) Citizens of Delhi killed some of his soldiers
(d) The citizens of Delhi did not pay him the required money

71. 'Ahmad Shah Abdali, who captured the throne of Afghanistan after the death of Nadir Shah, attacked India several times.' Which among the following, can NOT be counted as one of the results of his invasions?
(a) Helped in the downfall of the Mughal empire
(b) Gave rude shock to the Maratha power
(c) Helped in the rise of the Sikh-power in Punjab
(d) Paved the way for other invaders from the north-west

72. 'Bengal became independent of imperial control within a few years after Aurangzeb's death'. Who, among the following, was its first ruler?
(a) Murshid Quli Khan (b) Shujauddin Muhammad Khan
(c) Ala-ud-daulah Haider Jang (d) Alivardi-Khan

73. The Capital of the independent State of Bengal was:
(a) Dacca (b) Murshidabad
(c) Alinagar (d) Midnapur

74. Who, among the following Nawabs of Bengal, shifted his capital from Dacca to Murshidabad?
(a) Murshid Quli Khan (b) Shujauddin Muhammad Khan
(c) Sarfaraz Khan (d) Alivardi Khan

75. Who, among the following Nawab of Bengal, was the first one to whom the subedari of all the three provinces of Bengal, Bihar and Orissa was transferred?
(a) Murshid Quli Khan (b) Shujauddin Muhammad Khan
(c) Sarfaraz Khan (d) Alivardi Khan

76. During the later period of the reign of Shujauddin in Bengal, a clique of three principal advisors of the Nawab came into existence which seriously affected the politics of Bengal'. Who among the following was NOT a member of that triumvirate'?
(a) Haji Ahmed (b) Alamchand
(c) Jagat Seth Fateh Chand (d) Mir Jafar

77. After his death in 1756 A.D. Alivardi Khan, Nawab of Bengal was succeeded by:
(a) Siraj-ud-daulah (b) Mir Jafar
(c) Mir kasim (d) Nizamuddaulah

78. The Suba of Avadh (Oudh) became virtually independent in 1722 A.D. and its founder ruler was:
(a) Saadat Khan (b) Safdar Jang
(c) Shuja-ud-daulah (d) Asaf-ud-daulah

79. Who among the following rulers of Awadh was first appointed the Vazir of the Mughal emperor?
(a) Sadat Khan (b) Safdar Jang
(c) Shuja-ud-daulah (d) Asaf-ud-daulah

80. Who among the following rulers of Awadh, participated in the battle of Buxar (1764 A.D.) on behalf of Mir Kasim, the deposed ruler of Bengal?
(a) Saadat Khan (b) Safdar Jang
(c) Shuja-ud-daulah (d) Asaf-ud-daulah

81. Which, among the following was the cause of awarding the Subedari of Deccan to Nizam-ul-mulk, Asaf Jah by Emperor Mohammad Shah?
(a) He had helped Mohammad Shah in becoming the Emperor
(b) He defeated the Marathas
(c) He helped the Emperor in the overthrow of the Sayyid Brothers
(d) He had proved his capabilities as a good administrator

82. The Nizam-ul-mulk, Asaf Jah founded the virtual independent state of Hyderabad in:
(a) 1715 (b) 1724
(c) 1728 (d) 1735

83. The state of Hyderabad virtually became a dependency of the East India Company when the Governor General of the Company was:
(a) Warren Hastings (b) Cornwallis
(c) Sir John Shore (d) Lord Wellesly

84. After the death of Guru Govind Singh, the political leadership of the Sikhs went into the hands of Banda Singh. He has been credited with many achievements, However, which among the following was NOT achieved by him?
(a) Inspiring the Sikhs to found a political raj
(b) Carrying on offensive warfare against the Mughals with a view to establish Sikh raj in Punjab
(c) Assumption of royal authority and issue of coins in the name of the Guru
(d) Turning out the Mughals from Punjab

85. Banda Singh was tortured to death by the orders of the emperor
(a) Bahadur Shah I (b) Jahandar Shah
(c) Farrukhsiyar (d) Rafi-ud-daulah

86. Who, among the following, first inspired the Sikhs to establish an independent state of the Sikhs in Punjab?
(a) Guru Gobind Singh (b) Banda Singh
(c) Kapur Single (d) Ranjit Singh

87. Who, among the following, proved to be a determined enemy of the Sikhs once the Mughal hold over Punjab became weak?
(a) Ahmad Shah Abdali (b) Hindu Chiefs of Punjab
(c) Marathas (d) Saadat Khan

88. Who among the following appointed Ranjit Singh the governor of Lahore?
(a) Maha Singh (b) Marathas
(c) Ahmad Shah Abdali (d) Ruler of Afghanistan

89. Which among the following was the primary factor which helped Ranjit Singh in uniting a large number of Sikh Chiefs under his leadership?
(a) Fear of attack of Zaman Shah (b) Fear of the British-attack
(c) Fear of the Maratha-attack (d) Mutual rivalry among local chiefs

90. The primary cause of the first Carnatic war between the British and the French was:
(a) Participation of the English and the French in the native politics of Karnataka
(b) The ambition of Joseph Francis Dupleix to turn out the British from the South.
(c) The rivalry for trade between the French and the British
(d) The war of Austrian Succession because of which Britain and France became each other's enemies in every part of the world

91. The most important event of the first Carnatic war was the:
(a) Capture of Fort St. David by the French

(b) Capture of Pondicherry by the English
(c) Defeat of French naval commander, la Boundannias by the English Navy
(d) Defeat of the army of the nawab of Karnataka Anwar-ud-Din by the French at St. Thorne

92. Which among the following was NOT one of the results of the first Karnataka War?
(a) The French gained territories at the cost of the English
(b) The superiority of European arms and warfare as against the native rulers became clear
(c) Importance of Navy was clearly exhibited
(d) Political ambitions of Dupleix got further encouragement

93. Who, among the following native rulers received support of the French in the 2nd Karnataka war?
(a) Anwar-ud-din and Chanda Sahib
(b) Chanda Sahib and Nasir Jang
(c) Chanda Sahib and Muzaffar Jang
(d) Nasir Jang and Muhammad Ali and Muzaffar Jang

94. Who among the following native-rulers received the support from the English in the 2nd Karnataka war?
(a) Anwar-ud-din and Chanda Sahib
(b) Chanda Sahib and Nasir Jang
(c) Chanda Sahib and Muzaffar Jang
(d) Nasir Jang and Muhammad Ali and Muzaffar Jang

95. The turning point in favour of the fortunes of the English in the 2nd Karnataka-war was the:
(a) Battle of Ambur in 1749
(b) Capture of Arcot by Clive
(c) Failure of the French to capture Trichinopoly
(d) The dismissal of Dupleix in 1754

96. The battle of Wandiwash which sealed the fate of the French in India was fought between French and the English in the year:
(a) 1756 (b) 1758
(c) 1760 (d) 1763

97. Who, among the following French officers in India, ranks next to Dupleix in his successful dealing with native rulers in South India?
(a) La Bourdonnais (b) Goldehu
(c) Count de Lally (d) Bussy

98. Which among the following was Not one of the causes of the failure of Dupleix's schemes in India?
(a) Dupleix's negligence of French Trade and finances of the French Company
(b) Dupleix's failure to gain confidence and support of the French government
(c) Dupleix's interference in the native politics of Karnataka and Hyderabad at one and the same time
(d) Dupleix's neglect of French possessions in Bengal

99. Which, among the following was NOT an important item of trade available to the British in Bengal
(a) Cotton Textiles (b) Silk yarn
(c) Indigo (d) Sugar

100. The English came in conflict with Nawab Siraj-ud-daulah and Nawab Mir Kasim primarily on the question of their trade rights in Bengal.' Which, among the following was that right?
(a) To use their own currency
(b) To purchase and sell commercial goods without the permission of the Nawab
(c) To transport goods in their own ships
(d) To trade without payment of trade tax the right which they obtained from the Farman of Mughal emperor Farrukhsiyar in 1717 A.D.

Answers

1. (d)	21. (d)	41. (d)	61. (a)	81. (c)
2. (c)	22. (a)	42. (b)	62. (c)	82. (b)
3. (c)	23. (b)	43. (d)	63. (a)	83. (d)
4. (d)	24. (a)	44. (d)	64. (c)	84. (d)
5. (d)	25. (c)	45. (c)	65. (d)	85. (c)
6. (J)	26. (a)	46. (d)	66. (d)	86. (b)
7. (c)	27. (d)	47. (d)	67. (d)	87. (a)
8. (d)	28. (b)	48. (d)	68. (d)	88. (d)
9. (a)	29. (b)	49. (b)	69. (b)	89. (d)
10. (b)	30. (c)	50. (d)	70. (c)	90. (d)
11. (c)	31. (d)	51. (b)	71. (d)	91. (d)
12. (d)	32. (a)	52. (d)	72. (a)	92. (a)
13. (d)	33. (d)	53. (a)	73. (b)	93. (c)
14. (a)	34. (a)	54. (d)	74. (a)	94. (b)
15. (c)	35. (b)	55. (d)	75. (b)	95. (b)
16. (a)	36. (c)	56. (b)	76. (d)	96. (c)
17. (a)	37. (d)	57. (c)	77. (a)	97. (d)
18. (a)	38. (a)	58. (d)	78. (a)	98. (d)
19. (d)	39. (b)	59. (a)	79. (b)	99. (c)
20. (c)	40. (b)	60. (c)	80. (c)	100. (d)

Section III

SOLVED TEST PAPERS

MODEL TEST PAPER I

Note: Answer all the 50 questions Time: 1½ hrs.

1. The largest of all the Chaitya halls in India the Chaitya hall at Karle used for prayer, worship and meditation was constructed in:
   (a) Ist century B.C. (b) Ist century A.D.
   (c) 2nd century A.D. (d) 3rd century A.D.
2. The famous Jain caves excavated in Udayagiri and Khandegiri hills near Bhuvaneshwar in Orissa were constructed during the period ranging from:
   (a) 200 B.C. to 100 B.C. (b) 100 B.C. to 150 A.D.
   (c) 150 A.D. to 300 A.D. (d) 50 A.D. to 100 A.D.
3. Who among the following was the author of Natyashastra
   (a) Vasumitra (b) Nagarjuna
   (c) Asvaghosha (d) Bhasa
4. The first Christian missionary entered India in the
   (a) Ist century B.C. (b) Ist century A.D.
   (c) 2nd century A.D. (d) 3rd century A.D.
5. Mahavir died at
   (a) Kusinara (b) Vaisali
   (c) Rajagraha (d) Pava
6. In one of the following matters Jainism is different from Buddhism. Identify
   (a) Acceptance of the doctrine of Karma
   (b) Rejection of the authority of the Vedas as spiritual guides
   (c) Emphasising ethical rules of life
   (d) Attachment to severe asceticism
7. Untouchables, a category of people lower than the Sudras, came to be recognised during the Pre-Mauryan age primarily because of the development of:
   (a) Agriculture (b) Trade
   (c) Handicrafts (d) Nature of their economic occupations
8. Ashoka contributed to Indian polity and culture in several ways. However, which, among the following, was NOT his contribution
   (a) Reform in criminal justice
   (b) Attempt to provide cultural unity to the country

(c) A pacifist foreign policy
(d) Attempt for religious harmony among his subjects

9. One of them was not conquerred by Kanishka from China. Identify.
(a) Khotan (b) Yarkhand
(c) Kashgar (d) Kapisa

10. Demetrius, the foreign invader who was defeated by Pushyamitra was:
(a) A Saka Prince (b) A Huna Prince
(c) A Scythian Prince (d) A Bactrian Prince

11. Samudragupta was:
(a) Not educated (b) Educated
(c) Well learned (d) Well educated

12. Aryabhatiyam written by Aryabhata is primarily a treatise on:
(a) Astrology (b) Astronomy
(c) Metallurgy (d) Mathematics

13. The chief articles of export from India during the pre-Gupta age were:
(a) Glass-vessels, tin, lead, gold and silver
(b) Perfumes, medicinal herbs and precious stones
(c) Pearls, diamonds, muslin, ivory & indigo

14. Which, among the following statements, is NOT correct concerning the Varna system i.e. four-fold division of the India society during Ancient India?
(a) The emergence of sub-castes i.e. jati-system overruled the Varna system
(b) Strict rules were framed with a view to safeguard the purity of the Varnas
(c) Children as a result of mixed marriage were called Varna-Banker
(d) The untouchables or the Chandalas were not included in the Varna system

15. The Pallava-Dynasty was destroyed by:
(a) The later Chalukyas (b) The Rashtrakutas
(c) The Pandyas (d) Cholas

16. The Palas of Bengal patronized:
(a) Hinduism (b) Jainism
(c) Hinayana Buddhism (d) Tantrika Buddhism

17. Which, among the following scholarly works, was NOT written by Bhavabhuti?
(a) Venisanhara (b) Mahavir-Charita
(c) Uttar-Ram-Charita (d) Malti-Madhava

18. Who founded the Chandella dynasty of Bundelkhand?
(a) Jayasakti (b) Yasovarman
(c) Dhanga (d) Nannuka

19. Who were called the New Muslims?
(a) Hindu converts to Islam (b) Mongol converts to Islam
(c) Turkish converts to Islam (d) Persian converts to Islam

20. Among the images constructed during the rule of the Cholas, the most famous are:
(a) Stone images (b) Marble images
(c) Images carved out of rocks (d) Bronze images of Nataraja Siva

21. Iltutmish was the first legal Turk-Sultan of Delhi because he got the sanction of his title from:

(a) The Sultan of Gur (b) The Caliph
(c) The Sultan of Ghazni (d) All nobles of Delhi

22. Who, among the following modern historians, has argued that the primary aim of Alauddin in introducing his market system was not to pay less salary to his soldiers but to reduce the cost of articles?
(a) U.N. Day (b) K.S. Lal
(c) A.L. Srivastava (d) K.A. Nizami

23. The dismemberment of the Delhi Sultanate began during the region of:
(a) Mubarak Shah Khalji (b) Muhammad Bin Tughluq
(c) Firuz Tughluq (d) Successors of Firuz Tughluq

24. Sultan Mahmud of Gujarat earned the nick-name of Begarha because he:
(a) Defeated the ruler of Malwa
(b) Defeated the Portuguese
(c) Conquered the forts of Girnar and Champaner
(d) Killed a tiger single-handed

25. The number of the provinces of the Vijayanagara empire was:
(a) Three (b) Four
(c) Five (d) Six

26. Prataprudradeva-Yasobhusan, describing the glory of Prataprudradeva, ruler of Telingana was written in Sanskrit language by:
(a) Agastaya (b) Vidya Chakravartin
(c) Madhan (d) Vaman Bhatt Bana

27. What is biswa?
(a) a unit of area (b) a tax
(c) a tax collector (d) measuring rod

28. Who was called the Zar Baksha?
(a) Ahmad Shah (b) Qutb-ud-din Ahmad
(c) Muhammad Shah II (d) Mahmud Begarha

29. Which, among the features of architecture, was absent in the buildings constructed by the Sharqi rulers of Jaunpur?
(a) The dome (b) Square pillars
(c) Small galleries (d) Minarets

30. Which, among the following was not one of the early difficulties of Humayun?
(a) Brothers of Humayun
(b) Humayun's own character
(c) The Afghans
(d) The Rajputs

31. Jizya, the tax most hated by the Hindus, was abolished by Akbar in:
(a) 1562 (b) 1563
(c) 1564 (d) 1565

32. "Deccan ulcer ruined Aurangzeb." It is true because of the fierce resistance put up by:
(a) The State of Bijapur
(b) The State of Golkonda
(c) Shivaji
(d) The Marathas after the death of Sambhuji

33. Who, among the following historians, first described the rule of the Mughals as the 'Rule by Aristocracy'?
(a) Tara Chand (b) J.N. Sarkar
(c) A.L. Srivastava (d) S.R. Sharma

34. Which, among the following, did NOT constitute a handicap in the industrial progress during the Mughal period:
(a) Absence of Joint-stock companies
(b) Insecurity of property and its inheritance
(c) Mughal-emperors themselves established many Kharkanas (industries)
(d) shortage of capital-money for investment

35. Which, among the following was NOT a new feature of buildings constructed by Shah Jahan?
(a) Substitution of red sandstone by marble of a pure white texture
(b) Preference for curved lines in place of rectangular aspect in the buildings
(c) Addition of certain sensuousness to the building
(d) Creative design or form

36. 'The Geographical features of Maharashtra, particularly it being the plateau, helped in the rise of the Marathas in several ways.' However, which among the following, was one which was NOT conducive to their rise?
(a) It was a fit place for guerilla warfare
(b) Forts could be built easily which could be defended well but were not easily accessible by the enemy
(c) It made the Marathas simple, sturdy and courageous
(d) It provided good sea-ports which helped in foreign trade and made the Marathas economically self-sufficient

37. 'Shivaji used to collect taxes from the citizens of his neighbouring kingdoms as well'. These taxes were:
(a) Revenue and irrigation tax
(b) Custom duties
(c) Grazing tax and road tax
(d) Chauth and Sardeshmukhi

38. Who, among the following, helped Farrukhsiyar in snatching the throne of Delhi from the hands of Jahandar Shah?
(a) Sayyid brothers (Abdulla Khan and Hussain Ali)
(b) Chin Qilich Khan
(c) Murshid Quli Khan
(d) Sarfaraz Khan

39. Which, among the following was the cause of awarding the Subedari of Deccan to Nizam-ul-mulk, Asaf Jah by Emperor Mohammad Shah?
(a) He had helped Mohammad Shah in becoming the Emperor
(b) He defeated the Marathas
(c) He helped the Emperor in the overthrow of the Sayyid Brothers
(d) He had proved his capabilities as a good administrator

40. Which, among the following was the immediate cause of attack of Nawab Sirajuddaula on Calcutta in 1756?
    (a) Refusal of the English company to pay the overdue trade tax
    (b) English conspired against the Nawab with a view to depose him from the throne and that became known to him
    (c) Sirajuddaula desired to turn out the English from Bengal
    (d) Refusal of the English to demolish the fortifications of Calcutta
41. Yashwant Rao Holkar signed with English:
    (a) The treaty of Bassein
    (b) The treaty of Deogaon
    (c) The treaty of Surji-Arjangaon
    (d) The treaty of Rajpurghat
42. Dalhousie divided native States into three categories for the enforcement of the Doctrine of Lapse. Which, among the following, was NOT one of those categories?
    (a) States which were created or revived by the English
    (b) States which had accepted the English as their paramount power
    (c) States which had handed over their administration to English officials
    (d) States which were accepted as independent States by the English
43. Which, among the following, was NOT the one which exhibited racial arrogance of the British in India?
    (a) In several hotels and clubs the entry of the Indians was banned
    (b) The English misbehaved with their Indian servants
    (c) The English indulged in disrespecting Indian women
    (d) In many districts, even highly placed Indians were asked to respect even an English passer-by
    (e) The entry of the Indians was banned in Britain
44. The main item of import in Britain through the British East India Company in the late 17th century was cotton calicoes. Which, among the following, was the primary reason for it?
    (a) France and Holland had prohibited its import in their country
    (b) There were no import duties on it in Britain by that time
    (c) Improvement in the quality of calicoes by the Indians
    (d) Change in fashions in Britain
45. The industrial progress of India received impetus in the 2nd decade of the 20th century due to:
    (a) Rise in demand of Indian Industrial goods abroad
    (b) The British industrial progress reached an optimum point
    (c) Heavy investments were made in India by foreigners
    (d) 1st World War which created the necessity of production of certain goods in India
46. Swami Dayanand Saraswati established the first Arya Samaj in 1875 at:
    (a) Lahore (b) Nagpur
    (c) Ahmedabad (d) Bombay
47. 'Factory laws were passed in 1881, 1891, 1911, 1922 and 1930 well'. Which, among the following, was the cause of their beginning?

(a) Government felt that justice should be provided to the labour
(b) The factory owners were too much oppressive towards the labour
(c) Organisations of the labour had become strong
(d) Competition between British and India-made goods started and, therefore, these laws were used as levers to discourage that competition

48. Which, among the following provinces made a beginning of Municipal Institutions outside the presidency towns?
(a) Bengal (b) Madras
(c) Bombay (d) Uttar Pradesh

49. Who, among the following Marathi scholars, has been regarded as the Panini of Marathi?
(a) Sadashiv Kashinath
(b) Bapu Chhatra
(c) Hari Keshavji
(d) Dadoba Pandurang Tarkhadkar

50. The industrial progress of India received impetus in the second decade of the 20th century due to:
(a) Rise in demand of Indian Industrial goods abroad
(b) The British industrial progress reached an optimum point
(c) Heavy investments were made in India by foreigners
(d) First World War which created the necessity of production of certain goods in India

Answers

1. (c)	11. (c)	21. (b)	31. (c)	41. (d)
2. (b)	12. (d)	22. (a)	32. (d)	42. (c)
3. (c)	13. (c)	23. (b)	33. (a)	43. (e)
4. (b)	14. (a)	24. (c)	34. (d)	44. (b)
5. (d)	15. (d)	25. (d)	35. (d)	45. (d)
6. (d)	16. (d)	26. (a)	36. (d)	46. (a)
7. (d)	17. (a)	27. (a)	37. (d)	47. (b)
8. (a)	18. (d)	28. (c)	38. (a)	48. (a)
9. (d)	19. (b)	29. (d)	39. (c)	49. (b)
10. (d)	20. (d)	30. (d)	40. (d)	50. (a)

MODEL TEST PAPER II

Note: Answer all the 50 questions. Time: 1½ hrs.

1. To conquer and annex Peshwar and Punjab, Mahmud of Ghazni defeated
   (a) Ghurids (b) Arabs
   (c) Karkotakas (d) Hindushahis
2. Following are the lists of Harappan settlements and the river bents on which they were situated. Match List I with List II and select the correct answer with the help of the codes given below

List I	List II
I. Lothal	(A) Indus
II. Kalibangan	(B) Sutlej
III. Rupar	(C) Ravi
IV Harappa	(D) Ghaggar
V. Mohenjodaro	(E) Bhogava

   Codes
   (a) I-B, II-E. III-A, IV-D, V-C
   (b) I-E. II-D, III-B, IV-C, V-A
   (c) I-D, II-E, III-B, IV-C, V-A
   (d) I-E, II-D, III-C, IV-B. V-A
3. The Harappan deity not found in later Hindu pantheon is
   (a) Pasupati Siva
   (b) Seven Moths (Sapta Marikas)
   (c) Compound Creatures
   (d) Utlicom
4. Which among the following was NOT included as a seat of learning of the Sangams'
   (a) Old Madura (b) Kapatapuram
   (c) Modern Madura (d) Kaveripattinam
5. Mahavir had:
   (a) A daughter (b) A son
   (c) No issue (d) A daughter and a son
6. In one of the following matters Jainism is different from Buddhism. Identify
   (a) Extreme emphasis of ahimsa

(b) Doctrine of infallibility
(c) Soul theory
(d) Preaching in the language of the people

7. The author of Arthasastra was:
(a) Chanakya, Minister of Chandragupta Maurya
(b) Rakshasa, Minister of Dhana Nanda
(c) Not definitely known
(d) Chandragupta himself

8. Which of the following was the capital of Mauryan Empire?
(a) Gaya (b) Delhi
(c) Varanasi (d) Patliputra

9. Who was the Chinese general who defeated Kanishka?
(a) Pen-chao (b) Pan-yang
(c) Shi-huang-ti (d) Ho-ti

10. Menander, the Greek who ruled over North-West India is well known in Indian History because
(a) He issued beautiful coins of large variety
(b) He created an extensive empire in India
(c) Of a text known as the Milindapanha

11. The primary conquest of Chandragupta II was that of:
(a) Punjab and Kashmir (b) Gujarat & Kathiawar
(c) Malwa (d) Bengal

12. Navanitakam is a treatise on:
(a) Polity (b) Economics
(c) Medicine (d) Philosophy

13. The most famous city for production of cotton cloth during the period of visit of Hiuan Tsang was:
(a) Banaras (b) Mathura
(c) Pataliputra (d) Kanchi

14. Which, among the following statements, is NOT correct concerning the untouchables or the Chandalas during Ancient India?
(a) They lived outside towns
(b) They performed only menial works
(c) Even their shadow was regarded unclean by the higher castes
(d) Their status was linked with the Shudras

15. The main contribution of the Pallavas towards the history of South India was:
(a) Establishment of a system of administration similar to that of the Mauryas and the Guptas in the North
(b) Emphasis on local-self government
(c) Patronage to Hinduism
(d) Extension of Aryan culture in the South

16. The Sena-rulers of Bengal patronized:
(a) Hinduism (b) Jainism
(c) Mahayana Buddhism (d) Tantrika Buddhism

17. Which, among the following scholarly works, was NOT written by Kshemandra:
    (a) Vrahatakatha-Manjari (b) Dasavatara-charita
    (c) Kdla-Vilasa (d) Srikandh-charita
18. To which of the original clan are the Chandellas of Bundelkhand said to be related?
    (a) Gonds (b) Santals
    (c) Kols (d) Mundas
19. One of the following cannot be attributed to Ala-ud-din
    (a) Siri Fort (b) Hazar Sutun
    (c) Hauz-i-Khas (d) Purana Quila
20. Who, among the following Hoysala rulers, was persuaded to forsake Jainism and instead embrace Vaishnavism by saint Ramanuja:
    (a) Ballal I (b) Ballal II
    (c) Vishnuvardhan (d) Rajadhiraja I
21. The Mongol leader who threatened the safety of the Turkish rule in India during the rule of Iltutmish was:
    (a) Chingiz Khan (b) Halaku
    (c) Jalaluddin Mangbarni (d) Tajuddin Yildiz
22. The first Muslim commander who attacked South India was:
    (a) Alauddin Khalji (b) Malik Kafur
    (c) Nusrast Khan (d) Muhammad Tughlaq
23. Who, among the following historians has remarked: "the Saiyyads (Sayyids) could make no positive contribution to the king ship or to the system of civil administration"?
    (a) Khizr Khan (b) Mubarak Khan
    (c) Muhammad Shah (d) Alauddin Alam Shah
24. Who, among the following, was the founder ruler of the Khalji-rule in Malwa?
    (a) Mahmad Shah Khalji (b) Hushang Shah
    (c) Ghiyasuddin Shah (d) Nasiruddin Shah
25. Which, among the following was the duty of Mahanayakacharya, in the administration of Vijayanagara?
    (a) To supervise the observance of Dharma
    (b) To supervise the work of Nayakas
    (c) To supervise the village-administration
    (d) None of the above
26. Who, among the following, was the author of Narayana Vilas:
    (a) King Virupakya of Vijayanagara
    (b) King Krishnadeva Raya of Vijayanagara
    (c) Vidyapati
    (d) Divakara
27. By what name was the main instrument of transferring agrarian surplus called?
    (a) milk (b) inam
    (c) waqf (d) iqta
28. Where did Mahmud Begarha register a naval victory over the Portuguese?
    (a) Diu (b) Daman
    (c) Goa (d) Chaul

29. The Jama Masjid of Jaunpur was constructed by:
(a) Mubarak Shah Sharqi (b) Ibrahim Shah Sharqi
(c) Muhammad Shah Sharqi (d) Husain Shah Sharqi
30. When Humayun proceeded to fight against Bahadur Shah, the ruler of Gujarat, he wa engaged in fighting against?
(a) Malwa (b) Mewar
(c) Marwar (d) Bundelkhand
31. The only state in Northern India which Akbar failed to annexe or reduce to submission was
(a) Gondwana (b) Malwa
(c) Marwar (d) Mewar
32. Who, among the following Mughal emperors, was the most pious in his personal life?
(a) Akbar (b) Jahangir
(c) Shah Jahan (d) Aurangzeb
33. The rule of the Mughals has been described as the 'Rule by Aristocracy' because the Mughal nobility wielded large influence in matters of state by virtue of its:
(a) Extensive powers (b) Extensive jagirs
(c) Large armies (d) Hereditary status in most cases
34. During the rule of Mughals, wealth was mostly concentrated in:
(a) Temples & Mosques (b) Industrialists & Traders
(c) Emperors and nobility (d) Brokers & speculators
35. The Red Fort at Delhi was constructed by:
(a) Akbar (b) Jahangir
(c) Shah Jahan (d) Aurangzeb
36. Who, among the following nobles of one of the Deccani Muslim states first trained th Marathas in guerilla warfare?
(a) Malik Amber of Ahmadnagar
(b) Mir Zumla of Golkunda
(c) Madanna of Golkunda
(d) Afzal Khan of Bijapur
37. Chauth was a tax which Shivaji collected from the citizens of neighbouring kingdoms and i was:
(a) 1/5th of annual income of a territory
(b) 1/4 of the annual income of a territory
(c) 1/3 of the annual income of a territory
(d) 1/2 of the annual income of a territory
38. The first Mughal emperor who was put to death by the order of a nobel was:
(a) Bahadur Shah I (b) Jahandar Shah
(c) Farruk Siyar (d) Rafi-ud-darjat
39. The Nizam-ul-mulk, Asaf Jah founded the virtual independent state of Hyderabad in
(a) 1715 (b) 1724
(c) 1728 (d) 1735
40. 'When a strong British force under the command of Clive and Watson reached Bengal fron Madras, Nawab Siraj-ud-daula agreed for peace:' Where, among the following places, tha peace treaty was signed?
(a) Alinagar (b) Dacca
(c) Murshidabad (d) Patna

41. Which, among the following, was NOT one of the causes of the Third Anglo-Maratha War (1817-1818 A.D.)
    (a) The Maratha Chiefs, particularly, the Peshwa desired to throw off the restrictions imposed on them by the treaties with the English
    (b) The determination of Lord Hastings to give a final blow to the Maratha power
    (c) The united effort and desire of the Marathas to turn the English from India
    (d) The attack of Peshwa Baji Rao on the residency at Khirki
42. The right of every native ruler to freely adopt a child as his successor was restored to them by:
    (a) Lord Canning, the Governor-General of India
    (b) The Government of India Act, 1858 A.D.
    (c) The Queen's proclamation of 1858 A.D.
    (d) Sir Charles Wood in 1860 A.D. the then Secretary of State for India
43. Which, among the following, was NOT a measure which created doubt among the Indians that the English were trying to convert them to Christianity?
    (a) Introduction of Female education
    (b) Reading of the Bible was compulsory in Government and missionary schools
    (c) Official support to missionaries
    (d) Forceful conversions to Christianity
44. The British started economic exploitation of the Indians when:
    (a) There remained no fear of the Mughal emperor
    (b) There remained no fear of the might of the Marathas after the third battle of Panipat
    (c) There remained no European rival after the Third Anglo-French war
    (d) They captured political power in the provinces of Bengal, Bihar, and Orissa after the battle of Plassey
45. Which, among the following statements, is NOT correct concerning the growth of Industries in India?
    (a) There was regional disparity in industrial growth
    (b) The growth was extremely slow
    (c) All the industries were owned or controlled by British Capital
    (d) The government provided no help to them
46. Which, among the following, was the distinguishing feature concerning religion between Brahmo Samaj and Arya Samaj?
    (a) Anti idolatory
    (b) Anti ritualism
    (c) Separation of social evils from religion
    (d) Equal status to all religions
47. Which, among the following, was NOT one of the reasons of intensification of labour-movement after the First World War?
    (a) Rise in cost of living
    (b) Russian Revolution 1971
    (c) Non-cooperation Movement inspired the labour
    (d) The labour-movement of Britain inspired the Indian labour
    (e) Indian labour was under heavy exploitation

48. Which, among the following, was NOT included in Ripon's Resolution of 1882 concerning local self-government?
    (a) Local boards viz. Municipalities, Taluka Boards, District Boards were to be developed throughout the country
    (b) Local bodies were to have non official majorities coupled with a general system of election wherever possible
    (c) Local bodies were provided freedom to raise financial resources within their geographical limits
    (d) Official interference was to be reduced to the minimum
49. The outstanding novel of Marathi, Ranangam Apte was written by:
    (a) Hari Narayan Apte (b) Prof N.S. Phadke
    (c) P.V Deshpande (d) Vishram Badekar
50. Among the languages known to Raja Rammohan Roy, one of the following was not known to him. Identify.
    (a) Sanskrit (b) Persian
    (c) Hebrew (d) Malayalam

Answers

1. (d)	11. (b)	21. (a)	31. (d)	41. (c)
2. (b)	12. (c)	22. (a)	32. (d)	42. (c)
3. (d)	13. (b)	23. (a)	33. (d)	43. (d)
4. (a)	14. (d)	24. (a)	34. (c)	44. (d)
5. (c)	15. (d)	25. (c)	35. (c)	45. (c)
6. (d)	16. (a)	26. (a)	36. (a)	46. (d)
7. (a)	17. (d)	27. (d)	37. (b)	47. (d)
8. (d)	18. (a)	28. (d)	38. (c)	48. (c)
9. (d)	19. (d)	29. (d)	39. (b)	49. (d)
10. (d)	20. (c)	30. (b)	40. (a)	50. (d)

MODEL TEST PAPER III

Note: Answer all the 50 questions. Time: 1½ hrs.

1. Who among the following had written a treatise on fanciful technological devices?
   (a) Bhoja (b) Govindaraja
   (c) Chandravarman (d) Mahipala
2. Which one of the following communities of peasants revolted against the Pala rulers of Bengal?
   (a) Jats (b) Gurjaras
   (c) Kaivartas (d) Doms
3. A very important source for the political structure and social conditions of Gujarat from the 9th to the 13th centuries is the text known as
   (a) Rajatarangini (b) Panchatantra
   (c) Lekhapadhati (d) Sukraniti
4. The Chola inscriptions are found in the following languages:
   1. Sanskrit 2. Telugu
   3. Tamil 4. Kannada

   Their correct sequence in terms of the extent to which they were used (most frequently first, least frequent last) is
   (a) 1, 3, 4, 2 (b) 3, 1, 4, 2
   (c) 1, 3, 2, 4 (d) 3, 1, 2, 4
5. Match the temples in List I built by the Chola monarchs with the places in List II and select the correct answer:

List I	List II
A. The Koranganatha Temple	1. Tiruvalisavaram
B. The Rajarajeswara Temple	2. Dharasuram
C. The Airavatesvara Temple	3. Srinivasnallur
D. The Shiva Temple	4. Tanjore

	A	B	C	D
(a)	3	4	1	2
(b)	3	4	2	1
(c)	4	3	2	1
(d)	4	3	1	2

6. The capital-seat Gangaikondacholapuram was founded by
(a) Rajendra I (b) Rajaraja the Great
(c) Kulottunga I (d) Parantaka
7. Which one of the following pairs is correctly matched'?
(a) Krishnadevaraya: Manucharita
(b) Bukka 1: Vaidikamanggapravartaka
(c) Allasanipeddanna: Amuktamalyada
(d) Gangadevi: Amarasataka
8. Abdur Razzaq who left a detailed account of the Vijayanagara Empire in Persian, came to the Vijayanagara court as the envoy of Mirza Shah Rukh during the reign of
(a) Harihara II (b) Bukka II
(c) Deva Raya II (d) Krishnadeva Raya
9. What was the nature of the Nagaram settlements in South India?
(a) Villages inhabited by peasants castes
(b) Villages settled and dominated by combinations of traders and merchants
(c) Villages granted to the Brahmanas
(d) Villages having the local administrative units
10. The territorial revenue assignment in the Delhi Sultanate was known as
(a) tuyul (b) milk
(c) iqta (d) jagir
11. Sultan Alauddin Khalji claimed land revenue on
(a) one-fourth of the produce
(b) two-thirds of the produce
(c) one-half of the produce
(d) two-fifths of the produce
12. Gopis (cowherd girls) became an important part of the Krishna legend in art and literature in
(a) the Sunga period (b) the Kushana period
(c) the Gupta period (d) the early medieval period
13. Match List I with List II and select the correct answer:
List I (Sources mentioned)
A. Greek source
B. Jain source
C. Buddhist source
D. Brahmanical source
List II
(Information about Chandragupta Maurya, correct or incorrect, given in sources in List I)
1. He was born in a humble family
2. He was the son of a Kshatriya
3. He was a Sudra
4. He was the son of a village headman's daughter
5. He was a Jain

Codes:	A	B	C	D
(a)	4	5	3	1
(b)	1	3	4	2
(c)	1	4	2	3
(d)	3	5	2	4

14. Ashoka has been mentioned by name in his inscriptions at
(a) Maski and Gujarra only
(b) Dhauli and Rupnath only
(c) Nittur, Udegolam, Maski and Gujarra
(d) Kandhar, Bairat, Yerragudi and Maski
15. Which one of the following mentions Chandragupta Sabha, the Council of Chandragupta Maurya?
(a) Arthasastra (b) Mudrarakshasa
(c) Mahabhashya (d) Parisishtaparvan
16. In the Delhi Sultanate one silver tanka was the equivalent of
(a) 52 jitals (b) 48 jitals
(c) 45 jitals (d) 38 jitals
17. "I issue such orders to the people as I consider to be beneficial for them and the State. I do not know whether they are permitted by the shariat or not." This was said by
(a) Jalaluddin Khalji (b) Alauddin Khalji
(c) Ghiasuddin Tughlaq (d) Muhammad Tughlaq
18. Given below are two statements, one labelled as Assertion (A) and the other labelled as Reason (R):
Assertion (A): The Iqta system went a long way in establishing Islam in north India.
Reason (R): The Sultans, through this institution, wanted to control the Turkish nobles.
In the context of the above two statements, which one of the following is correct?
(a) Both A and R are true and R is the correct explanation of A
(b) Both A and R are true but R is not the correct explanation of A
(c) A is true but R is false
(d) A is false but R is true
19. Match List I and List II and select the correct answer:
List I (Years)
A. 1296 A.D.
B. 1336 A.D.
C. 1398 A.D.
D. 1504 A.D.
List II (Events)
1. The Mongols invaded Delhi
2. Harihara founded the kingdom of Vijayanagara
3. Timur's invasion
4. The city of Agra founded by Sultan Sikandar Lodi
5. Transfer of the capital to. Daulatabad from Delhi

Codes:	A	B	C	D
(a)	2	3	4	5
(b)	1	2	3	5
(c)	3	1	5	4
(d)	1	2	3	4

20. The main feature that distinguished the saqiya (Persian Wheel) from other water lifting devices during the Delhi Sultanate was the use of
    (a) lever-principle (b) pulleys
    (c) gear mechanism (d) leather bucket
21. During the thirteenth century the term fawazil denoted
    (a) the surplus revenue remitted to the State
    (b) a headman of a pargana
    (c) a military rank
    (d) the crown land
22. What was the total jama of the Delhi Sultanate as estimated by Husamuddin Junaidi in the reign of Sultan Feroze Shah Tughlaq?
    (a) Four crore and fifty lakhs (b) Five crore and thirty lakhs
    (c) Six crore and seventy-five lakhs (d) Seven crore and forty lakhs
23. The change of the capital of the Bahmani kingdom from Gulbarga to Bidar took place during the reign of
    (a) Shihabuddin Ahmad I (b) Ghiyasuddin Tahmtan
    (c) Shamsuddin Daud (d) Tajuddin Firoz
24. Which one of the following pairs is NOT correctly matched.
    (a) Baz Bahadur: Malwa (b) Sultan Muzaffar Shah: Gujarat
    (c) Yusuf Adil Shah: Ahmednagar (d) Qutb Shah: Golkunda
25. The central administration of the Vijayanagara kingdom maintained contact with the village through an officer called
    (a) naik (b) mahanayakacharyya
    (c) mahapratihara (d) dandapasika
26. Match List I with List II and select the correct answer:

List I	List II
A. Lakshmi Bat	1. Deported to 'Rangoon
B. Tantia Tope	2. Fled to Nepal
C. Nana Saheb	3. Captured and executed
D. Bahadur Shah	4. Killed in a battle

	A	B	C	D
(a)	1	2	3	4
(b)	2	3	4	1
(c)	4	3	2	1
(d)	4	2	3	1

27. The Indian Association played an important role in arousing national consciousness through the formation of the
    (a) Indian National Congress (b) Bengal British Indian Society
    (c) Indian National Conference (d) British India Association

28. The Moplah Rebellion (1921) took place in
    (a) Telengana (b) Malabar
    (c) Marathwada (d) Vidarbha
29. Who among the following was the first leader to organize labour movement in India?
    (a) B.P. Walia (b) Lala Lajpat Rai
    (c) N.M. Lokhandy (d) N.G. Ranga
30. Baba Ram Chandra organised peasants in
    (a) Oudh (b) Bihar
    (c) Bengal (d) Andhra
31. The first national news agency of India was
    (a) the Indian Review (b) the Free Press of India
    (c) the Hindustan Review (d) the Associated Press of India
32. Match List I with List II and select the correct answer:
    List I (Name of the reform movement)
    A. Satya Shodhak
    B. Self Respect
    C. Sarva Shodhak Samaj
    D. Namdhari
    List II (Name of its protagonist)
    1. Jotirao Govindrao Phule
    2. E. V. Ramaswami Naickar
    3. Shahu Maharaj
    4. Ram Singh

	A	B	C	D
(a)	1	2	3	4
(b)	2	3	4	1
(c)	3	4	1	2
(d)	4	1	2	3

33. What is the correct sequence of the following?
    1. Prohibition of Sati
    2. Education Resolution
    3. First University Act
    (a) 1, 2 and 3 (b) 1, 3 and 2
    (c) 2, 1 and 3 (d) 3, 2 and 1
34. The Act discouraging child marriage was passed in 1891 largely at the instance of
    (a) Ishwar Chandra Vidyasagar and Bhartendu Harishchandra
    (b) Mahadev Govind Ranade and Jotiba Phule
    (c) Keshab Chandra Sen and Behramji Malabari
    (d) Keshab Chandra Sen and Mahadev Govind Ranade
35. In early medieval south Indian polity the word Udankuttam meant
    (a) a group of small villages in the Chola kingdom
    (b) a body of officers under the Cholas
    (c) a tax levied in the Hoysala kingdom
    (d) the navy maintained by the Cholas

36. Which of the following were centers of Chahamana rule?
    1. Lata 2. Sakambari
    3. Naddula 4. Dhavagarta

    Choose the correct answer from the codes given below:
    (a) 1, 3 and 4 (b) 1, 2 and 3
    (c) 1, 2 and 4 (d) 2, 3 and 4
37. Dhavanyaloka is
    (a) an epic poem (b) a work on poetics
    (c) a play (d) a work on Buddhist epistemology
38. The Pala king Devapala claims to have defeated a Dravida king who is usually identified with
    (a) Dantidurga (b) Amoghavarsha
    (c) Dhruva (d) Krishna II
39. Mahakshapatalika was on official in charge of
    (a) chariots (b) navy
    (c) accounts (d) infantry
40. The Chandalla dynasty was founded by
    (a) Vakpati (b) Nannuka
    (c) Jayasakti (d) Harsha
41. Who was the ruler who was elected to the throne according to the Rajatarangini?
    (a) Gopala (b) Yasaskara
    (c) Nandivarman (d) Karikalan
42. Match List I with List II and select the correct answer by using the codes given below the lists:

List I	List II
A. Ajanta	1. Temples built by the Chandela rulers
B. Ellora	2. Cave paintings
C. Khajuraho	3. Kailasha temple
D. Elephants	4. Brahmanical sculptures

Codes:	A	B	C	D
(a)	2	3	1	4
(b)	2	4	1	3
(c)	1	3	4	2
(d)	3	2	1	4

43. Match List I with List II and select the correct answer using the codes given below the lists:

    List I
    A. Rudramal Temple
    B. Kandareya Mahadeva Temple
    C. Udayesvara Temple
    D. Lingaraja Temple

    List II
    1. Khajuraho
    2. Bhuvaneswar
    3. Kanchipuram

4. Siddhapur
5. Udaipur Codes:

	A	B	C	D
(a)	3	1	4	2
(b)	4	5	3	1
(c)	4	1	5	2
(d)	3	4	5	2

44. Who among the following had referred to the lost glory and splendour of Pataliputra?
(a) Cosmas (b) Fa-hien
(c) Huien-tsang (d) Megasthanese

45. Khwaja Ahdus Samad was the court painter of
(a) Babur (b) Akbar
(c) Jahangir (d) Shahjahan

46. The 'Fatawai Alamgiri' compiled at the order of Aurangzeb in 1663 by six persons headed by Shaikh Nizam was a:
(a) book of administrative rules
(b) set of military regulations
(c) set of religious regulations
(d) collection of sayings of Aurangzeb

47. Shaikh Ahmad Sirhindi was imprisoned by
(a) Humayun (b) Akbar
(c) Jahangir (d) Shahjahan

48. The statement that "both Agra and Fatehpur Sikri are bigger than London" was made by
(a) Bernier (b) Ralph Fitch
(c) Hawkins (d) Manucci

49. The author of the Das Bodh written during the Maratha period was:
(a) Dadaji Konddeva (b) Ramdas
(c) Tukaram (d) Eknath

50. Who among the following sons of Aurangzeb sought the help of Marathas against his father?
(a) Akbar (b) Muazzam
(c) Azam (d) Kambakhasha

Answers

1. (a)	11. (c)	21. (a)	31. (d)	41. (b)
2. (c)	12. (d)	22. (c)	32. (a)	42. (a)
3. (c)	13. (c)	23. (a)	33. (c)	43. (c)
4. (a)	14. (a)	24. (c)	34. (c)	44. (c)
5. (b)	15. (a)	25. (b)	35. (b)	45. (b)
6. (a)	16. (b)	26. (c)	36. (b)	46. (a)
7. (b)	17. (b)	27. (c)	37. (b)	47. (c)
8. (c)	18. (b)	28. (b)	38. (b)	48. (b)
9. (b)	19. (d)	29. (a)	39. (c)	49. (b)
10. (c)	20. (c)	30. (a)	40. (b)	50. (a)

MODEL TEST PAPER IV

1. Who was the Sunga Prince who arrested the tide of Yavanas(Greek) invasion ?
   (a) Agnimitra (b) Bhaga
   (c) Pushyamitra (d) Vasumitra
2. Demetrius, who was defeated by Pushyamitra was
   (a) A Bactrian Prince (b) A Huna Prince
   (c) A Saka Prince (d) None of these
3. The Capital of Kushana King Kanishka was
   (a) Kanishkapura
   (b) Sakal (Sialkot)
   (c) Purushapura (Peshawar)
   (d) Jalandhar
4. Har Dayal, Baba Hannam Singh, Tundilat, Baba Sohan Singh Bhakna and Gurdit Singh were associated with
   (a) India Independence League
   (b) Nowjawen Bharat Sabha
   (c) Ghadar movement
   (d) Akah movement
5. What is the correct chronological sequence of the following events?
   1. Guru-ka-Bagh agitation 2. Vaikom Satyagraha
   3. Kakori case 4. Nehru Report
   Select the correct answer using the codes given below
   (a) 1, 2, 3, 4 (b) 1, 2, 4, 3
   (c) 2, 1, 3, 4 (d) 2, 1, 4, 3
6. "We have now an open conspiracy to free the country from foreign rule and you, Comrades, and all our countrymen and countrywomen are invited to join it." Who among the following made this declaration ?
   (a) M. N. Roy (b) Jayaprakash Narayan
   (c) Subhash Bose (d) Jawaharlal Nehru
7. Match List I with List II and select the correct answer
   List I
   A. Sardul Singh Kaveeshar

B. Yusuf Meherally
C. T. Prakasam
D. Chowdhary Khahquzaman
List II
1. Muslim League
2. Forward Block
3. Indian National Congress
4. Congress Socialist Party

	A	B	C	D
(a)	2	4	1	3
(b)	4	2	1	3
(c)	2	4	3	1
(d)	4	2	3	1

8. Match List I with List II and select the correct answer
List I (Works)
A. Chaman Athaguntha (Oriya, 1921)
B. Jivanara Batat (Assamese, 1945)
C. Morali Mannige (Kamada, 1942)
D. Ranangan (Marathi, 1939)
List II (Authors)
1. Birinchi Kumar Barua
2. Fakir Mohan Senapati
3. Visram Bedekar
4. Sivaram Karanth

	A	B	C	D
(a)	1	2	3	4
(b)	2	1	3	4
(c)	2	1	4	3
(d)	1	2	4	3

9. Charak-Samahita is on
(a) Medicine (b) Astrology
(c) Sanskrit Grammer (d) None of these
10. Who was the founder of the Indo-Greek (Indo-Bactrian) dynasty in India ?
(a) Menander (b) Antialcides
(c) Demetrius (d) Alexander
11. The aim of Samudragupta in attacking the states of South India was
(a) Annexation
(b) Plunder
(c) Extension of his sphere of influence
(d) Acceptance of his suzerainty by their rulers
12. The Chinese pilgrim, Fa-hien who visited India during the rule of the mighty Guptas remained here for about:
(a) Five years (b) Seven years
(c) Eleven years (d) Fifteen years

13. The trade and industry during the pre-Gupta age were well-organised into:
(a) Srenis (b) Karshaoana
(c) Antarapana (d) Pada
14. The Upanayana Ceremony of children started:
(a) During the later Vedic age
(b) During the age of Buddha
(c) During the age of the Mauryas
(d) During the Gupta age
15. Who, among the following Pallava rulers, wrote the Mattavilasa-Prahasana?
(a) Mahendra Varman I (b) Narsingha Varman I
(c) Paramesvara Varman I (d) Narasingha Varman II
16. Who, among the following Pala rulers, succeeded most against his enemies-the Pratiharas and the Rashtrakutas:
(a) Devapala (b) Mahipala I
(c) Nayapala (d) Mahipala II
17. Which among the following was NOT a seat of learning during the Rajput age?
(a) Vikramsila (b) Vallabhi
(c) Mathura (d) Kanchi
18. Identify the correct chronological sequence:
(a) Lakshmi-Karna, Vijayasimhadeva, Yasah-Karna, Gangeyadeva Vikramaditya
(b) Gangeyadeva Vikramaditya, Lakshmi-Karna, Yasah-Karna, Vijyasimhadeva
(c) Yasah-Karna, Gangeyadeva Vikramaditya, Vijayasimhadeva, Lakshmi-Karna
(d) Gangeyadeva Vikramaditya, Yasah-Karna, Vijyasimhadeva, Lakshmi-Karna
19. Who was called the Lakh Baksha?
(a) Iltutmish (b) Qutb-ud-din Aibak
(c) Jalal-ud-din Khalji (d) Aram Shah
20. What is Vesara?
(a) an art style (b) a literary piece
(c) a painting (d) a work on music
21. Iltutmish became the Sultan of Delhi because he was:
(a) The son of Qutb-ud-din Aibak
(b) Son-in-law of Qutb-ud-din Aibak
(c) The nobles at Delhi chose him to be so
(d) The nobles at Lahore chose him to be so
22. Which, among the following was NOT one of the causes of the market-system introduced by Alauddin Khalji'?
(a) To reduce the cost of all necessary articles in the capital
(b) To maintain a large standing army at the centre at lower cost
(c) To provide better facilities of life to his subject at a cheaper cost
(d) To stop speculation and black-marketing in the capital by the traders
23. The Delhi Sultanate once enjoyed the most extensive territories during the reign of:
(a) Alauddin Khalji (b) Mubarak Shah Khalji
(c) Ghiyasuddin Tughluq (d) Muhammad-bin-Tughluq
24. Which, among the following kingdoms, was the bitterest enemy of Gujarat?
(a) Khandesh (b) Mewar

(c) Malwa (d) Marwar

25. The rule of the kings of Vijayanagara was:
(a) Rule by Council (b) Irresponsible despotism
(c) Benevolent despotism (d) Oligarchical rule

26. Who, among the following, was the author of Fatwah-i-Jahandari
(a) Sayyid Muin-ul-huq (b) Ibrahim Farukhi
(c) Khawaja Abu Malik Isami (d) Zia-ud-din Barani

27. What does the term Chaudhri indicate?
(a) Village headman
(b) Knights of the rais
(c) Governor
(d) Local magnate held answerable for collection of revenue in each Pargana?

28. What was the name of the old town near which Ahmedabad was built?
(a) Junagarh (b) Siri
(c) Asawal (d) Mandu

29. Alki Drawaza built by Alauddin Khalji is a gateway giving passage into the extension of:
(a) Qutub Minar (b) Dhai-din-ka-jaunpara
(c) Tomb of Iltutmish (d) Quat-ul-Islam

30. Which, among the following, was not one of the results of the battle of Khanua?
(a) It weakened the Rajput power
(b) It reduced the power of resistance of the Afghans against the Mughals
(c) The conquent of Rajasthan by the Mughals became easy
(d) It secured the position of Babar in India

31. The first reform introduced by Akbar was the:
(a) Abolition of the practice of Sati
(b) Abolition of the practice of enslaving the prisoners of war
(c) Abolition of pilgrims' tax
(d) Abolition of Jizya

32. The kingdom of Bijapur and Golkonda were annexed to the Mughal empire during the reign of:
(a) Akbar (b) Jahangir
(c) Shah Jahan (d) Aurangzeb

33. 'As compared to the rulers of the Delhi Sultanate the Mughal emperors brought a fundamental change in the policy of the State.' The change was:
(a) The rulers claimed divinity
(b) The administration was highly centralized
(c) There was no interference in the working of village-assemblies
(d) The state no more remained theocratic

34. The top-most industry of India during the Mughal period was:
(a) Cotton-cloth (b) Ivory-products
(c) Pearls-production (d) Silk-cotton

35. Akbar built Bulanda-Darwaza at Fatehpur Sikri to commemorate his conquest of:
(a) Malwa (b) Gujarat
(c) Bengal (d) Kashmir

36. The first French Governor who received the title of Nawab from the Mughal emperor was:
(a) Caron (b) Francois Martin
(c) Benoist Dumas (d) Joseph Francion Dupleix

37. 'Shivaji paid special attention towards the security of his forts and all officers of a fort had joint-responsibility.' Who, among the following, was NOT one of the officers in a fort?
(a) Havaldar (b) Jumaldar
(c) Sabnis (d) Sar-i-Naubat

38. Who among the following was primarily responsible for the capture of the Mughal throne by Jahandar Shah
(a) Asad Khan (b) Sarfaraj Khan
(c) Zulfigar Khan (d) Chin Qilich Khan

39. Who among the following rulers of Awadh, participated in the battle of Buxar (1764) on behalf of Mir Kasim, the deposed ruler of Bengal:
(a) Saadat Khan (b) Safdar Jang
(c) Shujauddaulah (d) Asafuddaulah

40. The English came in conflict with Nawab Siraj-ud-daulah and Nawab Mir Kasim primarily on the question of their trade rights in Bengal.
Which, among the following was that right?
(a) To use their own currency
(b) To purchase and sale commercial goods without the permission of the Nawab
(c) To transport goods in their own ships
(d) To trade without payment of trade tax the right which they obtained from the Farman of Mughal emperor Farrukhsiyar in 1717.

41. Who, among the following, has remarked about the consequences of the subsidiary alliance that "our policy and our aim have reduced all the power of India to the State of Sifars".
(a) Lord Wellesley (b) Arthur Wellesley
(c) General Lake (d) Lt. Col. Ochterlony

42. The Anglo-Afghan relations in the 19th century were mostly determined because of the fear of expansion towards India by:
(a) France (b) Russia
(c) Persia (d) Afghanistan

43. The Taluqdars of Avadh were annoyed by the British because:
(a) They were asked to pay higher revenue to the company
(b) Their hereditary privileges were abolished by the British
(c) Their share in the land-revenue was fixed
(d) They were asked to prove their claims over their respective jagirs and those who could not prove it were deprived of their Jagirs

44. Which, among the following items of Indian export, found the best market in Europe through the efforts of British East India Company?
(a) Cotton textiles (b) Silk-cloth
(c) Spices and pepper (d) Medicinal herbs

45. Heavy industries could not develop in India during the 19th century primarily because of:
    (a) Shortage of capital
    (b) Absence of skilled labour
    (c) Inadequate production of coal
46. Primarily, Ishwar Chandra Vidyasagar was an educationist and did much for female education but his name is attached with a social reform which, among the following, was that social reform?
    (a) Widow remarriages
    (b) Abolition of Sati
    (c) Prohibition of polygamy
    (d) Prohibition of child marriages
47. 'The first Factory Act was passed in 1881'. With what, among the following' was it concerned?
    (a) Female labour
    (b) Child labour
    (c) Fixation of working hours of adult male labour
    (d) Compensation to workers in case of accidents
48. In which, among the following presidency towns, the local body came into existence first?
    (a) Calcutta (b) Madras
    (c) Bombay (d) Delhi
49. Who among the following Hindi poets, is the author of Kamayan?
    (a) Sumitra Nandan Pant
    (b) Mahadevi Verma
    (c) Jayasankar Prasad
    (d) Suryakanta Tripathi Nirala
50. Where was Brahmo Samaj first established?
    (a) Bengal (b) The Punjab
    (c) Bombay (d) Madras

Answers

1. (a)	11. (d)	21. (c)	31. (b)	41. (b)
2. (a)	12. (c)	22. (c)	32. (d)	42. (b)
3. (a)	13. (a)	23. (d)	33. (d)	43. (d)
4. (c)	14. (a)	24. (c)	34. (a)	44. (a)
5. (a)	15. (a)	25. (c)	35. (b)	45. (c)
6. (c)	16. (a)	26. (d)	36. (c)	46. (d)
7. (c)	17. (c)	27. (d)	37. (b)	47. (b)
8. (c)	18 (b)	28. (c)	38. (c)	48. (b)
9. (a)	19. (d)	29. (d)	39. (c)	49. (c)
10. (a)	20. (a)	30. (c)	40. (d)	50. (a)

MODEL TEST PAPER V

Note: Answer all the 50 questions. Time: 1½ hrs.

1. The later Vedic-Aryans carried on sea trade
   (a) Yes (b) No
2. Who were the first people to paint their pottery?
   (a) Mesolithic (b) Chalcolithic
   (c) Neolithic (d) Iron age Men
3. Where was the 'Vanity case' found?
   (a) Harappa (b) Lothal
   (c) Rojdi (d) Mohenjo-daro
4. The literature produced under the patronage of Sangams was in
   (a) Tamil language (b) Kannada language
   (c) Telugu language (d) Malyalam language
5. The basic cause of difference between Svetambara and Diagambra Jains is
   (a) Whether women can get salvation
   (b) The important events concerning the life of Mahavira
   (c) Whether Jain-Monks should wear any garments or remain naked?
   (d) What garment should be worn by Jaina householders?
6. In one respect Jainism differs from Buddhism. Identify.
   (a) Preaching in public in the language of the people
   (b) Avoidance of ritual
   (c) Organisation of the Sangha for propaganda
   (d) Emphasis on nudity
7. Chandragupta Maurya was a base-born. It has been described by
   (a) Brahmanical-texts (b) Buddhist-texts
   (c) Jaina texts (d) Vedas
8. Ashoka was not responsible for the downfall of the Maurya dynasty because
   (a) Provincial governors rose in revolt only after his death
   (b) Brahmanical reaction against his policy took place after his death
   (c) There is no proof that Ashoka reduced the strength of his army
9. Identify the person other than Kanishka at whose instance the fourth Buddhist Council is supposed to have been held.

(a) Katyayaniputra (b) Asvagosha
(c) Nagarjuna (d) Vasumitra

10. The Capital of the Kushana ruler Kanishka was:
(a) Purushapura (Peshwar) (b) Sakal (Sialkot)
(c) Jalandhar (d) Kanishkapura

11. The foreigners who attacked India during the reign of Skandagupta were:
(a) The Sakas (b) The Scythians
(c) The Hunas (d) The Kushanas

12. Who, among the following Gupta-rulers, engraved horse of Asvamedha yajna on one of the coins issued by him:
(a) Chandra Gupta I (b) Samudra Gupta
(c) Chandra Gupta II (d) Kumar Gupta

13. Which, among the following, was the main item of trade of Indians with the Roman empire?
(a) Agricultural commodities
(b) Luxury goods
(c) Metals
(d) Raw material for industries

14. Which among the following statements is NOT correct regarding the position of slaves in Ancient India?
(a) The master of the slave had the right to sell him or her in the market
(b) Slaves had the right to inherit property
(c) Their condition was much better than their counterparts in the West
(d) A slave could not become a free-man in any condition

15. The highest seat of learning within the kingdom of the Pallavas was:
(a) Madura (b) Kanchi
(c) Mamallapuram (d) Mahabalipuram

16. The author of Gita-govinda was:
(a) Halayudha (b) Jayadeva
(c) Kalhana (d) Jona-raja

17. Who, among the following, wrote Prithviraj-Raso?
(a) Amara-Singh (b) Yadava
(c) Chandra Baradai (d) Jaya Singh Sura

18. Name the Pala who made the Pala dynasty a force in north Indian politics.
(a) Dharampala (b) Mahipala
(c) Gopala (d) Vigrahapala

19. Which one of these was built by Ala-ud-din Khalji?
(a) Alai Darwaza (b) Buland Darwaza
(c) Lal Quila (d) Qutub Minar

20. "It is the touchstone of Indian architecture as a whole." Who, among the following scholars has opined thus regarding the Rajarajesvara temple at Tanjore?
(a) V.A. Smith (b) Percy Bown
(c) Prof. Furgusson (d) Dr. K.A. Nilakanta Sastri

21. Who, among the following historians, has NOT accepted Iltutmish as the greatest ruler of the slave-dynasty?
    (a) Dr. A.L. Srivastav (b) Dr. Ishwari Prasad
    (c) Sir Woolsely Haig (d) Dr. S.R. Sharma
22. The Commander of Alauddin who subjugated the States of South India was;
    (a) Malik Kafur (b) Nusrat Khan
    (c) Ulugh Khan (d) Alp Khan
23. The first battle of Panipat between Ibrahim Lodi and the Mughal ruler Babar took place in the year:
    (a) 1525 A.D. (b) 1526 A.D.
    (c) 1527 A.D. (d) 1528 A.D.
24. The capital city of Malwa, Mandu was established by its ruler:
    (a) Hushang Shah (b) Mahmud Shah Khalji
    (c) Ghiyasuddin Shah (d) Nasiruddin Shah
25. What does the term Athavana stand for?
    (a) Land-revenue department (b) Land-revenue
    (c) Custom-duties (d) Trade-tax
26. Who, among the following, was the author of Jambavati Kalyan:
    (a) King Virupakya of Vijayanagara
    (b) King Krishnadeva Raya of Vijayanagara
    (c) Kirtiraja
    (d) Srivara
27. What was the main source of wealth of India during the Sultanate period?
    (a) industry (b) trade
    (c) agriculture (d) colonies
28. Who has been described as the pattern of excellence'?
    (a) Ahmad Shah (b) Muhammad Shah
    (c) Bahadur Shah (d) Mahmud Begarha
29. Who, among the following kings of Vijayanagara constructed the Vitthalswami temple?
    (a) Vijaya I (b) Devaraya II
    (c) Vir Narsingha (d) Krishnadevaraya
30. When Humayun ascended the throne of Delhi, Sher Khan, who ultimately drove him out of India, was
    (a) in the Mughal service
    (b) in the service of Jalal Khan, ruler of Bihar
    (c) master of South Bihar only
    (d) master of Bihar & Bengal
31. The one state of Southern India which was completely annexed by Akbar was:
    (a) Khandesh (b) Ahmadnagar
    (c) Bijapur (d) Golkonda
32. Who, among the following Mughal emperors, was NOT a lovable head of the family?
    (a) Akbar (b) Jahangir
    (c) Shah Jahan (d) Aurangzeb

33. The Mir Bakhshi of the Mughal-emperors was head of the department of:
(a) Finance (b) Army-organisation
(c) Foreign affairs (d) Intelligence
34. The most popular sect within Hinduism during the Mughal rule was:
(a) Vaishnavism (b) Saivism
(c) Tantrik cults (the Saktas) (d) Adi-vedantism
35. The Jama Masjid at Delhi, the largest and most well known masjid in the whole of India was constructed by:
(a) Akbar (b) Jahangir
(c) Shah Jahan (d) Aurangzeb
36. Shivaji was born in the year?
(a) 1617 A.D. (b) 1627 A.D.
(c) 1637 A.D. (d) 1647 A.D.
37. 'Sardeshmukhi was a tax which Shivaji collected from the citizens of neighbouring kingdoms and it was:
(a) 1/5th of the annual income of a territory
(b) 1/6th of the annual income of a territory
(c) 1/8th of the annual income of a territory
(d) 1/10th of the annual income of a territory
38. Who, among the following nobels, was/were regarded as King-maker during the period of the later Mughals?
(a) The Sayyid brothers - Abdulla and Husain Ali
(b) Sarbuland Khan
(c) Nizam-ul-Mulk, Asaf Jha
(d) Itiquab Khan
39. The state of Hyderabad virtually became a dependency of the East India Company when the Governor General of the Company was:
(a) Warren Hastings (b) Cornwallis
(c) Sir John Shore (d) Lord Wellesly
40. Who among the following Indians was NOT a party to the conspiracy of the English against Nawab Sirajuddaula with a view to despose him from the throne?
(a) Amichand (A Sikh merchant)
(b) Jagat-Seth Fateh Chand (A very rich trader)
(c) Mir Zafar (Mir-bakshi of the Nawab)
(d) Ghasiti Begum (Widow of one of the son-in-laws of Alivardi Khan)
41. Which, among the following was NOT one of the causes of the failure of the Marathas against the English
(a) Inept leadership
(b) Absence of unity among the Marathas
(c) Absence of stable economic policy of the Marathas
(d) Superiority of the English in arms, warfare, diplomacy and espionage
(e) The support of native-rulers, other than the Marathas, to the English
42. Which, among the following, was NOT a condition of the Permanent Settlement of Bengal?

(a) The Zamindars (landlords) were recognised hereditary owners of land
(b) They could not be displaced from their land so long they paid the revenue to the Govt.
(c) The revenue was fixed permanently with the landlords by the Govt.
(d) The share of the landlords out of the produce of the land was also fixed permanently

43. 'Certain measures of Dalhousie created serious discontentment in India which was also responsible for the revolt of 1857'. However, which among the following measures, was NOT one of them?
(a) 'Doctrine of lapse' and annexation of several states
(b) Introduction of Railways and Telegraph
(c) Abolition of titles and pensions of several rulers
(d) Educational reforms

44. 'After the occupation of Bengal, Bihar and Orissa, -the English used their power by several means for the betterment of their trade resulting in destruction of Indian handicrafts. However, which among the following means, was NOT adopted by them for that purpose?
(a) They monopolised the trade of Bengal by several legislations
(b) The English Company engaged Indian representatives gomashtas who registered Indian artisans particularly cloth weavers to work only for the company
(c) The weavers registered with the company were assigned fixed quantity and quality of work while were paid arbitrarily
(d) The English manipulated the prices of raw materials much against the interest of the artisans

45. 'British capital entered Indian industries extensively.' However, which among the following industries, was largely managed by the Indian capital?
(a) Jute (b) Coal
(c) Cotton-textiles (d) Sugar

46. Who, among the following was the founder of Ramakrishna mission?
(a) Ramakrishan Paramhansa (b) Devendra Nath Tagore
(c) Swami Vivekananda (d) Keshav Chandra Sen

47. The All India Trade Union Congress to further the interests of the Indian labour in matters of economic, social and political was first established in:
(a) 1915 (b) 1920
(c) 1925 (d) 1930

48. Which, among the following was NOT one of the recommendations of the Decentralization Commission, 1908 A.D.?
(a) Larger powers to Village Panchayats and establishments of Sub-District Boards with independent powers
(b) Withdrawals of restrictions on the powers of taxation of local bodies
(c) Unrestricted powers to raise loans by local bodies on their own credit
(d) All of the above were recommended

49. Who, among the following poets, has been called the Tagore of Punjabi?
(a) Puran Singh (b) Mohan Singh
(c) Amrita Pritam (d) Kartar Singh Duggal

50. In what language did Rammohan write his 'To Monotheists'?
(a) Sanskrit (b) Bengali
(c) Persian (d) Hindi

Answers

1. (a)	11. (c)	21. (b)	31. (a)	41. (e)
2. (b)	12. (d)	22. (a)	32. (d)	42. (d)
3. (a)	13. (b)	23. (b)	33. (b)	43. (d)
4. (a)	14. (d)	24. (a)	34. (a)	44. (a)
5. (c)	15. (c)	25. (a)	35. (c)	45. (c)
6. (d)	16. (b)	26. (d)	36. (b)	46. (c)
7. (a)	17. (c)	27. (c)	37. (d)	47. (b)
8. (a)	18. (a)	28. (d)	38. (a)	48. (d)
9. (d)	19. (a)	29. (d)	39. (d)	49. (a)
10. (a)	20. (b)	30. (c)	40. (d)	50. (c)

Section IV

GUIDELINES FOR PAPER III

COMPREHENSIVE HISTORY

Note:

Paper III will consist of descriptive type questions. These will include both short answer type questions and short essay type questions. This paper will be of 2½ hours durations and will carry 200 maximum marks. The questions in this paper will cover ancient, medieval and modern periods of Indian history. It will also include questions on research in history.

A. Ancient Period

1. Agraharas
2. Alvars/Nayanars
3. Bharatavarsha
4. Dandaniti
5. Dhammavijaya
6. Digvijaya
7. Mudra
8. Pre-history
9. Purusharthas
10. Sabha - Samiti
11. Sreni
12. Sallekhana
13. Samskaras
14. Sangam Age
15. Saptanga
16. Shadbhaga
17. Stupa
18. Varnashrama
19. Virgal (Hero-stone)
20. Vishti

B. Medieval Period

1. Amaram
2. Baluta
3. Bhai-bast
4. Chauth
5. Din-i-Ilalu
6. Ghatika
7. Iqta
8. Jangama
9. Jizyah
10. Khilafat
11. Khutba
12. Langar
13. Madad-i-maash
14. Maharashtra-dharma
15. Nishan
16. Raya-Rekho
17. Sulh-i-kul
18. Tasawwuf
19. Turkan-i-Chahlghani

C. Modern Period

1. Casteism
2. Colonialism
3. Communalism
4. Doctrine of Lapse
5. Dyarchy
6. Economic Drain
7. Economic Nationalism
8. Federalism
9. Filtration theory
10. Forward Policv
11. Indian Renaissance
12. Industrialisation
13. Leftism
14. Mercantilism
15. Modernisation
16. Paramountcy
17. Revivalism
18. Satyagraha
19. Swadeshi
20. Utilitarianism

SOURCES

Ancient Period

Archaeological sources

Exploration, excavation, epigraphy, numismatics, monuments

Literary sources

(a) Indigenous: Brahmanical, Buddhist, and Jaina literature, Kavya literature, Historical Kavyas, Scientific literature, Literature in regional languages.

(b) Foreign accounts: Greek, Chinese and Arab writers

Pre-history and proto-history

Stone age cultures of India : Paleolithic, Neolithic, Chalcolithic and Iron Age cultures

Indus Valley civilisation : Origin, date, extent, characteristics, contents, decline and survivals

Vedic Period

Migrations and settlements, date of the Rigveda, literary and archaeological evidences, evolution of social and political institutions, religious and philosophical ideas and practices, literature.

Period of Mahajanapadas

Sixteen Mahajanapadas, Republican States,-rise of urban centres, trade routes and economic growth, introduction of currency, origin and spread of Jainism and Buddhism, rise of Magadha, Nandas. Iranian and Mecedonean Invasions.

Mauryan Empire

Foundation of the Mauryan empire, Kautilya and the Arthashastra, Ashoka, Concept of Dhamma, Edicts, Brahmi and Kharosthi scripts, administration, economy, art, disintegration of the empire; Sungas and Kanvas

Post-Mauryan and Kushana Period

Indo-Greeks, Sakas, Kushanas, Western Kahatrapas; contact with outside world, growth of urban centres,economy, coinage, development of religions, Mahayana sect, social conditions, art and architecture, literature and science.

Early States in Eastern India and South India

Kharavela, The Satavahanas, Tamil states of the Sangam Age: economy, land grants and coinage. trade guilds, urbanisation, Buddhist centres, Sangam literature, administration, art and architecture.

Regional States

The Guptas and Vakatakas, Harsha; administration, Sanskrit literature, scientific literature, economic conditions, coinage of the Guptas, Varnashrama dharma, castes and sub-castes, position of women, education and educational institutions, contacts with neighbouring countries, central Asia, south east Asia and China, art and architecture.

The Kadambas, Gangas, Pallavas and the Chalukyas of Badami; Adminisration, role of the feudatory families, trade guilds, literature, growth of regional languages and scripts, growth of Vaishnava and Saiva religions, Tamil Bhakti Movement, Institution of temple and temple architecture.

The Rashtrakutas, Prathiharas, Palas and Senas, Kalachuri-chedis. Paramaras, Chahantanas, Chalukyas of Gujarat; Arab contacts, advent of the Turks, regional schools of architecture, religious sects and social conditions.

The Chalukyas of Kalyana, Hoysalas, Chola, Pandyas, Administration and local Government, growth of art and architecture, religious sects; Institution of temples and Mathas, Agraharas and Brahmadeyas, education and literature; economy and society; contact with Sri-Lanka and south east Asia.

Medieval Period

Archaeological Sources

Epigraphic and numismatic materials and monuments.

Literary Sources

Persian, Sanskrit and regional languages, Archival materials, Foreign travellers' accounts.

Political Developments

The Sultanate: The Turks, the Khaljis, the Tughlaqs, the Sayyids and the Lodis

Foundation of the Mughal Empire: Babur, Humayun and the Suris: expansion from

Akbar to Aurangzeb

Decline of the Mughal empire : political, administrative and economic causes

Later Mughals and disintegration of the Mughal empire

The Vijyanagara and the Bahamanis: rise, expansion and disintegration

The Maratha movement : The foundation of Swaraj by Shivaji; its expansion under the Peshwas; Maratha Confederacy; causes of decline

Administration

Administration under the Sultanate: civil, judicial, revenue, fiscal and military

Sher Shah's administrative reforms; Mughal administration; land revenue and other sources of income; mansabdari and jagirdari

Administrative system in the Deccan; the Vijayanagara, the Bahmanis and the Marathas; Malik Ambar's revenue system

Economic Aspects

Agricultural production ; village economy ; peasantry

Urbanisation ; urban centres and population

Industries : cotton textiles, handicrafts, agro-based industries; organisation, Karkhanas, technology

Trade and commerce: state policies, internal and external trade; European trade, trade centres and ports, transport and communication

Financial trade, commerce and industries; Hundi and Insurance Currency.

Socio-Religious Movements

The Sufis: their orders, beliefs and practices, the leading Sufi saints

Bhakti cult : Shaivism and its branches: Vaishnavism and its branches

The Saints of medieval period : north and south; their impact on socio-political and religious life

The Sikh movement: Guru Nanak Dev and his teachings and practices; Adi Granth; the Khalsa

Society

Classification : ruling class, major religious groups, the mercantile and professional classes

Rural society : petty chieftains, village officials, cultivators and non cultivating classes, artisans

Position of women

Cultural Life

Educational system and its motivations

Literature : Persian, Sanskrit and regional languages

Fine arts : major schools of painting and music

Architectural development of the north and south India; Indo-Islamic Architecture

Modern Period

Archival materials: biographies and memoirs, newspaper and oral histories

European traders in India in the 17th and 18th centuries : Portuguese, Dutch, French and the British

The establishment, expansion and consolidation of British rule in India

British relations with principal Indian powers: Bengal, Oudh, Nizam, Mysore, Marathas and Sikhs

Foreign Relations and Frontier Policy

Relations with Afghanistan and Persia

Relations with Burma

Relations with Nepal and Tibet

Administration under the East India Company and the Crown

Central and provincial adminsitration under the East India Company and the Crown

Development of local self-government

Constitutional development since 1773

Economic Development and Policy

Trade and commerce

Agricultural development and policy, land revenue administration, land tenures (Permanent Settlement, Ryotwari, Mahalwari, Taluqdari and Malguzari Settlements) - rural indebtedness

Decline of indigeneous industries

Famines and famine policy

Industrial development and policy, labour and trade union movements

Monetary policy- banking and currency

Growth of towns and cities

Social Policy and Social Changes

Impact of British rule on Indian society, emergence of the middle class, caste movements

Educational development and policy

Socio-religious reforms, emancipation of women

Press and public opinion

Western Impact on Indian culture,literatre, art, music and performing arts

National Movement

Rise of Indian nationalism, social and economic bases of nationalism

Revolt of 1857. civil rebellions, tribal movements

Indian National Congress, ideologies, programmes

Moderates, extremists, revolutionaries in India and abroad

Peasant movements

The Gandhian era, 1920-47

Genesis of Pakistan

Integration of Indian states

Constitution of India, 1950

Research in History

Scope and purpose of History

Objective and bias in History

History and its ancilliary sciences

Area of research - proposed

Sources - Primary/Secondary in the proposed area of research

Modern Historical Writing in his/her area research

Sample Questions

1. Explain the concept of Dandaniti in about 20 words.
2. Write the meaning and significance of Watan in about 20 words.
3. Write a short essay on Development of Local-self government. (Limit your answer to 50-60 words).